Dracula
FAQ

Dracula FAQ

All That's Left to Know About the Count from Transylvania

Bruce Scivally

Backbeat
Books

An Imprint of Hal Leonard Corporation

Published in 2015 by Backbeat Books
An Imprint of Hal Leonard Corporation
7777 West Bluemound Road
Milwaukee, WI 53213

Trade Book Division Editorial Offices
33 Plymouth St., Montclair, NJ 07042

The FAQ series was conceived by Robert Rodriguez and developed with Stuart Shea.

Printed in the United States of America

Book design by Snow Creative Services

Library of Congress Cataloging-in-Publication Data is available upon request.

ISBN 978-1-61713-600-9

www.backbeatbooks.com

To the children of the night
(you know who you are)

Contents

Acknowledgments

To dig up information on Dracula and other vampires beyond that which has appeared in countless other books required hundreds of hours of research in libraries in California, Illinois, and the UK. So, I must thank the extraordinarily patient librarians of:

- The Reuben Library of the British Film Institute
- The Evanston Public Library
- The Wilmette Public Library
- The Beverly Hills Public Library
- The Los Angeles Public Library
- The Margaret Herrick Library of the Academy of Motion Picture Arts & Sciences

Additionally, I wish to thank:

Harry Collett, for taking me on a tour of Whitby's Dracula sites

David Del Valle and the Del Valle Archives, for the bulk of the photos that illustrate the book

Timothy Grana, for providing a never-before-seen snapshot of Gloria Holden

John and Jools Hudson and Vanessa Way of The Chiltern Guest House, Whitby, for making me feel at home; Ted Newsom, for pointing me in the direction of David Del Valle; Jeanne Youngson, for moral support and encouragement

. . . and, of course, my friends and family, who saw precious little of me while I slaved away on the book. I have now returned from the land of the dead . . .

Introduction

It was a summer's evening at the end of June, but in Whitby there was a chill in the air. I had just arrived in the seaside town, and on a stroll from my hotel to the whalebone arch (literally, an arch made from two curving jawbones of a whale, rising perpendicularly out of the ground) there was a sign: "In Search of DRACULA—Tonight, 8 p.m." Of course, I had to go. After all, I was in Whitby to soak up some atmosphere while working on *Dracula FAQ*.

After a brief stroll around the hotels and shops on the West Cliff, I returned to the sign, and waited. And, at 8:00 p.m. there he was—Dracula (or, at least, a reasonable facsimile thereof). He's a retired teacher, Harry Collett, who leads ghost tours and Dracula tours through Whitby. Joined by over a dozen others, we set off, exploring the sights once traversed by Bram Stoker, who came to Whitby in 1890, just as he was beginning to work on his classic novel, *Dracula*.

Over 120 years later, Whitby still seems to be the quaint village described in Stoker's novel. There's the harbor, where—in the novel—the Russian ship *Demeter* crashes into the sand, all its occupants dead, and a "black dog"—Dracula—leaps onto British soil to begin his reign of terror. Up above the beach, atop the East Cliff, sits Whitby Abbey, whose ruins are said to have inspired Dracula's castle. Beside the abbey is a graveyard, filled with the graves of sailors, which is reached by climbing 199 steps from the beach, steps that are climbed by Mina and Lucy in the novel. The young women stay in a hotel in the Whitby Crescent, where Stoker

Bram Stoker's *Dracula* mentions the 199 steps, which lead up to Whitby Abbey.   © 2014 Bruce Scivally

himself lodged while in Whitby, and where there is now a blue plaque commemorating him.

Down in the shops of the West Cliff one can buy Vampire wine, or chocolate bars with little chocolate vampires on top of them, or Dracula refrigerator magnets, or postcards of the spooky-looking abbey ruins. Some of the restaurants also play up the Dracula connection: at Sherlock's Coffee House, a dessert called Dracula's Delight is served, and a delight it is—crushed meringue, raspberry coulis, fresh cream, and dairy vanilla ice cream, topped with a chocolate bat made of a milk chocolate heart for the body and chocolate wafers for the wings. And where better to walk off the sugar coma that induces than The Dracula Experience, a spook house that features recreated scenes from the novel, complete with animated Dracula mannequins that dart out from the darkness when you least expect them.

In short, Whitby is a Dracula mecca.

After taking the Dracula walking tour, I asked Harry Collett, who says that tourists from all over the world come to Whitby and take the tour, why he thought Dracula was still so popular after all these years. "I think people like to be frightened, but yet within a controlled environment," he replied. "They

Dracula's Delight is a goblet full of heaven: vanilla ice cream, chocolate, and raspberry sauce topped with a bat made from a cookie and chocolate wafers.   © 2014 Bruce Scivally

receive a little thrill from the fact that, in Whitby, you can see what's in the book. What Stoker wrote about is quite visible. And it puts you right into the scene, so you feel part of it."

Of course, Transylvania is another Dracula mecca, but I did not go there. For that matter, neither did Stoker. But my journey with Dracula began in a place just as remote from Whitby as Transylvania—Plevna, Alabama.

Some of my earliest memories are of staying up late on a Saturday night with my older brother, when we would each push a couple of chairs together and lie across them with the lights out to watch, on a small black-and-white TV, *Shock Theater*. Those late nights, seeing for the first time Bela Lugosi's Dracula and Boris Karloff's Frankenstein Monster and Lon Chaney Jr.'s Wolf Man scared the dickens out of me. And I loved it. I have been a lifelong fan of classic horror films since.

Walking among the ruins of Whitby Abbey supposedly inspired Bram
Stoker's conception of Dracula's castle. The abbey was established in
657 A.D. and fell into ruin when it was destroyed by Henry VIII in 1540.
© 2014 Bruce Scivally

My childhood, in the 1960s and '70s, was like many others who grew up
during that period: saturated with monsters. Besides the films on TV, there was
Famous Monsters of Filmland magazine, the Aurora model kits, and eight-inch
action figures. And as I got into my teens, I got a Super 8mm Kodak sound
projector and bought the heavily edited-down Castle Films versions of *Dracula*
and *Frankenstein* and a silent feature, 1922's *Nosferatu.* And I discovered Hammer
horror films, thanks to the *CBS Late Movie.*

When I turned eighteen, I left Alabama to go to Los Angeles and attend the
University of Southern California. There, I met Dr. Donald Reed, founder of
the Count Dracula Society, and through him was introduced to *Famous Monsters
of Filmland* editor Forrest J Ackerman. Many years later, I toured Ackerman's
home, which he called "the Ackermuseum," because it contained thousands
of items from horror and sci-fi films, including a cape and ring once worn by
Bela Lugosi as Dracula. Later still, assisting with a Romanian documentary, I
met Bela Lugosi Jr., who is just as commanding a presence as his famous father,
though less menacing. Working on a special edition DVD documentary, I met
Dracula himself, Christopher Lee, and was astonished to discover that he can
do a flawless imitation of the Looney Tunes character Yosemite Sam.

Now, here I was, sitting on Mina's Bench, a wooden seat on the West Cliff
of Whitby, from which one can see almost all the sights mentioned in Stoker's
Dracula, a novel that I first read as a teen and had revisited a couple of times
since, including re-reading it purely by coincidence before landing the job of
writing this book. It was surreal to sit there and think how the events of my life
had conspired to lead me to that place, and this job.

And what a job it was! I thought I would spend a couple of months researching Dracula, but my digging through newspaper and magazine archives and
libraries and my own extensive collection of Dracula books consumed me until

I had to force myself to stop researching and start writing. And once I began writing, having waited so long, it consumed practically all of my waking hours. By the end, I felt I was under the curse of Dracula—I ate, slept, and breathed Dracula. I only watched Dracula- or vampire-related movies and TV shows, while simultaneously typing away on chapters. I began staying up late, writing, keeping vampire hours, sleeping until late in the day. I consumed so much caffeine that I eventually became a monster myself, more coffee than man.

And now, the book is done. It is time for me to become the tour guide, leading you on a journey through centuries of vampire history. Hang on—things might get a little batty.

Dracula
FAQ

He, Who Commanded Nations

Bad Vlad, Dangerous to Know

Vlad the Impaler

When was the first Dracula horror story written? Many would say 1897, the year that Bram Stoker's seminal Gothic novel *Dracula* was published, but the first stories featuring a character named Dracula committing gruesome acts were published over four hundred years earlier.

In 1432, Vlad III became the prince of Wallachia, a region of modern-day Romania north of the Danube River and south of the Southern Carpathian mountains. With the help of Holy Roman Emperor Sigismund, Vlad III seized control of Wallachia and defended his country against the Ottoman Turks, whose empire was spreading through the Balkan Peninsula. Though Vlad III's reign was relatively short and notoriously bloody, many of his countrymen—the ones he didn't torture or impale—regarded him as a hero during the six years when he exercised the most control over the region. Even today, Vlad III is regarded as a leading light who held the line against the Turks after the fall of Constantinople.

Nonetheless, Vlad III remained a historical footnote, largely forgotten, until 1890, when an Irish author, vacationing in Whitby, England, was looking for a name for the vampire character in a horror story he was writing. At the Whitby Library, he opened up William Wilkinson's 1820 book, *An Account of the Principalities of Wallachia and Moldavia*, wherein he read about "the Voïvode Dracula" who formed an alliance with Ladislas, King of Hungary, to fight against the Turks. But Stoker may have been guided in his research by a man he met at the Lyceum Theatre, Arminius Vambery. A Hungarian scholar who was said to have been a spy, Vambery is mentioned within the text of *Dracula* as a friend of Van Helsing's. He was certainly a friend of Stoker's, and supposedly told the author about a ruler named Vlad Tepeş, whose nickname was Draculya. This led Stoker to library research in Whitby and, when he returned to London, at

Copy of a portrait of Vlad III by unknown artist, dating from the second half of the sixteenth century. In their book, *Dracula: Prince of Many Faces*, McNally and Florescu write that the portrait on which it is based was likely painted after 1462, when Vlad III was imprisoned at Buda.

Courtesy of Kunsthistorisches Museum, Vienna. Author's collection.

the British Museum. Mixing a few facts in with his fiction, Stoker created his vampire, Dracula.

Many years later, in the 1950s, a professor from Boston College, Raymond T. McNally, saw the 1931 film *Dracula* on television and became intrigued by its central character. He then read Stoker's novel, which began with Jonathan Harker's travels through Cluj and Bistrita. Finding that these places actually existed, he wondered if perhaps Dracula did, too.

McNally began his research by asking Hungarian scholars if there had, in fact, ever been a leader named Dracula. They told him he was crazy, that he was wasting his time, that Dracula was only a figment of Bram Stoker's imagination. But, in 1967, he met and teamed up with Boston College's professor of Balkanese empire history, Romanian-born Radu Florescu, who had also been interested in the search for a historical Dracula. The two men agreed to pool their resources and work as a team.

After digging through all the available documentation in the archives of four countries and conferring with historians, archaeologists, genealogists, and folklorists from the University of Bucharest and the University of London, the pair eventually succeeded in piecing together the complicated story of Dracula's life. They collated all the information in their 1972 book, *In Search of Dracula.*

The book revealed that Vlad III's father, Vlad II, was a member of the Order of the Dragon, a religious military order created in 1408 by Holy Roman Emperor Sigismund to defend the region against the Turks. In the Romanian language, "Dracul" meant dragon, and as head of the Order of the Dragon, Vlad II became popularly known among his countrymen as Vlad Dracul. Also, the way Romanians denoted a nobleman's son was to add an -*a* to the end of his name, so Vlad III, son of Vlad II, became known as Vlad Dracula, or "Vlad, son of the Dragon." In modern times, "dracul" became accepted as the Romanian term for "devil," leading to the misconception that Dracula thus means "Son of the Devil."

In his memoirs, *A Book Hunter's Holiday*, book collector Dr. A. S. W. Rosenbach—who eventually purchased Bram Stoker's original manuscript of *Dracula* for his Philadelphia library, now a museum—said that he was able, after a long search, to get his hands on a rare manuscript called *Dracole*, published by Peter Wagner in Nuremberg around 1488, over a decade after the death of Vlad III. Page forty of the book featured a woodcut of "Dracole Waida." The woodcut showed the head and shoulders of Vlad III as a man with cruel eyes, a thick mustache and long, flowing hair under a high hat.

Following up on Rosenbach's research, Florescu and McNally found other manuscripts detailing the evil deeds of Vlad III, particularly pamphlets found in various monasteries and archives in France and Switzerland.

These early manuscripts enumerated many atrocities attributed to Vlad III, proving, if nothing else, that the reading public has always had a great interest in stories of sex, violence, and perversion. The Vlad III stories focused on his cruelty and a taste for violence that suggested insanity. For instance, when a visiting delegation of Turkish

Woodcut portrait of Vlad III, "Dracole Waida," from the pamphlet *Dracole*, published by Peter Wagner in Nuremberg around 1488.

The Marsden Archive, UK/Bridgeman Images

ambassadors refused to remove their hats in his presence, saying that it wasn't their custom to doff them in deference to anyone, Vlad ordered the hats nailed to their heads.

It was also written that to end the suffering of the poor in his vicinity, Vlad invited all of them to a great feast. Once they were inside the banquet hall, he barred the doors from the outside and set fire to it. Another version of this story substitutes boyars, or ruling aristocrats, for the poor. Whatever their social rank, Vlad ended their suffering, permanently. A German pamphlet from 1521 depicts Vlad roasting children alive and feeding them to their mothers, and slicing off the breasts of women and forcing their husbands to eat them.

In another Dracula tale, a merchant came to Vlad complaining that a sack containing 160 ducats of gold had been stolen. Vlad put out the word: return the money by dawn, or else. Sometime during the night, the sack of gold was returned. But when the merchant counted the coins, he found that there were now 161 ducats. He went to Vlad's castle and told the prince that the money had been returned, but that when he counted it, there was an extra coin. Vlad informed the merchant that had he not been honest about the extra gold, he would have been impaled.

According to the pamphlets, impaling was Vlad III's pastime. Victims were impaled by having a post with a rounded—not sharp—end forced up through their rectum and into their chest cavity, leaving them to die a slow, agonizing death. At one point during his reign, Vlad III commanded the local peasants to construct a castle in South Transylvania, near Curtea de Arges. When they expressed reluctance, he prepared a banquet. Halfway through the festivities, Vlad ordered his men to round up the elderly villagers and impale them. The remaining younger villagers immediately agreed to build the castle.

Further, it was written that Vlad III enjoyed dining among the rotting corpses of his impaled victims. He even sometimes dipped his bread in their blood. In one tale, a nobleman dining with him among the decomposing bodies complained of their stench. Vlad impaled him on an unusually tall stake, raising him high among the fresh breezes, so he couldn't be offended by the odor of the rotting corpses below.

In 1462, the Sultan mounted an offensive against Vlad III. As the Turkish troops closed in, they came upon what appeared to be a forest of oddly shaped trees. Coming closer, they saw that it wasn't trees, but rather a forest of over twenty thousand impaled bodies. Horrified, the Turks fled.

It was Vlad's predilection for impaling his enemies that gave him his nickname, "Vlad Țepeș," meaning "Vlad the Impaler." However, in a time when such acts were commonplace, Vlad's countrymen regarded him as a hero for saving Romania from foreign invaders. Impaling was, in fact, a method of execution Vlad likely learned when, as a boy, he was held prisoner by the Turks. Outside Romania, impalings were recorded through the years in Russia, Germany, Austria, and neighboring countries.

Eventually, the Turks laid siege to Vlad's castle, and he was forced to flee. According to legend, he shod all of his horses backwards, so that the horseshoe prints of the escaping party would seem to be leading to his castle rather than away from it. It didn't help. Vlad III was captured, imprisoned, and beheaded by the Turks in 1477.

After his death, Vlad III's body was supposedly taken by Orthodox monks to their monastery at Snagov, a wooded island in a large lake roughly twenty-five miles north of Bucharest. To facilitate prayers for his troubled spirit, he was buried under a heavy stone slab set in the floor immediately in front of the chapel altar.

While writing *Dracula*, Bram Stoker never actually set foot in Transylvania, and thus erred in the location of the historical Dracula's castle. Stoker placed it on a one-thousand-foot rocky crag in North Transylvania. The actual castle is located in South Transylvania, near Curtea de Arges, a thousand feet up in the Wallachian Mountains overlooking the Arges River Valley. The discovery of the castle was the highlight of McNally and Florescu's investigations. They wrote that it was an eerie place, which the local peasants felt was evil; they never got up the courage to stay there overnight.

The Dracula legends studied by Florescu and McNally were written by German monks and merchants fleeing Vlad III's wrath. Since the stories were written by his enemies, naturally they emphasized his worst qualities. When the tales proved popular new ones were concocted, further distorting Vlad III's image.

Although no one doubts that Vlad III actually lived and impaled both his enemies and his own countrymen, some of the other atrocities attributed to him may be lies spread by

Typical of the woodcuts used to illustrate pamphlets featuring stories of Vlad III, this one, published by Ambrosius Huber in Nuremberg in 1499, shows Vlad feasting among impaled bodies.

The Marsden Archive, UK/Bridgeman Images

his enemies to slander him. Vlad III seemed intent on ridding his country of parasites, which included German Saxon merchants. It was the stories of these merchants—who were often the victims of Vlad's cruelty—that were published as pamphlets in Germany shortly after Vlad III's death. And, at a time when such pamphlets were the primary form of entertainment, publishers learned that the more lurid the stories, the more pamphlets they sold. So, to make money, they printed the legend.

Vlad the Vampire

As barbaric as he was, the real Prince Dracula was no supernatural bloodsucker. So how did his legacy become intertwined with that of vampires? Professor McNally noted that belief in vampires dated as far back as 2,500 B.C.; there were manuscripts about vampires and frescoes depicting bat gods in Tibetan monasteries. McNally theorized that the Magyars, who originally came from East Asia, brought vampire stories with them when they migrated into Transylvania. Because Vlad III was so tyrannical and cruel, the peasants saw him as the living personification of the Magyar vampire god.

Newspaper ad for Calvin Floyd's documentary *In Search of Dracula*, inspired by Radu Florescu and Raymond T. McNally's book of the same name.

Author's collection

McNally's colleague, Radu Florescu, felt that Vlad III's association with vampirism was clinched by the fact that after his death his body was never found. In 1931, a party that included Florescu's uncle carried out excavations on the island in Snagov Lake where Vlad III was presumed to be interred. They unearthed many skeletons of bodies that had been buried upright where they had been impaled. However, inside the monastery, in the supposed grave of Vlad III, they found only ox bones and artifacts. An unmarked grave was located near the door of the chapel that contained human bones, scraps of red silk and jewelry with Vlad's emblem. It is theorized that these were Vlad's remains, moved to the second grave to prevent them from being disturbed by the prince's enemies. They were taken to the national historical museum in Bucharest, and have since gone missing.

Down through the years, Vlad III remained a legendary folk bogeyman in Romania, but it wasn't until the 1970s that the locals associated him with Bram Stoker's fictional vampire, because it wasn't until 1971 that Stoker's novel was translated into the Romanian language. At first astonished that Stoker in-

In 1975's *In Search of Dracula*, Christopher Lee not only played Dracula but also Vlad III, the historical Dracula.
© 1975 Aspekt Films. Author's collection.

ferred that his evil vampire was, in fact, their own national hero, they soon embraced the confusion of the literary icon with the historical figure for the sake of attracting Western tourists.

When *In Search of Dracula* was published, it generated a great deal of publicity, much to the surprise of the two Boston college professors. They made the most of it. Their numerous appearances on TV talk shows helped bring Vlad the Impaler into the popular mainstream, and also helped resuscitate sales of Bram Stoker's novel; in the first four months of 1972, a Dell paperback edition went through two reprints of twenty-five thousand copies each. With the popularity of the book and a renewed interest in Dracula and vampires, a documentary film, also called *In Search of Dracula*, was put into production, with Christopher Lee not only acting as host but also acting as Vlad Tepeș and Dracula. Directed by Calvin Floyd, the Swedish/French/American co-production was released in 1975.

Vlad the Tourist Attraction

The interest in the historical Dracula led to a tourist boom that is still thriving today. In 1972, Pan American World Airways began offering an eighteen-day escorted tour of Transylvania and central Romania. Two years later, the Communist Government of Romania promoted package tours of "Dracula country."

The island in Snagov Lake became a destination for tourists hoping to find Dracula's tomb. Away from the lake and its shores, they wandered about the decrepit foundations of ancient torture chambers, and heard folk tales about a sunken church beneath the lake and Vlad's ghost rising from the murky waters. In 1975, the floor of Snagov Chapel was excavated, in hopes of locating the headless body of Vlad III. Nothing was found.

Besides being a bicentennial year in America, 1976 was also the five hundredth anniversary of the death of Vlad III. In Transylvania—then a part of Romania—1976 was called "Dracula Year." The event was celebrated with studies, sculptures, paintings, and poems. The Communists then in power didn't whitewash Vlad's cruel actions, but explained them as being necessary in that medieval age; a forceful politician whose ends justified his means, Vlad III was celebrated as a ruler who used extreme measures to enforce the law and protect his people from oppressors.

As Westerners began touring Vlad III's castle, his alleged tomb, and other historical sites, the Romanian government took the Dracula phenomenon seriously and the country's Tourist Board, at great expense, restored buildings associated with Vlad.

In April of 1979, a radio commercial began airing in New York City promoting Romanian tourism. Although Dracula wasn't mentioned by name, he appeared in the ad, proclaiming—after a wolf's howl—"Welcome to Transylvania." At that time, Americans accounted for only thirty thousand of Romania's five million yearly tourists. The country hoped that the ads would bump the figure up to forty thousand, and used the popular image of the vampire Count Dracula in the ads because that was what most Americans thought of when they thought of Transylvania.

Catering to tourists, the seventy-room, three-story Hotel Tihuta in the Carpathian Mountains began promoting itself in the mid-1980s as "Hotel Dracula." The walls were adorned with bats and wolves, the concierge's desk was located in a second-floor tower, and the hotel cook also doubled as a vampire, springing from a coffin to scare tourists in the basement "torture chamber." When construction of the $2 million facility began in 1976, Romania hoped to attract thousands of Western tourists, but business was bad in the beginning and by 1985 the hotel was only operating at 70 percent capacity. Originally, as noted above, the establishment was to have been named Hotel Dracula, although local authorities vetoed the idea. But the operators knew what would attract the tourists, and began offering visitors the chance to sleep in a coffin and to order a snifter of plum brandy called "Elixir Dracula."

While in power, Romanian president Nicolae Ceaușescu downplayed Vlad III's part in his country's history, but once the Communist ruler was deposed in 1989, Romanian tourist officials used Vlad Tepeș and his ties to the fictional Dracula even more aggressively to lure Western tourists to their East European cities. Visitors to Romania in the early 1990s were encouraged to join package tours rather than trying to navigate the territory themselves in rented vehicles, since gasoline supplies were undependable and the wait at the Hungarian-Romanian border was sometimes hours long.

In 1993, four years after the collapse of Communism in Romania, Nicolae Paduraru, a former Romanian tourism official, founded the Transylvanian Society of Dracula in his hometown of Sighişoara. He hoped the society would attract scholars and historians to explore both the historical figure of Vlad III and the Dracula of Stoker's novel. To that end, Paduraru started Mysterious Journeys, a company that organized tours of sites associated with Vlad III.

At the turn of the new century, Romania announced plans to create a Dracula theme park in Sighişoara. The park was expected to include a golf course, a Ferris wheel, a ghost castle with torture chambers, a restaurant serving "scary meat jelly," a petting zoo, and other family attractions. However, the park faced opposition from environmentalists who feared for the ancient oak forests surrounding the area and conservationists who wished to preserve the town's medieval character. They also feared that calling it Dracula Park would further erase the distinction between Bram Stoker's fictional creation and the historical figure who kept the Turks at bay.

In June of 2002, the Romanian tourist board hired PricewaterhouseCoopers to help find the $30 million it still needed to fund Dracula Park. After doing a feasibility study, PricewaterhouseCoopers decided the park would be a bad idea.

Romanian officials weren't deterred. They next proposed building the theme park in Bucharest, and in October 2003, the Romanian government established Dracula Park S. A. to find investors and create designs for the amusement park, whose costs were now expected to range from $47 million to $82 million. Two early sponsors for the idea were the Coca-Cola Hellenic Bottling Company, who pledged $150,000, and Brau Union, Austria's largest brewery, who pledged $500,000. Local residents and investors remained pessimistic, however, and the remaining funds were never raised.

In May of 2014, it was reported that Castle Bran near Braşov, Romania, which is often referred to as "Castle Dracula" on tours of Romania's Dracula-related sites, was up for sale. The link to Vlad III was tenuous; he didn't live there, but rather was imprisoned there for a couple of months. In 1920, the Romanian royal family gave the fortress to Queen Victoria's granddaughter Queen Marie. When Queen Marie died in 1938, the castle was bequeathed to her daughter, Princess Ileana, who held it until 1948, when the Communists came to power and gave the royal family just twenty-four hours to flee the country. After the fall of Ceauşescu, the castle was returned to the royal family; it is now owned by Ileana's children, Archduke Dominic and his sisters Maria Magdalena and Elizabeth. The royals, now in their seventies, are looking for investors to help bring the castle into the twenty-first century. It was offered for sale to the Romanian government for $80 million, but they passed. Handling the sale of the property is New York attorney Mark Meyer, who also happens to be the honorary American consul for Moldova.

Skeleton in the Closet

Although Vlad III died centuries ago, his descendants are still roaming the earth, such as Polish-born Count Wladyslaw Kuzdrzal-Kicki, whom German magazines dubbed Count Dracula XV. "I remember the whispering going on in the family about some cruel ancestor whose deeds were not exactly fit to be immortalized on a tombstone," said Kuzdrzal-Kicki in a 1979 interview with Alice Siegert of the *Chicago Tribune*. Kuzdrzal-Kicki learned of his ancestral ties to Vlad III while doing genealogical research for a book he was planning to write, when he discovered that a great-granddaughter of Vlad III married his forebear Petr Kicki around 1535.

Kuzdrzal-Kicki believed Bram Stoker, looking for a name for his vampire character, seized on Dracula because it sounded similar to the Gaelic-Irish word for bloodsucker, "dreagul."

Ulick O'Connor, a poet and biographer from Dublin, had his own encounter with Dracula on the occasion of his first visit to New York's Chelsea Hotel, as he related to Maureen Dowd in a 1983 article in the *New York Times*. While checking into the hotel, he inquired about another guest's identity. O'Connor said, "I was told he was Dracula's cousin and, naturally, I thought it was a joke. But then it turned out the guy was Count Roderick Ghyka, the son of the crown prince of Romania and a direct descendant of Count Vlad, the real Dracula. And the funny thing was when I talked to him I found out his mother was Maureen O'Connor, a distant relative of my father. The Chelsea Hotel is the only place in the world where you meet Dracula's cousin and he turns out to be your cousin, too." Ghyka died in 1978.

In 1982, Sir Iain Moncreiffe, the former chairman of Debrett's, published *Royal Highness*, a book in which he claimed that Prince Charles was a great grandson sixteen times removed to Vlad III. According to Moncreiffe, the Prince of Wales's great grandmother, Queen Mary, consort of George V, was descended from Vlad IV, half-brother of Vlad III. Rather than take offense at the news, Prince Charles embraced it. In 2006, he purchased a farmhouse in the rural Transylvanian village of Viscri, and became a patron of the Mihai Eminescu Trust, an organization working to restore the cultural heritage of Transylvania's Saxon villages. In a 2013 video for the Romanian National Tourist Office, Prince Charles was seen saying, "Transylvania is in my blood. The genealogy shows I am descended from Vlad the Impaler, so I do have a bit of a stake in the country."

Vlad the Legend

Once the media discovered Vlad the Impaler, the image of the Wallachian prince began to crop up in attractions such as the London Dungeon where, in 1988, visitors could gaze at a recreation of Vlad dining among staked corpses. Vlad Tepeș also turned up at Madame Tussauds wax museum in London, where

In the Chamber of Horrors of London's Madame Tussauds Wax Museum, the first figure one encounters is Vlad the Impaler.

he remains one of the first figures visitors encounter as they enter the Chamber of Horrors.

In Los Angeles in September 1988, the Shakespeare Society of America premiered a new play by Ron Magid, *Dracula Tyrannus*, subtitled *The Tragical History of Vlad the Impaler*. To Magid's knowledge, it was the first time anyone had dramatized the life of Vlad III. The play starred Christopher Nixon; the staging included a mound of smoking skulls.

Inevitably, filmmakers also became interested in the story of Vlad the Impaler. The first film adaptation of *Dracula* to appear after the publication of Florescu and McNally's book was the CBS telefilm *Bram Stoker's Dracula*, directed by Dan Curtis and starring Jack Palance. At the conclusion of the telefilm, the camera moves in on a painting of Dracula as a warlord astride a horse, a clear reference to Vlad III.

In September of 1977, the *Los Angeles Times* reported that a film about Vlad III was being produced in Romania, with the intention of promoting Vlad Dracula as a national hero. *Vlad the Impaler*, starring Ştefan Sileanu as Vlad III, was released in Romania on January 8, 1979. The film focused mainly on Vlad's military campaigns against the Turks, playing down the impaling and veering away from the most lurid tales, although it did show highwaymen and beggars being burned in a banquet hall and Turkish emissaries with their hats nailed to their heads. Despite those actions, Ştefan Sileanu's Vlad III came across as a heroic figure rather than a crazed psychopath.

In the 1980s, Hollywood film production kicked up in Eastern Europe. At the time, the Romanian government reportedly turned down hundreds of proposals for Dracula movies to be filmed in the region, on the grounds that Bram Stoker's conception of the vampire count was an insult to the memory of the historical Dracula.

To Die For (1989), directed by Deran Sarafian, presented Brendan Hughes as vampire Vlad Tepish in modern-day Los Angeles, searching for his one true love. But then his nemesis arrives, determined to put an end to Vlad's long reign of terror. The film spawned a sequel, 1991's *Son of Darkness: To Die For II*, with TV's Robin Hood Michael Praed taking on the role of Vlad Tepish, now going by the rather obvious alias Dr. Max Schreck, in another story that portrayed Vlad as a modern-day vampire.

Screenwriter James V. Hart and producer/director Francis Ford Coppola began their 1992 film *Bram Stoker's Dracula* with scenes of Vlad in battle. In their romantic retelling, Vlad returns from the battlefield only to discover that his beloved wife, believing he has been killed, has committed suicide (in reality, she leapt to her death from Vlad's castle at Poenari because she feared being tortured by the Turks). Vlad then renounces God, which leads to his curse of immortality. Like the Dan Curtis TV movie, when Dracula then goes to nineteenth-century London, he encounters a reincarnation of his lost love.

The following year, Roger Corman unleashed his own Vlad/Dracula mash-up, *Dracula Rising*. Filmed in Bulgaria and directed by Fred T. Gallo, it featured *Blue Lagoon* heartthrob Christopher Atkins as Vlad. The film begins in modern-day America, with art historian Theresa (Stacey Travis) meeting a mysterious man at a party to whom she feels strangely attracted. She meets him again when she arrives in Romania to restore artwork in an ancient monastery. Flashbacks reveal that Theresa is a reincarnation of a peasant woman who was a monk's lover five hundred years earlier. When she was burned at the stake for witchcraft, the monk swore to avenge her death, and was cursed with vampirism. Now, in the modern day, he believes he has found his lost love. Although the vampire is called Vlad, he is a far cry from the Vlad III of history, who—whatever he was—was certainly no monk.

The Kushner-Locke Company produced 2000's *Dark Prince: The True Story of Dracula*, directed by Joe Chappelle and starring Rudolf Martin as a clean-shaven Vlad the Impaler. The TV movie, filmed in Bucharest and Transylvania, aired in the U.S. on October 31, 2000, just about a month after an episode of *Buffy the Vampire Slayer* in which Martin played Dracula. Like the earlier Romanian film, *Dark Prince: The True Story of Dracula* portrays the life of Vlad III, focusing equally on his love for a woman named Lidia (Jane Marsh) and his military campaigns against the Turks, receiving advice along the way from Father Stefan

(Peter Weller) and King Janos (rock star Roger Daltrey of the Who). The telefilm showed Vlad's progression from ruler to impaler, presenting a man who attained absolute power and was corrupted absolutely; the more lurid aspects of Vlad's history were discarded as the "forgeries and lies" of his enemies.

The 2003 film *Vlad* starred Billy Zane as Adrian, a modern-day disciple of the Order of the Dragon, aiding four foreign exchange students who have been brought to the Carpathians, where they are chased through the stunning scenery (shot on location in Romania) by a clearly vampiric Vlad Tepeș. Francesco Quinn, son of actor Anthony Quinn, exudes pure evil as the black-clad vampire. With a storyline that traverses back and forth from the fifteenth century to modern day, and has characters that bounce back and forth across time, the plot is rather muddled; the film was notable primarily as an example of how completely Stoker's *Dracula* and the historical Vlad III had become intertwined in popular culture by the turn of the century.

Saint Dracula 3D, written and directed by Rupesh Paul and produced by BizTV Network of the United Arab Emirates, was filmed in Wales and featured British actor Mitch Powell as Dracula. The 2012 film has the historical Dracula, Vlad III, reawaken in modern day and fall for a nun who is—you guessed it!—a reincarnation of his lost love. It also includes a completely out-of-left-field musical number that seems to have no connection to the rest of the film. When it was shown in Kerala, a state in the southwest region of India, the film drew protests from the Kerala Catholic Youth Movement, who found its depiction of Dracula as an actual saint and inferences of nuns having sex "vulgar," particularly given that the film was released there on March 29, 2013—Good Friday.

Dracula: The Dark Prince (2013), directed by Peary Teo, creates an entirely fictional backstory of a clean-shaven, blond-haired Vlad going to battle and leaving his wife to rule in his place. When the boyars kill his wife, he renounces God and is cursed with immortality. Luke Roberts plays the rather Nordic-looking Vlad, who—in his search for "the Lightbringer," a magical stick that can defeat the "creatures of the night"—eventually, in modern times, discovers a female crusader named Alina (Kelly Wenham), who is the reincarnation of his lost love (sound familiar?). Ultimately, Vlad, who has a slimy chancellor named Renfield (Stephen Hogan), is opposed by Leonardo Van Helsing (Jon Voight). With its mixture of elements from the historical Vlad and Stoker's novel, as well as images borrowed from Hammer horror films, Coppola's *Bram Stoker's Dracula*, and TV's *Xena: Warrior Princess*, *Dracula: The Dark Prince* emerged as a rather mindless comic-book blending of historical and horror elements.

In 2009, *Entertainment Weekly* reported that Summit Entertainment had purchased a spec script called *Vlad* from Charlie Hunnam, an actor as well as a scriptwriter who was then appearing in the American TV series *Sons of Anarchy*. Produced by Summit and Brad Pitt's production company, Plan B, the film was to be directed by Anthony Mandler. However, another film beat it to the punch.

Luke Evans stars as a clean-shaven Vlad III in *Dracula Untold*, a
film meant to reboot the Dracula character for a new generation of filmgoers.

© 2014 Universal Pictures. Author's collection.

Vlad Untold

On October 10, 2014, *Dracula Untold* hit American theaters. The project got its
start in 2006, when producer Michael DeLuca optioned the script *Dracula Year
Zero* by Matt Sazama and Buck Sharples. Alex Proyas was initially set to direct
with Sam Worthington in the title role, but when the film finally went before
the cameras in 2013, Luke Evans had won the role of Vlad Dracula and Gary
Shore, a director of commercials, was set to make his feature film debut. Filmed
in Northern Ireland, the $70 million production charts Vlad III's journey from
warlord to vampire. Universal Pictures, which released the film, hoped it would
revive their popular monster franchises.

Evans, who starred in the West End musical *Rent*, sought to play Vlad the
Impaler as more man than monster. "The film is about the transition Vlad made

on a human level, after being taken captive by the Ottoman court and reared as a child by his father's enemy, the first sultan," he said. "There he trained as a Turkish warrior, and learnt the gruesome torture techniques he went on to use against them as an adult . . . I don't think he was born evil. So the idea is to make him if not likeable then at least understandable."

Anyone hoping for a realistic portrayal of Vlad III's life would have been sorely disappointed by *Dracula Untold*, which used only the broadest strokes of Vlad's story and melded it with a comic-book–level vampire story. Before his transformation, Vlad is shown as being a kind, gentle ruler with hints of a dark, brutal past. When faced with a vastly superior invading army of Turks, he purposely seeks out an ancient vampire who lives in Broken Tooth Mountain to give him the supernatural power he needs to defeat his enemies. The vampire makes Vlad drink his blood, and then tells him that if he can resist the yearning to drink blood for three days, he will revert back to being human. After his transformation, Vlad's story becomes tragic—despite his newfound power, he is unable to save his wife, Mirena (Sarah Gadon), who falls from a cliff and, as she is dying, begs Vlad to drink her blood so that he will have the power to rescue their son, who has been kidnapped by the sultan. A vampiric Vlad confronts the sultan and defeats him, leaving his son to be crowned king of Transylvania. The film then cuts to an epilogue, in which Vlad, in modern day, encounters a woman named Mina (Sarah Gadon again), who is a reincarnation of Mirena (yet another film using the "Vlad's reincarnated lost love" trope). As they walk away together, we see that the vampire from Broken Tooth Mountain has also survived.

This is neither a very good film about Vlad, nor is it a very good Dracula film. One expects Dracula to be the king vampire of his story; in that sense, the real Dracula of *Dracula Untold* isn't Vlad, but the old vampire of Broken Tooth Mountain, played by Charles Dance. The ending hints at a sequel that will pit Vlad against the elder vampire, which points at the basic problem that undercuts the film: it's Dracula as heroic protagonist. In traditional Dracula films, the vampire is the villain, the antagonist, the force of darkness to be defeated by the forces of good. In *Dracula Untold*, there are moments when Vlad is almost cuddly; a force of darkness he is not. The film proved popular with audiences, however, collecting over $200 million at the worldwide box office before ending its run.

More than a century after the publication of Bram Stoker's *Dracula*, it appears that the more recently unearthed story of Vlad III, brought to light largely through the efforts of Radu Florescu and Raymond T. McNally, has supplanted the traditional image of a tuxedo-clad vampire and replaced it with a combination of history and fantasy. Like Stoker's fictional creation, Vlad III—Vlad the Impaler—has risen from the shadows of history, immortal and shape-shifting.

2

Dead and Undead

Vampire Myths Through the Ages

Vampires of Antiquity

In *Dracula*, Bram Stoker codified vampire myths and beliefs that have since become gospel, though the movies have added their own twists to the popular conception of bloodsuckers. But when Stoker wrote his novel, he was drawing on ideas that had been around for centuries; almost every culture, it seems, has their own version of reanimated, often blood-drinking corpses.

In their book *In Search of Dracula*, professors Raymond T. McNally and Radu Florescu wrote about vampires being found on Babylonian pottery and in ancient Peruvian rites. The ancient Greeks believed in the lamiai, creatures that suck the blood of children and have the ability to change their ghastly appearance to something more desirable to lure young men to their ruin or their deaths. According to Greek mythology, these monsters came into being when Zeus had a love affair with the Libyan princess Lamia, who—depending on which account one reads—was either the daughter of the sea god Poseidon or of Poseidon's son, Belus. When Hera, Zeus's jealous wife, found out about the illicit affair, she killed all of Lamia's children and sent her into exile. Since Lamia couldn't exact revenge upon the gods, she set about destroying mankind by stealing the babies of humans and sucking their blood. Later versions of the story changed the princess Lamia into beings called the *lamiai*, who were half-women, half-snake.

Many believe that India may be where vampire myths originated. The rich mythology of India includes hundreds of gods and demons, some of which still thrive in modern lore. It is believed that the stories spread through conquest and caravans into Europe, where they became intermingled with and modified local superstitions, myths, and legends. From the Indian underworld came the *rakshasas*, who seemed human but had fangs, lived in cemeteries, and wandered about at night, killing pregnant women and small children. Any human remains left by the rakshasas would be eaten by the hatu-dhana (also spelled yatu-dhana), who were less evolved demons than the rakshasas.

When the Greeks converted to Christianity, a new monster entered the imagination. The *vrykolakas* was a recently deceased person who returned to life as a virulent demon, either because they led a sacrilegious life, were excommunicated from the church, were buried in unconsecrated ground, or were just unlucky enough to have eaten meat from a sheep that had been wounded by a werewolf. Though essentially a vampire, the word *vrykolakas* is derived from the Bulgarian *vărkolak*, which is itself a compound of words that roughly translated mean "wolf hair," or werewolf.

Vampires of Europe and Eurasia

Similar creatures are found among the folklore of rural Czechs and Slovaks, where they are called *upir* or *nelapsi*. The upir, believed to have two hearts and two souls, is a particularly nasty monster that can kill with its evil eye, but also sucks the blood from its victims while crushing them in its embrace.

The Russians have a variant of the upir, which they call the *uppyr*. Anyone who holds beliefs that run counter to the teachings of the Russian Orthodox Church or who leads a less than saintly life can become an uppyr, or a corpse that refuses to stay buried.

Bulgarians have their *vampir*, a corpse that rises from its grave, appearing just as healthy as when it was living. The vampir sometimes move to new locales where they aren't recognized, so they can live relatively normal lives by day and wreak havoc by night. In Bosnia, the *lampir* is a disease-carrying corpse that leaves its grave to infect others.

In the Romanian principality of Transylvania, where Stoker set the beginning and end of his novel, the locals believed in two types of vampires: the *strigoi vii*, which look like living persons, and the *strigoi mort*, which leave their tombs and take the forms of animals to terrorize the living. Strigoi is taken from the word *striga*, or witch; when witches die, they are doomed to become vampires. Of the two types, the strigoi mort are the deadliest, rising from their graves to first suck the blood of their families and livestock and then moving on to their village neighbors.

In Romania, it is believed that suicides may become vampires, as well as those who lead sinful lives. And if a pregnant woman allows a vampire to look at her, she'll give birth to a vampire. Other candidates for vampirism include children who die before baptism, children born out of wedlock, and anyone born with an amniotic membrane, or caul, clinging to their head. Some say that the seventh son of a seventh son, or the seventh child of the same sex, may become a vampire.

Albanians had the *shtriga*, a term derived from the Latin *strix*, for screech owl. The shtriga was thought to be a witch who seemed like a normal person during daylight hours, but when night fell, it transformed into a flying insect like a fly or moth, attacking victims and drinking their blood. To trap a shtriga, one had

Bat Woman, painted by Albert Penot in 1890.

Author's collection

to construct a cross of pig bones and attach it to the doorway of a church during a religious service. If a shtriga was among those inside, they would be unable to exit past the pig-bone cross. If you suspected someone of being a shtriga, it paid to follow them after dark and wait for them to vomit the blood of their victims. If you soaked a coin in the blood, you'd have a charm to protect you against future shtriga attacks.

In northern Germany, one could fall victim to the *nachtzeherer*, or night waster, a creature that, once it died and resurrected, chewed on its own arms, hands, and clothing. Suicides were likely to become nachtzeherer, as well as those who suffered sudden unexplained deaths or people buried with their names attached to their clothing. Southern Germany had a similar creature called the *blutsauger*, or bloodsucker.

Early myths from Scotland gave rise to the *baobhan sith*, beautiful women who appeared from nowhere and danced with young hunters by moonlight. In the morning, the hunters would be found drained of their blood.

Vampires of the Americas

In Latin America, the Mayan *Camazotz* had the body of a man but the head of a bat. A symbol of death and sacrifice, the Camazotz supposedly inhabited caves, like the vampire bats that likely inspired them.

A particularly mean-spirited creature was the *tiahuelpuchi*, a bloodsucking variety of the *bruja*—or witch—that had the power to transform into a number of different animals so it could roam about freely. The tiahuelpuchi sucked blood from infants, killing them, and also was able to hypnotize adults into committing suicide. To protect infants from tiahuelpuchi attacks, garlic, onions, and metal were placed in or around the crib. It is said that even today, in the more remote areas of Mexico, infant deaths are believed to be caused by the tiahuelpuchi.

Vampires of Asia and Africa

In China, the *jiang shi* (sometimes spelled *chiang shih*), also known as the hopping ghost, is the undead corpse of a victim of suicide, hanging, drowning, or smothering. These creatures, known for ripping the limbs and heads from their victims, are—like the Mexican tiahuelpuchi—repelled by garlic, salt, and metal filings. But it's not likely you'd encounter one on a stormy night; if they hear the sound of thunder, they die.

The *kappa*, a Japanese monster, has greenish-yellow skin, large round eyes and webbed fingers and toes and is said to look like a hairless monkey. It hides in waterways and ponds, from which it springs onto its victims, pulls them under and drowns them. It then sucks their blood through their intestines, and may eat the victim's liver. A variant of the kappa occurs in Malaysia, where if a mother dies in childbirth, she becomes a *langsuyar* and her child a *pontianak*. Both seek revenge on living victims by tearing open their bellies and sucking their blood.

In Arab countries, a murder victim could become an *afrit*, a spirit that rose in smoke from a dead body to seek revenge on its murderer. To prevent someone from becoming an afrit, a spike was driven into the ground at the murder site.

West Africa's vampire is the *obayifo*, a creature that assumes human form by day, but by night goes about sucking the blood from children, causing them to sicken and die. They also kill livestock and cause poor crops.

From Whence Do Vampires Come?

In pre-industrial times, villagers had no knowledge of airborne diseases or micro-organisms that could infect food sources or water supplies, thus it seemed plausible that the first person to succumb to a disease would come out at night and spread it to others. Nor did primitive societies have an understanding of how bodies decompose. In their attempts to explain such things through superstition, vampire myths developed.

Stages of Death

When a person dies, the body undergoes certain stages of decomposition. As the internal organs deteriorate, they release gases that can bloat the body, making it appear as if it has just fed. Blood or other reddish fluid may be forced out through the mouth, nostrils, or other orifices. As water in the skin evaporates, it causes dehydration that can cause the fingertips to shrink back from the nails and gums to shrink back from the teeth, giving the appearance that the nails and teeth have grown. When staked, a bloated corpse releases the gases and fluids, giving the appearance of bleeding and emitting a noise that might sound like a groan, if the released air passes through the vocal cords, or like flatulence, if the air passes through the anus. Either sound is proof of life for, as any self-respecting vampire hunter will tell you, dead men don't groan, and they certainly don't fart.

Some disinterred bodies may seem more lifelike than others due to temperature affecting the speed at which decomposition occurs. A body buried in cold, dry weather will decompose more slowly, showing fewer signs of decomposition than a body buried for a similar length of time in a hot and humid climate. If a dead body placed in cold ground is dug up and seems not to have decomposed, the vampire hunters may jump to the conclusion that it is still alive.

During times of plague, it is likely that people were buried who appeared to be dead but who were, in fact, simply unconscious. Should such a person have cause to be unearthed, there might be signs that they tried to escape their coffin upon awakening, bloodying their hands or faces in their efforts to gain freedom (in the nineteenth century, coffins were devised with a pull-string that traveled up a tube to the top of the gravesite, where it was attached to a bell, allowing anyone unfortunate enough to be buried alive to signal that they were still among the living). Also, if grave robbers disinterred someone, they might do a sloppy job of putting them back in the earth, giving the appearance that the corpse had left its grave under its own volition.

Identifying Vampires

In European cultures, many rituals for identifying a vampire developed through the years. If any holes appeared over a grave, they were considered a sign of vampirism. But how could one be sure the grave contained a vampire without digging up the corpse? One method was to put a virgin boy astride a virgin horse and lead them through the graveyard; the horse would balk at the vampire's grave. Black horses were thought best for the job, except in Albania, where white horses were preferred (a point to remember if you're trying to pass yourself off as a qualified vampire hunter in Albania).

In the 1700s, there were reports in Eastern Europe of vampires being exhumed, who, though dead for years, looked as though they'd just gone to sleep. They hadn't decomposed, and when stakes were plunged into their hearts or their heads cut off, warm blood spurted out. It was thought that the devil had given them supernatural powers, permitting them to leave their undisturbed graves and prey upon the living, especially members of their own families. As Douglass McFerran, an author and professor of philosophy at Pierce College in Woodland Hills, California, pointed out, they did not look like Bela Lugosi in evening clothes. "The real horror of the historic[al] vampire is that he looks normal," McFerran said in an interview with Gerald Faris of the *Los Angeles Times*. "He has a heartbeat, his eyes are normal and he never looks abnormal. The semi-corpse is Hollywood."

McFerran said that, historically, vampirism was part of the religious persecution that happened in Eastern Europe after the Turks were driven out and the area came under the control of Roman Catholic Austria. For instance, in

Hungary in the early 1700s, dead people were sometimes put on trial, accused of leaving their graves and assaulting their neighbors. The targets of these trials were usually Greek Orthodox adherents or excommunicated Catholics. Accounts of vampirism in the eighteenth century were more detailed and were sometimes accepted as official documents, though McFerran viewed them with skepticism, saying many were frauds.

Stoker's Vampires

Today, most of what we know of vampires we learned from Bram Stoker's *Dracula* and the countless vampire books, plays, and films it spawned. In the book, Stoker mentions that in Eastern Europe, the word *nosferatu* means undead. Stoker found the word in Emily de Laszkowski Gerard's 1888 book, *The Land Beyond the Forest*, or perhaps from her 1885 essay, "Transylvanian Superstitions." Stoker accepted Gerard's assertion that nosferatu was a Romanian word for vampire; he wasn't aware that she got it wrong. According to Mark Dawidziak, author of *The Bedside, Bathtub & Armchair Companion to Dracula*, the word seems to have derived from the Greek *nosphoros*, which means "plague carrier" or "disease bearing," though some say it is a corruption of the Latin word for "not breathing" or the Romanian words for "unclean" and "insufferable."

Stoker's Dracula and other vampires of his ilk are easily recognized. They have hair in the palms of their hands. They have long, pointed ears. Their red eyes glare out from under thick eyebrows that meet over a prominent nose. Their lips are red and swollen. Their face has an "extraordinary pallor." They have prominent canine teeth. Their breath stinks. They tend to dress in nothing

Long before *True Blood* and *The Vampire Diaries*, *Varney the Vampire* kept people coming back for more vampire thrills, for 109 successive issues, published as "penny dreadful" pamphlets from 1845 to 1847.   *Author's collection*

but black. They generally spend their days in their coffins, preferring to move about at night, though they are able to go about in daylight; in the novel, Jonathan Harker spots Dracula during the daytime on a London street. They can command wolves, bats, and rats to do their bidding. They can turn into mist, dust motes, moonbeams, bats, or wolves. They are unnaturally strong. And though they may be centuries old, drinking blood can make them appear young; Dracula is an old man when Harker first sees him in Transylvania, but appears decades younger by the time he encounters him again.

But the classic, Stoker-inspired vampire is not all-powerful. A vampire cannot cross the threshold of a residence unless someone inside invites them in. And, in Dracula's case, they can be repelled by the symbols of Christianity, like a crucifix or holy water. They're also repelled by the smell of garlic. Despite having researched vampire traditions, Stoker added a few new twists, such as the vampire's inability to cast a reflection in a mirror (presumably because its body is just a re-animated shell, with no soul inside), and its ability to change locations so long as it takes along a coffin filled with soil from its native burial site.

Whatever its abilities, the vampire in its myriad forms has long haunted humankind. Even in our scientific, less superstitious age, vampires are seen in popular entertainment—books, movies, and games. It seems that as long as human beings have an imagination and fear death, the creatures that dwell in the dark recesses of our subconscious will exist among us.

3

Precursors of Dracula

Victorian Vampires

The Vampire in Verse

Although Bram Stoker's *Dracula* most influenced the popular conception of vampires in the twentieth and twenty-first centuries, he was certainly not the first bloodsucker to emerge in literature. Besides drawing upon centuries of folklore, Stoker also drew upon decades of literary precedent.

One of the first mentions of a vampire in popular literature occurred in Heinrich August Ossenfelder's poem *Der Vampir* (*The Vampire*), which appeared in 1748. The poem is told from the point of view of a man in love with a respectable young woman who rejects his affection. In return, he threatens to come to her in the night, drink her blood, and turn her into a vampire, proving that his beliefs are stronger than her mother's Christianity. Linking, from the outset, vampirism and erotic yearning, the poem contains the lines:

> And as softly thou art sleeping
> To thee shall I come creeping
> And thy life's blood drain away.

Though not strictly a vampire poem, Gottfried August Bürger's poem *Lenore* (1773) involves a character who returns from his grave. It is thought to have had an influence on future Gothic literature; it was later translated from the German into English by William Taylor, who called it *Ellenore*. In the latter poem, when her husband William does not return from the Seven Years' War, Ellenore curses God. That evening, at midnight, a stranger resembling William knocks on her door and asks her to come on a horseback ride with him to their marriage bed. She goes with him on the moonlight ride, speeding through eerie landscapes. When she asks why he is riding so fast, he responds that it is because "the dead travel fast," a line familiar to anyone who has read Stoker's *Dracula*.

Esteemed German poet and novelist Johann Wolfgang von Goethe made his contribution to vampire literature with his 1797 poem *Die Braut von Corinth* (*The Bride of Corinth*), in which a traveler beds down in the room of a house only to be visited by a pale, white-robed maiden who makes love to him and takes his life. The poem contains the lines:

> From my grave to wander I am forc'd
> Still to seek The Good's long-sever'd link,
> Still to love the bridegroom I have lost,
> And the life-blood of his heart to drink . . .

In 1810, John Stagg published *The Vampyre*, in which a husband tells his wife he is being visited at night by his former friend, now a vampire, and—knowing that he will soon suffer his friend's fate—begs her to put an end to him:

> But to avoid this horrid fate,
> Soon as I'm dead and laid in earth,
> Drive thro' my corpse a jav'lin straight;
> This shall prevent my coming forth . . .

The poem ends with both the husband and his friend being staked, freeing the village from the vampire curse.

George Gordon, Lord Byron, presented a revenant of his own in *The Giaour* (1813). *Giaour* is a Turkish insult meaning infidel (non-believer); the main story has a woman from Hassan's harem, Leila, who is in love with the infidel, punished by being thrown into the sea. The infidel takes his revenge by killing Hassan, an act for which, the Ottoman narrator tells us, the infidel will be punished by being condemned to become a vampire after his death, preying upon his own family:

> But first on earth, as Vampyre sent,
> Thy corse shall from its tomb be rent;
> Then ghastly haunt thy native place,
> And suck the blood of all thy race;
> There from thy daughter, sister, wife,
> At midnight drain the stream of life . . .

The Byronic Vampire

Having won fame for his poem *Childe Harold's Pilgrimage*, Byron was considered something of a vampire himself, luring married women into torrid affairs and leaving them emotionally drained. One of his lovers, the married Lady Caroline Lamb, who famously labeled Byron "mad, bad and dangerous to know," wrote a novel in 1816 called *Glenarvon*, whose main character, Ruthven Glenarvon, was a thinly disguised Byron with vampiric characteristics: he was a nocturnal wanderer who "howls and barks, whenever the moon shines bright," had an

George Gordon, Lord Byron, as painted by Thomas Phillips in
1813. Dashingly handsome but well-known as a rake, the poet
coined an adjective *Byronesque.*   *Wikimedia Commons*

ancestor who "drank hot blood from the skull of his enemy" (a reference to a
real-life event—Byron once drank wine from a skull in Newstead Abbey), and
tells Calantha (the novel's avatar for Lady Caroline), "My love is death."

After *Glenarvon*'s publication, Byron went on a tour of Europe, taking with
him his physician and personal secretary, Dr. John Polidori. It was a rather one-
sided friendship; Lord Byron enjoyed playing cruel practical jokes at the
expense of his traveling companion, whom he nicknamed "Polly-Dolly." Polly-
Dolly played along, but he was only laughing on the outside. Inwardly, he was
harboring a smoldering resentment for Byron.

In 1816, Byron and Polidori arrived at the Villa Diodati, Byron's summer
house in Geneva. They were soon joined by Byron's friend and fellow poet
Percy Shelley and Shelley's girlfriend, Mary Godwin, with whom Shelley,
estranged from his wife, had a son. Mary Godwin's sister, Claire, who was
pregnant with Lord Byron's child, arrived sometime later. It was a rainy summer,
and one gloomy June night, during a period when the weather kept them
indoors, the group amused themselves by sitting around the fire reading from
Fantasmagoriana, a French collection of German horror stories. After a while,

Byron suggested that they each write a ghost story of their own. Shelley wrote "A Fragment of a Ghost Story" and jotted down five ideas that were published posthumously as *Journal at Geneva.* Mary's contribution would become her novel, *Frankenstein, or the Modern Prometheus,* published in 1818. Lord Byron began a story, "Fragment of a Novel," which he later abandoned. But Polidori picked up Byron's unfinished tale and used it as the basis for his novel, *The Vampyre.* The main character, Lord Ruthven (a name that alludes to Lady Caroline Lamb's Ruthven Glenarvon), is—like Byron—an aristocrat who is exceedingly handsome, though very pale; the very sight of him is enough to make women swoon. Also like Byron, Ruthven has a flaw in his beauty; for the poet, it was a club foot; for the vampire, it is a dead grey eye.

Byron eventually tired of Polidori and dismissed him. Polidori returned to England where *The Vampyre* was published, without his permission, in the April 1819 issue of *New Monthly Magazine.* The story was erroneously attributed to Byron, who released "Fragment of a Novel" to clear up the confusion. Depressed and deeply in debt, Polidori was found dead on August 24, 1821. It was rumored that he had committed suicide. He was only twenty-five, but he left a lasting legacy: the first published modern vampire story.

After its magazine publication, *The Vampyre* was released as a novel, selling so well it was translated into other languages. In 1820, Frenchman Cyprien Bérard wrote a sequel, *Lord Ruthven ou les Vampires.* Polidori's original was dramatized for the Paris stage as *Le Vampire,* opening at the Théatre de la Porte-Charles Nordier on June 13, 1820. Written by Charles Nordier, the play changed the story's locale from Greece to Scotland and the name of the vampire from Ruthven to Rutwen. Like the later stage adaptations of *Dracula,* it took a critical drubbing but was a success with the public, sparking a "vampire mania" in the arts.

Soon, several other plays about vampires opened in Europe, including *Le Fils Vampires* by Paul Féval, the comedy *Le Vampire* by Martin Joseph Mengals, and the opera *Der Vampyr* by Heinrich Marschner, which was based on Heinrich Ludwig Ritter's play *Der Vampir oder die Totenbraut,* which in turn was based on Polidori's novel. The Nordier play was adapted into an English-language production by James Robinson Planché as *The Vampire, or, The Bride of the Isles,* which premiered on August 9, 1820, at the English Opera House (later to become the Lyceum Theatre, managed by *Dracula* author Bram Stoker). To affect a quick disappearance for the bloodsucker, a special trap door with spring leaves that immediately reclosed was built into the set. The cast members took to calling it the "vampire's trap," a name by which actors and stagehands still refer to that particular type of trap door.

Alexandre Dumas *père* was in the audience of a revival of the Nordier play in 1823, and in 1851 wrote his own adaptation of the novel, also called *Le Vampire.* In Dumas's version, a group of travelers stop at a haunted castle, where the vampire Lord Ruthven begins to prey on them (a plot similar to the 1966 Hammer film, *Dracula, Prince of Darkness*).

Dion Boucicault wrote his own version of Polidori's story, called *The Vampire*, which was presented on June 19, 1852 at the Princess Theatre in London, with Boucicault himself essaying the lead role of vampire Alan Raby. Raby dressed all in black with a velvet cloak and hat; forty years later, Bram Stoker would describe Dracula as being "clad in black from head to foot."

After seeing Boucicault's *The Vampire*, one London critic wrote that he had no objection to "an honest ghost," but "an animated corpse which goes about in Christian attire, and although never known to eat, or drink, or shake hands, is allowed to sit at good men's feasts; which renews its odious life every hundred years by sucking a young lady's blood, after fascinating her by motions which resemble mesmerism burlesqued . . . such a ghost as this passes all bounds of toleration." In her diary, Queen Victoria dismissed the play as "very trashy."

Varney the Vampire

In 1845, *Varney the Vampire* arrived on the scene, in a series of 109 "penny dreadful" pamphlets. The story continued for two years, totaling 220 chapters in 876 double-columned pages. In 1847, it was published in book form. Though no author was credited, the story is believed to have been written by James Malcolm Rymer (some thought it the work of Thomas Preskett Prest, whose 1846 *The String of Pearls*, co-authored with Rymer, introduced the character of Sweeney Todd, the demon barber of Fleet Street). Cursed with vampirism after betraying a royalist to Oliver Cromwell and then accidentally killing his own son in a fit of anger, Sir Francis Varney dies and is revived several times throughout the convoluted, often confusing storyline. Though Varney can walk in sunlight and has no aversion to garlic or crosses, the story did establish that

Cover of the "penny dreadful" *Varney the Vampire*, or the *Feast of Blood*, showing the vampire as a rather unappealing living corpse. *Author's collection* vampires have fangs, leave two puncture marks on the necks of their victims, have hypnotic powers, and possess unnatural strength. It is believed to be the first story to show a vampire coming in through a window to victimize a sleeping woman; it also has a vampire make his way from Eastern Europe to England on a vessel that is shipwrecked in a storm. Additionally, Varney is the first sympathetic vampire, despising the condition with which he's cursed; at the tale's end, he commits suicide by throwing himself into Mount Vesuvius.

The Mysterious Azzo

In 1860, *The Mysterious Stranger* was published in England. Translated from the 1844 story *Der Fremde* by Karl Adolf von Wachsmann, it concerned a family traveling from Germany to Hungary to take possession of a castle they've inherited. Passing through the Carpathian Mountains, they encounter the knight Azzo von Klatka, who becomes attracted to Franziska, one of the young women in the party. After several visits from Azzo, Franziska becomes progressively weaker. When her cousin, Woislaw, returns from fighting the Napoleonic war in Russia, he recognizes that Azzo is a vampire and works with Franziska to destroy him. Given the similarities to the plot of Stoker's vampire tale, it is believed that Stoker read *The Mysterious Stranger* prior to writing *Dracula*.

Stoker himself admitted to having read Dublin author Joseph Sheridan Le Fanu's story *Carmilla*, which first appeared in the short story collection *In a Glass Darkly*, published in 1872. The story concerns a young woman, Laura, who falls under the spell of another woman, Carmilla. A close bond develops between Carmilla and Laura, who grows progressively weaker. Carmilla is eventually deduced to be Countess Mircalla Karnstein, and is staked and beheaded after being located in her blood-filled coffin in Karnstein Castle. *Carmilla* later inspired a trio of films from Hammer Film Productions, which are collectively known as the Karnstein trilogy: *Vampire Lovers* (1970), *Lust for a Vampire* (1971), and *Twins of Evil* (1971).

Like a nineteenth-century Quentin Tarantino, Bram Stoker seemed to have ingested the best elements of all of these seminal works and reshaped them into a vision that was similar and yet uniquely his own, more captivating, more exciting, and more spine-chilling than any vampire tale that came before it. After Glenarvon, Ruthven, Raby, Varney, Azzo, and Carmilla, the stage was set for Stoker to unleash Dracula.

Un-Dead on Arrival

Bram Stoker and *Dracula*

In the Beginning . . .

Imagine, if you will, a young Irish boy of such sensitivity that he is frightened by everything. His father, Abraham, a stern, strict man who works as a clerk at Dublin Castle (the center of the city's administration), is away most of the day. His mother, Charlotte, from County Sligo, tells him stories of the plague, famine, Irish superstitions, banshees, and premature burial. The boy's anxieties manifest themselves in a strange way: they render him unable to walk. In his formative years, he has to be carried from room to room, and is sometimes taken outside and lain on the grass, where he observes his older brother and sister at play.

This was the story of Abraham Stoker the younger. It was only later, after three other brothers and a sister came along, that Stoker's illness mysteriously lifted and, at age seven, he took his first steps.

Stoker, born in Clontarf, Ireland, on November 8, 1847, grew up attending private school. His father sometimes took him to the theater. The boy Stoker fell in love with the fantasy world of the stage, a world of imagination, mystery, and dreams. When he finished his private school education, he went to university at Trinity College, Dublin, from 1864 to 1870. At Trinity, he joined the debating team and fell in love with the works of Walt Whitman, defending the controversial poet's *Leaves of Grass*. He wrote a long letter to Whitman, speaking of how moved he was by his writing, saying, "How sweet a thing it is for a strong, healthy man with a woman's eyes and a child's wishes to feel that he can speak so to a man who can be if he wishes father and brother and wife to his soul." Stoker was perhaps looking for a literary mentor, or at least longing to be accepted by a writer he admired. Whitman eventually responded, and years later, when Stoker made a tour of America with the actor Henry Irving, Whitman and Stoker met.

Despite his childhood infirmity, Stoker grew to be six feet two, a large man for his time, and was quite an athlete while at Trinity College. After he graduated with honors, earning a BA in mathematics, his father arranged a job for him at Dublin Castle; the son was following in the father's footsteps.

Dracula author Bram Stoker, circa 1906, photographed at the studio of Victorian portraitists William and Daniel Downey.   *Author's collection*

The Call of the Stage

When Henry Irving came through Dublin on a theater tour in August of 1867, Stoker—halfway through his studies at Trinity—saw him as Captain Absolute in *The Rivals*. Stoker was so smitten by Irving's performances that he himself became an actor for a short while, even appearing as Captain Absolute in another production of *The Rivals*. When not acting, Stoker spent his days working at Dublin Castle, and his nights working on his master's degree. And, in November 1871, when Henry Irving returned to Dublin, performing as Digby Grant in James Albery's *Two Roses*, Stoker made sure to be there.

When the local papers failed to praise Irving's performance, Stoker decided that he should become a drama critic and champion talents overlooked by the establishment. He submitted reviews of theatrical performances to the *Dublin Evening Mail*, a newspaper co-owned by J. Sheridan Le Fanu, the author of the vampire tale *Carmilla*. Aside from reviews, Stoker also began writing stories. His first published tale, "The Crystal Cup," appeared in *The London Society* in 1872. Three years later came his first horror story, a four-part serial called *The Chain of Destiny*, published in *The Shamrock*.

As a lover of theater, as well as being an aspiring author, Stoker began attending the weekend salons of surgeon Sir William Wilde and his colorful wife, Lady Jane Wilde, who wrote poetry under the name Speranza and was an ardent nationalist and collector of Irish folk tales. The salons attracted the cream of Dublin's artistic and intellectual elite, including J. Sheridan Le Fanu and the young Stoker, who—in his final year at Trinity—recommended the Wildes' son, Oscar, for membership in the Philosophical Society. Oscar later left Trinity for Oxford, leaving behind a young woman named Florence Balcombe, who was celebrated as a great beauty. In Oscar's absence, she began seeing Stoker. Though he was upset at Florence's decision, Wilde eventually resumed friendships with both Balcombe and Stoker.

On October 12, 1876, Stoker's father died. Shortly afterwards, the younger Stoker decided to change his name from Abraham to Bram, a signal that, without the parental influence, he was now his own man. Having now become an Inspector of Petty Sessions at Dublin Castle, he was nevertheless still writing theatrical reviews. Though he received no pay for them, they would soon pay big dividends.

Lord of the Lyceum

In December 1876, Henry Irving made yet another tour of Ireland, this time performing *Hamlet*. When he passed through Dublin, Stoker wrote a glowing notice. Irving was impressed enough, or flattered enough, that he requested dinner with Stoker. Kindred spirits, the two men talked until dawn. On their second meeting, in Irving's rooms at the Shelbourne Hotel, the actor gave Stoker a special gift, a recitation of *The Dream of Eugene Aram* performed with such gusto that, upon finishing, Irving collapsed in a chair. Stoker was left in hysterics, moving Irving so that he presented Stoker with a photo of himself autographed, "My dear friend Stoker. God bless you! God bless you!! Henry Irving, Dublin, December 3, 1876." Writing about the evening later, Stoker said, "Soul had looked into soul! From that hour began a friendship as profound, as close, as lasting as can be between two men."

In the winter of 1878, Irving made yet another tour of Ireland. By now, he had become acting manager of the Lyceum Theatre, and he convinced Stoker to join him as business manager. Stoker accepted. In December of 1878, he arranged a hasty marriage to Florence Balcombe and, after the briefest of honeymoons, left Dublin for London and the Lyceum.

In his new position, Stoker oversaw the administrative and artistic management of the Lyceum, becoming Irving's confidante and right-hand man. The Stokers were now rubbing shoulders with the cream of British society. They lived in a fashionable house in Chelsea, at Cheyne Walk, with such neighbors as James McNeill Whistler; Dante Gabriel Rossetti; John Singer Sargent; Alfred, Lord Tennyson; W. S. Gilbert; and, for a time, Mark Twain. On December 31, 1879, the Stoker's son, Noel Thornley, was born.

Henry Irving (left, in top hat) and his devoted theater manager, Bram Stoker (second from right) exit the stage door of the Lyceum Theatre, as seen in the publication *Tatler*, October 1902.   *Author's collection*

The Birth of Dracula

Stoker held memberships in the National Liberal Club, the Authors' Club, and the Green Room Club. John J. O'Connor, writing in the *New York Times* sixty-five years after Stoker's death, claimed that the author also belonged to "the Order of the Golden Dawn, an occult society whose members included William Butler Yeats, the poet, and Aleister Crowley, the notorious Satanist."

A collection of Stoker's rather morbid short stories, *Under the Sunset*, was published in 1881, but his next novel, *The Snake's Pass*, didn't appear until 1890. That year, Stoker had a dream that would fuel his most lasting creation. He saw a man reclining, sleeping, while three vampire women hovered over him. They kissed him, not on the mouth, but on the neck. Then, a man tore into the room and savagely pushed the women away, saying, "This man belongs to me. I want him." The dream simmered in Stoker's imagination, and he began developing a story around it. In early August 1890, he took his family for a holiday in Whitby, in North Yorkshire. The seaside town fired the imagination of the author.

Whitby is situated on two cliffs, split in the middle by the River Esk. Stoker wrote parts of the novel while vacationing in the town, and wove the location into his story. In his new novel, the vampire's ship runs aground at Whitby, an episode based on a real-life incident—the Russian ship *Dmitry* out of Narva ran aground there during a storm in October 1885; in the novel, it is the *Demeter*, out of Varna. But it was the East Cliff, with its 199 steps leading up to a graveyard and the ruins of Whitby Abbey, that made the greatest impression on the author. It's said that in the Abbey ruins, Stoker found the inspiration for Castle Dracula.

Most importantly, in the Whitby Library, Stoker found a book called *An Account of the Principalities of Wallachia and Moldavia*, in which there was a footnote about a fifteenth-century warlord named Dracula. Stoker had thought of calling his villain Count Wampyr, from Styria (a location mentioned in J. Sheridan Le Fanu's *Carmilla*). Now, he changed his vampire's name to Count Dracula, and situated his castle in Transylvania.

Some of the most evocative writing in *Dracula* comes at the beginning and end, the portions set in Transylvania. In reality, Stoker never visited the country, relying instead on information gleaned from books and from his friend Arminius Vambery, a professor from the University of Budapest. After conversations with Vambery, Stoker conducted further research in the British Library, uncovering facts about Vlad III.

While collecting information and working out the plot of *Dracula*, Stoker also wrote two other novels, *The Watter's Mou'* and *The Shoulder of Shasta*, both of which appeared in 1895. In May of 1897, Stoker sent the manuscript of his latest novel to Constable, his publisher. There was some uncertainty about the title; in his working notes, he had jotted down three possible titles: "The Un-Dead," "The Dead Un-Dead," and "Dracula." Stoker submitted it under the title "The Un-Dead." Before publication, the title changed to *Dracula*. The book arrived at booksellers on May 26, 1897.

Since its publication, Stoker's book has been subject to all kinds of interpretations of the author's unconscious influences. Some have seen it as an exploration of the fear of foreign immigration, with a malicious invader from Eastern Europe attempting to spread his evil influence over civilized cosmopolitan London. Others view it as a misogynistic fantasy of male power dominating the "New Woman," as women with progressive, liberated ideas were referred to at the time; Mina Murray, with her aspirations to work alongside her husband-to-be, Jonathan Harker, and her mastery of shorthand and the typewriter

An advertisement for the novel, *Dracula*, from the *New York Times*, August 24, 1901.

Author's collection

is definitely an exemplar of this progressive female, Others say the novel's vampirism is a metaphor for the sexuality that Victorians were prohibited from expressing, with the vampire's bite being symbolic of penetration, and the "blood disease" of vampirism being a metaphor for syphilis. But Stoker may have thought he was simply writing an exciting thriller, given verisimilitude by its presentation as a series of journal entries and letters.

Dracula as Irving?

Given Stoker's slavish devotion to Henry Irving, many biographers have drawn parallels between the Renfield-Dracula relationship of the novel and the real-life relationship of Stoker and Irving. The physical description of Dracula—tall, thin, charismatic, mesmeric—could apply equally as well to Irving, though the actor had no facial hair, nor any on the palms of his hands. Whereas the vampire depleted the blood of his victims literally, Irving only expected his sycophants— Stoker chief among them—to figuratively give their blood to his productions.

By the time *Dracula* was published, Irving had become the theater's brilliant interpreter of Hamlet, Shylock, Mephistopheles, and Faust. It's only natural that Stoker, who put Shakespearean elements into Dracula, would begin thinking of how to get his boss interested in doing the book as a play. But Irving would have none of it; he saw his factotum's novel as a "shilling shocker," unworthy of his exalted talents.

Stoker himself penned the first stage version of *Dracula.* Hastily done, it was intended primarily to protect the copyright of the book for stage productions. At that time, many authors did quick play adaptations of their novels for that very reason, and the Lyceum Theatre often rented out its facilities, usually on a Saturday morning, for the required staged reading, which counted as a performance. Stoker's *Dracula* adaptation reportedly began at 10:30 in the morning and lasted until the final curtain rang down at 6:15 that evening. A "Mr. Jones" played Dracula; it is presumed that this was Whitworth Jones, an actor with the Lyceum company. Irving reportedly saw a portion of the reading and, to Stoker's supreme disappointment, pronounced it, "Dreadful!"

Stoker's affiliation with Henry Irving lasted until the actor's death in 1905. Afterwards, Stoker wrote an extensive two-volume account of Irving's life, *Personal Reminiscences of Henry Irving,* drawing upon the extensive notes and diaries Stoker kept during their twenty-seven-year-long association. Indeed, it was this book for which he thought he would be best remembered, and during the remainder of his lifetime, he was right.

Stoker's Twilight Years

After Irving's death, with the Lyceum under new management, Stoker eked out a meager living serving on the literary staff of the *London Daily Telegraph.* Still interested in theater, he also acted as manager of David Bispham's light opera, *The Vicar of Wakefield*. But his best years, the Lyceum years, were behind him.

Between 1898 and 1911, he published seven more books, including *The Jewel of Seven Stars* (1903) and *The Lair of the White Worm* (1911), both of which would eventually inspire film adaptations. Doubleday and McClure Co. published *Dracula* in the United States. In March 1900, the company placed advertisements in the *New York Times* offering the book for sale ("a thrilling book for the jaded reader") for a dollar fifty. The following month, an advertisement in the

This cover illustration from a 1916 edition of *Dracula* depicts the vampire, in black cloak, scaling the wall of his castle.

Author's collection

Chicago Daily Tribune offered it as one of the "famous books of the year" at the bargain sale price of sixty-eight cents.

Dracula was serialized in *The Washington Times* of Washington, D.C., in 1900, and again from September 1917 into early 1918. It was said that the publication of the story caused the newspaper to sell out daily, and that instead of shouting the news, the newsboys just announced that there was a new instalment of *Dracula*.

Stoker died in London on April 21, 1912, at age sixty-four. The *New York Times*, in their obituary, noted "his best-known publication is *Personal Reminiscences of Henry Irving*, issued in 1908." In 1914, two years after Stoker's death, his widow, Florence, took the original first chapter of *Dracula*, which had been omitted prior to the book's publication, and included it with other Stoker tales, published as *Dracula's Guest and Other Weird Stories*.

Dracula's Legacy

Dr. A. S. W. Rosenbach, who bought and sold decorative objects, opened the Rosenbach Company with his brother in 1903. Besides buying rarities that ended up in several major libraries, he began a personal collection that, through the 1920s, grew to include James Joyce's original handwritten manuscript for *Ulysses*, Lewis Carroll's own copy of an 1865 edition of *Alice's Adventures in Wonderland*, and handwritten notes and an outline for Bram Stoker's *Dracula*. They now reside in the Rosenbach Museum Library in Philadelphia.

A *New York Times* article published in 1927 asserted that in the thirty years since its first publication, *Dracula* had sold on average thirty thousand copies a year. But despite the novel's steady sales, *Dracula* didn't really begin to enter the popular consciousness until 1922, the year that F. W. Murnau's *Nosferatu* was released, setting off legal action from Florence Stoker. This was also the year that Mrs. Stoker granted permission to Hamilton Deane for a stage adaptation of *Dracula*; he premiered it in Derby, England, in 1923. An Americanized version of the play opened on Broadway in 1927, and was adapted into a film in 1931. From that point on, *Dracula* would seem ubiquitous.

A new series of Dracula novels was introduced in 1973 by Pinnacle Books, at the instigation of publisher Lyle Kenyon Engel. Written by Robert Lory, the modern-day science-fiction–tinged stories debuted with *Dracula Returns*, in which the titular character, described as being more like Bela Lugosi than Stoker's character, is resurrected by Dr. Damien Harmon, who wants to use the vampire in a war on crime. In order to control the Count, Harmon has implanted a device in his chest that can, at a moment's notice, inject a sliver of a stake into Dracula's heart. The series ran for a total of nine books as Dracula worked to gain control over his masters. Though initial sales were strong, they dropped off significantly by the final book, leading to the cancellation of the series.

The year 1975 saw the release of Dracula scholar Leonard Wolf's *The Annotated Dracula*, published by Clarkson N. Potter/Crown, with Stoker's text accompanied by illustrations by Sätty as well as photographs, maps, etchings, and numerous notes adding insight, analysis, and historical context. The book eventually sold thirty thousand copies, with a paperback edition appearing in October 1976.

Author Nicholas Meyer, whose Sherlock Holmes pastiche *The Seven Per-Cent Solution*, pairing Holmes with Sigmund Freud, had been a publishing success in 1974, returned to Baker Street for his 1976 novel *The West End Horror*, in which Holmes investigates a mystery in the theater world, encountering Bram Stoker, George Bernard Shaw, and Henry Irving. The book spent eleven weeks on the *New York Times* bestseller list. Two years later,

In Stoker's *Dracula*, Lucy and Mina, while on summer holiday, stay at this hotel on Whitby's Royal Crescent. In reality, Stoker stayed here while working on his novel.

© *2014 Bruce Scivally*

Holmes encountered the creation, not the creator, in Loren D. Estelman's 1978 book, *Sherlock Holmes vs. Dracula*, published by Doubleday. That same year Fred Saberhagen concocted *The Holmes-Dracula File*, published by Ace paperbacks. In that story, Sherlock Holmes was revealed to be a blood relative of Dracula, who assisted the detective in solving the case of "The Giant Rat of Sumatra," a plot to bring the plague to London.

Stoker's Legacy

In 1977, eighty years after the publication of *Dracula*, the Greater London Council erected a blue plaque at 18 St. Leonard's Terrace, London, Stoker's former home. Six years later, Ireland honored him with a commemorative blue plaque at No. 30 Kildare Street. Though Stoker only lived at the location for a brief period, it was chosen as the site of the memorial because the owners of the house in which he was born, at 15 Marino Crescent in the suburb of Clontarf, refused the honor, not wishing to have sightseers on their lawn.

Another plaque was placed at 6 Royal Crescent in Whitby, where Stoker visited between 1890 and 1896, while writing *Dracula*. In the novel, it became the guesthouse where Mina Murray and Lucy Westenra spent the summer, and Lucy fell under Dracula's spell. In 1980, the London-based Dracula Society, in conjunction with town officials, dedicated the Bram Stoker Memorial Seat, a wood-and-iron bench at the south end of Spion Kop on the West Cliff. The location of the bench on a high grassy bluff gives a panoramic view of every Whitby location mentioned in Stoker's novel.

At the nearby Royal Hotel, modern visitors will find a framed, hand-colored portrait of Stoker, one of two such portraits the Dracula Society presented to hotels; the other is in Romania. In the East Cliff's tourist section, numerous shops sell Dracula-themed items, including postcards, refrigerator magnets, T-shirts, and chocolate bars adorned with vampire bats. Along the pier, one can enter The Dracula Experience, a spook-house attraction with recreations of scenes from the novel.

In April of 1979, Sotheby's auctioned off a first edition of *Dracula*, inscribed by Bram Stoker and dated June 1897. Auctioneers had expected it would go for about $150, but when the bidding stopped, it sold for fifteen hundred dollars. The buyer was not identified.

In February of 1984, Oxford University Press released the one hundredth title in the paperback line of their acclaimed World's Classic series: *Dracula*. The book was advertised with an announcement proclaiming, "Sink your teeth into a World's Classic." The *New York Times* noted that since the novel was published in 1897 it had never been out of print.

In December of 1987, Guernsey's auction house in New York held a specialty auction of science fiction, fantasy, and horror memorabilia, collected over sixty years by Forrest J Ackerman, editor of *Famous Monsters of Filmland* magazine. Among his nineteen hundred books, posters, and paintings were two first editions of Bram Stoker's *Dracula*, the Constable Westminster's British version of 1897, which was expected to bring up to fifteen hundred dollars, and the American edition of 1899, expected to bring as much as three hundred dollars.

In 1991, science-fiction author Brian W. Aldiss wrote *Dracula Unbound*, a novel that saw vampires as cold-blooded descendants of relatives of the dinosaurs. Stoker himself is featured as a character in the time-travel novel that jumps from the distant past to Victorian London to modern-day America to the future.

When Francis Ford Coppola's *Dracula* was released to theaters in the fall of 1992, the Signet paperback edition of *Dracula* jumped to number nine on the *New York Times* list of Paperback Best Sellers, where it remained for two weeks.

In 1993, author Kim Newman published a novel, *Anno-Dracula*, in which the vampire count, having finally defeated Van Helsing and his merry band of vampire hunters, had survived to marry Queen Victoria. The tyrannical ruler's

London is disrupted by the murders of Jack the Ripper, who is revealed to be Dr. Jack Seward. Reviewing the book for the *New York Times*, Nina Auerbach wrote, "*Anno-Dracula* is the definitive bleak *Dracula* for the age of AIDS and the England of John Major."

The following year, Roderick Anscombe, a psychiatrist and teacher at Harvard Medical School, published his debut novel, *The Secret Life of Laszlo, Count Dracula*. Unlike Stoker's vampire, who possessed supernatural powers, Anscombe's Dracula is an ordinary man, albeit one with a penchant for cutting the throats of women he loves and drinking their blood; it is Dracula re-imagined as Hannibal Lecter.

At the same time, another Dracula appeared in print, in debut novelist Jeanne Kalogridis's *Covenant with the Vampire: The Diaries of the Family Dracul*. In Kalogridis's novel, Stoker's Dracula becomes Uncle Vlad, controlling patriarch of an extended family; it is Dracula as The Godfather.

In 1997, one hundred years after its founding by Frank Doubleday, the Doubleday publishing company released a list of the ten most influential books it had published, "10 Books That Shaped Our Century," based on a survey of authors, educators, journalists, and booksellers. Included, along with Anne Frank's *The Diary of a Young Girl*, Alex Haley's *Roots*, Aldous Huxley's *Brave New World*, and T. E. Lawrence's *The Seven Pillars of Wisdom*, was Bram Stoker's *Dracula*.

Having been an amateur actor, Bram Stoker would likely have been delighted to know that he had, himself, become a character in a play. In 2014, Michael Theodorou wrote *There Are Such Things*, a play set in 1906, which found Stoker temporarily blind after a stroke, experiencing strange visitations as his wife, Florence, nurses him back to health.

A century after Stoker's death, his creation has become a perennial Halloween bogeyman, as much a symbol of the yearly holiday as Santa Claus is of Christmas. But, as we shall see, this resurrection may not have happened without the vision of another Irish-born theatrical impresario and the ineptitude of a German film producer.

5

The Curtain Rises

Dracula on Stage

The Vaudeville Dracula

As a lifelong lover of the stage, Bram Stoker had always imagined *Dracula* as a stage vehicle. It had been his fervent desire that, once the book was published, it would become a stage production at the Lyceum Theatre, with Henry Irving starring as the vampire. But it was not to be. Irving didn't particularly care for Stoker's "shilling shocker," and aside from Stoker's own hastily produced one-time only presentation to protect the stage copyright, there were no theatrical adaptations of the novel in the author's lifetime.

But Dracula did appear from time to time on playbills. At the turn of the century, performers looking for hooks to attract audiences to their vaudeville acts often adopted the names of characters from popular fiction, as in August of 1903 when a performer emerged on the vaudeville circuit in Chicago going by the name "Dracula." In May 1904, he appeared at Luna Park in New York billed as "Dracula, Aerial Contortionist." A listing of "New Acts of the Week" in *Variety* of March 2, 1907, noted that his twelve-minute act at Pastor's was billed as "Dracula, The Frolicsome Demon." The trade paper described him as being a contortionist whose act depended heavily on his stage setting and "corkscrew stunts" under a spotlight, finishing with trapeze work.

Hamilton Deane's *Dracula*

The first dramatic stage adaptation of Stoker's *Dracula* came from an actor who, in his way, was very much like Henry Irving. Hamilton Deane had been a bank clerk until he took up acting, making his stage debut in 1899—two years after the publication of *Dracula*—in the Henry Irving Vacation Company. Working in the company meant that Deane got to know Stoker, and undoubtedly read the author's book; his family also owned an estate in Dublin next door to Stoker's father. But unlike Henry Irving, who refused Stoker's overtures to do a *Dracula* play, Deane saw the novel's potential to become a theatrical success.

Over the years, Deane approached several writers with the idea of adapting the book. They were all put off by the novel's expansive structure, dense storyline, and its epistolary format. The problems of condensing and simplifying the narrative and limiting the telling to just a few locations seemed insurmountable.

By 1923, Deane had become a respected actor and the head of his own theater troupe, the Hamilton Deane Company. He once again sought a writer to adapt *Dracula*, and when he was rebuffed, his leading lady, Dora Mary Patrick (who later became Mrs. Deane), suggested he adapt the book himself. When he was sidelined by a severe cold, Deane finally began writing a draft. As he became immersed in it, he sought Florence Stoker's permission. Receiving her blessing, he completed the play in four weeks.

Stoker had always envisioned the play done in the best Lyceum style, with massive sets, special effects, moody lighting, and a huge cast, giving it all the spectacle of the Lyceum's Shakespeare productions. But at the close of the nineteenth century that kind of theatrical grandeur gave way to plays by dramatists who, with the advent of Freud and his theories of psychology, were exploring human relationships on a much smaller scale; castles and moors gave way to drawing rooms, and casts of dozens became casts of four, or five, or six, meaning that the plays could now be performed almost anywhere—the expensive production values of a Lyceum Theatre were no longer needed. It was in this tradition, the drawing room drama, that Deane refashioned *Dracula*, dropping the beginning and end sections in Transylvania and concentrating the entire story in London.

We can thank Deane for the conception of Dracula as a vampire in evening clothes and a black cape. Stoker's vampire was dressed entirely in black, and only on occasion is there mention of him wearing a cloak; he was also described, in the beginning of the book, as an elderly man with hairy palms, pointed fangs, and bad breath. For the stage, Deane dressed his vampire in white tie and tails, making him presentable enough to be allowed into an English drawing room. He also draped him in an opera cape, which served a practical purpose: it helped to hide the actor's descent through a trap door when Dracula needed to make a quick disappearance.

Deane first produced the play at the Grand Theatre in Derby, England, in the summer of 1924, and later brought it to Wimbledon for a tryout, with Edmund Blake playing the vampire; Dora Mary Patrick as Mina; and the writer as Van Helsing. It has been said that though Deane intended to play Dracula, he eventually decided on playing Van Helsing because the latter part had more lines. *Weekly Variety* reported that the production resulted in women fainting and men urging the actors to "desist from their blood-thirsty conduct." But the houses sold out; the shilling-shocker was a hit. Many theaters made offers for the London rights. Deane refused all of them, fearing the play would not be a success in metropolitan London. Instead, he took it on the road, building up its reputation as a crowd-pleaser. It was such a success that he eventually organized a second touring company; there were also productions in Vienna, Budapest, Paris, and Rome.

By 1926, Deane had made enough money from his vampire play that he felt safe risking a London run. It opened at the Little Theatre on February 14, 1927, with twenty-two-year-old Raymond Huntley as Dracula, and Bernard Jukes as Renfield. As in the provinces, the critics rebuked the play, but the public came in droves.

The Little Theatre appointed a trained nurse to tend to those who were overcome by the onstage frights. A reporter from the *New York Times* witnessed a woman in the audience go into hysterics, and four others faint. The theater's lessee, Jose Levy, said five men collapsed to every woman, so a nurse was regularly engaged from a nearby hospital. Upon coming to, some victims returned to their seats to see the play's conclusion, while others left the theater only to return on another night. The Little Theatre did well from *Dracula*. *Variety* reported that while the play had originally been expected to have a four-week run, it soon extended to three months. It was the first time in three years, according to the trade paper, that the theater turned a profit.

A second adaptation of Stoker's novel, produced by Harry L. Warburton, also toured in England in 1927. It reportedly featured scenes from the book that had been omitted from Deane's version. In addition, Florence Stoker commissioned her own stage version of the novel. At one point, three different productions were running in London simultaneously.

After a five-month run at the Little Theatre, *Dracula* closed on July 22, 1927. Since white mice had been required for the play, one of the stagehands kept a colony of them, which multiplied during the run. Once the play closed, an advertisement ran in London papers saying that any boy who came to the Little Theatre and asked for a white mouse would be given one. The result was another *Dracula*-inspired queue at the theater, as young boys lined up for the free pets.

Dracula wasn't really finished, however; the play simply transferred to a larger venue, the Duke of York's Theatre, where it continued running through December of 1927. After its initial run, the play remained popular in the provinces, with actors such as Keith Pyott, Gerald Neville, Frederick Keen, W. E. Holloway, and Ivan Butler in the title role. From April 25 to May 13, 1939, Deane brought the play to the Lyceum Theatre, the professional home of Dracula's creator, Bram Stoker, and for the first time Deane essayed the role of the vampire king himself.

Dracula on Broadway

It would take another eccentric dreamer to bring the play to America: Horace Liveright. A colorful Jazz Age figure, Liveright was born in 1884, growing up in the mining town of Osceola Mills, Pennsylvania. After a few years as an office boy for a stock brokerage firm, he decided, at age sixteen, to become a playwright. A year later, he finished the book and lyrics for a comic opera, *John Smith*, which was put in rehearsal by Edward E. Rice at Wallack's Theater in New York.

Unfortunately, Rice went bankrupt before opening night. But Liveright, now stage-struck, moved to New York, where he spent several years selling bonds for Sutro Brothers until becoming manager of the bond department of Day Adams & Co.

In 1910, at age twenty-six, Liveright wed the daughter of the founder of the International Paper Company, becoming an instant millionaire in the process. He quit the bond business and, using his wife's dowry, began a small company for the manufacture and sale of paper products. He teamed with Albert Boni, the owner of a Greenwich Village bookstore, to start a publishing company in 1917. Facing resistance from the "gentlemen's club" of the publishing world, the two Jewish upstarts started publishing the works of Greenwich Village radicals, including John Reed's *Ten Days That Shook the World*. They then kicked off the paperback publishing industry with the Modern Library, a series of reprints of classic books, which would eventually include *Dracula*.

Liveright hired Edward Bernays, an innovator in public relations, to promote his firm's catalogue. The two men felt that books could be sold like any other commodity, with aggressive newspaper and magazine advertising, and that the publication of new books could be hyped like the opening of a new play, generating free advertising through press announcements. As a result, Boni & Liveright soon became one of the most famous publishing houses in America.

Horace Liveright, the Broadway impresario whose publishing empire funded his often foolhardy ventures into producing plays; *Dracula* was one of his few hits.

The Billy Rose Theatre Collection, New York Public Library at Lincoln Center, Astor, Lenox, and Tilden Foundations

In one six-year span, the firm published books from seven Nobel Prize winners. By the fall of 1925, they had published works by William Faulkner, Hart Crane, and Dorothy Parker, as well as Anita Loos's *Gentlemen Prefer Blondes* and Eugene O'Neill's *Desire Under the Elms*. These and other hits put Boni & Liveright on the map. With the business going like gangbusters, Liveright bought out Boni's share. Now in sole charge, he took an interest in new writers like Ben Hecht and Ernest Hemingway, and he put together one of the most brilliant editorial staffs in history, with names like Louis Kronenberger, Bennett Cerf, and Lillian Hellman.

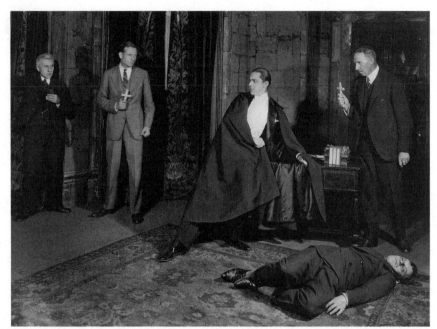

A promotional still from the stage production of the Broadway play features Van Helsing (Edward Van Sloan), Jonathan Harker (Terence Neill), and Dr. Seward (Herbert Bunston) confronting Dracula (Bela Lugosi) with crosses; their efforts appear to have come too late for Renfield (Bernard Jukes, on the floor).   *Courtesy of Del Valle Archives*

Liveright was at the pinnacle of his success, but he had a potent enemy: himself. With huge appetites for booze, gambling, ladies, and theater, he poured money from the publishing business into a five-story brownstone in the speakeasy district of Manhattan. It had been his office since 1923; now it became party central, renowned for star-studded gatherings and free-flowing booze. Feeling invincible, he began backing Broadway plays, but while he was lucky with literature, he was dreadful at drama. Though Liveright brought such plays as *The Firebrand* and *An American Tragedy* to the New York stage, before long the failure of other plays siphoned off his publishing company's profits.

In 1925, when Liveright was strapped for cash, Bennett Cerf offered to buy the Modern Library for two hundred thousand dollars. While it solved Liveright's money problems in the short term, ultimately it was a huge mistake; the Modern Library was the cash cow whose profits covered losses from the Broadway and publishing flops. Becoming more desperate as his debts mounted, Liveright needed a hit. On a trip to London in March of 1927, he saw a play at the Little Theatre that he thought was the answer to his prayers: *Dracula*. Though he thought it was the worst company of actors he had ever seen, he believed the play could be rewritten into a New York success. He asked

Lucy (Hazel Whitmore), Dracula (Bela Lugosi), and Renfield (Bernard Jukes) in the 1927 Broadway production of *Dracula*. Lugosi and Jukes went to Los Angeles with the play the following year.   *Author's collection*

other New York producers then in London for their opinions; they warned him that it would never find an audience in America. Liveright didn't listen.

Acquiring rights to the play, he hired John L. Balderston, London correspondent of the *New York World* and author of *Berkeley Square*, to prepare an Americanized version of *Dracula*. Balderston switched the character names of Lucy and Mina, and set the events in the library of Dr. Seward's sanatorium in Purley, London; Lucy's boudoir; and a secret vault. And in Balderston's version, Van Helsing repels Dracula not with garlic but with wolf's bane.

Raymond Huntley, who played Dracula in London, and Bernard Jukes, who played Renfield, were offered the chance to reprise their roles on Broadway, but Huntley asked for more money than Liveright was willing to pay, so the only British performer imported to America was Jukes.

When Liveright arrived back in New York on May 14, 1927, he announced that his first production of the new Broadway season would be *Dracula*. Rehearsals began August 29, with the New York premiere scheduled for October 5, 1927, at the Fulton Theater. Staged by Ira Hards, the play had its tryouts in New Haven, Connecticut, at the Shubert Theater. It was first presented on September 19, with Edward Van Sloan playing Van Helsing; Dorothy Peterson as Lucy Harker; and, in the title role of Dracula, a Hungarian-born performer named Bela Lugosi. Lugosi was seen as a Continental matinee idol; the *New York Times*' Jim Koch later called him "an undead Valentino."

One of
Broadways
Six Hits

Take her to DRACULA.
She'll hug you for
protection.

FOR DETAILS SEE
THEATRICAL PAGE

The Prince of Darkness on the Great White Way: an ad
for *Dracula* from the *New York Times*, December 1, 1927.

Author's collection

Louis Cline, Horace Liveright's publicist, began ballyhooing *Dracula* early. On the opening night of the New Haven tryout, drama editors at the New York newspapers received a bulletin that the stage manager, having seen how the play went over with an audience, was said to have been driven out of his mind; it wasn't that the play was that bad, but that it was that good. Most newspaper editors realized the story wasn't true, but it made good copy. Cline, himself an old newspaper man, was just getting warmed up.

When *Dracula* came to the Fulton Theater, Cline hired a nurse to prowl up and down the aisles, occasionally plucking "unconscious" spectators out of their seats and escorting them away for treatment. There were whispers that not all the faintings were genuine. New York drivers also found traffic tickets on their automobiles that turned out to be, instead of a summons to court, a summons to appear at the Fulton Theater. For the sports-minded, he had *Dracula* baseball schedules printed. There were also stickers, hats, masks, heralds, "throw-aways," and a limerick contest.

The play's official Broadway premiere was on Wednesday, October 5, 1927. Unlike in London, the play received good reviews, assuring it a long run. The relatively new medium of radio was employed to generate publicity, with cast members interviewed on WRNY and WGBS. A radio version of *Dracula*, featuring actors from the Fulton Theater cast, including Bela Lugosi, Dorothy Peterson, and Edward Van Sloan, aired on station WJZ on March 30, 1928.

One of the sensational hits of the season, *Dracula* closed following the performance of Saturday, May 19, 1928, with plans to re-open in Los Angeles three weeks later. It had run in New York for thirty-three weeks, racking up 241 performances.

The Ghoul Goes West

O. D. Woodward purchased rights to present *Dracula* on the West Coast, and the play opened at the Biltmore Theater in Los Angeles on June 25, 1928. Bela Lugosi, Edward Van Sloan, and Bernard Jukes reprised their New York roles, but Hazel Whitmore now took on the part of Lucy Harker. Among the movie stars present on opening night were Dolores Del Rio, Richard Dix, and Al Jolson; others who subsequently saw the play were Douglas Fairbanks Jr., Richard Barthelmess, and Ruth Chatterton. The critical response in Los Angeles was just as glowing as in New York, with Bela Lugosi being particularly praised for his measured malevolence.

As the play went into its second week in the film capital, Woodward borrowed a page from the Liveright playbook and hired a nurse to be on duty to tend to those who fainted—or pretended to—during performances. The success of the play resulted in a run on copies of the book in local bookstores, with virtually every downtown bookstore selling out.

Though originally booked for a four-week engagement, *Dracula* proved so popular that it was held over double that period, finally closing August 18, 1928. By then, its combined New York and Los Angeles run totaled fifteen hundred performances. The Los Angeles cast then took the play north to San Francisco.

While Lugosi continued playing *Dracula* in the city by the bay, Raymond Huntley was brought from England to head a touring company. A second road company, featuring acclaimed tennis player Bill Tilden, started from Long Island on October 11, 1928, and Howard Sinclair took the role at the Ohio Theater in Cleveland in March 1929. Over the next three years, *Dracula* became known as "The *Abie's Irish Rose* of mystery plays"—a perennial that was always in production somewhere.

Lugosi was due to be back in the cape in Los Angeles on April 22, 1929, appearing at Hollywood's Music Box Theater. A few days later, Horace Liveright filed suit in Los Angeles Superior Court demanding an accounting of receipts from the touring companies of *Dracula*, contending

Bela Lugosi, in less severe eye makeup than he normally wore onstage as Dracula, poses for a glamour portrait as the vampire. *Courtesy of Del Valle Archives*

Dracula comes to the Windy City, as this ad from the *Chicago Daily Tribune* of April 14, 1929, attests.

Author's collection

that O. D. Woodward owed him considerable back royalties.

Liveright, who hoped to have two touring companies on the road for the 1930 season, was once again in financial straits. Most of the Broadway shows he backed failed—*Dracula* was one of the few hits—and his new publishing company, Horace Liveright, Inc., became a pyramid scheme; he kept it afloat by getting young wealthy men to become vice-presidents, a privilege for which they paid him five-figure sums. Liveright eventually lost control of his company to his accountant and was forced out in 1930. Meanwhile, Liveright's former employee, Bennett Cerf, used the Modern Library, which he bought from Liveright, as the cornerstone to build his publishing company, Random House.

The Liveright vs. Woodward litigation delayed the play's Los Angeles revival; it began at the Music Box on May 19, 1929, almost a month later than originally announced. (Appearing with Lugosi in this production was Frederick Pymm as the cockney asylum attendant; he would graduate to playing Dracula in a 1938 Los Angeles revival.) The play ended its Los Angeles run on June 9, 1929. In Chicago, it continued for thirteen weeks. Meanwhile, in Australia, the play premiered June 1 at the Palace Theatre in Sydney, with Ashton Jarry as Dracula.

On June 25, 1929, the legal battle between Horace Liveright and O. D. Woodward entered its second phase, when Liveright and playwright John L. Balderston filed suit against Woodward in the U.S. District Court in Los Angeles, asking for an injunction to restrain Woodward from mounting any further productions of the play and asking for damages in the amount of ten thousand dollars from the Music Box Theater production. The plaintiffs asserted that Woodward's license had expired and he had no authority to continue presenting *Dracula*. As with Liveright, Woodward's luck with theatrical productions eventually ran dry. By 1935, he was on the relief rolls in Los Angeles County, one of twelve hundred former stage personnel in the L.A. County Relief Administration Drama Project, a federally financed program that gave productions in high-school auditoriums and other venues for audiences who were admitted free. Six years later he was directing *Dracula*, with Frederick Pymm starring, at L.A.'s Beaux Arts Playhouse in a production that also featured Dwight Frye as Renfield.

Dracula—The Middle Years

Victor Jory, who had been playing Dracula in stock company productions, essayed the role when the Pasadena Community Playhouse offered *Dracula* beginning August 14, 1930. Another actor in the cast just starting out on his career was Robert Young. Meanwhile, Courtney White took on the role when the play began its third touring season in Wilmington, Delaware, in September 1930. Liveright had, by that time, turned over management of the play to his publicist, Louis Cline.

After Chicago, *Dracula* moved on to Boston, where it opened at the Lyric, a theater the *New York Times* called a "death warrant for any play consigned to it," yet the play sold out for four weeks. This was particularly remarkable since it was making its fourth Boston visit in three seasons.

At the end of 1930, O. E. Wee took over management of the *Dracula* touring companies, which in a single year raked in $350,000. Even after years on the road, the play was still capable of grossing from $11,000 to $13,000 on a schedule of eight performances. Wee felt obligated to keep up the ballyhoo of Liveright and Cline, including people fainting at performances, nurses in attendance, and men arising at the end of the second act to scream for their mothers.

Horace Liveright, meanwhile, was reeling from the stock market crash and the failure of his publishing company. He went to Hollywood, serving as an adviser at Paramount Pictures in 1931, then returned to New York and began dictating his memoirs. Near the end of September 1933, he contracted pneumonia, and on September 24, 1933, he died at his New York home. He was only forty-nine years old.

Liveright's most successful legacy was *Dracula*, which kept rolling along into the 1930s and beyond. In December of 1933, Bela Lugosi, having now starred in the film version, was the headliner at the Loew's State Theater in New York, performing a condensed version of the play for a vaudeville audience.

Whenever his film career lulled, Lugosi reprised his most famous role in road company tours. In November of 1941, the actor signed up for a two-year tour of 124 cities in a revival of *Dracula*. Though he felt his typecasting as a vampire had severely limited his career, he was nonetheless glad to have the work.

Another revival, by a company headed by Leo Shull called Genius, Inc., was to have opened December 16, 1942, at the Malin Studios in New York, with Dracula portrayed by an actor wearing an Adolf Hitler mustache. However, the play was suddenly postponed at the last minute, ostensibly because the operators of the theater didn't feel it was ready. It opened a week later, on the 23rd, with Hitler/Dracula arriving just in time for Christmas.

Stiano Braggiotti played the vampire count at the Flatbush Theater in Brooklyn in November of 1942, and the following year Lugosi took up the cape again for another national tour of the play in the spring of 1943. The revival made its way eastward from California before ending up in New York.

Beginning his twentieth year of association with *Dracula*, Lugosi again hit the road with the play in 1947. Hedda Hopper reported that his stage program now also included a dramatization of Edgar Allan Poe's "The Tell-Tale Heart." Lugosi toured again in 1948.

The following year, J. Edward Bromberg, who had appeared as a Van Helsing–type character in the 1943 film *Son of Dracula*, played Van Helsing in a production of *Dracula*, with John Drew Devereaux as the vampire, at the Robin Hood Theater in Arden, Delaware. Lugosi took up the cape again in 1949, appearing at the "Midnite Spook Show" at the Hammond Outdoor Theater, near Chicago, at the end of August.

Dracula Burlesque

Beginning June 30, 1951, John Carradine, who supplanted Bela Lugosi as Dracula in two movies for Universal Pictures in the 1940s, took to the stage of Chicago's Drury Lane Theater for a two-week engagement in *Dracula*. The play then moved on to Detroit, where everything seemed to go wrong. The prop bat malfunctioned. The audience laughed at scary lines. Carradine decided to stop fighting the gaffes and just go with it. When the play ended, he strolled in front of the curtain and addressed the audience, saying, "If I'm alive, what am I doing here? On the other hand, if I'm dead, why do I have to wee-wee?" The audience roared, so Carradine repeated the line after every performance from then onward.

Frank Langella first sank his teeth into the role of Dracula beginning August 7, 1967, starring in the Deane-Balderston play at the Berkshire Playhouse in Stockbridge, Massachusetts. However, the original play now seemed like a creaky relic. William Gibson, director of the Berkshire, said it was the worst play of the season at the box office.

A burlesque of *Dracula*, called *Fangs Ain't What They Used to Be*, debuted in 1969 at the Horseshoe Stage Theater in Los Angeles. Written and directed by Jerry B. Wheeler, the campy, low-humor spoof featured Murray Langston as a homosexual Dracula. Critics panned it, finding it more boring than bawdy.

Another horror farce came along in the spring of 1970. *I'm Sorry, the Bridge Is Out, You'll Have to Spend the Night,* by Sheldon Hillman and Bob Pickett, premiered at the Coronet Theater in Los Angeles. The play featured the Frankenstein Monster, Dracula, his wives, the Mummy and the Wolf Man trying to lay claim to the same nice young couple. The height of its humor was the Monster referring to Dracula, played by Peter Virgo Jr., as "Batman."

A more serious take on the story debuted at the John Drew Theater in East Hampton, Long Island, in August 1970, with a Yale Repertory Summer Theater show called *Cops and Horrors*, featuring two one-acts, one based on *Flypaper* by Dashiell Hammett, and the other a new version of *Dracula*, both adapted by Kenneth Cavander. In the latter production, directed by Larry Arrick, Robert Drivas played Dracula as a boyishly handsome seducer rather than a monster.

James Naughton was Dr. Seward, and a pre-*Happy Days* Henry Winkler performed as a thickly accented Dr. Van Helsing.

A very different take on the story arrived with *Dracula Sabbat*, written by Leon Katz and directed by Lawrence Kornfeld at the Judson Memorial Church in Washington Square, New York, beginning September 20, 1970. With a cast that included Duane Tucker as Dracula and a young Rhea Perlman as one of his attendants, this "theater of ritual" production by the Judson Poets' Theater was basically a scripted black mass spiced with a great deal of nudity and simulated sexual acts.

The Deane-Balderston *Dracula*, which seemed to be in performance every year since its debut at some theater or other, turned up again at the Coconut Grove Playhouse in Chicago on July 27, 1971, with Hurd Hatfield, star of the 1945 film *The Picture of Dorian Gray*, in the title role.

That same year, when Stage West in Springfield, Massachusetts, lost its production rights to the Deane-Balderston play, Ted Tiller was asked to write a replacement, in just three weeks. The result was *Count Dracula*, a comic treatment of Stoker's novel that quickly became a staple of summer stock as well as college, community, and dinner theater productions.

A new staging of the Deane-Balderston warhorse premiered in Massachusetts in July 1973, when the Nantucket Stage Company, an experimental summer theater troupe formed by producer/playwright/painter John Wulp, began its first season at the Cyrus Pierce Theater with a three-week run of *Dracula*. A New York native, Wulp moved to Nantucket in 1959 in search of the good life. That same year, he won an Obie as best director for the Arnold Weinstein play *The Red Eye of Love*. Wulp was now the director of the Cyrus Pierce Theater, a 200-seat venue converted from a pool house by designer Roger Morgan with a tiny nine-by-eighteen-foot stage. With a budget of $125,000 for three plays, he was determined to give each one the best production possible.

Wulp was already familiar with *Dracula*, having designed a production of the play for Bela Lugosi in the late 1940s. For the Nantucket run, he asked illustrator Edward Gorey to design the settings. It was the first time the artist had ever worked in the theater, but the combination of Dracula and Gorey, known for his macabre drawings, was inspired. Gorey drew the settings in a half-inch to one-foot scale, and the designs were then enlarged to life-size by the theater company. Gorey had been concerned that his cross-hatched style of drawing wouldn't translate well to the stage, but he needn't have worried. Reproduced full-size, they converted the stage into a giant black-and-white Gorey environment, with lots of bat and skull imagery. The costuming continued the black-and-white motif, but each scene contained at least one element of red, such as a decanter of wine, a rose, or a ruby.

The Nantucket production featured Lloyd Battista as Dracula, and shortly after it closed, the theater burned down. The play later moved to New York, where it was presented at the Cherry Lane Theatre beginning October 23, 1973.

In London that same fall, *The Rocky Horror Show* began at the Royal Court's Second Auditorium before transferring to the Classica Cinema in Chelsea, quickly establishing itself as the trendy show to see. A mixture of rock concert and horror movie, the book, music, and lyrics of *The Rocky Horror Show* were provided by Richard O'Brien. The plot involves two young travelers trapped in a castle by transvestite alien Frank-N-Furter, who has put together a creation that looks more like a male centerfold than a monster.

The Fiftieth Anniversary Broadway Revival

In the summer of 1977, producer Eugene Wolsk was prepping several shows for Broadway, including revivals of *Man of La Mancha* and *Dracula*, the latter being the Nantucket production of four years earlier, with the Edward Gorey–designed sets. Several producers had vied for the rights to present the play, including one who envisioned it with Tab Hunter as Dracula and Twiggy as Lucy. Wolsk and the Jujamcyn Company, which owned and managed theaters, produced the play in association with John Wulp, the original presenter, as well as Victor Lurie, Elizabeth McCann, and Max Wietzenhoffer. The Martin Beck Theater, owned by the Jujamcyn Company, was booked for the play, with the run set to begin October 20, 1977.

For the lead role, the producers cast Frank Langella, a tall, darkly handsome actor who had played the part a decade earlier and who had the kind of syrupy voice that could read the Congressional Record and make it sound seductive.

Langella grew up in Bayonne, New Jersey, in a wealthy family as the son of the president of the local barrel and drum company. At ten years old, knowing he wanted to become an actor, he often snuck off to Times Square to buy John Gielgud records, imitating the British actor as a way of making his thick New Jersey accent disappear. As Langella matured, his tall, lanky frame, good looks, and sonorous voice made him a natural for the theater, so he studied drama at Syracuse University, graduating in 1959, and began working in regional theaters. At age twenty-two, he landed a role off-Broadway in *The Immoralist*, directed by George Keathley.

His feature film debut came in 1970's *Diary of a Mad Housewife*, playing a narcissistic writer. He followed that up with a comedic turn in Mel Brooks's *The Twelve Chairs*. Despite critical plaudits for the film roles, Langella chose to work mostly in the theater, with only occasional forays into film and television, including starring in a TV-movie remake of *The Mark of Zorro* in 1974.

In 1975, Langella made his Broadway debut and won a Best Supporting Actor Tony Award for playing the role of a talkative lizard in Edward Albee's *Seascape*. During the play's run, he had an opportunity to meet the idol of his youth, John Gielgud. When the esteemed English actor went backstage, Langella told him how he had listened to his records to help lose his accent. Gielgud responded, "Well, you've grown out of it now, dear boy. You don't sound like me at all."

Langella was first approached about the role of Dracula in November of 1976, but didn't make up his mind until January of the following year, after the producers convinced him that the show would not be camp but rather would be done with integrity and style. Seeing the play as a love story, the actor insisted that there be no fangs and no red contact lenses; his Dracula would not be a ghoul, but a Byronic hero, more Bronté than Stoker. When he took the role, the general consensus was that with so many past productions of the play, another wasn't needed. Roger Stevens, chairman of the Kennedy Center, told Langella that staging the play again was the most ridiculous idea he had ever heard. Langella had, in fact, turned down other offers to play the

Ann Sachs, as Lucy, awaits a late-night rendezvous with Dracula (Frank Langella), in a scene from the 1977 Broadway revival of the Deane-Balderston play.
Courtesy of Del Valle Archives

vampire, including one that had Dracula living in a penthouse in New York, cruising ladies in Bloomingdale's and paying them five thousand dollars each to bite their necks.

Dennis Rosa, who directed the original Nantucket production, was retained to shepherd the Broadway presentation. Previews were set to begin October 11, following a Boston trial run. On October 3, 1977, during the sold-out Boston tryouts, a power failure blacked out three square miles of the city for more than two hours. Onstage as Dracula, Langella quipped, "Obviously there are forces much greater than mine working."

When *Dracula* had its opening night performance at Broadway's Martin Beck Theater, receipts went to benefit the Parks Council. Afterwards, there was a Macabre After-Theater Dinner Party at the Harvard Club, where patrons were asked to wear black and white with a touch of red. The next day's reviews were full of praise for Gorey's sets and for Langella's performance, which reclaimed the vampire from a decade of camp and parody and presented Dracula with grace, dignity and a healthy dose of sex appeal.

Langella felt the play's love scene was one of the most erotic he'd ever played. In an interview with Judy Klemesrud of the *New York Times*, he said, "People still tell me it's the hottest scene in years. Actually, I can't think of a woman who doesn't like to be taken, if it's with love. If you take a woman by force and at the same time gently, you can't fail, even if some American men feel they can't be aggressive and tender at the same time." Dracula's aggressive tenderness certainly appealed to women; during the play's run, when Langella was recognized by women on the street, they often exposed their throats and asked him to take a bite. Speaking to Ellen Farley of the *Los Angeles Times*, he noted that "it's always done with a certain degree of affection and sweetness that's nice."

Dracula sold out its first two weeks and generated long lines at the box office. A number of celebrities came to see what the commotion was about, including Claudette Colbert, Barbra Streisand, Lena Horne, Anne Bancroft, Cicely Tyson, Sissy Spacek, Alexis Smith, Tony Bennett, Lee Radziwill, Candice Bergen, and Jean Simmons.

Shortly after *Dracula* began its run, on the Sunday afternoon of November 6, 1977, following a matinee performance, Langella took his longtime fiancée, Ruth Weil, outside the city to be wed. It was the first marriage for the thirty-seven-year-old actor; Weil, thirty-six, was divorced. Langella's wedding was almost as much of a nightmare as the play he'd just performed. The car was late, the driver was stopped for speeding, the couple couldn't hear their favorite song because the record player was broken, and Weil couldn't get the ring over her finger. After a one-day honeymoon, Langella returned to *Dracula*. A year later, during the making of the *Dracula* film, Langella related all of these events to his onscreen co-star Laurence Olivier, who was portraying Van Helsing. When the esteemed actor learned that the ceremony took place in the town hall of Wilton, Connecticut, he replied, "Oh my God, I was married to Vivien Leigh in that same town hall in that little town."

By year's end, *Dracula* went from being a success to being a sensation, creating a tsunami of *Dracula* merchandising, including Edward Gorey–designed wallpaper and *Dracula: A Toy Theatre*, composed of drawings that replicated the set and characters of *Dracula* that could be cut out with scissors and assembled. The success of *Dracula* also prompted a short-lived fashion fad in Manhattan—men wearing capes, though, naturally, only after sundown.

The revival of the Deane-Balderston play wasn't the only *Dracula* in New York in the fall of 1977. Off Broadway, the Dracula Theater Company presented *The Passion of Dracula* at the Cherry Lane Theatre, starting September 14, with the official opening set for September 28 at midnight. Peter Bennett directed, and Eric Krebs produced the new play by Bob Hall and David Richmond, with Christopher Bernau as Dracula. The play cost thirty thousand dollars to mount, a tenth of the cost of the Langella *Dracula*, but while the Martin Beck auditorium had 1,280 seats, the off-Broadway Cherry Lane had only 180—and a top ticket price half that of the Martin Beck.

The Passion of Dracula

For *The Passion of Dracula*, a dentist took casts of Christopher Bernau's mouth and jaw to create properly fitted fangs. And, to better understand his character, Bernau consulted with a parapsychologist as well as with the president of the Vampire Research Center of America, Dr. Stephen Kaplan, who instructed Bernau on the best areas of the neck to bite a victim. Bernau noted that Dracula was the only role he ever had in which he could chew not only the scenery but also the rest of the cast.

Once the play opened, critics derided it for having an inconsistent tone, comical one moment and scary the next, with flashes of Romanticism and Freudian psychology. To lure people to the theater, the producers tried a little old-fashioned Liveright-style ballyhoo. On Halloween, the theater dropped ticket prices to ten dollars and asked playgoers to come in costume for a post-show party where they could mingle with cast members and sample Bloody Mary Quiche. Those who stayed till midnight saw Dr. Silkini perform his horror-themed magic show. When the play celebrated its five hundredth performance on January 12, 1979, playgoers each received a complimentary vampire cocktail. The following month, a party after the play celebrated the publication of Countess Marina Polvay's *Dracula's Cookbook*, with recipes for omelet of capon's blood, duck's blood soup, and Transylvanian doughnuts.

Despite mostly negative reviews, *The Passion of Dracula* racked up 735 performances, making it off-Broadway's twenty-first longest-running show. The play was also videotaped for Showtime's *Broadway on Showtime* series in 1980, directed by Bob Hall and starring Bernau as Dracula and Malachi Throne as Van Helsing.

In February 1978, two more Dracula plays opened in New York. *Dracula, A Modern Fable* played weekends in February at the Troupe Theater on West 39th Street, while Ted Tiller's 1971 play *Count Dracula* opened February 16 for an eleven-day run at the Equity Library Theater. Although it had been performed all over the world, this was *Count Dracula*'s first production in New York. Directed by Robert Lanchester, it featured William Shust as Dracula.

In March 1978, Frank Langella appeared as Dracula in an "I Love New York" TV commercial, directed by Stan Dragoti, touting the city's Broadway attractions. After brief bits from the actors and dancers of *A Chorus Line*, *The Wiz*, *Grease*, and other shows, Dracula snapped his cape and proclaimed, "I love New York . . . especially in the evening." The New York State Commerce Department hired ad agency Wells, Rich, Greene to create the commercial to attract tourists to Broadway. According to the League of New York Theaters and Producers, the commercial, which aired during the nationwide Tony telecast on June 4, was responsible for a $2.87-million increase in Broadway's weekly gross, and a 19.9 percent increase in attendance.

In the spring of 1978, Langella announced that though he was originally contracted to perform in *Dracula* only until July, he had agreed to stay with the play until October, when he was due to begin work on the film version. In the meantime, he gamely engaged in a public service–oriented promotional stunt: in April, two Greater New York Blood Program mobile units parked outside the Martin Beck Theater while the *Dracula* cast gave blood, encouraging passersby to join them.

When awards season came, Langella picked up the Delia Austrian medal, the annual award of the Drama League of New York, for most distinguished performance of the year. He was also the recipient of a 1978 award from the Count Dracula Society, along with Louis Jourdan, who played the Count in a PBS-TV version of the story. Edward Gorey's sets for *Dracula* were honored with a special award at the thirty-third annual Edgar Allan Poe Awards dinner in March 1978. Since Gorey was not present to accept the award, Dracula accepted it for him—Dracula being sci-fi author Isaac Asimov, wearing a cape. Though many felt Langella's performance was deserving of a Tony, when the awards were handed out in June, the actor lost to Barnard Hughes, starring in *Da*. Edward Gorey, however, won a Tony for the show's costumes, and the show itself won for Most Innovative Revival.

Having proved a smashing success on Broadway, the Deane-Balderston *Dracula* was chosen to be the opening attraction of the Center Theater Group Ahmanson's 1978–79 season in Los Angeles, with Dennis Rosa directing. The Edward Gorey sets were duplicated for the West Coast run, but they didn't come cheaply; the mock-macabre castle interior, which often elicited spontaneous applause from audiences, cost eighty-four thousand dollars.

While Langella continued to wow the New York audiences, George Chakiris was hired for a production of *Dracula* at the Little Theater on the Square in Sullivan, Illinois, in July 1978. But Chakiris was never seen by Chicago audiences as the vampire count. Before the show opened, the London producers of *The Passion of Dracula* bought him out of his contract. Producer Guy Little was unfazed. While English audiences now had an American Dracula, his American audience would have an English Dracula; he brought John Phillip Law from the UK to replace Chakiris. *The Passion of Dracula* also came to Illinois, with José Greco starring as the vampire count at the Paramount Arts Centre in Aurora, in a one-night-only presentation on November 5, 1978.

Dracula arrived in Los Angeles on September 29, 1978, without Frank Langella, who couldn't do the role because of his commitment to star in the film. The next logical choice seemed to be Raul Julia, who received rave notices in the role in Baltimore, except that Julia was taking over from Langella on Broadway. The producers' next choice was Barry Bostwick, but he had just shot a television pilot, and wouldn't be available if the series was picked up.

There was talk of casting an actual Romanian in the title role. When producer Elizabeth McCann put together a second touring company of *Dracula*, she met with the managers of tennis star Ilie Nastase to see if he would be available. Nastase had such a "bad boy" attitude on the tennis courts that sports writers of the time often referred to him as "Dracula," but he didn't end up as the vampire on stage.

When the *Dracula* touring company moved to Los Angeles, English actor Jeremy Brett stepped into the role. He then toured with it around the U.S. In 1984, he took on the role for which he is best remembered, as Sherlock Holmes in the Granada TV series.

Author's collection

Finally, in August of 1978, it was announced that the Ahmanson's Dracula would be British actor Jeremy Brett. At that point, Brett was best known to American audiences for playing Freddie Eynsford Hill in the 1964 film *My Fair Lady*; Sherlock Holmes was still six years away. Brett appeared in full dress as Dracula at the Hope USO Club in Hollywood for Actors Blood Drive '78; newspapers noted that Brett was not allowed to sample the goods.

Once Langella left to begin work on the *Dracula* film, Raul Julia took up the cape on Broadway. Born in San Juan, Puerto Rico, Julia seemed fated to become Dracula: his first acting role, at age five, was playing the devil in a church play. He played Dracula with such gusto that, in the scene where the vampire forces Lucy to drink blood from his chest, he sometimes actually scratched his chest with his fingernails and drew real blood. Women found his vampire just as delectable as Langella's; like his predecessor, he was deluged with letters, many of them containing propositions. But Julia's evenings off were already spoken for: he used them to speak to college groups on the issue of world hunger.

After Raul Julia gave his last performance in *Dracula* on Sunday, June 17, 1979, he was replaced by Canadian actor Jean LeClerc, making his Broadway

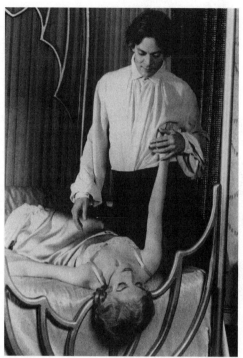

The first actor to don the cape when Frank Langella left the play was Raul Julia, who would later breathe life into another macabre character, Gomez Addams, in two *Addams Family* movies.

Courtesy of Del Valle Archives

debut. LeClerc had previously played the title role in the national company of the play. In analyzing the vampire role, LeClerc, a Frenchman from Montreal, felt that Dracula was distant, remote, and a lover; he considered the play, with its sensuality and neck-biting, a woman's fantasy.

In a typical publicity stunt, before the performance on August 15, 1979, LeClerc and others from the production donated blood for the Greater New York Blood Program. For a Halloween promotion in 1979, the first one hundred patrons who lined up in costume were given free tickets to the show. Following the performance, Jean LeClerc chose four lucky individuals to join him for free dinners at Backstage.

The revival of *Dracula* outstripped its original in terms of staying power. The 1927 *Dracula* ran for 281 Broadway performances, while the production at the Martin Beck closed January 6, 1980, after 925. It also spawned two national touring companies, and its reception was at least partially responsible for the notion of doing a *Frankenstein* revival next; the adaptation of Mary Shelly's story opened on Broadway in 1980. Ultimately, from its original three-hundred-thousand-dollar investment, *Dracula* turned a profit estimated at $2 million, making it one of Broadway's major profit earners. The producing team of Nelle Nugent and Liz McCann, two of the six producers of *Dracula*, put their *Dracula* earnings into other productions and had three more Broadway hits, with *The Elephant Man*, *Home*, and *Mornings at Seven*.

Vampires Over Chicago

With *Dracula* doing well in its revival, Chicago's Wisdom Bridge Theater decided the time was ripe to revive David Campton's 1972 adaptation of *Carmilla*, a melodrama about a female vampire, based on J. Sheridan Le Fanu's Gothic novel. It opened May 24, 1978, with Dawn Davis as the title vampiress, who seeks to coerce her distant female relative into keeping her company in the crypt. At intermission, tomato juice was served in champagne glasses.

Other Draculas came to Chicago in 1979. George Hamilton, having finished filming *Love at First Bite*, took the title role in *Count Dracula* at the Drury Lane Martinique in Evergreen Park on January 30, 1979. Meanwhile, the touring company of the Broadway *Dracula*, complete with its Edward Gorey set designs, came to the Shubert Theater on February 28, 1979, with Jeremy Brett starring and Dennis Rosa continuing as the play's director.

In an unusual publicity stunt to promote the play, at the February 13, 1979, staging of *Dracula*, twenty-six residents from the Chicago area who all shared the last name Blood were invited to a free performance. The *Chicago Tribune's* Jeff Lyon interviewed Brett after one show and was surprised to see how different the actor was out of costume. Brett admitted that at a recent cocktail party, a woman invited him to bite her neck, and he consented. Before the evening was over, he'd had to bite several other women. Even the hostess of the TV program *AM Chicago* asked him to give her a nibble.

And Then There Were ... Lots

The 1970s ended with an explosion of vampire plays that continued into the next four decades. At a 1978 production of *Dracula* at the Peninsula Players of Fish Creek in Door County, Wisconsin, "America's oldest professional resident summer theater," live bats nesting in the wooden roof occasionally swooped over the audience. Some patrons thought they had been specially trained for the play.

Still another adaptation of Stoker's novel, *Dracula, The Vampire King* by Anthony Scully, was to have opened at the Terrace Theater in Long Beach, California, on November 17, 1978. Produced by Jerry Mancus and David Plattner, the four-hundred-thousand-dollar production was supposed to have laser beams for Dracula's eyes, rear-projection screens, a fireplace from which Michael Ansara, who played Dracula, would emerge hanging upside down, escape couches, smoke pots and a mirror that cracked. Werner Klemperer played Van Helsing as a priest instead of the usual doctor figure, and in the climax, Dracula's head was cut off and thrown into a picnic basket, which then exploded. Before the play began its five-performance run, it was canned. Reasons for the cancellation ranged from lack of enough advance sales to suggestions of dwindling funds and problems with a complicated set. *Dracula, the Vampire King* eventually skipped Long Beach and headed for San Francisco, where it faltered and closed early.

Michael Bogdanov directed *Dracula, or a Pain in the Neck*, a production of the New Vic Theatre of London, at the Beacon Theater in New York in March 1984. Bogdanov adapted the audience-participation play with Phil Woods. Anthony Milner played Dracula. Having already performed the play in London, the company expected to tour it around the U.S. It was scheduled for a one-week engagement in New York, but closed after two performances.

In the early 1980s, when the Barnstormers Theater Group in Tamworth, New Hampshire, presented *Dracula*, the vampire was dressed in a black cape

Michael Ansara hovers over Catherine Erhardt in the short-lived 1978 play, *Dracula, the Vampire King.*
Photo by David Talbert. Author's collection.

that had belonged to the director's father. The director, Francis Grover Cleveland, was the youngest son of Grover Cleveland, who was president of the United States in 1885–89 and 1893–97.

Daniel Day-Lewis appeared as Dracula in 1984 at London's Half Moon Theatre, with a blond-and-black haircut. Soon after the play ended, Stephen Frears cast Day-Lewis in *My Beautiful Laundrette*, and asked the actor to retain the unusual hairstyle for the film.

The Deane-Balderston revival of *Dracula*, complete with Edward Gorey sets, rose again at the Arlington Center for the Performing Arts in Santa Barbara, California, on January 8, 1985, with Martin Landau in the title role. The original director, Dennis Rosa, again did the honors. Reviewing the play for the *Los Angeles Times*, Dan Sullivan wrote that Landau, rather than suggesting a sensual vampire, seemed more like "a friend of your father's who drops by on the way to a fancy dress ball with some papers for him to sign—something about title insurance."

The production next moved to the Chicago suburbs, where it played the Rialto Square Theater in Joliet, Illinois. The February 15 opening was followed by a pre-show candlelit "Dine with Dracula Buffet." The "taste of Transylvania" menu included gulyas, Szekely ghoulash, red beet salad, plum dumplings, and strudel.

Another vampire-related play, *Vampire Lesbians of Sodom* by Charles Busch, was presented by Theater-In-Limbo and Gerald A. Davis at the Provincetown Playhouse in New York in June 1985. Filled with flashy costumes, outrageous lines and bad puns, it was thought to be the cult-favorite successor to *The Rocky Horror Show*.

Another comedic take, *Dracula, A Tale of the Nosferatu* by George Lace and George McGuire, had its Orange County premiere September 18, 1985, at Harlequin Dinner Playhouse in Santa Ana, California. The *Los Angeles Times* called it "a fun chilling tale for the entire family."

A different take on *Dracula* was offered by *Renfield*, a drama by Fred Hunter which was directed by Jean Marie Conway and produced by the Red Key

Productions troupe at the Immediate Theater Studio in Chicago in May 1986. The play centered on Paul, a schizophrenic character who arrives on his brother's doorstep after a two-year disappearance. Interspersed with the brother's attempts to help him are Paul's musings on the Renfield of myth and his interactions with Miss Mina, in a play that explored facets of human loneliness.

The BayWay Arts Center in East Islip offered Ted Tiller's *Count Dracula* in November 1989. Directed by Reva Kaufman, the revival starred Bob Dorian, who was a host on the American Movie Classics (AMC) cable channel, in the title role. Like Martin Landau before him, Dorian's performance was said by critics to resemble an insurance salesman rather than a dark Lothario of the night.

In an unusual bit of theatrical casting, for a performance of a radio drama adaptation of *Dracula* by Mac Wellman at the Classic Stage Company in Greenwich Village, New York, on November 1, 1993, the role of Van Helsing was played by Jean Stapleton, an actress best remembered for playing Edith Bunker on TV's *All in the Family*. Wellman's play was eventually performed by the SoHo Repertory in New York in May 1994, under the direction of Julian Webber, with a cast that included Tim Blake Nelson as Harker, who is driven mad by Dracula, played by Thomas Jay Ryan.

After scoring a success with his *Dracula*, playwright Mac Wellman remained in the vampire vein. In November 1994, his play *Swoop* premiered at the SoHo Repertory Theater in the Tribeca area of New York. The play featured a trio of vampires—Lucy Westenra (Lauren Hamilton), Wilhelmina Murray (played by two actors, Zivia Flomenhaft and Jan Leslie Harding, since her character is split into ego and id) and Dracula (John Nesci)—transplanted into the present, where they hover over the New York metropolitan area, contemplating the world beneath them in a quartet of monologues.

In October of 2000, Rod Barnes wrote and produced *The Gotham Chronicles*, a soap-opera-style play based loosely on real-life activities of New York's vampire clans, at the Raw Space Theater on 42nd Street.

With the success of *Twilight*, along with the TV shows *True Blood* and *The Vampire Diaries*, suddenly it seemed like a good idea to bring *Dracula* back to Broadway. In February of 2010, two sets of producers fought for the rights. One hoped to do it off-Broadway with a young actor in the lead and Academy Award–winner F. Murray Abraham as Van Helsing; theirs was to be a modest half-million-dollar production expected to play at the Little Shubert before going on a national tour. The other set of producers wanted a Broadway production with another Oscar winner, Javier Bardem, as Dracula. As of this writing, both productions seem to have withered like a vampire in daylight.

6

Music of the Night

Vampire Musicals

Dearest Dracula, A Musical Nightmare

At the Dublin Theater Festival in the fall of 1965, a new musical comedy, *Dearest Dracula*, premiered. The Jay Landesman production, with a book by Margaret Hill, Charlotte Hill, and Jack Murdock, lyrics by Fran Landesman and music by Gordon Caleb, was described as an "elaborate musical extravaganza" by Robert B. Byrnes of the *Los Angeles Times*. Byrnes wrote that the musical contained fifteen songs, and was "well acted, well sung with all that was formerly terrifying in this work now turned into funny episodes and macabrely humorous incidents." In the post-nuclear, post-Beatles world of Roy Lichtenstein prints and Andy Warhol soup cans, even Dracula had gone camp.

On July 21, 1978, nine years after they had premiered *Fangs Ain't What They Used to Be*, the Zephyr Theater staged *Dracula, A Musical Nightmare*. The play originated four years earlier at the Berkeley Rep, with books and lyrics by Douglas Johnson and music by John Aschenbrenner. As he did in the earlier version, Joe Spano played dual roles: Chauncey, a music hall entertainer, and Dracula.

Dracula, the Musical?

Jack Sharkey, a prolific writer of dinner theater musicals, penned *Dracula, The Musical?* in 1982, under the pen name of Rick Abbot, for a premiere in Australia. When it was presented at the Westminster Community Theater in Westminster, California, in June of 1988, *Los Angeles Times'* reviewer Mark Smith said, "Abbot, known primarily for a slew of lightweight comedies that find unending life on small stages, has lampooned the Dracula story into coffin dust. To get the tone of this show, just look at some of the gags: When someone remarks that the vermin-eating Renfield is not an attractive house guest, the reply is: 'Just think what we save on fly swatters.' When Dracula makes his big entrance, Renfield does an Ed McMahon 'Heeeeeerrrre's Dracky!' When Van Helsing reminds everybody that their lives are in 'jeopardy,' the theme song from the television game show comes blaring through." Smith did admit, however, that "the audience during a recent performance seemed to enjoy it quite a lot."

Another musical adaptation of the book came in May 1983, at the Olio Theater on Hollywood's Sunset Boulevard. In this version, written by Carol Knapp, Francesca Miller, and Gary O'Brien, the tale was set in 1930s Hollywood.

Possessed, The Dracula Musical

Possessed, The Dracula Musical, produced Off-Broadway by the American Stage Company at a cost of over $1 million, had its world premiere at the Becton Theater at Fairleigh Dickinson University in Teaneck, New Jersey, on December 2, 1987. Jason Darrow, who wrote the lyrics and co-authored the book with Robert Marasco (author of the horror novel *Burnt Offerings*), got the idea after reading Bram Stoker's novel. A songwriter and record producer for artists such as Melissa Manchester and Gilbert Bécaud, Darrow

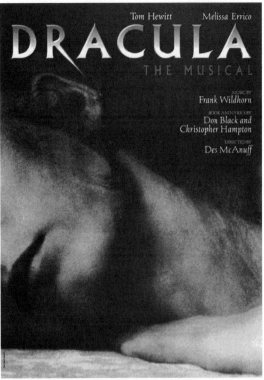

Poster for *Dracula, The Musical* at the Belasco Theater, New York. *Author's collection*

re-imagined the story as a musical set in a modern-day asylum, seen mostly through the eyes of Renfield. Morton Da Costa, a veteran of musicals such as *The Music Man* and *Auntie Mame*, was signed to direct, and Carter Cathcart wrote the music.

Set in Purley, England, the play had Renfield as a rock musician committed to a sanitarium. Mr. Webb—a.k.a. Dracula (played by Michael Zaslow)—drops in, presenting himself as a music promoter with connections and money, and offers Renfield stardom in return for a few small favors. Reviewing the play for the *New York Times*, Alvin Klein said, "It is difficult to find in the American Stage Company's *Possessed*, subtitled *The Dracula Musical*, plausibility or validation on its own terms or entertainment on any level, but it is easy to be offended by it. . . . Perhaps there are no bad ideas for musicals, only bad musicals, like this one."

Another musical take on Stoker's vampire, *Dracula, Another Bloody Musical*, opened at the Westminster Theatre in London in March 1988. Harry Herbert played Dracula, and Princess Diana visited with cast members after seeing one performance. That same year, Halifax's Neptune Theatre premiered

Dracula—A Chamber Musical, with music by Marek Norman and lyrics and book by Richard Ouzounian. It had a popular run at the Stratford Festival the following year.

Another spoof, *Miami Beach Monsters*, was presented by RE Productions at the Triad Theater in Manhattan in January of 2000. Conceived by Helen Butleroff, Georgia Bogardus Holof, Robert Leahy, George Robert Minkoff, Ellen M. Schwartz, and Carol Spero; with a book by Holof, Schwartz, and Dan Berkowitz; music by Michael Brown, Dick Gallagher, David Mettee, Steven Silverstein, and David Strickland; lyrics by Brown, Holof, Schwartz, and Stephen Cole; the musical was directed and choreographed by Butleroff. The show featured a group of movie creatures—Frankenstein's Monster (Steve Elmore), his Bride (Laurie Gamache), Dracula (Craig Mason), the Wolf Man (Richard Rowan), Killer Tomato (Diane J. Findlay), and a lizard-like character called Catskilla (Jimmy Spadola) living in retirement in Florida when their commemoration on a set of postage stamps leads to their rediscovery by a younger generation. Reviewing the production for the *New York Times*, Lawrence Van Gelder felt that despite its moments of cleverness and show business savvy, the show fell "well this side of parody paradise."

Dracula, The Musical

At the end of October 2001, *Dracula, The Musical* premiered at the La Jolla Playhouse, staged by Des McAnuff and composed by Frank Wildhorn, with book and lyrics by Don Black and Christopher Hampton. Tom Hewitt starred as Dracula. Interviewed by Jan Breslauer of the *Los Angeles Times*, Des McAnuff said that in approaching Stoker's novel, "I think there's been a tendency to parody it or to not trust it. We all felt that if we really tapped into what made the book powerful, that really would translate on stage."

McAnuff had been thinking about doing a Dracula musical for several years. "I met with a couple of composers, and from time to time I would mention the project," he told Breslauer. "Then when I got really consumed with doing movies, I didn't give it too much more thought." Coincidentally, Wildhorn had also been thinking about it for some time. "I actually thought of doing *Dracula* when I was a student at USC in 1979–80 when I saw Frank Langella do the play," he recalled to Breslauer. "But it wasn't the time to do it because the play had just come out. So instead I found this little book called *Dr. Jekyll and Mr. Hyde* and that then took seventeen years of my life to get it to Broadway." Wildhorn was not exactly a critical favorite. The *New York Post* referred to Ben Brantley, the theater critic for the *New York Times*, as the composer's own personal Van Helsing; Brantley once wrote that Wildhorn's scores were like bottles of "pop, all carbonated fizz and syrup."

Once they were brought together, McAnuff and Wildhorn discussed how to proceed with the adaptation. They agreed that it shouldn't be a series of pop ballads and it shouldn't be a parody, but rather something with a touch of nineteenth-century influence, a little more classical and sober.

Hampton, who had previously penned *Dangerous Liaisons*, worked closely with Don Black on both the book and lyrics. The challenge for Hampton was to collapse the novel in such a way that he kept everything essential, making the musical the fast-moving equivalent of a page-turner. Dracula's role was expanded for the play, and he was turned into a more sympathetic vampire, with lyricist Don Black striving to illuminate his humanity.

When the musical was produced at the La Jolla Playhouse in 2001, it played to 115 percent paid capacity, the highest for any world premiere production in the playhouse's history. However, plans for a Broadway production were sidelined by less-than-glowing reviews. The *Los Angeles Times* said "the ultra-familiar story never opens up into a realm of satisfying musical escapism, or even satisfying schlock," while the *San Diego Union-Tribune* said, "*Dracula* lacks bite."

Nonetheless, in 2004, after Dutch entertainment mogul Joop van den Ende saw a workshop of *Dracula, The Musical*, he was so pleased that he underwrote a Broadway production. The show premiered at the Belasco Theater on August 19, 2004, having undergone some changes since its La Jolla Playhouse days, with the addition of new songs and different staging. In an interview with Lisa Tolin of Salt Lake City's *Deseret News*, Tom Hewitt said, "It's more passionate, it has more drive, it moves like—if I may say—a bat out of hell. I think we have a better show."

Though fearsome onstage, Hewitt was more timid offstage. "I'm a pussycat," he told Tolin. "I'm a spineless, weak little man. Seriously, I lack a backbone." When the air conditioner in his dressing room broke during a ninety-degree summer heat wave, Hewitt was reluctant to ask for another. His hair and makeup people eventually told him, "You're above the title, you're getting an air conditioner."

"I have to learn how to be an aggressive, forceful star guy," Hewitt told Tolin. "I'm not that. I get embarrassed that I get a car service after the show."

Hewitt, six feet three with graying hair, made his Broadway debut at age forty as Scar in *The Lion King*. He then earned a Tony nomination as Dr. Frank 'N' Furter in a revival of *The Rocky Horror Show*. Now, at forty-six, he found himself being buckled into a harness and flown fifty feet above an audience. He loved it, and also loved his on-stage clinches with co-star Melissa Errico, though he admitted it was a challenge to maintain an aura of sensuality while choreographing the surreptitious insertion of fangs and deployment of fake blood in the midst of passion and romance.

The critics were not kind. In *The Hartford* (CT) *Courant*, Malcolm Johnson wrote, "High-flying special effects and seductive art nouveau scenery fail to rescue a bloodless book and hollow pop opera music in the new Frank Wildhorn extravaganza, a *Dracula* unworthy of the name. The composer, who reached his apex with the stagy but rarely credible *Jekyll & Hyde*, has shifted his minor talent to another tale of gothic horror and verboten sex, with strangely empty results."

In *The Record* (Bergen County, New Jersey), Robert Feldberg said, "Bram Stoker wrote *Dracula* 107 years ago. The bloodless musical made from his novel seems about as old. . . . It plays as a frantic, shorthand version of the book, jumping hastily from Transylvania to London and back. . . . Presenting, with a relatively straight face . . . a horror story in the language and style of the turn of the 20th century doesn't work. It isn't scary. It's quaint and often silly."

Peter Marks of the *Washington Post* wrote, "It turns out there's a fate for Dracula more terrible than undead. Uninteresting. . . . This somber new musical drama is a plodding, bloodless affair. . . . Fans and commentators have always remarked on the Count's fatal powers of attraction. Who knew that included the ability to bore you to death?"

The show closed after 154 performances, but proved a hit in Europe.

Dance of the Vampires

In the fall of 1997, Roman Polanski's 1967 film, *The Fearless Vampire Killers or: Pardon Me, But Your Teeth Are in My Neck*, was adapted into a stage musical, *Tanze der Vampire*, which premiered at the twelve-hundred-seat Raimund Theater in Vienna, Austria. Polanski directed the musical, which was produced by Andrew Braunsberg and featured music by Jim Steinman (who had composed hit songs for Meat Loaf) with book and lyrics by Michael Kunze. "It's a big, Wagnerian musical with lots of humor," Steinman told George Hamilton of the *London Financial Times*. "A lot of it is pure Mel Brooks, and a lot of it is Anne Rice." The score featured a song written by Steinman that had previously been a hit for Bonnie Tyler, "Total Eclipse of the Heart." "I couldn't resist using it," said Steinman. "I actually wrote it for another vampire musical that was based on *Nosferatu*, but never got produced." The musical ran until mid-January.

After the show went on to become a hit in the German cities of Stuttgart, Hamburg, and Berlin, New York producers Elizabeth Williams and Anita Waxman made plans to bring it to Broadway. Steinman was involved in transferring it, co-writing the book with playwright David Ives, and co-directing with John Caird; Polanski was prohibited from directing the play, since he had fled the U.S. in 1979 after being charged with statutory rape and would be arrested upon his return. A staged reading was held in New York in May of 2001. "The German production is a fairly humorless show, with people getting hit on the head with salami," Ives told Patrick Pacheco of *Newsday*. "And I've been brought in to take out the salami and put in the chorus girls. We were very pleased with the reading, and now it's just a question of getting a theater, which, needless to say, isn't easy."

By July of 2001, Steinman was clashing with producers Williams and Waxman over the artistic direction of the show, so he turned over producing responsibilities to his manager, David Sonenberg. The show was originally scheduled to go into rehearsals in December and open in April at the Minskoff Theater. It would end up taking considerably longer to reach the stage.

After approaching David Bowie, John Travolta, Richard Gere, and Placido Domingo to star, the production got a boost when it was announced that Michael Crawford, Tony Award–winning star of Andrew Lloyd Webber's *The Phantom of the Opera*, had signed on to play Count Von Krolock.

In February of 2002, John Rando took over as director of *Dance of the Vampires*. "This show isn't camp," Rando said in an interview with Robert Feldberg of the Bergen County, New Jersey, *Record*. "It takes the vampire myth and pokes fun at it, but it also embraces it. Its message is about the excesses of appetite. It has wit and an edge to it."

Comparing the Broadway version to the one that premiered in Vienna, Rando told Feldberg, "The main character in our production will be vastly different, a much more multifaceted, dynamic, complete figure. We've also made other changes and cuts and restructured the show into a book musical, with dialogue; the original is [all sung]. I think we've made it a much more interesting story. The German production is probably more faithful to the film."

The $14 million show got off to a rocky start. During a tech rehearsal in early October 2002, Michael Crawford's dresser fell through a trap door on stage and was rushed to the hospital with minor injuries. One of the highlights of the show was a six-ton graveyard, a piece of scenery designed to descend fifty feet from the theater's fly space, tilting upward so that the audience could see the coffin lids being removed and the vampires emerging for a big song-and-dance number. There was also a coffin that popped up out of the ground to emit Count Von Krolock, a red-eyed bat that flew over the audience, and lots of flying vampires. Technical difficulties in getting all of those computer-controlled elements to work smoothly caused cancellation of the show's first two preview performances, which were originally scheduled for October 2002. Despite the setbacks, with Crawford's name above the title, the advance sales were nearly $10 million.

By Halloween, after its first full week of previews, *Dance of the Vampires* took in $730,000. The musical was set to open November 21. However, it was postponed for eighteen days when director John Rando went to Texas to be with his mother, who was recovering from open-heart surgery.

When the show finally opened, the critic for the *London Daily Mail* enthused, "Instead of Lloyd Webber's pungent operatics, we have knockabout Gothic rock with a twist by Jim Steinman. . . . Crawford presides over this camp nuttiness like a longhaired loon, grinning at the fun and singing gloriously, like a fallen angel, in a swirl of dry ice and a panoply of candles, just as he did in *Phantom*. . . . Crawford has been the biggest British musical theater star of the past 30 years, from *Billy* to *Barnum* to *Phantom*. He still is. He flies like a bat out of hell."

Other critics were far less generous. Malcolm Johnson, of the *Hartford* (CT) *Courant*, wrote, "A fine line divides satire and plagiarism, and *Dance of the Vampires* crosses it all too often . . . the elaborate horror spoof . . . frequently raises the specter of its superior neighbor, the long-running *The Phantom of the Opera*."

In the *New York Daily News*, Howard Kissel wrote, "Few musicals in recent years have created the expectations of *Dance of the Vampires*. No one, mind you, expected anything good. . . . What's hard to understand is why Michael Crawford, its star, would want to appear in a show that spends so much energy sending up the work he did in *Phantom of the Opera*."

Ben Brantley in the *New York Times* said, "Theater disaster cultists, a breed that makes Vlad the Impaler look small-time, have had their fangs at the ready ever since the early buzz began on *Vampires*. . . . *Vampires* exudes the less exalted, simply embarrassed feeling of a costume party that everyone got all dressed up for and then decided wasn't such a good idea. . . . The overall effect is of a desperately protracted skit from a summer replacement variety show of the late 1960's, the kind on which second-tier celebrities showed up to make fun of themselves."

When the show closed, there was plenty of blame to go around. Some pointed the finger at producer David Sonenberg, who bought an opera but decided to make it something else, reportedly insisting that there be five jokes on every page of the script.

Others looked at Michael Crawford, who—in his zeal to not be compared with his role in *Phantom of the Opera*—insisted on writing his own jokes as Count Krolock, and didn't want his co-star, René Auberjonois, to upstage him, so he cut Auberjonois's laugh lines; they ended up stepping on each other's punch lines in performances. Then there was the choreographer who wasn't accustomed to dealing with such big troupes, and the composer who became so disgusted with the process that he stopped coming to rehearsals and skipped opening night. After its premiere, the show had daily ticket sales of between forty thousand and sixty thousand dollars; to support the weekly operating overhead of six hundred thousand dollars, it needed daily sales of one hundred thousand. By January, the $6 million of advance sales had evaporated. Giving in to the popular perception of the show, and desperate to sell tickets, the producers resorted to running ads that called *Dance of the Vampires* "the one new Broadway musical that really sucks." But it was too late. The show closed on January 25, 2003, after only fifty-six performances. The investors lost everything.

Lestat

In May of 2003, it was announced that Elton John and his longtime lyricist, Bernie Taupin, would be collaborating on a Broadway musical version of Anne Rice's vampire novels, to be called *The Vampire Lestat*. The original plan was for a Broadway debut in 2005. In a press conference to announce the musical, Elton John took pains to say that it would not be a spoof, it would not be a rock musical, and wouldn't have the clichéd capes and garlic, trying his best to distance the project from the colossal flop, *Dance of the Vampires*. And, although the book was to be written by Linda Woolverton and the director was to be Robert Jess Roth, both of whom collaborated on *Beauty and the Beast*, it was not going to be a Disney musical. It would, however, be the first Broadway production from Warner Bros. Theater Ventures, who were also preparing a *Batman* musical with Jim Steinman that recycled a tune from *Dance of the Vampires.*

When the $10 million *Lestat* began its out-of-town tryout in San Francisco in early January 2006, it received blistering reviews. *Variety* noted that the production had "too much plot to wade through. Titular figure aside, characters come and go without creating involving narrative or emotional arcs." The *San Francisco Chronicle* called *Lestat* "didactic, disjointed, oddly miscast, confusingly designed and floundering," dismissing Elton John's songs as "unrelentingly saccharine, banal and virtually indistinguishable." The *Modesto Bee* called it "laborious, vague and bloated, leaving the cast heroically emoting to little effect."

Nonetheless, the producers decided to persevere in their quest to bring it to Broadway's Palace Theater in April. Gregg Maday, overseeing the musical for Warner Bros. Theater Ventures, told Michael Riedel of the *New York Post*, "Everybody likes to get good notices, to hear how wonderful they are. But the reality is we know there are things that need fixing, and we are in the process of making a very complicated and difficult story come to life on stage."

"There is a lot of philosophical information in the first act," Maday told Riedel. "It drags and the audience is confused. I think we're going to focus on making the storytelling more streamlined. We have been juggling a lot of intellectual ideas that are in the novel, but I think what has to come to the forefront is Lestat's story: 'How do I survive, I don't want to be alone.'"

After being retooled with the aid of a new song from Elton John and Bernie Taupin, *Lestat* opened at Broadway's Palace Theater on April 25, 2006. Hugh Panaro starred as Lestat, with Jim Stanek as Louis, and Allison Fischer as Claudia. After thirty-three previews, it ran for only thirty-nine performances before closing.

The critics came with knives sharpened. Malcolm Johnson, in the *Hartford Courant*, said, "Time was when folklore blamed the rays of the sun for burning vampires to cinders. Of late, the fabled white lights of Broadway have been doing the incineration. *Lestat* looks like the new ash man. . . . *Lestat* will most likely burn out like a New Orleans house afire."

In the *Chicago Tribune*, Chris Jones wrote, "The opening number of *Lestat*, the first Broadway musical to feature both music by Elton John and lyrics by Bernie Taupin, features the titular hero killing a pack of wolves, mostly with his mouth. 'My blood it roars like thunder in this mortal breast,' sings poor Hugh Panaro, personally snuffing out a big, bad doggie and just starting out on what is destined to be a very bad night for him, 'purified by battle and the smell of death.' Ah, yes, the seductive smell of death. In the case of *Lestat* that will come through the perfume of paper. Upon which is etched a closing notice."

Howard Kissel of the *New York Daily News* praised the play with faint damns, writing, "These days, it might be accurate to say musicals are marketed, rather than created. Take *Lestat*, the third vampire musical in the last 3½ years. To call it the best of the three is not much praise, since its short-lived predecessors were abysmal. . . . The advantage it has, however, over Frank Wildhorn's *Dracula* and Jim Steinman's *Dance of the Vampires* is that it is based on the work of two brand names with huge followings—Elton John and Anne Rice. . . . The one novelty in the treatment of the vampire theme is the introduction of a pre-pubescent vampire, a sort of bloodsucking Eloise, snarkily played by Allison Fischer. . . . Otherwise the material itself is flat."

When all was said and done, Elton John hated *Lestat*; he wanted to close it out of town. When it came to Broadway, it lost $10 million. *Variety*'s David Rooney may have had the right idea. After the musical opened, he wrote, "It might be time to nail the coffin lid shut on all belting bloodsuckers."

7

Symphonies of Horror

Vampires in the Fine Arts

Vampire Opera

One of the most popular German operas of its day was Heinrich Marschner's *Der Vampyr*, composed in 1828. A key composer in the development of German opera between Carl Maria von Weber and Richard Wagner, Marschner based *Der Vampyr* on John Polidori's 1819 novella, *The Vampire*. The opera centers on Lord Ruthven, who has been condemned to Hell but makes a pact with the Devil by which he will be able to stay on earth, provided he obtains the souls of three virgins. As the opera progresses, he succeeds with Emmy and Ianthe, but when he goes after Malvina, her beloved Edgar Aubry intervenes to save her from the vampire's clutches.

In the latter part of the twentieth century, other composers were tempted to try vampire themes. A recording of the Hoffnung Astronautical Music Festival of November 28, 1961, was released in August 1962, on which the longest work was a "Horrortorio," in which the marriage of Frankenstein's son to Dracula's daughter was turned into a respectable Victorian oratorio.

A "non-opera" by Sue Ellen Case, *Johnny Appleseed/Dracula—the Universe in Infancy*, was presented by students of the California Institute of the Arts at the First Unitarian Church of Los Angeles in April 1970. Case, who was an instructor in art history at the school, described her work as "melodic and danced"; the cast included "four-foot walking chickens."

John Deak of the New York Philharmonic Orchestra presented two scenes from his *Lucy and the Count* for string quintet at Cooper Union in February of 1983. Reviewing for the *New York Times*, Bernard Holland wrote that it was "a musical version of *Dracula* in which Mr. Deak both narrated and joined his colleagues in lurid background music and squeaky-door sound effects. . . . It was amusing and a little more—intentionally absurd, but at the same time making us think just a little bit harder about the enigmatic ties between instrumental sound and human speech."

NORTHERN
BALLET
THEATRE

Northern Ballet
Theatre's seductive
new production

What would you
give to live forever?

DAVID NIXON'S

Dracula

WY PLAY
HOUSE
Box Office: 0113 213 7700   Fri 2 – Sat 10
www.wyp.org.uk   September 2005

Poster for a 2005 British ballet adaptation of *Dracula*.
Author's collection

In 1970, La Mama E. T. C., an avant-garde theatrical company in New York, presented the chamber opera *Carmilla: A Vampire Tale*, then a work in progress by composer Ben Johnston and writer Wilford Leach, who also directed with John Braswell. It returned in 1972 and 1976 and toured widely in 1977. Adapted from J. Sheridan Le Fanu's novella, it concerned a young woman, Laura, who dreamed as a child of having a dark-haired soul mate who appears on her doorstep when both appear to be eighteen years old. The soul mate, Carmilla, ensnares Laura into a vampiric half-life. Nancy Heikin sang the role of Carmilla, with Margaret Benczak as Laura.

Robert Moran was commissioned by the Catalyst label to create *The Dracula Diary*, an "opera macabre" with a libretto by James Skofield filled with murder, jealousy, and lust, and whose central character is an eighteenth-century diva-turned-vampire. The work was recorded in 1994 on the Catalyst label, with the Houston Opera Studio conducted by Ward Holmquist. Reviewing it for the *New York Times*, K. Robert Schwardz wrote, "Generic chord progressions, clumsy text setting and cheesy synthesized sound effects all conspire to create an ambiance closer to *Phantom of the Opera* than to opera itself."

In March of 1999, Jonathan Sheffer and the Eos Orchestra premiered Pulitzer Prize–winning composer David Del Tredici's *Dracula*. Specially commissioned by the orchestra, the work was based on Alfred Corn's poem, *My Neighbor, the Distinguished Count*, which told the story from the perspective of the woman next door, alternating humor and chills as it told of her seduction and transformation by the vampire. The piece was set for soprano and thirteen instruments, including the theremin. The concert took place in the auditorium of the New York Society for Ethical Culture in Manhattan.

Dance of the Vampires

A protégée of Agnes deMille, Katherine Litz created a pantomime/dance version of *Dracula*, set to the *First Symphony* of Charles Ives, which she premiered at the Hunter Playhouse in New York on February 1, 1959. Approaching the Bram Stoker text respectfully, the piece had Jonathan Harker, danced by Ray Harrison, as the hero who saves Mina (Litz) from the clutches of Dracula (Charles Weidman). In the *New York Times*, John Martin wrote, "It was an extremely stylish bit of theater, which captured the flavor of Bram Stoker and the Victorian period in which he wrote, without burlesque or condescension . . . penetrating with real pity below the ridiculous surfaces of things and people to the essential truths and tragedies beneath." After this premiere, Litz went on to produce two more dance versions of Stoker's tale.

Another dance version of *Dracula* came with the premiere performance of Ping Chong's *Nosferatu*, a comic danse macabre inspired by F. W. Murnau's 1922 film, by Chong's Fiji Company at New York's La MaMa Annex. Subtitled "a symphony of darkness," the piece combined live actors, projections and an architectural environment in an audio-visual tapestry. Reviewing it for the *New York Times*, Mel Gussow wrote, "On one level, this is a stylish hi-tech comedy about a contemporary married couple named Harker, as in the *Dracula* story, and their circle of fashion-conscious friends. While they exchange self-parodying mod-ish remarks, on a wall screen, we see titles and still pictures from the original film, climaxing with Dracula rising from his crypt. Demons also inhabit the stage, a chorus of lively corpses, unseen by the characters who are so concerned with their own affairs that they would not notice a bloodsucker if he sat on their couch. The evening, of course, ends infernally, with a lifelike, long-nailed vampire on the attack. Until that point, however, Mr. Chong is equally interested in orchestrating his social criticism." In an interview with Sid Smith of the *Chicago Tribune*, Chong called it "a drawing-room comedy, very Noel Coward."

In 1985, the California Ballet Association commissioned Charles Bennett to design a dance drama based on *Dracula*. Bennett had wanted to do the ballet for twenty years. "I'm fascinated by the subject and by its enormous popularity over the years, so I've immersed myself in as much vampire lore as I could," he told Eileen Sondak of the *Los Angeles Times*. The ballet was performed at Symphony Hall in San Diego in October 1987. Bennett utilized a tri-level stage to depict the twenty-four scenes in his three-act ballet, creating overlapping activities to drive the melodrama at a snappy pace. "It's so complex, it's mind-blowing for me," Bennett told Sondak. "We do every kind of movement, from Transylvanian Gypsy dancing to the tango." The ballet required a forty-four-member cast, many of whom were fitted with fangs. Paul Sanasardo, coaxed out of retirement for the role of Dracula, told Sondak, "Dracula was my chance to do a self-portrait. The critics labeled me the dark poet, because I have a history of playing Death.

I stopped dancing three years ago, but I'm an intense performer and I just couldn't say no to this role." Martin Bernheimer in the *Los Angeles Times* called the ballet "a hard-working, ponderous, ultra-lugubrious semblance of the Bram Stoker novel as conceived and choreographed by Charles Bennett . . . and performed by a cast that included Paul Sanasardo . . . flapping his cloak in the title role. . . . Some of the show was so awful it was fun. Almost."

Another dance version of Stoker's novel appeared in October of 1990, when the Wilkes-Barre–based Ballet Theater Pennsylvania brought their dance theater version of *Dracula* to the State Theater of the New Brunswick Cultural Center in New Brunswick, Connecticut. Choreographed by Mary L. Hepner, the two-act ballet featured music by Verdi, Puccini, and Philip Glass. The production included a tango performed by Dracula in a crimson-lined black cape, and masked demons, gargoyles, and vampires dancing a stylistic mix of ballet, jazz, and modern dance. *Dracula* was chosen as a subject because the sixteen-dancer troupe needed a vehicle to promote itself on a national level for its six-week tour of thirty-eight cities. Depending on the tastes of the particular market, in less conservative areas the ballet featured a sexually suggestive bar scene.

A year later, the American Repertory Ballet Company, formerly the Princeton Ballet, presented *Dracula* as a dramatic ballet in two acts, choreographed by Stuart Sebastian, at the State Theater in New Brunswick on October 30, 1991. Barbara Gilford of the *New York Times* wrote, "The ballet disturbs, offering a quite literally enthralling evocation of the well-known story in dance scenes that contain passion and violence that might distress children under the age of 10 or 12. Set to a collage of musical selections associated with death, *Dracula* . . . involves a mature theme presented with a sometimes spine-chilling theatricality." Stuart Sebastian was the director of the Dayton Ballet, which offered the premiere of *Dracula* in 1990. It was the last ballet Sebastian created before he died of AIDS in January 1991, at the age of forty.

A new *Dracula* ballet came along in 1996, this time a $4 million three-act piece with elaborate special effects and costumes by Jean-Paul Gaultier. Madonna's promoter, Zev Eizik, guaranteed the booking fees for a sixty-three-week international tour.

The Houston Ballet staged a new *Dracula* in March of 1997, in time for the centennial of the novel's publication, by the company's artistic director, Ben Stevenson. In the *New York Times*, Sam Howe Verhoek said the ballet "could well be subtitled *Sex and Death in Transylvania*. . . . It is a haunting extravaganza of neo-classical dance, set to the music of Franz Liszt on a stage bathed in maroon, red, deep blue and black to evoke a village living in the shadow of evil. Dracula is wicked, but as he swoops around in a cape that is nearly 23 feet from tip to tip, he is not without erotic allure for his 18 captive wives, the corps de ballet. *Swan Lake*, it's not." Reviewing the ballet for the *New York Times*, Jennifer Dunning wrote, "Ben Stevenson's *Dracula* is spectacle of an order ballet audiences seldom see today. The sets, costumes and lighting are not just lavish but exquisitely beautiful and atmospheric. . . . Dracula and his ghostly undead brides fly. The Count dies in a flash of light atop a candle lighted chandelier. And a rattling old coach careers on and off the stage in the ballet. . . . For once, $1 million, the cost of *Dracula*, looks like a million."

The Royal Winnipeg Ballet's globe-trotting production of *Dracula*, presented in 1998 and choreographed by Mark Godden, was later turned into an International Emmy-winning film by Winnipeg-based experimental filmmaker Guy Maddin. *Dracula: Pages from a Virgin's Diary* was produced in 2002 for Canadian television. A silent, black-and-white adaptation of *Dracula*, the film featured dancer-actors Zhang Wei-Qiang as Dracula, Tara Birtwhistle as Lucy, CindyMarie Small as Nina, and David Moroni as Dr. Van Helsing, all emoting in the evocative style of silent melodrama while dancing the elegant choreography of Godden. Stephen Holden in the *New York Times* wrote, "As Mr. Zhang's suave, swashbuckling count seduces and poisons his victims, you think of

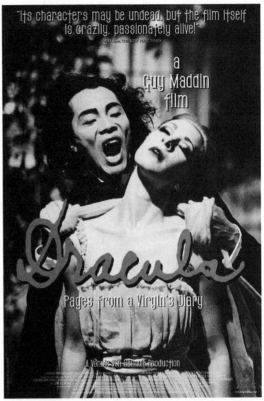

Poster from Guy Maddin's film, *Dracula: Pages from a Virgin's Diary*. Part dance, part silent film, all mood and menace. Zhang Wei-Qiang danced the part of Dracula, with Tara Birtwhistle as Lucy.   *Author's collection*

Attila the Hun as a Valentino-like voluptuary luring them to surrender to the intoxicating rhythm of the tango in his hard, unsmiling eyes. Radiating an avid sexual intensity that carries a whiff of sadism, Mr. Zhang is as charismatic a Dracula as has ever been shown on the screen. . . . His final pose is sensual and heroic. This Dracula may be dangerous, he is also a martyr in an antisexual, xenophobic witch hunt."

When Maddin was first approached about filming *Dracula*, he hadn't read the book. "I had no real love of Dracula," he told Mike Rubin of the *New York Times*. After agreeing to the job "strictly from hunger," Maddin viewed every vampire film he could find, and decided his adaptation would be the most faithful to Stoker's novel, even if it was ballet. Maddin found working with dancers rather than actors beneficial. "When they quit doing bourrées and pas de deux," he told Rubin, "they ended up doing mimed narrative action exposition, and that's basically silent-movie acting much like Buster Keaton or

Chaplin would do, but far more elegant, because dancers learn to mime with every fiber of their bodies."

After its Canadian telecast, the film became the centerpiece of the 2002 New York Video Festival. A. O. Scott of the *New York Times* said it was "crazily, passionately alive. The blurry shadows at the perimeter of the frames and the jerky movements of the actors . . . uncannily simulate the look of the very oldest movies, and the head-tossing, throat-baring displays of lust and dread are at once parodic and grandly, operatically earnest. . . . The contemporary resonances of this *Dracula* are obvious enough—fear of foreigners, fear of AIDS, sexual anxieties of every variety—but it never departs from its own strange, captivating world."

8

Silent Screams

Nosferatu

A Symphony of Horror

hat's the result when a German occultist produces a movie based on a popular vampire novel without first bothering to acquire the rights? Answer: the first classic vampire film.

The same year that Bram Stoker's *Dracula* was published, Robert Paul and Birt Acres, who built the first 35mm movie camera in Britain, also made the first film shot in the UK, *Incident at Cloverly Cottage*. By the turn of the century, motion pictures were being produced around the globe, and filmmakers turned to literature for inspiration. One of the first known celluloid appearances of Dracula came in 1921, in the Hungarian film *Drakula halála*, or *The Death of Dracula*. Although the film is lost, it appears to have been a Dracula film only tangentially. The story concerns a woman who visits an insane asylum where one of the inmates claims to be Count Dracula. Afterwards, she begins experiencing frightening visions, which may be real, or may simply be nightmares. After opening in Vienna, the film, which starred Paul Askenas as Dracula, was recut and shown in Budapest in 1923.

After the First World War, Berlin became the cultural center of Germany. Many theatrically minded artists gravitated to the city and became involved in the productions at Max Reinhardt's Deutsches Theater. Reinhardt, rebelling against the naturalism of Otto Brahm, his mentor and the theater's former owner, embraced a bold new style of Expressionist theater which used every element of stagecraft—set design, painting, costuming, music, lighting and actors' performances—to express the inner, psychological states of the characters, making subjective emotions tangible, even if achievement of that effect required distortion. Many future film directors received their training in Reinhardt's theater, including F. W. Murnau, Paul Leni, and Ernst Lubitsch.

As these theater directors moved into film, they took the stage techniques of Expressionism with them. One of the directors, Robert Wiene, made what is considered to be the first true horror film, *The Cabinet of Dr. Caligari*, in 1919. Told from the point-of-view of a madman in an asylum, the film relates the tale of a mesmerist using a somnambulist to carry out crimes on his behalf. The

Max Schreck as Count Orlok in F. W. Murnau's
Nosferatu (1922).   *Author's collection*

success of the film showed that audiences were willing to accept stories of the weird and supernatural, and that such stories didn't need to be explained away as having been a nightmare or a hoax, as had previously been the fashion in both film and theater.

One of those inspired by *Caligari* was a painter and designer named Albin Grau. Serving in the German Army in World War I, Grau had a conversation with a Serbian farmer who confided that his father was one of the undead, a vampire. Grau, a self-described spiritualist and devotee of the occult, was intrigued by the idea, and began thinking about making a supernatural film featuring a vampire as the main character.

In 1921, Grau teamed with Enrico Dieckmann to form a new company, Prana-Film. The name comes from the Buddhist concept of *prana*, or "breath-as-life." With an initial capitalization of twenty thousand marks, the company announced a slate of upcoming projects that all had elements of the fantastic and the occult; besides Grau's long-simmering vampire idea, they intended to make *Der Sumpfteufel* (*The Devil of the Swamp*) and *Hollenträume* (*Dreams of Hell*).

The executives of Prana-Film did not know much about filmmaking, but Grau and his scriptwriter Henrik Galeen apparently did know about Stoker's *Dracula*, at least enough to lift the broad strokes of their story from Stoker's pages. Galeen changed the names of the major characters, so that Dracula became Graf (Count) Orlock, Harker became Hutter, Mina became Ellen, and so on. Grau and Galeen also changed Stoker's ending. Instead of the vampire being pursued back to his castle, where he is killed after being beheaded, Galeen's script has Ellen luring Orlock to her bedside, keeping him there until sunrise. When the vampire is caught in the searing light of the sun's rays, he disintegrates. This went counter to Stoker's book, in which Dracula is seen in daylight in London, but it had a lasting impact on the conception of vampires in books and movies—henceforth, the vampire's aversion to sunlight became accepted lore.

Galeen had been part of the Berlin theater company of Max Reinhardt, and may have suggested another Reinhardt alumnus to Grau to direct the film:

F. W. Murnau. Murnau, whose real name was Freidrich Wilhelm Plumpe, studied at Heidelberg University where he directed plays in which students were actors. After graduating, he went to Berlin, acting in plays directed by Reinhardt. It wasn't long before he went into the movies. One of his early films, *Der Januskopf*, was an adaptation of Robert Louis Stevenson's *Strange Case of Dr. Jekyll and Mr. Hyde*, featuring Conrad Veidt and a newcomer to the movies named Bela Lugosi.

Though Murnau was the director, Grau was the real visionary behind *Nosferatu*. Before filming began, he created production sketches of key scenes. These sketches dictated not only the look of the vampire but also the Expressionistic use of stark shadows and geometric compositions. Murnau combined this with his own penchant for stylized naturalism and compositions inspired by classic paintings to create a film that begins with a realist approach but becomes more Expressionistic as Hutter travels from his homeland to the Land of Phantoms, and encounters the evil that will come to plague his village.

Filming of *Nosferatu* began in the summer of 1921, with much of the film shot on location. Max Schreck—another alumnus of the Reinhardt company—portrayed Orlock as a kind of walking pestilence. With his nearly bald head, pointed ears, bushy eyebrows, and two rat-like fangs protruding from the center of his mouth, as well as a tall but hunched frame and long talons for fingers, he evoked a rat more than a bat. Murnau shot the latter part of his film in Lübeck, a German port city with canals, which became Wisborg in the film. When the vampire's derelict ship glides into the port, an army of rats follows him off,

Count Orlok (Max Schreck) arrives in Wisborg, bringing the plague of vampirism.
Courtesy of Del Valle Archives

drawing a metaphoric connection between the spread of plague and the spread of vampirism.

Throughout the film, cameraman Fritz Arno Wagner made good use of shadows. When Ellen has a vision of Orlock, we see his shadow come up over her body, his hand squeezing over her heart as she spasms. In the final scene, as the vampire goes up to Ellen's bedroom, we see only his shadow ascending the stairs and turning the doorknob.

Once the film was completed, Grau and Dieckmann spared no expense promoting it. On March 7, 1922, Prana-Film Co. gave a ball in the buildings of the Berlin Zoo, along with a screening of the film, called "The Festival of Nosferatu." It kicked off the most expensive publicity campaign ever waged in Berlin. In fact, the producers spent more in publicizing the film than they did in producing it; shortly after the glitzy premiere, it was revealed that Prana-Film could no longer pay its bills.

When the film opened in Berlin in April of 1922, C. Hooper Trask of *Weekly Variety* covered the event, calling the film "a still-born *Caligari*," while acknowledging that the plot was lifted from Bram Stoker's *Dracula*.

The publicity surrounding the screening at the Berlin Zoo and the resultant reviews of the film drew the attention of Stoker's widow, Florence. She immediately joined the British Incorporated Society of Authors, sending along with her membership check the program of the event at the Zoological Gardens and advertisements featuring drawings of Count Orlock. The program noted that *Nosferatu, Eine Symphonie des Grauens* was "freely adapted" from Stoker's *Dracula*, yet the author's widow had never signed any agreement with the filmmakers. It was an oversight they would soon come to regret.

Florence Balcombe as sketched by her admirer, Oscar Wilde. Though she left Wilde for Bram Stoker, all three remained friends until Wilde's death in 1900.   *Author's collection*

The British Incorporated Society of Authors hired an attorney in Germany to pursue Florence Stoker's claims, but by that time Prana-Film had gone into receivership. The attorney advised Mrs. Stoker that while they wouldn't be able to get any money out of the company, they might at least get ownership of the film, or an injunction against anyone who would purchase it.

The legal struggles went on for the next two years, as Prana folded and their receivers, the Deutsch-Amerikanisch Film Union, appealed all the decisions in the German courts that went in Florence Stoker's favor. Becoming increasingly aware that she would never receive any money for the copyright infringement, she decided the next best thing would be to see that all copies of the film were destroyed. The German court issued the destruction orders in July of 1925.

Luckily, the film survived, in prints that had been secretly moved out of Germany, and then pirated. One such print ended up in America, where, through an oversight, Stoker's *Dracula* novel was in the public domain and the destruction orders had no effect. After directing *Nosferatu*, Murnau helmed such films as *Tartuffe, Faust*, and *The Last Laugh*. The latter brought him acclaim in the United States, and William Fox, president of Fox Films, brought him to Hollywood in 1926, where he directed *Sunrise—A Song of Two Humans* (1927) , regarded as one of the finest silents ever made.

At the end of May 1929, *Nosferatu the Vampire* (as the film was called in U.S. newspaper announcements) was shown at the Film Guild Cinema in New York's Greenwich Village. Mordaunt Hall, a critic who appears not to have understood the ideas behind Expressionism, reviewed it for the *New York Times*, writing, "It is the sort of thing one could watch at midnight without its having much effect upon one's slumbering hours. . . . The backgrounds are often quite effective, but most of it seems like cardboard puppets doing all they can to be horrible on papier-maché settings. . . . It is a production that is rather more of a soporific than a thriller."

When sound arrived in Hollywood and Fox began ordering Murnau to make allowances for the new technology in his films, the director became disenchanted with the film capital. For his next project, he partnered with Robert Flaherty on the documentary *Tabu*, filmed in the South Seas. He was reportedly contemplating a return to Germany when he was killed in a car accident on March 11, 1931, on the Coast Highway near Santa Barbara. After his car ran off an embankment, it rolled twice, ending bottom-side up. Murnau's valet, who was driving, escaped injury, but his chauffeur was killed instantly. Murnau, who had been pinned beneath the car, was taken to a local hospital where he succumbed from his injuries. His death came just days before the release of *Tabu* in New York.

Nosferatu's fame and reputation grew over the years. In October of 1960, Daniel Talbot and Peter Bogdanovich began a ten-film Monday Night Film Society series at the New Yorker Theater in New York. On January 9, they screened Murnau's *Nosferatu*. Later in the year, on September 28, 1961, highlights from *Nosferatu* were presented on the half-hour TV series *Silents Please*, which showed edited versions of silent films introduced by comedian Ernie Kovacs and narrated by archivist Paul Killiam.

New York's Museum of Modern Art began a ten-week series devoted to "The Horror Film" in February 1965. The series began with *The Cabinet of Dr. Caligari* and continued with *Nosferatu* and 1931's *Dracula* and *Frankenstein*, among others.

By the 1960s, anyone interested in owning early silent films could buy copies of them in 8mm, Super 8mm, and 16mm gauges from a variety of distributors who advertised in publications like *Famous Monsters of Filmland*. The home movie editions of *Nosferatu* routinely replaced the original German intertitles with English-language ones that changed the characters' names to those in Stoker's novel—Count Dracula, Harker, Mina, etc.

In May 1985, Dr. Enno Patalas of the Munich Film Museum, who had presented a restored version of the 1922 *Nosferatu* at the Berlin Film Festival the previous year, brought the film to Los Angeles, where it was screened at the Bing Theater of the County Museum of Art as part of the *Films of F. W. Murnau* series, with live musical accompaniment. In 1989, the film was presented at the American Museum of the Moving Image in Astoria, Queens, with live musical accompaniment provided by the Club Foot Orchestra, a San Francisco group. Another score composed for the silent classic was presented in October of 1991, when the Metropolitan Museum of Art presented *Nosferatu* with live orchestral accompaniment featuring a score by Armin Brunner, conductor and composer of the Orchestra of St. Luke's, based on the works of Bach. The film resurfaced again in early April of 1993, when "one of the rarest prints available" with newly translated English intertitles and a live piano accompaniment was presented at the Joseph Papp Public Theater.

Jim Shepard's 1996 short story collection, *Battling Against Castro*, offered a tale called "Nosferatu" that was an imagined diary kept by director F. W. Murnau while filming the silent classic. Two years later, Shepard expanded the idea, writing a fictional "biography" of Murnau, titled *Nosferatu: A Novel*, encompassing the director's entire life.

In his book, Shepard describes Murnau setting off for Berlin to pursue his higher education and falling in love with Hans Ehrenbaum-Degele, a Jewish banker's son, with whom he travels to the ski resort of Murnau for a romantic holiday. They eventually end up going to war, where Hans is killed on the Eastern Front. Murnau, believing his lover joined the war because of Murnau's infidelity, is shattered, forever after riddled with guilt and shame. The book received mixed reviews, with most praise reserved for the chapters dealing with the filming of *Nosferatu*, which were the book's most evocative passages.

Phantom of the Night

When the fiftieth anniversary revival of the Hamilton Deane-John Balderston play *Dracula* became a surprise hit on Broadway in 1977, a number of Dracula films went into production. One of the most intriguing was filmmaker Werner Herzog's remake of *Nosferatu*.

Nosferatu the Vampyre took shape after Herzog was approached by 20th Century-Fox, who were looking to collaborate with the celebrated director. Wishing to finance Herzog's next three pictures, they offered him a home in Beverly Hills and several hundred thousand dollars to write a screenplay. He

Lucy (Isabelle Adjani) sacrifices herself to destroy Count Dracula (Klaus Kinski) in Werner Herzog's eerie, atmospheric 1979 remake of F. W. Murnau's 1922 *Nosferatu.*
Courtesy of Del Valle Archives

replied that he needed only two dollars to write a screenplay—the cost of the paper. The director was reluctant to take on a long-term, three-picture commitment to one studio, but he made them a counter-offer. Aware that Hollywood studios feared financing European "art-house" directors who were prone to deliver films with running times much too long to be successfully marketed, Herzog agreed that he would deliver a film with a running time between one-and-a-half and two-and-a-half hours in length or else the studio would get final cut, meaning they could edit it as they wished.

The director hoped a remake of *Nosferatu* would propel him from art-house status to mainstream success in America. Shot simultaneously in English and German, the film was only partly financed by its American distributor, 20th Century-Fox; Germany's Zweites Deutsches Fernsehen (ZDF) and France's Gaumont put up the rest of the funding.

Herzog thought of *Nosferatu* as a link between the new German cinema, of which he was one of the chief exponents, along with Wim Wenders, Rainer Werner Fassbinder, and Volker Schlondorff, and the early German directors such as Fritz Lang, Paul Leni, G. W. Pabst and F. W. Murnau. Those earliest filmmakers and the filmmakers of new German cinema were separated by World War II and the atrocities of the Nazis. The filmmakers of Herzog's generation

Werner Herzog directing Clemens Scheitz for 1979's *Nosferatu the Vampyre.*   *Author's collection*

grew up mostly without fathers and mentors, so he sought a paternal connection by reaching back to the generation of the grandfathers, the film pioneers.

Herzog was never a filmmaker to take the easy, conventional route. For his film *Heart of Glass*, he hypnotized his actors. For *The Mystery of Kaspar Hauser*, he cast a former mental patient in the title role. For *Aguirre, the Wrath of God*, he hacked through the jungles of South America, a monomaniacal director making a film about a monomaniacal conquistador.

For *Nosferatu*, Herzog set out to do a remake as faithful as possible to the original, yet he couldn't help but inject into it some of his own idiosyncrasies. Where Murnau's vampire was soulless and moved with the rapidity of a crab, Herzog explored Dracula's sadness, suffering, and longing; he wanted audiences to feel the pain of the vampire so acutely that they would forget about his ghastly appearance.

Herzog had only one actor in mind for the lead role: Klaus Kinski, the star of the director's previous film, *Aguirre, the Wrath of God*. However, the director and star had a tempestuous working relationship during the making of that film. When it was finished, they didn't speak to each other for four years. Finally, Herzog called Kinski one morning at 1:00 a.m. and said, "You have to make two films with me—*Woyzeck* and *Nosferatu*." Without hesitation, Kinski said yes.

A prolific actor in European cinema as well as the occasional English-language film (he had appeared as Kostoyed in 1965's *Doctor Zhivago*), Kinski shaved his head for the role of the vampire and endured makeup that left him with ears like a bat's wings, sharp-nailed talons for fingers, and rat-like fangs close together in the front of his mouth. *Nosferatu* was not Kinski's first encounter with *Dracula*; he had previously played Renfield in Jess Franco's 1970 adaptation of Stoker's novel, *Count Dracula*, starring Christopher Lee in the title role.

For the part of Lucy, Herzog chose French actress Isabelle Adjani, star of François Truffaut's *Adele H.*, whom he considered a "female genius." Adjani brought a sense of suffering to her role that matched Kinski's, making Dracula and Lucy kindred spirits.

Unfortunately, Lübeck, the city where Murnau filmed in 1921, was destroyed in World War II, so Herzog chose Delft, a picturesque city of canals and cobbled streets, as his location; its gabled houses were almost identical to those seen in Murnau's Lübeck. However, there was one drawback—in the 1960s, Delft got rid of all its rats. When Herzog informed the town burghers that his film required ten thousand rodents that he was importing from Hungary, they balked. Even though Herzog assured the Burgomeister that the rats were sterilized, the city refused permission. Consequently, Herzog had to truck his rodents to the neighboring town of Schiedam, filming the scene with fewer rats than he originally hoped.

While filming in Delft, Herzog rented a huge house for the entire crew on the Oude Delft Canal and divided both the rooms and the domestic chores equally among them. In the communal atmosphere, crewmembers found themselves cooking dinner for everyone, pitching in to sew costumes and make props.

In *Nosferatu*, Herzog tried to evoke a sense of spiritual malaise through his imagery, such as a vampire with billowing cloak carrying a coffin underneath his arm through the town's imposing main square. Herzog filmed the shot through a soft violet filter to give it the look of a Gothic-Romantic painting. Some of the simplest shots were the most difficult to achieve. A slow-motion shot of bats flying against a white background that punctuates the film took more than a year to capture. But for the director, it was worth the effort to get an image that added to the trancelike feel.

In the final scene, when the vampire lovingly strokes Lucy as he bites her, a moment both erotic and repulsive, both Kinski and Adjani chose to improvise. Kinski decided on the spur of the moment to stroke Adjani; her reaction was to thrust her head back in a mixture of pleasure and pain, creating a moment of both sacrifice and sexual surrender.

Nosferatu the Vampyre had its world premiere in Paris on January 17, 1979. Audiences used to cheesy depictions of vampires laughed early on, hearing lines like "Count Dracula has written from Transylvania." Herzog shrugged it off. He had invested the film with a sense of the ethereal, which eventually won over the audience.

In August of 1979, the film was selected to screen at the New York Film Festival. The following month, it screened at the Telluride Film Festival, where a special tribute was paid to Klaus Kinski, who hosted a seminar at the festival entitled, "Was Hitchcock Right When He Said 'Actors Are Cattle'?"

Nosferatu the Vampyre opened in New York on October 4, 1979. Writing in the *New York Times*, critic Vincent Canby called it "a kind of charming diversion . . . funny without being silly, eerie without being foolish and uncommonly beautiful in a way that has nothing to do with mere prettiness."

Kinski avoided seeing Murnau's original *Nosferatu* until he had completed work on Herzog's version, which he defended against critics who shrugged it off as simply a remake of a classic film. *Hamlet*, he said had been done a hundred thousand times, and each time it was a remake. By year's end, the film was on many critics' Top Ten lists. It also made number eight on a list of top kisses in films compiled by the *New York Times*' Lisa Zeidner in 2000.

In September of 1980, PBS stations aired *Werner Herzog and the Making of Nosferatu*, a documentary by filmmakers Jim Whaley and Michael Hack. In the half hour presentation, Herzog said in an interview, "[A]ll my films come out of pain . . . not from pleasure."

In E. Elias Merhige's 2000 film, *Shadow of the Vampire*, Willem Dafoe portrays Max Schreck, an actual vampire hired by F. W. Murnau (John Malkovich) to star in his film, *Nosferatu*.

Courtesy of Del Valle Archives

Shadows of the Vampire

Klaus Kinski returned to the *Nosferatu* role, sort of, for 1988's *Nosferatu in Venice*, also known as *Vampire in Venice*, an Italian production originally planned as a sequel to *Nosferatu*. The film, however, was fraught with troubles. The original director, Maurizio Lucidi, who began filming before the script was completed, was sacked after shooting crowd scenes in Venice. Pasquale Squitieri was then hired to write and direct, but his script was deemed too expensive. When filming resumed, B-movie veteran Mario Caiano was at the helm, until Kinski arrived for his first day of shooting. The erratic actor got into a violent argument with Caiano and refused to work with him. Caiano left the set, and the picture. Getting desperate, producer Augusto Caminito took over, helped by his assistant Luigi Cozzi. It was rumored that Kinski, who refused to shave his head and undergo the lengthy makeup sessions he'd endured for Herzog, directed portions of the film.

Filmmaker E. Elias Merhige, perhaps taking inspiration from novelist Jim Shepard, created his own meditation on the making of F. W. Murnau's *Nosferatu* with his film *Shadow of the Vampire*, which was screened in the Directors' Fortnight at the Cannes Film Festival in May of 2000. In Merhige's film, Murnau, having been unable to find a suitable actor to portray the vampire of *Nosferatu*, hires an actual vampire, who begins to feed on his cast and crew. John Malkovich portrayed Murnau, while the vampire was played by Willem Dafoe.

In June 2000, the HERE Arts Center in New York's South Village presented a dramatic version of *Nosferatu*, a presentation of the Telluride Repertory Theater of Colorado adapted from Bram Stoker's *Dracula* and F. W. Murnau's film *Nosferatu: A Symphony of Horror* by Rene Migliaccio, who also directed. The play took its storyline from the silent film, whose style it attempted to evoke by having actors in clown-white makeup. However, the ending was changed; instead of Mina dying from Nosferatu's bite, the play ends as she stands astride the vanquished vampire, who was played by Nikolai Kinski, Klaus Kinski's son.

Had Florence Stoker succeeded in her attempts to quash *Nosferatu*, the world would have been robbed of a film now recognized as one of the seminal classics of cinema. Not only was it the first film version of Stoker's *Dracula*, it also set the template for how to condense and adapt Stoker's tale for future filmmakers, and set the precedent for film vampires to be not just ghouls but longing, yearning, romantic figures, a conception as old as *Nosferatu* yet as fresh as *Twilight* and *The Vampire Diaries*. Within every vampire film or TV show resides the shadow of the original vampire, *Nosferatu*.

9

"I Am . . . Dracula"

Bela Lugosi, Vampiric Valentino

The Early Years

One actor is associated with Dracula more than any other. He first played the part on Broadway, then in the movies, and then toured as Dracula almost until his dying day. The role was both a blessing and a curse, bringing him fame while at the same time typecasting him. So strong was the association that for decades, whenever anyone thought of Dracula, they thought of a thickly accented, ruby-lipped, heavy-browed, pale-faced man with a Brilliantined widow's peak, wearing a dinner jacket and cape. They thought of Bela Lugosi.

Béla Ferenc Dezsö Blaskó, the youngest of four children of banker István Blaskó and his wife, Paula, was born in Lugos, Hungary (now Lugoj, Romania), on October 20, 1882. He dropped out of school at age twelve, and at the turn of the century appeared in provincial theaters, playing small roles in plays and operettas. In 1903, embarking on a stage career, he took the name "Lugossy," later spelled "Lugosi," in honor of his birthplace. He eventually ended up in Budapest, where he acted in dozens of roles with the National Theater of Hungary from 1913 to 1919.

During World War I, Lugosi served in the Austro Hungarian Army as an infantryman, rising to the rank of captain in the ski patrol; serving on the Russian front, he was wounded. When the war ended, he wed his first wife, Ilona Szmick, and returned to the theater. He also made his first film, 1917's *Az ezredes* (*The Colonel*) and, using the name Arisztid Olt, appeared in a dozen silent films in Hungary. After participating in an effort to form an actors' union, he was forced to flee the country. He made his way to Vienna, at which point his wife decided she couldn't leave her family behind and returned to Hungary; they divorced in July 1920. Lugosi went on to Berlin, appearing in eighteen films from 1919 to 1920, including *Der Januskopf*, a version of *Dr. Jekyll and Mr. Hyde* directed by F. W. Murnau, who, two years later, made *Nosferatu*.

In October of 1920, Lugosi left for the United States, working his way across the ocean as the boat's third engineer. In December, he entered the country at New Orleans and made his way to New York where, in March 1921, he was

Bela Lugosi in *Dracula* (1931). Lugosi's Dracula did not wear fangs, setting a precedent that other films followed until the late 1950s.

© *1931 Universal Pictures, Inc. Author's collection.*

legally inspected for immigration at Ellis Island. After appearing in plays in the Hungarian émigré community, he formed a small stock company that toured Eastern cities, playing to immigrant audiences. During this time, he performed with actress Ilona Von Montagh, another Hungarian expatriate. They began a romance and, in September of 1921, were married. The union soured over Lugosi's wish for Montagh to quit the stage and be a traditional wife, and after fourteen days (as he claimed) or two months (as she said), they separated, though they didn't finalize a divorce until February 13, 1925.

On Broadway

Lugosi's first Broadway role came in 1922, as Fernando in *The Red Poppy*. He made a deal with the play's producer to give him an English actor to coach him in his lines, and by opening night, he had phonetically memorized the entire part. However, when he received cheers from the audience, he could only bow; he didn't know enough English to speak off the cuff. Playing a Spanish Apache, he claimed that his onstage lovemaking was so "hot" that in his embraces with actress Estelle Winwood he broke two of her ribs. In 1925, he had a five-month run in the comedy *The Devil in the Cheese*, then appeared as an Arab sheik in *Arabesque*; by then he had learned to speak English, albeit with a pronounced accent.

His American film debut came in 1923, when he played a saboteur out to blow up the Panama Canal in *The Silent Command*. He continued appearing in other silent films made in the New York area, as well as taking stage roles.

Around this time, according to a 1925 article in the *Los Angeles Times*, a producer in Hollywood was thinking of making a film of Bram Stoker's *Dracula*. It was rumored that Arthur Edmund Carew, who played the Persian in Universal's *The Phantom of the Opera*, was under consideration for the role of the vampire. Fate had other plans.

After German filmmakers scored hits with supernatural thrillers like *The Cabinet of Dr. Caligari* and *The Golem*, Universal decided to try their luck with films of the macabre. First up was Lon Chaney as *The Hunchback of Notre Dame* (1923), with the actor under heavy makeup as Quasimodo. The producers wondered if such a grotesque character would catch on, but when the film was completed, it was a hit. The studio followed it up with *The Phantom of the Opera* (1925), which did even better.

It was said that Lon Chaney wanted to star as *Dracula*, and often discussed the part with his frequent collaborator, director Tod Browning. Reportedly, during the years of their silent film collaborations, Chaney—known as The Man of a Thousand Faces—had a full scenario and a secret makeup worked out for the role, but as sound film emerged Browning held out for a talkie production.

When Horace Liveright produced the Hamilton Deane–John L. Balderston adaptation of *Dracula* on Broadway in October 1927, Bela Lugosi won the lead part. It was the perfect union of actor and role. The play ran throughout the season and was followed by a tour of two years.

Universal Pictures became interested in *Dracula* almost as soon as the play became a box-office sensation in London. They had five story editors take a look at the book in June 1927; one was enthusiastic, another felt it too gruesome, a third said it would be an insult to audiences, and a fourth said "ABSOLUTELY NO!" The fifth and final reader said that while *Dracula* was always good material for a film from the dramatic and pictorial angle, it was not from the standpoint of box-office or industry ethics.

On April 28, 1928, Universal Pictures founder Carl Laemmle gave production control to his son, Carl Jr., as a twenty-first birthday present. Junior, as he was known, made periodic trips to New York looking for material that would be good for films, and on one trip he saw *Dracula*. He thought it might make a good project for Lon Chaney, who had left Universal for MGM; with the right part, Junior hoped to be able to lure him back.

Junior heard that Chaney was negotiating a new contract at MGM and talks were at an impasse over the actor's demand to be paid more for talking films. Laemmle offered the one-time Universal star a three-picture deal that would include a remake of his 1921 silent *Outside the Law*, a sequel to *The Phantom of the Opera* called *The Return of the Phantom*, and *Dracula*, although at this point the studio had not yet purchased the rights to either the play or Stoker's novel. But MGM refused to loan out Chaney's services, and Chaney eventually re-signed with the more prestigious studio, having used the Universal offer as leverage to get a more generous contract. Junior then alienated Chaney by releasing a "talking" version of *The Phantom of the Opera*, in which another actor dubbed dialogue to go over shots of Chaney's shadow. Chaney sued Universal.

Meanwhile, Bela Lugosi came to Los Angeles in 1928, when the Broadway adaptation of *Dracula* opened at the Biltmore Theater on June 25. While in Los Angeles, Lugosi stayed at the Ambassador Hotel, enjoying the swimming pool and tennis court. Alma Whitaker, a reporter for the *Los Angeles Times*, interviewed the actor and asked if he was a bachelor. Lugosi replied, "Oh, surely, madame. And 'open for business,' you think, yes?" The reporter noted that he made his reply with "a gentle hilarity that reeked of potential victory," and observed that Lugosi "kisses ladies' hands with natural savoir-faire, and oozes polished charm."

Lugosi was "adopted" by the Hollywood social set and spent time with other Hungarian expatriates, including Vilma Banky, Alexander Korda, and Michael Curtiz. Though glad to be doing the play, he complained to the *Los Angeles Times* that his theatrical engagements were "seriously interfering with his social activities."

After finishing his run in *Dracula* in Los Angeles, Lugosi appeared in a film for Fox, *The Veiled Woman*. A few months later, he co-starred with Corinne Griffith in First National's *Prisoners*, for director William A. Seiter. The *Los Angeles Times* reported that Lugosi, due to long experience on stage, spoke his English language lines with ease.

Lugosi was then cast as a Scotland Yard detective in *The Thirteenth Chair*, directed by Tod Browning. According to the *Chicago Daily Tribune*, Browning was "elated over what he considers a discovery for the screen ."

After finishing his work on the film, Lugosi traveled to San Francisco, where he continued performing in *Dracula.* On July 27, 1929, he married San Francisco socialite Beatrice Woodruff Weeks, whom he had been dating for the previous year. The union was short-lived. At the end of the year, Weeks testified in divorce court that Lugosi was unable to leave his "irascible role" on the stage and brought it into the home, where he displayed his violent temper to both her and the servants. Confidentially, it was rumored that the marriage faltered because of Lugosi's affair with actress Clara Bow, who had been swept away after seeing his performance as the vampire king.

Dracula in Tinseltown

In the spring of 1930, several studios were interested in the *Dracula* rights, including Universal, MGM, and Paramount. All were put off, however, by the story's supernatural aspects. In most previous "mystery" dramas, there was usually a rational explanation for the terrors in the denouement. *Dracula* expected its audience to accept a five-hundred-year-old vampire as a reality. Despite misgivings, Junior Laemmle asked Fritz Stephani to write up a potential film treatment based on Bram Stoker's novel. When the treatment was submitted in June, Laemmle began to see the property's box-office potential. He decided to go ahead with *Dracula*, and began negotiating for the rights with representatives of the play and Bram Stoker's widow, Florence. The studio announced that the film would be directed by Tod Browning and would star John Wray. Lugosi campaigned for the lead, but Universal wanted a name actor; at that time, despite numerous film appearances, Lugosi was still a relative unknown.

On June 21, 1930, the *Los Angeles Times* reported that Universal Pictures had purchased the rights to *Dracula*, intending to make it as an "important" picture in the next year. The studio paid forty thousand dollars for the rights to both the novel and play of *Dracula* on August 22, 1930. To quell theatrical producer Horace Liveright's concerns that a film version would hurt future box-office returns of the play, he was paid thirty-five hundred dollars. Universal also purchased the one copy of *Nosferatu* then known to be in the United States; it is obvious that they screened the film, since some moments of *Dracula* are copied almost exactly from Murnau's earlier film.

Universal budgeted *Dracula* at $355,050. To keep it to a reasonable level, the latter half of the film would reflect the play more than the novel, keeping the action in England instead of ending with a chase through the wilds of Transylvania. Fritz Stepani's thirty-two-page treatment was handed off to writer Louis Stevens, and then to Louis Bromfield, who handed in a script on August 7, 1930. In Bromfield's script, Dracula is an old man in the beginning, but when he comes to England (by airplane, as in the play, except Bromfield envisioned one with scalloped bat's wings), he goes by the name Count de Ville and becomes younger with the blood of his new victims. Dudley Murphy next worked on the adaptation, paring back some of Bromfield's ideas to make it more economical to film, and inserting more dialogue from the play. Still unsatisfied, Universal turned the script over to Garrett Fort, who worked closely with director Tod Browning; only Fort is credited with "Play Script" in the credits of the film.

Two actors from the stage production were hired immediately: Edward Van Sloan, as Van Helsing, and Herbert Bunston, as Dr. Seward; early in his career, Bunston performed at the Lyceum Theatre and met Bram Stoker. Bernard Jukes hoped to reprise the role of Renfield, but instead it went to Dwight Frye. First under consideration for the role of Jonathan Harker was Lew Ayres, who won acclaim for his role in *All Quiet on the Western Front* (1930). Ayres expressed more interest in playing Renfield, so the part of Harker went to Robert Ames. When Ames dropped out, it was given to David Manners. Helen Chandler and Frances Dade were cast as Mina and Lucy, respectively. Young English actress Moon Carroll had a small part as Briggs, a nurse in Seward's asylum, having previously appeared with Lugosi in Browning's film *The Thirteenth Chair* (1929).

Lugosi continued to campaign for the role of Dracula, and during the final days of July 1930, writers Louis Bromfield and Dudley Murphy and Universal producer E. M. Asher went to Oakland, California, to see him in a local production of the play. Their reaction is unknown, but whatever it was, Junior

Van Helsing (Edward Van Sloan) confronts Count Dracula (Bela Lugosi). Van Sloan, Lugosi, and Herbert Bunston, who played Dr. Seward, appeared in both the Broadway play and Universal's film version. © *1931 Universal Pictures, Inc. Author's collection.*

Laemmle remained unconvinced. On September 3, *Variety* reported that a "number of actors" had been tested, and the studio had narrowed the list down to William Courtney, Bela Lugosi, and Paul Muni. *Hollywood Filmograph* magazine, which had been actively championing Lugosi, wrote in its September 6 issue, "It seems like everybody that is anybody is pulling for Bela Lugosi to play Dracula. . . . Those who have seen his performance in New York, on the West Coast and abroad, say that the story is made to order for him, since he has the voice along with the appearance that is necessary for the part."

In an interview with the *Los Angeles Examiner,* Tod Browning said he preferred an unknown for the role, since he thought a well-known actor would take "away from the thrilling effects of the story." Ultimately, Universal agreed, and on September 12, 1930, after doing several camera tests, Bela Lugosi was signed for the role that would not only haunt movie audiences but also haunt the actor for the rest of his career. Since he was so desperate to take the part, he was offered only five hundred dollars per week; his total salary for the film came to thirty-five hundred dollars. David Manners, meanwhile, in the smaller role of Harker, was paid two thousand dollars per week.

Filming got underway on September 29, 1930. At a time when dubbing was still in its infancy, Universal—wishing to produce a version of *Dracula* for foreign audiences—simultaneously filmed a second version, with a Spanish-speaking cast, as they had done with *The Cat Creeps.* Photographed at night by director George Melford, the Spanish-language *Dracula* starred Carlos Villarias (billed

Here, Dracula (Carlos Villarias) recoils from the cross held by Van Helsing (Eduardo Arozamena). © *1931 Universal Pictures, Inc. Courtesy of Del Valle Archives.*

as Carlos Villar) as Conde Dracula. Though it is often assumed that Browning shot during the day and Melford filmed the same scenes on the same sets at night, such was seldom the case. Melford began filming on October 10, over a week after Browning, and filmed some scenes prior to the English-speaking crew. Melford was also able to use some of Browning's footage, so there were scenes that he didn't have to restage.

During filming, Helen Chandler began suffering appendicitis, but put off an operation for six weeks so that she could finish filming her part as Mina. After receiving daily treatments from a studio doctor, on November 13, 1930, she filmed her final scene around noon and went directly from the studio to Hollywood Hospital.

Vocal artist D. G. Del Valle, adept at imitating animal sounds, provided some of the soundtrack of the film. He told Flora M. Darling of the *Los Angeles Times* that he impersonated "a wolf's baying and howling and such ungodly sounds as frogs, bats and owls." Another voice artist, Sarah Schwartz, lent her voice to the film, providing the screams. According to a 1938 *New York Times* profile, Schwartz was guaranteed work at Universal in return for an act of heroism. According to the paper, on July 18, 1917, Schwartz came to the Universal casting office looking for work as a film extra when a fire broke out in one of the studio's editing rooms. Rushing to the blaze, she dashed in to see if anyone needed help. Seeing reels of celluloid on the cutting room floor, she grabbed several armfuls, getting seriously burned in the process. Studio head Carl Laemmle was so grateful that he promised her she would always have a job at Universal. Schwartz went on to work as an extra or in bit parts in practically every Universal Pictures production, but found her true calling when sound came in: she was best at screaming, and Universal was best at producing horror films. It was a perfect match.

Tod Browning finished filming on November 15, after forty-two shooting days (the schedule originally called for thirty-six). Added scenes were filmed on December 13, and retakes on January 2; the final cost was $441,984.90. The Spanish version finished on November 8, after twenty days of filming.

Dracula premiered at the Roxy in New York on February 12, 1931 (not, as has often been reported, on February 14—Valentine's Day). It was originally scheduled to open February 13—Friday the 13th—but was moved back one day at the studio's behest. The full program began with an overture of Gershwin's *Rhapsody in Blue*, a Movietone newsreel, and a stage show, *Hello, New York!*, with Santry and Norton, Leonide Masine, and the Roxyettes. Reviewer Mordaunt Hall of the *New York Times* reported that audiences broke into applause when Van Helsing produced a little cross that caused Dracula to fling his cloak over his head and flee. Hall called it "the best of the many mystery films."

Initially, Universal Pictures felt somewhat ashamed to be unleashing a monster on the public and played down the horror aspects in their advertising. Newspaper ads for the film proclaimed: "His kiss was like the icy breath of death . . . yet no woman could resist!" and "The story of the strangest passion the world has ever known!" But Andrew J. Sharick, Universal's field exploitation representative, and Arthur Frudenfeld, the manager of RKO's Down Town Theater in Detroit, Michigan, thought that playing up the terrors would scare people into the theater instead of scaring them away. They were right. At the Roxy, the film took in over $120,000 in eight days.

When the film opened at the State-Lake Theater in Chicago in March, the *Chicago*

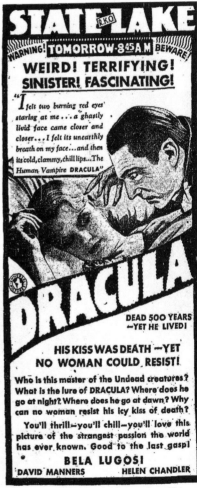

This newspaper ad, from the *Chicago Tribune* of March 18, 1931, besides evoking the supernatural aspects of the story, also positions it as a romance, with the line "the strangest passion the world has ever known." *Author's collection*

Daily Tribune wrote that while the film was not as scary as the play, the theater was nonetheless packed. In the "Letters" section of the *Chicago Daily Tribune*, "Katherine R. E." wrote about going to a matinee where *Dracula* was shown. She said children screamed and hid their faces, yet stayed to the very end. She admonished parents for bringing their children to such an "over-stimulating" picture that would undoubtedly ruin their lives.

On March 27, *Dracula* arrived in Los Angeles, opening at the Orpheum Theater. Philip K. Scheuer, reviewing *Dracula* for the *Los Angeles Times*, wrote that the film was a careful—perhaps *too* careful—visualization of a horror story, slow-paced and occasionally laughter-inducing. To help promote the film, Lugosi appeared on Los Angeles radio station KHJ on March 27, 1931.

When Carl Laemmle Jr. released *Dracula*, the Great Depression was in full swing, and many felt there were horrors enough in real life, so the public would not want to also experience them on the screen. They were wrong. *Variety* reported that throughout the country, *Dracula*'s receipts exceeded the box-office records established by Universal's *All Quiet on the Western Front*. In the U.S. alone, *Dracula* brought in half a million dollars.

From the *New York Times*, March 27, 1931. *Dracula* was Universal's first horror film of the sound era, and set off a barrage of horror stories from other studios, as well.

Author's collection

The Horror Boom

William Manchester, looking back on the golden age of horror films in a 1975 article for the *New York Times*, wrote, "[T]he worst years of the Depression were great years for horror movies. What was sick in these films seemed to appeal to what was sick in the country. . . . Depression America was able to find parables of its plight in bizarre films."

Dracula kicked off a spate of horror films—now officially its own genre—at Universal. Lugosi was next slated to play the monster in *Frankenstein*, but he dismissed the part as dumb show, all makeup and no dialogue. Both he and director Robert Florey moved on to *Murders in the Rue Morgue* (1932). It was a decision that would have lifelong consequences for Lugosi. By refusing *Frankenstein*, he opened the door for another actor to supplant him as Universal's top horror star. Character actor Boris Karloff took the role, and the brilliance of his sensitive portrayal, under James Whale's direction, brought him instant stardom. When *Frankenstein* was released, print ads compared it to *Dracula*, saying "A Sensation That Makes *Dracula* Look Like a Pink Tea! Come, Shudder!"

On May 8, 1931, the Spanish-language version of *Dracula* opened at the California Theater in Los Angeles. A reviewer for the *Los Angeles Times* wrote that it was "rather good entertainment."

After amassing an enormous debt of $2,615,844 in 1930, largely as a result of the failure of the over-budget, underperforming pet project of Junior Laemmle's, *King of Jazz* (featuring bandleader Paul Whiteman), Universal showed a profit of $462,570 in 1931, about half of which was due to the success of *Dracula*.

The studio decided to further capitalize on the popularity of horror films by pairing their two new horror stars. Lugosi was supposed to star with Karloff in an adaptation of Robert Louis Stevenson's *The Suicide Club*, but when that project failed to get off the ground, he was courted by other studios. Warner Bros. First National considered him for the lead in *Doctor X*; the film was ultimately made with Preston Foster. Lugosi, instead, went to Hawaii, co-starring with Warner Oland in Fox's Charlie Chan film, *The Black Camel*, in which Lugosi appeared as a fortune-teller.

The actor was just as active offscreen as on. On February 1, 1932, forty-nine-year-old Bela Lugosi and nineteen-year-old Lillian Arch eloped to Las Vegas, Nevada, to be married. The bride was the daughter of one of Lugosi's friends from the Hungarian community.

With his heavy accent, along with the lingering *Dracula* image, Lugosi found his choice of roles limited. In 1932, he starred in the independent film *White Zombie*, portrayed the Sayer of the Law in Paramount's *Island of Lost Souls*, and took on the role of the villain Roxor in Fox's *Chandu the Magician*.

The year 1933 found the actor once again putting on the Dracula cloak. After his success in the vampire role, Charles Pressley's Motion Picture Museum and Hall of Fame included a wax figure of Lugosi as the Count. Later, Paramount Pictures filmed a short subject based on the Hall of Fame exhibits called *Hollywood on Parade*, in which some of the figures come to life. At one point, Betty Boop (Bonnie Poe) is singing "My Silent Love," when the figure of Dracula begins to move and slowly stalks over to her. Taking Betty in his arms, Dracula says, "Betty—you have booped your last boop!" The camera cuts away as he goes in for the bite and she screams.

In January of 1934, Universal announced plans to finally get both of their horror stars into one film, with Lugosi and Karloff set to appear in *The Black Cat*. The film provided Lugosi with one of his best roles.

In December of 1934, Lugosi again found himself working with Tod Browning, in a film that began shooting as "The Vampire of Prague." It was, in fact, a remake of Browning's earlier film, *London After Midnight*, which starred

Lon Chaney as a pointy-toothed vampire. By the time MGM released the film, it had undergone a title change to *Mark of the Vampire*. Lugosi, in a Dracula cape and with a bloody bullet wound in his temple (presumably to indicate he was a suicide, and thus doomed to become a vampire), had little to do except skulk around the cavernous sets and glower. The finale revealed that he was, in fact, an actor hired to trick a murderer into confessing his crime.

In March of 1935, Universal unveiled plans for a sequel to *Dracula*, to be called *Dracula's Daughter*. Carl Laemmle Jr. announced that it would be made with Lugosi, Boris Karloff, Claude Rains, and Colin Clive. The younger Laemmle apparently decided to produce the movie after the success of *Bride of Frankenstein*. In the end, Dracula was written out of the script; he made only a brief appearance in the final film, played not by Lugosi but rather by a wax dummy. The film also did not feature any of the other stars originally announced for the cast. Nonetheless, Lugosi was soon back before the cameras at Universal, co-starring with Boris Karloff in *The Raven*.

When a *New York Times* staffer interviewed Lugosi in July of 1935, he found a tall man who, without his Dracula cloak and makeup, seemed "like a senior master of an English public school." The reporter noted that despite Lugosi's accent and formal manner of speaking, he peppered his speech with Yankee idioms, as when he offered the reporter "an eye-opener." Lugosi noted that since he had played Dracula, he received more fan mail—90 percent of it from women—than when he played romantic lovers on the stage.

In the mid-1930s, Universal Studios president Carl Laemmle, nearing seventy and ready to retire after twenty-seven years in the film industry, sold his studio. By October of 1936, his son, Junior Laemmle, was eased out of the company and into independent production.

The Second Wave of Horror

On January 5, 1938, Lugosi's son, Bela George Lugosi, was born. Many years later, Lugosi Jr. spoke to Frank del Olmo of the *Los Angeles Times* about what it was like going to see his father's horror films with his friends as a child. While the other kids got scared and hid under the seats, he was unfazed; to him, it wasn't a monster on screen, it was just dad. Lugosi Jr. recalled that his father, a self-educated man, spent his time between making movies reading books from morning until night.

Between 1936 and 1938, Lugosi found it difficult to get roles in Hollywood, having been typed as Dracula. He tried for dramatic parts in other films, but the response was always the same—"You're a bogeyman." He had become typecast as a horror actor.

When he first came to Hollywood, he bought a home for thirty-two thousand dollars. With no income, he mortgaged it to the hilt, until he finally lost the property. When his money ran out, he began borrowing from friends. During

His horror film roles typed Bela Lugosi as a bogeyman, an image he played up in personal appearances. *Courtesy of Del Valle Archives*

those two years, his only employment was eight weeks of touring with the road company of *Tovarich*, playing the commissar.

Then one night he received a call from Eric Umann, manager of the little Regina Theater on Wilshire Boulevard in Los Angeles. Umann was about to open Universal's *Dracula* and *Frankenstein*, along with RKO's *Son of Kong*, for a four-day revival, and asked Lugosi if he would make a personal appearance. Umann said he thought the pictures would drum up some business with a newer generation who were too young to have seen them in their original runs. Needing the cash, Lugosi agreed to make an appearance. Umann opened the triple feature on August 4, 1938. He had lines around the block. Instead of four days, the films played for five weeks, and always to capacity business. Others theaters followed suit, and Universal soon netted nearly a half-million dollars in rentals and percentage deals on their two old horror films. Even after five weeks, the box-office take was still strong enough that Umann would have extended the engagement, but Universal—now aware that they had two golden geese—raised the rental prices. By September, other theaters in Los Angeles were showing double features of *Dracula* and *Frankenstein* that ran for weeks and did overflow business.

Theaters in other cities also booked the two old stalwarts. When the Victory Theater in Salt Lake City announced the double feature, tickets were sold out by ten in the morning. The *New York Times* reported that four thousand Mormons outside the theater broke through a police line, smashed the plate glass box office, bent the front doors in and even tore one of the door checks in their frenzy to get into the building. Not wanting to turn away such an enthusiastic crowd, the theater's manager rented an empty theater that was across the street and packed it to the rafters, bicycling film reels to it as soon as they had played at the Victory. Still, the street was full of eager patrons waiting to get in and be frightened.

In Waterbury, Connecticut, a 3,800-seat theater played to 6,500 customers the first day the doubleheader opened there. At Warner's Theater in Fresno, California, the double bill became the first repeat engagement in the theater's history. Six policemen were needed at the Fox Uptown in Kansas City to keep the avid horror fans in line at the box office. The St. Louis Theater in St. Louis, Missouri, did twice the business of any other theater in the city, so the double bill was held over there a second week. By the end of October 1938, the double feature of *Dracula* and *Frankenstein* was the seventh-highest-grossing release in the country.

For Lugosi, the demand for *Dracula* proved that although the studios had shunned him, audiences had not. It also proved that there was still a strong demand for well-produced horror films, an observation not lost on Universal Pictures.

The studio decided the time was ripe to do a third *Frankenstein* movie, one that would feature both Karloff and Lugosi. The actor also had offers for film work in England. "I owe it all to that little man at the Regina Theater," he told Ed Sullivan of the *New York Daily News*. "I was dead and he brought me to life."

The new Universal project, *Son of Frankenstein*, featured Lugosi playing Ygor opposite Boris Karloff's Monster, with Basil Rathbone in the title role. Lugosi told Sullivan that he would have turned down the role in *Son of Frankenstein* if he hadn't been desperate for money. Having played every manner of role in his younger days in Budapest, he found it discouraging that in America, the only parts he could get involved "scaring children." Universal didn't skimp on their new horror production; the *Los Angeles Times* reported that the studio spent a half-million dollars on it.

Lugosi did appear in one straight role in 1939, as a Communist commissar at the conclusion of *Ninotchka*, starring Greta Garbo and directed by Ernst Lubitsch. But with the continuing re-releases of *Dracula*, his identification with the vampire role was complete. In the spring of 1940, when he joined a host of celebrities on a war bond tour through the Southwest, children would point at him and whisper, "Dracula."

Lugosi reprised his role as Ygor in 1942's *Ghost of Frankenstein*. Since the film ended with Ygor's evil brain being put into the Frankenstein Monster, it seemed only logical to cast Lugosi as the now-talking Monster in the following year's *Frankenstein Meets the Wolf Man*. In 1931, Lugosi had considered the role of the Monster beneath him; now, he was happy to have the work. Sadly, his

During the filming of *Bud Abbott and Lou Costello Meet Frankenstein*, proud papa Bela Lugosi introduces his son, Bela G. Lugosi, to Frankenstein's Monster (Glenn Strange).

© *1948 Universal Pictures. Author's collection.*

performance was undercut by the studio's decision to cut all of the Monster's lines before the film's release.

In 1944, even low-budget Columbia Pictures got into the vampire game, starring Lugosi in *Return of the Vampire*, in which a Nazi bomb unearths centuries-old vampire Armand Tesla (Dracula by any other name) during the London Blitz. Lugosi played Tesla during the day, then rushed off at night to the Music Box Theater in Los Angeles, where he was appearing in *Arsenic and Old Lace*. He had taken the comedic stage role without hesitation. He told the *Los Angeles Times* that if the producers had known how eager he was to play comedy, they could have had him without salary. "It's my first break since the *Dracula* curse hit me," he said. When *Return of the Vampire* opened to generally good notices and respectable box office, Columbia toyed with the idea of doing a sequel with Lugosi, "Bride of the Vampire," but the film never went forward.

Through the remainder of the 1940s, while Universal made Dracula films with Lon Chaney Jr. and John Carradine, Lugosi's only starring roles were at bargain-basement studios like Monogram, usually playing mad doctors, as in *Voodoo Man*, *Return of the Ape Man*, and *Zombies on Broadway*. His last onscreen collaboration with Boris Karloff came in 1945's *The Body Snatcher*, an RKO film produced by Val Lewton and directed by Robert Wise, in which Lugosi, as a not-very-bright servant, is murdered early in the proceedings by Karloff's body-stealing cabman.

In Lugosi's final film for Universal, he returned to the role of Dracula for *Bud Abbott and Lou Costello Meet Frankenstein* (1948). It was only the second, and last, time he played the role in a feature film.

The 1931 *Dracula* was back in the news in the summer of 1950, when scriptwriter John Balderston, who also worked on *Frankenstein*, sued Universal for unpaid royalties he felt were due him for sequels made after the success of those films. Balderston estimated that, altogether, the monster movies had grossed more than $10 million. The case was settled out of court in 1953, with a resolution Balderston found "highly satisfactory." The playwright didn't have long to enjoy his windfall; he died March 8, 1954, of a heart attack.

The Final Days

Lugosi returned to the stage in the summer of 1950, in a touring production of *Dracula* that played at St. Michael's Playhouse in Winooski Park, Vermont, in June and July. In May of 1953, Lugosi and his wife, Lillian, separated. She said her husband frequently accused her of associating with other men, even though he knew the accusations were untrue. Even when she went to the dentist, he called the dentist's office to verify she was there. Without acting roles on which to focus his attention, the aging idol was focusing on his wife, to an unhealthy degree.

The following month, Lillian brought a divorce suit against Lugosi, charging the actor with cruelty. Lugosi, then seventy, and his forty-one-year-old wife negotiated a settlement of the community property, which included a car, lots at Lake Elsinore, and fifteen thousand dollars in a life insurance policy. Lillian was awarded custody of their son, Bela Jr., then fifteen. When the divorce was finalized on July 17, 1953, Lillian's divorce petition charged Lugosi with "unfounded jealousy."

Feeling that her husband, now retired, should not be burdened with financial obligations at his advanced age, Lillian, a bookkeeper, initially intended to waive support for her son. However, the judge refused to approve such an agreement, saying no court could relieve a father of his responsibility. The court mandated Lugosi to pay fifty dollars per month in child support; Lillian asked for only a dollar a month as token alimony for herself.

During these years, Lugosi's only film work came from Edward D. Wood Jr., a filmmaker whose ambition far outdistanced his talent. Despite the bottom-of-the-barrel nature of the work, Lugosi—ever the professional—still performed with as much gusto as he could muster. After acting as an onscreen narrator for Wood's *Glen or Glenda*, Lugosi played a mad doctor in the inept director's *Bride of the Monster*.

On April 22, 1955, the seventy-two-year-old actor committed himself to a state hospital, hoping to cure his twenty-year drug addiction, first to morphine and then to methadone, which he took to ease "lightning-like pains" in his legs, owing to his injuries from World War I. Superior Court Judge Wallace L. Ware, on signing the order, congratulated Lugosi for voluntarily asking for treatment.

Too ill to go to court, Lugosi was given a hearing in a ward of Los Angeles General Hospital. He voluntarily signed himself into the institution on April 21, saying he needed help to overcome the drug habit, and admitting that he had become dependent on the goodness of friends for his food, as his small old-age pension barely covered the rent.

Judge Ware ordered Lugosi committed to the Metropolitan State Hospital at Norwalk. After three months of rehabilitation, the actor appeared before the staff physicians for consideration of release. When he was admitted on April 22, he weighed just 125 pounds. After three months, he was twenty pounds heavier.

During his stay in the hospital, he received letters from a fan who signed them, "a dash of Hope." The writer was Hope Lininger, who became Lugosi's fifth wife on August 24, 1955.

In mid-November of 1955, Lugosi testified before a federal committee investigating narcotics trafficking. He described becoming addicted to prescription methadone and Demerol, saying that he had to increase the doses and eventually lost the ability to memorize lines of dialogue, causing him to lose his film career.

Soon after, in 1956, he played a mute in a low-budget independent horror film, *The Black Sleep*, along with John Carradine, Lon Chaney Jr., Tor Johnson, and Basil Rathbone. His last appearance before a film camera was test footage for a proposed Ed Wood project. Lugosi was filmed in front of Tor Johnson's house, in a graveyard, and in front of his own apartment. Shortly thereafter, on August 16, 1956, he died in his Los Angeles home, at age seventy-three.

At his funeral two days later, about sixty mourners passed his bier to pay their respects, while a priest said a prayer, and a Hungarian violinist played a farewell dirge. The mourners were mostly family members and friends from Los Angeles's Hungarian community, not celebrities, though Scott Beal, associate director of *Dracula* was there, along with directors Zoltan Korda and Ed Wood. Ralph Staats,

August 24, 1955: Wedding day for Hope Lininger and Bela Lugosi.   *Author's collection*

vice-president of Utter-McKinley mortuary, was heard to whisper, "There never was a broken-down actor in Hollywood who couldn't get a ten or a twenty from him when he had it." Lugosi was laid to rest at the Holy Cross Cemetery in Culver City, wrapped in his black Dracula cape. Though some have reported that it was his last request to be buried in his vampire cloak, it was actually his wife, Hope, and his son, Bela Jr., who felt it would be an appropriate gesture.

Shortly after his death, comedian Jonathan Winters said, "I don't feel that Bela is really dead; he's just gone home." The snippets of Lugosi footage filmed by Ed Wood were eventually used in the notoriously bad *Plan 9 from Outer Space*, released in 1959.

The Lugosi Legacy

Bela Lugosi Jr. became a lawyer, being admitted to practice in California in June of 1964. Lillian Arch Lugosi eventually married again, when she and actor Brian Donlevy wed in Indio on February 25, 1966.

In the late 1950s and early 1960s, as the older horror films were shown on television, a new legion of Lugosi fans emerged, and the original *Dracula* came to be regarded as a bona-fide classic. Along with F. W. Murnau's *Nosferatu*, the 1931 *Dracula* and *Frankenstein* were among the films shown during a ten-week series devoted to "The Horror Film" screened at the Museum of Modern Art in New York from February to April of 1965.

On February 3, 1966, Bela Lugosi Jr. joined his father's widow, Hope Lininger Lugosi, in filing suit against Universal Pictures for exploiting Lugosi's likeness as Dracula, which they asserted was not a right granted in his 1930 contract to play the role. In 1960, four years after Lugosi's death, Universal began licensing makers of cards, games, clothing, kites, and Halloween masks to reproduce the Lugosi likeness as Dracula without consent of his heirs.

On February 1, 1972, a Los Angeles Superior Court ruled that Universal Pictures had to account to Lugosi's heirs for profits made from licensing his likeness as Dracula. However, the court felt that under the statute of limitations, the heirs could only recover money from licensing agreements made since February 3, 1964. When the accounting was completed in 1974, Bela Lugosi Jr. and Hope Lininger Lugosi were awarded $53,023.23 for their share of the royalties from licensing of the actor's likeness.

On June 9, 1977, a Court of Appeals decision overturned the earlier decision, ruling that the "right to exploit the name and likeness is personal to the artist and must be exercised, if at all, by him during his lifetime." In August 1977, the Lugosi case was accepted for review by the California State Supreme Court, and was argued orally before the court in May 1978. The majority decision rejected the idea that Lugosi had developed a property right to his horror movie portrayal of Dracula so extensive that it could be passed on to his heirs for their exclusive commercial use. In a fifty-eight-page dissenting opinion, Chief Justice Rose Elizabeth Bird argued that the studio had infringed on Lugosi's "right of publicity" and that his heirs, inheriting that right, were entitled to collect from the studio for exploiting his name and likeness.

Justice Stanley Mosk, however, noted that other actors—Lon Chaney Jr. and John Carradine—had played Dracula for the studio, therefore Lugosi's portrayal created no inheritable property right. In his concurring opinion, Mosk wrote, "May the descendants of George Washington sue the secretary of the Treasury for placing his likeness on the dollar bill? May the descendants of James and Dolly Madison recover for the commercialization of Dolly Madison confections?" Mosk summarized the case by saying, "Lugosi rises from the grave twenty years after death to haunt his former employer."

Nonetheless, the Lugosi case was among those that led, in 1985, to California passing the Celebrity Rights Act, declaring that a celebrity's personality rights can survive after their death, and pass on to their heirs. In 1994, it was reported that Bela Lugosi's heirs were earning twenty-five thousand dollars a year from advertising and licensing deals.

Director Tim Burton's 1994 film *Ed Wood* told the story of the offbeat friendship between Wood, played by Johnny Depp, and Lugosi, played by Martin Landau, with a makeup assist from Rick Baker. Though his performance as Lugosi earned Landau an Academy Award for Best Supporting Actor, friends of Lugosi such as *Famous Monsters of Filmland* publisher Forrest J Ackerman and the actor's widow, Hope Lininger, said Landau's portrayal was inaccurate, if not slanderous. They maintained that the actor did not swear (especially in the presence of ladies), didn't sleep in coffins, and never owned small dogs.

In September of 1997, Bela Lugosi's Dracula was immortalized on a U.S. postage stamp, along with other classic movie ghouls, including Frankenstein's Monster, the Wolf Man, the Mummy, and the Phantom of the Opera. The thirty-two-cent stamps were unveiled at a ceremony at Universal Studios in California.

In October of 1998, The Kronos Quartet performed in a program called "Ghost Opera" that concluded the Next Wave Festival at the Brooklyn Academy of Music. Among the music they premiered was a work-in-progress by composer Philip Glass: a score to Tod Browning's *Dracula*. The 1931 film was reissued on home video in September of 1999, with the new Glass music. The complete score was performed by the Kronos Quartet at the Brooklyn Academy of Music at the 1999 New Wave Festival in October 1999. A year later, in a concert called *Dracula: The Music and Film*, the experiment of projecting the film while the Kronos Quartet played live accompaniment was repeated, this time in New Jersey at Englewood.

Each year since 1988, the Library of Congress has selected twenty-five films it regards as culturally, historically, or aesthetically significant and preserved them as part of the National Film Registry. In December of 2000, the Registry inducted Lugosi's *Dracula*.

More recently, the actor was the subject of the radio play *There Are Such Things*, written by Steven McNicoll and Mark McDonnell, broadcast on BBC Radio 4 in 2001. Telling the story of Lugosi's efforts to break free of his *Dracula*

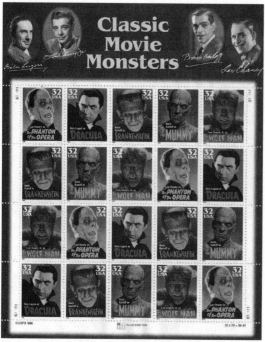

In October of 1997, the United States Postal Service saluted Bela Lugosi, Boris Karloff, Lon Chaney, and Lon Chaney Jr., with Classic Movie Monsters postage stamps, painted by Colorado Springs artist Thomas Blackshear. *Author's collection*

typecasting, the drama received the Hamilton Deane Award for best dramatic presentation from the Dracula Society in 2002.

In June of 2011, Michael Theodorou, who in 1994 had penned his own adaptation of *Dracula*, introduced a new play: *Lugosi*, set during the actor's 1951 British tour of *Dracula*, exploring the co-dependent relationship between Lugosi and his wife, Lillian. Theodorou saw Lugosi as a classically trained actor "whose style of acting was, if anything, too big for the screen."

In 2006, Dark Horse published *Universal Studios Monsters: Dracula*, with a vampire who looked a lot like Bela Lugosi. Lugosi became a comic-book character himself in 2013, when Monsterverse introduced *Bela Lugosi's Tales from the Grave*, with the iconic horror star acting as host and introducing horror tales in the style of the EC horror comics of the 1950s, with the aid of his assistant, Hugo, and vampire groupie, Nosferina. The series, officially licensed by Lugosi Enterprises, is still continuing, introducing a new generation to the horror icon.

With the advent of the Internet, there are now numerous websites and Facebook pages devoted to Bela Lugosi. Like the five-hundred-year-old vampire he most famously portrayed, it now appears the actor who once feared being forgotten will haunt our screens forever.

10

Bogeymen in Black and White

The Universal Draculas

Dracula's Daughter

The initial success with *Dracula* led Universal Pictures to do *Frankenstein,* followed by a spate of other horror and sci-fi stories over the next four years: *Murders in the Rue Morgue, The Mummy, The Invisible Man, The Black Cat, The Raven,* and *Werewolf of London.* Having pretty well exhausted the pantheon of vampires, man-made monsters and werewolves, the studio made their first direct sequel to a monster film in 1935: *Bride of Frankenstein.* When that proved to be a success, a sequel to the film that began the horror cycle in the first place seemed a foregone conclusion.

But *Dracula's Daughter* did not have its genesis at Universal Pictures. Instead, it originated with producer David O. Selznick, who would become famous for his 1939 Oscar-bait epic, *Gone With the Wind.* In 1933, Selznick negotiated with Florence Stoker, widow of *Dracula* author Bram Stoker, for the film rights to Stoker's short story "Dracula's Guest." Securing an option, he then hired John L. Balderston, who had adapted Hamilton Deane's *Dracula* stage play for American audiences, to write a treatment. Balderston did so, and Selznick took the project to MGM, but was unable to persuade the studio to produce it; MGM was worried about a potential lawsuit arising from infringement on Universal Pictures' title to the original novel. In fact, their discussions were considered so sensitive that in all cables and letters referring to the project, they called it by a code name: "Tarantula." Ultimately, MGM passed, after which Selznick sold the treatment to Universal.

Two years later, Universal finally decided to make a movie called *Dracula's Daughter,* but instead of using the Balderston treatment, they commissioned an entirely new screenplay from Garrett Fort, who had adapted Balderston and Deane's *Dracula* for the movies four years earlier.

Dracula's Daughter was first announced in the *Los Angeles Times* on November 20, 1935. At that time, the director was reported to be Edward Sutherland, who had helmed the 1928 W. C. Fields comedy *Tillie's Punctured Romance* and the 1933

The lovely Gloria Holden as Countess Maria Zaleska, otherwise known as *Dracula's Daughter*.
© *1935 Universal Pictures.*
Courtesy of Del Valle Archives.

horror mystery *Murders in the Zoo*, with Lionel Atwill. The newspaper reported that Bela Lugosi would star in the film, which was to go into production "in the next two weeks" from a script by John L. Balderston and R. C. Sheriff. Lugosi posed for publicity photos with producer David Diamond and actress Gloria Holden, who had been selected for the title role of Countess Maria Zaleska, a.k.a. Dracula's daughter. It was reported that Universal cast the unknown "exotic stage beauty" Holden because they wanted to ensure that the public would accept the title character as a reality, and not identify her as an actress they had just seen in a "sweet girl" role.

Born in England in 1903, Gloria Holden came to America when she was a child. With her classical beauty, she gravitated to the stage, studying at New York's American Academy of Dramatic Arts and appearing on Broadway before going to Hollywood. She played a party guest in the first chapter of the 1934 serial *The Return of Chandu*, starring Lugosi, and two years later turned up in a small role in MGM's *Wife Versus Secretary*, a comedy-drama with a cast headlined by Clark Gable, Jean Harlow, Myrna Loy, and James Stewart. Then Universal offered her a screen test and a seven-year contract. Holden signed the contract, took an apartment, and sent for her furniture.

The actress was put off by Garrett Fort's script, saying that having created such a "poisonous role" as the insatiable vampire, the author must be a monstrous, horrible person. In fact, screenwriter Garrett Fort had become a devotee of Indian guru Meher Baba, who claimed to be God in human form and had not spoken a word since 1925. Since Fort was becoming preoccupied with spiritual pursuits, in December of 1935, Finley Peter Dunne Jr. was brought in to collaborate on the screenplay.

As 1936 dawned, Edward Sutherland dropped out as director. In February, Lambert Hillyer took up the reins, inheriting a cast that included not only Gloria Holden but also Cesar Romero, Marguerite Churchill, and Irving Pichel. Apparently, since his name was no longer appearing among the cast, it had already been decided to drop Lugosi. In the film, Dracula's corpse would only be glimpsed for a brief moment before being immolated by Countess Zaleska;

so a wax dummy was used. When Cesar Romero moved on to *She Married a Million*, Otto Kruger was hired to replace him.

The final film owed more to J. Sheridan Le Fanu's *Carmilla* than to Stoker, particularly a sequence in which Zaleska's servant, Sandor (Irving Pichel) lures a young woman named Lili (Nan Grey) back to Zaleska's apartment. Zaleska asks the young woman to pose for her. After Lili partially undresses and nervously exposes her shoulder, Zaleska is overcome with her vampiric yearning and approaches. The camera moves up to a leering mask on the wall as we hear Lili scream. As Jim Koch wrote in a 1994 *New York Times* article, "Gloria Holden as the title character showed a decided preference for female victims, quite a feat in the same year that Lillian Hellman's play *The Children's Hour* was transferred to the screen with all references to lesbianism deleted by order of the Hays Office."

Snapshot of Gloria Holden, sans vampiric make-up, sent to an admirer.
Courtesy of Timothy Grana

Variety reviewed the film on May 2, 1936, calling it "a chiller with plenty of ice." It opened in New York two weeks later to strong reviews, although Frank S. Nugent of the *New York Times* wondered how Dracula's daughter was able to preserve her attractive appearance, when vampires cast no reflections in mirrors.

By the time the film reached Los Angeles theaters a couple of weeks later, it was paired on a double bill with a Technicolor musical, *Dancing Pirate*. An ad in the *Los Angeles Times* proclaimed that *Dracula's Daughter* was "More Sensational Than Her Unforgettable Father." The newspaper's Philip K. Scheuer called the film "a chiller generally superior to its over-rated predecessor, plain *Dracula*."

The *Chicago Daily Tribune's* "Mae Tinée" (a name used by several staff reviewers) reviewed the film in July of 1936, giving it a favorable notice but admonishing readers, "LEAVE THE CHILDREN AT HOME."

After her star turn at Universal proved successful, Gloria Holden realized the studio was planning on grooming her to be another horror star, in the vein of Boris Karloff or Bela Lugosi. Offered the role of a leopard woman, she refused and her contract was revoked. Jobless, she rented out her apartment and lived in a hotel room for nearly six months. Then, just as she was contemplating a return to New York, Holden was offered a role in Warner Bros.' *The Life of Emile Zola* (1937). She continued to appear in supporting roles in films for Warner Bros., RKO, MGM, and other companies until 1958; she died in 1991.

In November of 1938, with production of *Son of Frankenstein* running behind schedule and Universal's promotional department eager to get a horror film into theaters, the studio decided to re-release *Dracula's Daughter* on a double bill with *Bride of Frankenstein*. The films were shown in New York's Rialto Theater beginning May 18, 1939.

Son of Dracula

Once *Son of Frankenstein* was released and became a hit, the studio revisited Dracula. Although he had been definitively put to his eternal rest at the end of the 1931 film, they began investigating how they could bring the vampire to life again. Occult expert Manly P. Hall suggested that driving a stake through Dracula's heart would only work so long as the sun was above the horizon, but if Van Helsing had done the deed just one minute after sundown, then Dracula would have survived. With that premise, Hall wrote a scenario that would resurrect Dracula in Buenos Aires. The film, however, failed to materialize.

When Universal announced its 1942–43 production schedule in June of 1942, among the fifty-five films they planned to make were two horror pictures, *Frankenstein Meets the Wolf Man* and *Son of Dracula*. Within days, the *New York Times* reported that Curt Siodmak was writing the script of *Son of Dracula*, and in July, Lon Chaney Jr. was announced as the film's star, with production due to begin in September.

Count Alucard (Lon Chaney Jr.), prepares to put the bite on Louise Allbritton in *Son of Dracula* (1943).
© *Universal Pictures, Inc.*
Courtesy of Del Valle Archives.

The son of actor Lon Chaney, Creighton Tull Chaney was born February 10, 1906, between curtain calls in Oklahoma City, where his parents were playing in a stock company. When his father moved west and became an iconic actor in silent films, Creighton went to Los Feliz School and Hollywood High. He worked for a plumbing company until his father died of throat cancer. He then took up acting, appearing in small roles in Westerns and serials and even a couple of Charlie Chan mysteries, becoming typed as a "heavy." He appeared under his own name of Creighton Chaney until 1935, when a producer hoping to capitalize on the marketing value of his famous father's name re-christened him Lon Chaney

Jr. Chaney hated the "Jr." but realized taking his father's name could help his career.

His break came with the 1939 film version of John Steinbeck's *Of Mice and Men*, in which Chaney Jr. received critical plaudits for his moving portrayal as Lennie, the brute with the mind of a child, opposite Burgess Meredith's George. In 1940, Universal signed Chaney Jr. to a contract. They put him in a Western, *Riders of Death Valley*, but then decided to trade on his lineage and put him in the kinds of roles his father made famous, grooming him to be their next horror star. After playing the lead in *Man Made Monster* (1941), he essayed his signature role in *The Wolf Man* (1941). Chaney Jr. was never as good an actor as Karloff or Lugosi, but he had a sincerity that worked well for the emotionally tortured Larry Talbot, who became a wolf under the light of the full moon.

When *The Wolf Man* became a hit, Chaney Jr. was then cast as practically every creature in the Universal Pictures pantheon. He played Frankenstein's Monster in *The Ghost of Frankenstein* (1942) and took over the role of the Mummy with 1942's *The Mummy's Tomb* (he would continue for two more films, *The Mummy's Ghost* and *The Mummy's Curse*, both in 1944). But his own personal favorite was the Wolf Man, the character he first breathed life into, which he regarded as "my baby." However, in the summer of 1942, the studio wanted him to become their new Dracula.

Pre-production dragged through the winter, with director George Waggner overseeing the writing of Eric Taylor's script. Taylor based the story on an original idea by Curt Siodmak, who concocted a tale that had Count Alucard (Dracula spelled backwards) causing havoc in the modern-day American South (judging from the swamps and the fortune teller, most likely Louisiana, though every character speaks with proper mid-Atlantic, not Southern, accents).

Lon Chaney Jr. and Evelyn Ankers (Chaney's co-star in *The Wolf Man*) were the first to sign on to *Son of Dracula*, which was called "Destiny" when it went into production. In January 1943, Louise Allbritton and Alan Curtis joined the cast. Allbritton was the

Louise Allbritton is more prominent on this poster for *Son of Dracula* than the vampire of the title.   *Author's collection* wife of CBS broadcaster Charles Collingwood; she later had the lead role in the Broadway production of *The Seven Year Itch*.

The film was directed by Robert Siodmak, brother of scriptwriter Curt Siodmak, who placed the emphasis on thrills rather than chills. Unlike the previous two Dracula films, *Son of Dracula* actually showed the vampire not only materializing out of mist but also turning into a bat. Special-effects wizard John P. Fulton achieved the latter effect by filming a shot of a mechanical bat suspended by piano wire, then replacing the bat with Chaney Jr. and filming from the same position. The transformation stages in-between were achieved with traditional animation, showing the wings of the bat enlarging and assuming the shape of Dracula.

In June of 1943, while *Son of Dracula* was in production, Universal announced plans to bring together several of their monster characters in a film to be called "The Chamber of Horrors." It was thought the film would include Dracula, Frankenstein's Monster, the Wolf Man, the Invisible Man, the Mummy, and the Mad Ghoul. Curt Siodmak was assigned scripting duties, while George Waggner was tapped to produce (he had both produced and directed *The Wolf Man*, and produced *The Ghost of Frankenstein* and *Frankenstein Meets the Wolf Man*). The studio hoped to get all of the actors who had made the parts famous for this "super-horror picture."

Even crusty Bosley Crowther of the *New York Times* liked that idea, writing, "The pure and simple thought of a cinematic convention of all those scourges is enough to tickle our fancy for a week." However, when Universal announced their plans for the 1943–44 season, the horror titles included were *The Invisible Man's Revenge*, *The Mummy's Chest*, and *Son of Dracula*; "The Chamber of Horrors" failed to make the list.

Son of Dracula arrived at New York's Rialto Theater on November 5, 1943. Reviewers found it a mediocre thriller, but the film performed well enough to be held over for a second week. It was due to finish its run definitively after three weeks, but when the Rialto's managers looked at the receipts, they kept it for a fourth rather than replacing it, as had been scheduled, with Laurel and Hardy's *Dancing Masters*. When the film opened in Los Angeles at the Hawaii Theater on November 18, 1943, it was accompanied by Universal's B-movie thriller, *The Mad Ghoul*.

House of Frankenstein

Next up for Chaney Jr. was *Frankenstein Meets the Wolf Man*. In the previous Frankenstein film, 1942's *The Ghost of Frankenstein*, Chaney Jr. played the Monster, who was given the brain of Ygor, voiced by Bela Lugosi. The new film, as scripted, had the Monster blind and speaking (as he had been at the climax of *Ghost*, when given Ygor's brain), hence it was decided to offer the role to Lugosi. When *Frankenstein Meets the Wolf Man* was finished, Universal executives felt the Monster speaking with Ygor's raspy voice was laughable, and all of Lugosi's dialogue was cut. *Frankenstein Meets the Wolf Man* performed well at the box office, especially among the young demographic that now made up the primary audience of horror films. The studio once again felt the only way to top a film with two monsters was to make a film with all of them, so they returned to their earlier idea, "The Chamber of Horrors." The job of producing the film fell to Paul Malvern, who had entered show business as a child acrobat with the Ringling Bros. circus before becoming a silent movie stuntman. In the 1930s, he began Lone Star Productions, which produced a bevy of B-Westerns, many starring a young John Wayne. When he moved to Universal in the 1940s, he introduced the studio to Deanna Durbin, whose musicals were among Universal's top moneymakers throughout the decade, and brought with him expertise for making brisk, low-budget, crowd-pleasing programmers.

Anne Gwynne and John Carradine take a break from filming *House of Frankenstein* (1944).
Courtesy of Del Valle Archives

George Waggner, originally set to produce "The Chamber of Horrors," whose title had now changed to "Destiny" (seemingly a stock title the studio used for any film whose title was undecided; it had also been floated for *The Wolf Man*), was now producing *The Climax*, a Technicolor thriller that brought Boris Karloff back to the studio. Karloff returned after three years in New York and on tour with *Arsenic and Old Lace*, and now vowed that he was done with playing monsters. But he wasn't averse to appearing in thriller films, especially if they required no special makeup, so Universal signed him for two films, *The Climax* and "Destiny."

By 1943, Universal had relegated horror films and thrillers to B-movie status, as opposed to *Dracula*, *Frankenstein*, *The Mummy*, *Bride of Frankenstein*, *Dracula's Daughter*, *Son of Frankenstein*, and others, which were all considered A-productions with higher budgets and higher production values. Now, monster movies were produced to be half of a double bill presentation, and Universal was facing competition in that arena from other studios. The most serious competition came from RKO, who set up a horror division under producer Val Lewton that was redefining the horror film, beginning with the atmospheric

Cat People, directed by Jacques Tourneur and released on December 6, 1942, in New York City before opening in other American cities on Christmas Day. The following year, RKO released Tourneur's *The Leopard Man* and *I Walked with a Zombie*, and Mark Robson's *The 7th Victim*, all produced by Lewton.

Now, Universal fought back, unleashing an army of their greatest monsters all in one film. Curt Siodmak came up with a storyline which featured mad Dr. Neimann and his hunchback assistant, Daniel, taking over a traveling horror show, whose main exhibit is Dracula's skeleton. Seeking revenge upon the men who sent him to prison, Niemann temporarily revives Dracula, only to later expose the vampire to sunlight when they are being pursued by the authorities. The Frankenstein Monster, the Wolf Man and a gypsy girl also figure into the proceedings, which were also supposed to include the Mummy, but that idea was dropped early on. Edward T. Lowe wrote the final screenplay, which was titled "The Devil's Brood."

Lon Chaney Jr. was brought back for another turn as the Wolf Man, J. Carrol Naish was tapped for the role of the hunchback, Elena Verdugo played the gypsy girl, and Karloff took the role of Dr. Niemann. The Monster, reduced to only a few minutes of screen time, was enacted by Glenn Strange, a former cowboy-turned-stuntman who had doubled John Wayne in many of the Westerns produced by Paul Malvern. While working on another film at Universal, the six-foot-five-inch Strange went to makeup man Jack Pierce to have a scar applied. Pierce took a long look at Strange and called Malvern, whom Strange knew from working in the producer's Westerns. Feeling that Strange had the contour they'd been looking for, the imposing actor was chosen to become Frankenstein's Monster. Having won the role, Strange turned to Boris Karloff to school him in the Monster's walk and mannerisms.

Bela Lugosi was originally announced for the role of Dracula, but was ultimately passed over for reasons that remain unclear. Instead, the role went to John Carradine. Born on February 5, 1906, to an attorney-poet-painter father and surgeon mother, Richmond Reed Carradine grew up in Poughkeepsie, New York. After attending Christ Church School and Philadelphia's Graphic Art School, where he studied sculpture, the tall, gaunt actor traveled the South selling sketches until 1925, when he landed a part in a New Orleans theater production of *Camille*. He arrived in Hollywood in 1927, where he cultivated a reputation as a hammy eccentric; he was said to stroll the streets of Los Angeles reciting Shakespeare while wearing a red-lined satin cape and wide-brimmed hat, a practice that earned him the nickname "the Bard of the Boulevard." Carradine later denied that he did so, claiming instead that he went to the Hollywood Bowl every night at midnight for five years, bellowing Shakespeare at twenty-thousand empty seats to improve his elocution and projection.

In 1932, according to Carradine, he was noticed by one of Hollywood's most important producer/directors, when Cecil B. DeMille saw him passing by, reciting the gravedigger's lines from *Hamlet*, and cast him in his 1932 epic, *The Sign of the Cross*. Carradine then appeared in bit parts for various studios, including playing a villager in 1933's *The Invisible Man* and a hunter in *Bride of Frankenstein* in 1935, the year that he signed a contract with 20th Century-Fox and changed his professional name to John Carradine. By the end of the 1930s, he was receiving larger parts: President Lincoln in *Of Human Hearts* (1938), Barryman in *The Hound of the Baskervilles* (1939), Bob Ford in *Jesse James* (1939). He became a favorite of director John Ford, who featured him as the gambler Hatfield in 1939's *Stagecoach* and as Preacher Casy in 1940's *The Grapes of Wrath*; he eventually appeared in ten of the director's films. He was also well known at Universal, having just appeared in supporting roles in *The Invisible Man's Revenge* and *The Mummy's Ghost* (both 1944).

At the time he agreed to take the Dracula role, Carradine was getting back on his feet after having formed, in 1943, a Shakespearean repertory company. He toured with the company, directing and playing Hamlet, Iago, and Othello, but in wartime it was difficult for actors to travel cross-country, so the company folded. Now, he was taking on a role indelibly associated with another actor. Carradine chose to play it straight, rather than do a Lugosi imitation.

Bucking Universal's current trend, producer Paul Malvern attempted to boost the film to A-picture status so it could be exhibited in first-run houses in major cities. He claimed the film had a budget of five hundred thousand dollars, twice what the company usually spent on its monster pictures. Malvern noted that having so many monsters in one film created some difficulties, chief among them scheduling the filming so that they were all allowed sufficient time in Jack Pierce's makeup chair; it took Pierce three-and-a-half hours to transform Lon Chaney Jr. into the Wolf Man, and a similar length of time to make up Glenn Strange as Frankenstein's Monster. J. Carrol Naish's hunchback makeup only took one hour to apply, but the actor reported that under the strain of it, he lost four pounds the first two days he wore the hump.

In April 1944, as "The Devil's Brood" was going into production, the *New York Times* reported that Ford Beebe had been given producing and directing chores for Universal's "The Wolf Man vs. Dracula," with Bernard Shubert writing the screenplay. As summer approached, Universal observed its usual custom of announcing its film program for the coming year. In 1944–45, the studio planned to release five horror films, including "The Devil's Brood," "Dracula vs. the Wolf Man," "Dead Man's Eyes," "The Frozen Ghost," and "The Mummy Returns," all of them to feature Lon Chaney Jr., whom the studio was keeping busy in horror roles. Another monster mashup was announced in November, when the *New York Times* reported that Ben Pivar would produce "The House of Horrors" for Universal, with "the Creeper" (Rondo Hatton) appearing with the studio's other monsters, including Dracula, the Mummy, the Mad Ghoul, and Frankenstein's Monster.

"The Devil's Brood" completed filming on May 8. With a backlog of movies, Universal held off releasing it until December 15, 1944, when it premiered at New York's Rialto Theater. By that time, the title had undergone yet another change, ending up as *House of Frankenstein*. A. H. Weiler of the *New York Times* wrote that with its all-star lineup of monsters, *House of Frankenstein* was like a baseball team with nine Babe Ruths. But most reviewers were unimpressed; they dismissed the film as juvenile.

House of Frankenstein opened at the Hawaii Theater in Los Angeles on December 22, 1944, on a double bill with *The Mummy's Curse*. West Coast reviewers were kinder to it than their East Coast cousins. John L. Scott in the *Los Angeles Times* called it a "super-shocker."

The Hollywood Citizen-News gave it a thumbs-up, raving, "*House of Frankenstein* is a thriller deluxe. . . . It's a film guaranteed to provide an acute case of jitters."

House of Dracula

House of Frankenstein entered national release in February of 1945, and helped Universal achieve a profit of $4 million by year's end. The success of their monster rally encouraged Universal to rush another one into production. The *New York Times* reported in March 1945 that Boris Karloff had signed a new three-picture contract with Universal, under which his first film would be *The House of Dracula*, featuring all of the studio's horror characters. But Karloff moved on, and in September, it was reported that John Carradine would have the title role in the film, co-starring with Lon Chaney Jr., Lionel Atwill, and Onslow Stevens. Behind the cameras was the same team from *House of Frankenstein*: producer Paul Malvern, director Erle C. Kenton, and scriptwriter Edward T. Lowe, who made no attempt to explain how the monsters had survived their certain deaths from the previous film.

Economy was the watchword on the production, so much so that footage from previous films was recycled, including a brief shot of Karloff as the Monster from *Bride of Frankenstein* seen in a nightmare montage, and the monster's fiery demise being lifted directly from the climax of *The Ghost of Frankenstein*.

House of Dracula breezed through production, with shooting ending on October 15, 1945. The film was previewed at Universal on November 28, and opened at the Rialto Theater in New York on December 21, where the Gotham critics attacked it like a mob of angry villagers with pitchforks. The reviewer for the *New York Daily News* called it "a cold-blooded experiment to determine audience saturation point," while the *Chicago Daily Tribune* dismissed it as a "tale of half-witted horrors."

When it arrived in Los Angeles on February 6, 1946, it was on a double bill with a Western, *The Daltons Ride Again*, which also starred Lon Chaney Jr. Reviewing the horror offering in the *Los Angeles Times*, John L. Scott wrote, "Universal may have ended a profitable series of horror pictures with *House of Dracula*, since the vampire Count, Frankenstein's Monster and the Wolf Man are liquidated (and about time, too!)."

In March, the film continued its run in New York and Chicago, now on a double bill with another Chaney Jr. vehicle, *Pillow of Death*, the final instalment of the *Inner Sanctum* series. By then, the studio had officially dropped many of

1945's *House of Dracula* gave John Carradine a more substantial showcase for his interpretation of Dracula as a vampire of palpable loneliness and yearning.   *Author's collection*

its contract players, including Chaney Jr. The studio merged with International Pictures on October 1, 1946, to become Universal-International, a company now dedicated to making "high quality pictures." Monster movies, serials and B-Westerns, once the studio's bread and butter, were dumped from future production rosters.

But not for long . . .

Abbott and Costello Meet Dracula and Company

By 1947, Universal-International was almost bankrupt. Although Ronald Colman won an Academy Award for his starring role in the studio's *A Double Life* (1947), mass audiences preferred the lowbrow antics of *The Egg and I*, which starred Claudette Colbert and Fred MacMurray and introduced Ma and Pa Kettle, played by Marjorie Main and Percy Kilbride. *The Egg and I*'s $5.75 million gross kept the studio afloat, and the Kettles kept going for nine profitable sequels. The studio's other popular moneymakers were the comedies of Bud Abbott and Lou Costello, much to the chagrin of Universal-International's erudite production chief, William Goetz, who considered such films "tacky."

Abbott and Costello became a team in 1936 when both were appearing at Minsky's Burlesque. A hit on the nightclub and vaudeville circuits, where they refined their "Who's on First?" routine, the duo arrived in Hollywood in 1941.

Bela Lugosi, though typecast as Dracula, only played the character twice in feature films. The first time was in 1931; the second was in 1948's *Bud Abbott and Lou Costello Meet Frankenstein*, which featured cowboy actor Glenn Strange as Frankenstein's Monster.

Courtesy of Del Valle Archives

Universal put them into a comedy musical with the Andrews Sisters called *Buck Privates*; budgeted at $180,000, the film grossed more than $10 million, establishing Abbott and Costello as the nation's newest comedy sensation. By the following year, the pair was earning $150,000 for each film they made, plus 10 percent of the profits. Their radio show on NBC brought in an additional $20,000 per week.

On December 3, 1942, the *Los Angeles Times'* Edwin Schallert reported that Abbott and Costello were planning a return to the stage with a musical show that would feature Universal's popular monsters, including Frankenstein's Monster, Dracula, Dracula's daughter, and the Wolf Man. Their plan was to first do the Broadway revue, then turn it into a film for Universal, not unlike Olsen and Johnson had done with 1941's *Hellzapoppin!*, released by the studio. The comedy duo was scheduled to have a five-month break after filming "Oh! Doctor" (released in 1943 as *Hit the Ice*), but ultimately they didn't feel that would give them enough of a window to do a Broadway engagement which, if it caught on, could run for a year. Eventually, they dropped the idea and instead embarked on a tour of military camps with their radio show, raising some eighty million dollars for the war effort.

Now, nearly five years later, the studio was in trouble, and the powers-that-be decided that maybe the solution lay in a return to their "tacky" comedy team and "tacky" monsters. So, on July 29, 1947, the *New York Times* revealed that Universal-International was producing a comedy called "The Brain of Frankenstein," pairing Abbott and Costello with the studio's most famous monsters. Robert Arthur was set to produce and Charles Barton to direct, from a screenplay being prepared by Robert Lees and Fred Rinaldo. Charles Van Enger, the cinematographer of the silent Lon Chaney Sr. classics *The Hunchback of Notre Dame* and *The Phantom of the Opera*, was hired to shoot the movie. Filming was set to begin in October, once the comedy duo had completed *The Noose Hangs High*, a film for Eagle-Lion also directed by Barton, which they made under a clause in their Universal contract permitting them to do one film a year for another company.

Producer Robert Arthur, who had previously been a writer and associate producer of MGM musicals, originally thought of pitting the comedians against not only the Frankenstein's Monster, Dracula, and the Wolf Man, but also Kharis the Mummy, Dracula's son Alucard, and the Invisible Man. By the time Frederic Rinaldo and Robert Lees, as well as gagman John Grant, were finished with the script, Kharis and Alucard were gone, and the Invisible Man was reduced to an end-of-film cameo. The offbeat plot had Dracula and Frankenstein's Monster brought to America as part of a wax museum exhibit, summoned by Dracula's acolyte Sandra, who is helping the Count find the perfect servile brain for the Monster to make him Dracula's slave. She has chosen Costello's brain, but their plans are interrupted when Larry Talbot, determined to stop Dracula, finds them.

On January 12, 1948, Universal-International announced that Bela Lugosi had signed for Dracula; Lon Chaney Jr. to reprise his role as Talbot, the tormented Wolf Man; and Glenn Strange as the Frankenstein's Monster. "The Brain of Frankenstein" was expected to begin filming on February 2. When Ella Raines realized that the studio was going to put her in the film, she asked to be released from her contract. The studio hired Jane Randolph to take the role instead. Lou Costello also balked at doing the film, until Arthur offered him a fifty-thousand-dollar advance on his percentage. With that incentive, Costello relented.

Makeup maestro Jack Pierce had been among those shown the door by the new administration. In his place, Universal-International hired Bud Westmore, who streamlined the process of making up the Wolf Man and Frankenstein's Monster by using foam rubber appliances. Instead of two or three hours, Lon Chaney Jr. and Glenn Strange now had only about an hour in the makeup chair. Westmore also did his best to erase the years from the sixty-five-year-old Lugosi by applying heavy powder to his face, dark rinse to his hair, and rouge to his lips.

Lugosi was happy to be back at Universal. With no film work since making *Scared to Death* two years earlier, he had been making ends meet by touring with yet another revival of *Dracula*. The new film marked the first time he had played Dracula in a feature since he originated the role in 1931 (though he had played plenty of other vampires in-between, who were essentially Dracula-by-another-name). The actor felt the script preserved his character's dignity, since Dracula himself was not lampooned.

When filming began, it became clear that the monsters were not the real terrors on the set. Abbott and Costello resorted to their usual antics, sometimes failing to show up or, if they did, spending the day playing cards on the sidelines instead of working in front of the camera. Director Charles Barton said the only thing that really caused overages on the production was when Abbott and

Bud Abbott and Lou Costello Meet Frankenstein arrives in Chicago, and receives some welcome publicity from the *Chicago Tribune* of August 10, 1948.   *Author's collection*

Costello got their collective dander up and refused to come to work, but he never had any trouble with Chaney Jr., Strange, or Lugosi; the "monsters," he said, "were as sweet as little babies."

Remembering Lugosi, Barton told Gregory William Mank, the author of *It's Alive! The Classic Cinema Saga of Frankenstein*, "He was a hell of a good actor. He was very helpful to Lon, and to me, and to everybody. Particularly that wonderful, beautiful girl, Lenore Aubert. I remember in the scene where Lugosi told her, 'Look into my eyes,' how he tried to help her look as if she were really hypnotized. It was a hard scene to do, and damn, he worked with her like a real pro. He was a lovely, lovely guy."

During the first week of March, Lou Costello celebrated his thirty-eighth birthday on the set, partying with Dracula, Frankenstein's Monster, and the Wolf Man. As the comedy duo relaxed and settled into the film, they sometimes indulged in pie fights. Barton said there were always pies ready on the set, in case the mood suddenly struck Bud and Lou; the pie bill was between $3,800 and $4,800. Chaney Jr. enjoyed the pastry battles, but Lugosi and Strange remained on the sidelines; neither had to worry about becoming targets, because Abbott and Costello had great respect for them, regarding them as old pros.

Filming came to a close on Saturday, March 20, 1948. While "The Brain of Frankenstein" was in post-production, Universal-International re-released *Son of Dracula* on a double bill with *The Ghost of Frankenstein*. The films appeared in Los Angeles theaters at the end of May 1948. The following month, on June 25, the new film was previewed at Los Angeles's Forum Theater, with its title now changed to *Bud Abbott and Lou Costello Meet Frankenstein*.

The Hollywood Reporter wrote that the film was "a crazy giddy show that combines chills and laughs in one zany sequence after another."

Variety's reviewer was of the same opinion, writing, "Combination of horror and slapstick should pay off brilliantly. . . . Producer Robert Arthur and director Charles T. Barton can chalk it up as one of the best for the comedians."

Bud Abbott and Lou Costello Meet Frankenstein opened on July 24, 1948, in Los Angeles, where it proved popular enough to be held over for a second week. Four days later, it opened at Loew's Criterion in New York, playing the city during an air-conditioning engineers' strike that left the theatergoers sweltering. Nonetheless, houses showing the film enjoyed sell-out crowds. In the *New York Star*, critic Cecilia Ager wrote, "It's heart-warming to see all our favorite monsters once more. . . . It's kind of like a class reunion . . . everybody connected with this nostalgic travesty of horror movies deserves credit . . . they have made *Abbott and Costello Meet Frankenstein* a broad, friendly comedy, good to see. It's real American folklore; look at it that way." Bosley Crowther of the *New York Times* was less amused, writing that most of the comic invention in the film was embraced in its title.

To help promote *Bud Abbott and Lou Costello Meet Frankenstein*, Universal-International sent Bela Lugosi and Glenn Strange on a personal appearance tour. In Chicago, the film opened in August, playing at the RKO Palace along with Chapter 5 of the popular Columbia Pictures serial *Superman*. By year's end, the film proved to be one of Universal-International's "Big 3" moneymakers.

The Universal monster films came to television in the late 1950s, and remain popular TV fare right up to the present day. More than eighty years since *Dracula* kicked off the Universal Pictures horror series, the classic monsters are still filling the studio's coffers, with multiple releases on home video, DVD, and Blu-Ray. As the old films demonstrated time and again, you can't keep a good ghoul down.

Hammer Time!

Christopher Lee

Horror of Dracula

After being lampooned by Abbott and Costello, it seemed the classic monsters were done for good. As the 1950s dawned, American horror movies were no longer being produced by major studios, but by smaller companies like American International Pictures and Lippert, companies that made cheap black-and-white "quickies" for the entertainment of teenagers at drive-ins. But in England, one company decided to take a chance on reviving the old gothic monsters in lurid, living color.

In November of 1934, comedian William Hinds, whose stage name was Will Hammer, registered the name for a new film company: Hammer Productions Ltd. Hammer's first film, *The Public Life of Henry the Ninth*, a spoof of the previous year's *The Private Life of Henry the Eighth*, was completed in January of 1935. In May of that year, Hinds joined a former cinema owner named Enrique Carreras to form a distribution company called Exclusive Films. Hammer made four more films distributed by Exclusive, including *Mystery of the Mary Celeste* (1936) starring Bela Lugosi, before going into bankruptcy in 1937.

In 1938, James Carreras joined Exclusive and revived Hammer Film Productions with himself, Enrique Carreras, William Hinds, and Hinds's son Anthony as directors. James Carreras and Anthony Hinds were soon off to fight in World War II, but returned after the war to begin producing "quota quickies"—low-budget films usually presented as the lower half of double bills. They found limited success producing films based on BBC radio thrillers and, by the mid-1950s, had formed a partnership with an American distributor, ensuring that their films would play on both sides of the Atlantic.

It was an adaptation of the BBC TV sci-fi serial *The Quatermass Xperiment* that became one of the company's biggest hits and showed the way for the future. Feeling the film's popularity came from public response to the horror element, Hammer decided to make a series of "shilling shockers" intended for release in both Britain and America, the first of which was 1957's *The Curse of Frankenstein*. When the film opened at the Warner Theater in London there were lines around the block. The same thing happened in Tokyo and Berlin. By the time it ended its run, *The Curse of Frankenstein*, budgeted at approximately $150,000, took in a reported $3.5 million. Its success led Hammer to think about following it up with an adaptation of the other great gothic novel: *Dracula.*

James Carreras found the rights to *Dracula* were cloudy; another British company, Associated Rediffusion Ltd., had planned to do a six-part TV adaptation of Bram Stoker's novel, but their investigation showed the rights were still held by Universal Pictures. Hammer then began negotiations with Universal, which continued until March 1958, by which time their *Dracula* film was already in post-production.

Given its limited budget of £81,000, Jimmy Sangster pared the story to the bone, deleting many of Stoker's characters and the book's multiple locations. Instead of an elderly Dutchman, Van Helsing became more youthful and energetic. So did Dracula; this was not a courtly, mesmeric, thickly accented Dracula in the Bela Lugosi tradition, but a sensual, robust predator who spoke in clipped Oxford tones.

In *Horror of Dracula,* Christopher Lee is on screen for only seven of the film's eighty-two minutes, but his menace is felt throughout.
© *1958 Hammer Film Productions/Universal Pictures. Courtesy of Del Valle Archives.*

The picture was directed by Terence Fisher, who had also helmed *The Curse of Frankenstein.* To star, Hammer returned to the two actors who had headlined the Frankenstein picture—Peter Cushing and Christopher Lee. Cushing was given the role of vampire hunter Abraham Van Helsing, while Lee was set to play Count Dracula. "The part called for another big, tall guy," Lee told Bill Kelley in a 1992 *Starlog* magazine interview. "I looked darkly European and presentable enough."

Born in 1922, the six-foot-four-inch Lee served in the RAF in World War II. Following the war, his cousin Count Nicolo Carandini, the Italian ambassador to Great Britain, suggested Lee should become an actor and introduced him to the head of Two Cities Films. It was there that he made his first onscreen appearance, in 1947's *Corridor of Mirrors.* After ten years of appearing in a variety of small roles, Lee was offered the part of the monster in *The Curse of Frankenstein,* which led to *Dracula.*

The film was originally to begin shooting on November 4, but production issues delayed the start until November 11. It continued for six bitterly cold weeks at Bray Studios, where production designer Bernard Robinson designed elegantly Spartan sets in contrast to the expressionistic sets of the 1931 film.

As in Stoker's novel, Dracula hardly appears in the film; the plot centers more on Van Helsing and his attempts to foil the vampire. Consequently, Lee, who was paid £60 per day, eventually earned £750 for his work on the picture, while Peter Cushing, who had considerably more screen time, received £2,500 for six weeks' work. Nonetheless, when Lee is onscreen, he is a commanding presence, a more primal creature than the refined, cultured gentleman presented by previous interpreters of the role.

Unlike the horror films of the 1930s and '40s that relied on the suggestion of horror, Hammer Films put the horrors onscreen, for the audience to experience firsthand. Lee was the first actor to play Dracula in a color film, and the first to be seen wearing fangs, dripping bright red blood. The makeup man, Phil Leakey, had two sets of fangs prepared for the actor, which clipped onto his eyeteeth. He also took Lee to an oculist to be fitted with contact lenses that gave Dracula bloodshot eyes. Despite being specially fitted, the lenses irritated Lee's eyes terribly, leaving him practically blind. On the first take of the scene when Dracula snatches the vampire woman away from Harker, the actor overshot his targets and ran far past the camera.

In Lee's Dracula films, his powers are more limited than previous screen vampires. He is unable to turn into a bat or wolf or wisp of smoke, remaining always in human form. Yet Lee's performance is more feral than any previous Dracula; he emphasizes the vampire's savage ferocity and intensely masculine physical allure. The latter is witnessed in the scenes of Dracula descending on his female victims, who wait for him expectantly, willfully surrendering themselves to his love bite with expressions of sexual ecstasy that were quite titillating for 1950s audiences. Indeed, when Melissa Stribling,

From the *New York Times*, May 28, 1958: A throwback to Horace Liveright-style publicity. Besides having stars Christopher Lee and Peter Cushing appear in person, when *Horror of Dracula* opened at New York's Mayfair Theater, there was "first aid if you chicken out" and "courage cocktails if you lack the nerve to see the picture." *Author's collection*

as Mina, exited her bedroom after being bitten by Dracula, she was unable to express the particular smile that director Terence Fisher wanted and flubbed several takes. Finally, he took her aside and said, "Just imagine you've had the best sex of your life, all night long!" When the cameras rolled again, she nailed it.

In an interview with Donald Glut for 1975's *The Dracula Book*, Lee said he tried to remain true to Stoker's conception, adding, "What came onto the screen was a combination of my having read the book and trying to invest the character with his dignity and nobility, ferocity and sadness."

Despite the gravity of the proceedings onscreen, there were some light moments behind the scenes. Filming the scene in which Dracula throws Mina into an open grave, Lee recalled that he picked up stuntwoman Daphne Baker, charged across the graveyard, flung her into the grave, and fell straight in on top of her.

Principal photography ended on Christmas Eve 1957, when Lee and Cushing and their stunt doubles filmed the final showdown of Dracula and Van Helsing in the castle library, including Van Helsing's leap from the refectory table to the curtains, tearing them down to let in the stream of sunlight. After the holiday, special-effects man Syd Pearson returned to the library set to film the final stages of Dracula's disintegration using dummies, balloons, and copious amounts of Fuller's earth (a type of fine clay powder).

When the film was screened for the British Board of Film Classification, the censorship board demanded that cuts be made. Shots of Lucy's staking were trimmed, as were shots of Dracula seducing and biting Mina, and the more graphic shots of Dracula's disintegration. On April 15, 1958, the film was passed with an *X* certificate, classifying it in the UK as being for adults only.

Dracula had its premiere at the Gaumont, Haymarket, on May 20, 1958. A giant billboard outside was rigged to continuously drip blood from Dracula's lips through ingenious trip-lighting. At peak hours, audiences lined up for a quarter of a mile beyond the box office; the film earned more than any movie shown at the Gaumont since its opening in 1925.

Universal Pictures obtained the distribution rights for the United States, changing the title for American audiences so as not to confuse it with their 1931 *Dracula*. The newly christened *Horror of Dracula* reached New York's Mayfair Theater at the end of May 1958. British actors Peter Cushing and Christopher Lee, along with Anthony Hinds and James Carreras, traveled to New York on May 25, 1958, to help promote the May 29th premiere, signing autographs at the eleven thirty a.m. and seven forty-five p.m. showings. During the trip, Cushing celebrated his forty-fifth birthday (May 26) at the top of the Empire State Building, while Lee celebrated his thirty-sixth birthday (May 27) at a press conference arranged by Universal Pictures, where he was presented with a cake.

For American audiences used to the black-and-white no-visible-fangs approach of Bela Lugosi, Lon Chaney Jr., and John Carradine, the impact of seeing Christopher Lee's Dracula in red-eyed, blood-dripping-from-pointed-teeth Technicolor was shocking. In a letter to the *New York Times*, Manfred George (the editor of *Aufbau*, a journal for German-speaking Jews) wrote that as "a fanatic moviegoer" he'd seen numerous films, but "none has ever disgusted me as much as *Horror of Dracula*." He described what he witnessed at a preview of the film:

> A boy of eight who sat in the same row with me became hysterical with fear and had to be led out by his mother. On the other side of the aisle, two children crouched low under the seats to escape the impact of horror emanating from the screen. In the rear, a little girl suddenly began to scream; she too left the movie house with her parents soon after.

The film remained at the Mayfair well into June.

Horror of Dracula came to Chicago's Oriental Theater on Friday, June 20, 1958, paired—as in some New York showings—with *The Thing That Couldn't Die*. With this latest version of *Dracula* a success, Hammer began promoting itself as "the company that is putting fresh blood into the film industry."

Some countries got more blood than others. Japanese audiences saw shots cut from Dracula's seduction of Mina, and a shot of him clawing at his face as he fades to dust that were denied British audiences. The film was restored by the British Film Institute in 2007. Afterwards, the final four reels, comprising the final forty minutes of the film with many of the "lost" scenes intact, were discovered in Japan. Once restored, they were added to the BFI restoration for release on Blu-ray in the UK in March of 2013.

With the release of *Horror of Dracula*, Christopher Lee became recognized as the new king of horror cinema, a reputation he cemented with his portrayal of *The Mummy* for Hammer in 1959. That same year, he played a "straight" role as Sir Henry in Hammer's *The Hound of the Baskervilles*, with Peter Cushing as a first-rate Sherlock Holmes, a role that would later be played by Lee himself. Lee and Cushing appeared together frequently in horror films over the next twenty-five years, until 1983's *House of the Long Shadows*, in which they co-starred with American horror stars Vincent Price and John Carradine.

The Brides of Dracula

Even as Christopher Lee and Peter Cushing were traveling to New York to promote *Horror of Dracula*, Hammer was already preparing a sequel to their Frankenstein film, and also a sequel to Dracula, to be called "Disciple of Dracula." The new horror stars realized that they had inherited the mantle of Boris Karloff and Bela Lugosi. Christopher Lee, well aware of how Lugosi's association with Dracula had typecast him, decided to prove his abilities in other roles before putting on Dracula's black cloak again; a sequel with Lee would have to wait seven years.

Instead, Lee appeared as a vampire in Italian director Stefano Vanzina's comedy *Tempi duri per i vampiri* (*Hard Times for Vampires*) in the spring of 1959.

Lee did not play Dracula, but rather Baron Roderigo de Braumfürten. Also known as *Uncle Was a Vampire*, the film was met with a chilly reception when it opened in Rome in October, with the reviewer for *Intermezzo* writing, "The director attempts to disguise the weakness of the comedy with a parade of beautiful women, but even the participation of specialist Christopher Lee doesn't produce the desired result."

In the summer of 1960, Universal was clamoring for the promised sequel to *Horror of Dracula*. With Christopher Lee refusing to return to the role, Anthony Hinds put a new vampire film into production. He dusted off Jimmy Sangster's script for "Disciple of Dracula," and had *The Hound of the Baskervilles* scriptwriter Peter Bryan redraft it in a way that totally removed Dracula from the proceedings. Peter Cushing was unsatisfied with the changes, so a third writer, Edward Percy, was brought in for a polish. To Hammer's relief, Cushing now signed on.

The Brides of Dracula was unusual in that instead of further chronicling the adventures of the vampire king, it focused instead on a new exploit of his adversary, Van Helsing. A prologue explains that while Dracula has been destroyed, his many disciples are still perpetrating his evil. *The Brides of Dracula* presented David Peel as Baron Meinster, a kind of Dracula-lite, who succeeds where Dracula failed in *Horror of Dracula*—in a climactic battle with Van Helsing inside a windmill, Meinster manages to put the bite on the vampire hunter. Van Helsing effectively cures himself with the aid of a red-hot metal rod and holy water before setting the mill ablaze and creating a giant shadow of a cross with the mill's windmill vanes, destroying Meinster.

The Brides of Dracula opened at the Odeon Marble Arch on July 4. It made its way to America two months later, opening in New York on September 5, 1960, on a double bill with *The Cossacks*. In Los Angeles, the film was paired on a double bill with *The Leech Woman*. In both cities, the film garnered disappointing reviews.

Hammer's horror productions generally earned back their cost on their London release alone; the rest was profit. By the mid-1960s, Hammer owned its own studios, controlled its own finance and had distribution deals with both Columbia Pictures and Universal. James Carreras found it profitable to follow a "bread and butter formula" of making two films a year for $450,000 each.

Prince of Darkness

On Wednesday, December 16, 1964, a double bill of *The Curse of Frankenstein* and *Horror of Dracula* opened in New York City. On February 10, 1965, the horror combo landed on twenty screens in Los Angeles. On both coasts, the double feature did good business. The box-office returns of the *Horror of Dracula* re-release showed Hammer that there were still profits to be derived from the character, so the studio decided to once again pursue turning Dracula into a franchise, as they had with their Frankenstein films starring Peter Cushing (which, unlike the Universal series of the 1930s and '40s, followed the exploits

Dracula—Prince of Darkness (1966) was filmed on the same sets that were used for *Rasputin: The Mad Monk*, which was shot immediately afterwards to save costs.
© *1966 Hammer Film Productions/Warner Bros./ Seven Arts. Courtesy of Del Valle Archives.*

of Dr. Victor Frankenstein rather than the exploits of his monster). Given the disappointing reception of *Brides of Dracula*, the studio realized that in order to create a Dracula series, they would need to secure the services of Christopher Lee. In the years since the actor had starred in *Horror of Dracula*, however, his star status and salary had increased. Consequently, Hammer decided that for the next film, like Lee's first, he would get paid on a daily rate, with his participation in the film kept to a minimum. He also received a small percentage of the producer's gross.

The new Dracula film was announced to the trades as "The Disciple of Dracula," the title of the script that had become *The Brides of Dracula.* The script was actually the one prepared years before for the proposed sequel, "The Revenge of Dracula." When refurbishment of Bray Studios caused the production to be delayed, Peter Cushing had to bow out of the cast. The scenes with Van Helsing were rewritten for Father Sandor, played by Andrew Keir. By the time the film finished shooting, so little of Jimmy Sangster's original script remained that he replaced his name in the credits with a pseudonym, "John Sansom."

The film went into production in 1965 as "Dracula III" (the film title on the clapperboards was simply "Dracula"), scheduled so that the same crew and much of the cast could go immediately from the Dracula film into another picture, *Rasputin—the Mad Monk,* made on the same sets. Terence Fisher again took up the directing reins, in a story that involved four travelers happening upon Dracula's castle. Once revived, Christopher Lee's Dracula becomes a demonic presence, but one without dialogue. In interviews, Sangster maintained that he had not written any dialogue for Lee; Lee maintained that the dialogue was so ludicrous he refused to speak it. Whatever the case, the end result—Dracula hissing like a rabid cat—was disappointing.

At the film's climax, Dracula stands atop his frozen moat until Father Sandor shoots the ice surrounding him, causing the piece upon which Dracula is standing to break free and tilt up, depositing the vampire in the freezing water. The scene was truly agonizing for Lee; while filming it, one of his red contact lenses popped out. It was hastily reinserted, with some of the salt from the fake ice still clinging to it, which irritated his eye to no end. Stuntman Eddie Powell, doubling Lee, fared worse when he did the fall into the water; he nearly drowned when he was temporarily trapped under the faux ice.

On Wednesday, April 13, 1966, 20th Century-Fox released a double bill of *Dracula, Prince of Darkness* and *The Plague of the Zombies* to theaters and drive-ins throughout Los Angeles. In the *Los Angeles Times*, reviewer Kevin Thomas called *Dracula, Prince of Darkness* a "handsomely-mounted movie," saying, "It is always rewarding to discover a high degree of polished professionalism in a picture aimed deliberately at the most undiscriminating audiences." The double feature hit New York screens on Wednesday, May 4, 1966.

Rising from the Grave

The next entry in the Dracula series began shooting on April 22, 1968, at Pinewood Studios rather than Bray Studios. Just four days earlier, it was announced that Hammer had been honored with the Queen's Award to Industry. The award was formally presented by the Lord Lieutenant of the County of Buckinghamshire on May 29, as Lee filmed his death throes impaled on a cross, struggling "like a fly on a pin." As the actor recalled, after the Lord Lieutenant and his wife, who had never been in a studio before, watched his death throes without any expression at all on their faces, there was a prolonged

May 29, 1968—the directors, executives, and production heads of Hammer Films, along with Christopher Lee (top row, left, in Dracula suit) and Peter Cushing (bottom row, seated second from left) on the occasion of Hammer receiving the Queen's Award to Industry.   *Author's collection*

silence and then, very clearly and penetratingly, the Lord Lieutenant turned to his wife and said, "You know, my dear, that man is a member of my club."

The script was by Hammer producer Anthony Hinds, writing under the *nom de plume* of "John Elder." The actual producer, however, was Aida Young, one of only a small number of women producers in the industry at the time. Young had worked as an assistant director on the 1955 Hammer film *The Quatermass Xperiment*, and then segued into TV as production supervisor on *The New Adventures of Charlie Chan* (1957–58), and *Danger Man* (1960–61). She returned to Hammer as associate producer of *She*, with Ursula Andress and Peter Cushing, rising to producer with its sequel, *The Vengeance of She*. In 1968, Young took charge of Hammer's Dracula series.

The director was to have been Terence Fisher, but when Fisher broke his leg in a car crash, the reins were handed over to Freddie Francis. Francis began his career as a cinematographer with 1956's *Hell in Korea* and went on to photograph the classic *Saturday Night and Sunday Morning* (1960) and *Sons and Lovers* (also 1960, for which he won the Academy Award for Best Black-and-White Cinematography) before turning to directing full-time in the early 1960s. He made several films for Hammer, including 1964's *The Evil of Frankenstein*, before taking up the reins of the new Dracula film. In the 1980s, he returned to camerawork, photographing *The Elephant Man* (1980), *The French Lieutenant's Woman* (1981), *Dune* (1984), and *Glory* (1989, for which he won his second Best Cinematography Oscar), among other prestigious films.

The new Dracula film was positioned for a young demographic, with the protagonists, Paul and Maria, being in their early twenties (the next two films in the series also had a youthful protagonist named Paul). The film also rewrote some of the established vampire mythos. Now, it was not enough to simply drive a stake in the vampire's heart; the vampire hunter had to be devoutly religious, and say a prayer. Otherwise, Dracula could remove the stake and instantly heal. Christopher Lee loudly voiced his displeasure at such tinkering with the legend, and played the scene under protest.

Christopher Lee objected to this scene in 1968's *Dracula Has Risen from the Grave*, in which the vampire is staked but, rather than disintegrate into dust, is able to remove the stake from his chest because Paul (Barry Andrews), an atheist, can't bring himself to say a prayer after doing the deed.   *Author's collection*

By the time it was finished, the new Dracula film carried the title *Dracula Has Risen from the Grave*. As with *Dracula, Prince of Darkness*, the vampire's role in the proceedings was minimal, but at least this film gave him some melodramatic dialogue, the first time Lee had spoken as Dracula since the opening scenes of 1958's *Horror of Dracula* a decade earlier. The vampire's attire also changed; his cape was now lined with scarlet, and Lee wore a ring which had been given to him by Forrest J Ackerman, editor of *Famous Monsters of Filmland* magazine, which was a duplicate of the one worn by Bela Lugosi in his 1931 *Dracula*. Lee wore the ring in all of his subsequent Hammer Dracula films.

Dracula (Christopher Lee) has the lovely Maria (Veronica Carlson) in his clutches. Besides being Hammer's biggest moneymaker, 1968's *Dracula Has Risen from the Grave* was the very first film given a rating by the Motion Picture Association of America in the U.S. under their newly introduced ratings system; it earned a "G."

© 1968 Hammer Film Productions/ Warner Bros./ Seven Arts. Author's collection.

Their affiliation with Universal having ended, *Dracula Has Risen from the Grave* was released by Warner Bros.-Seven Arts with a campy poster campaign that showed a close-up of Veronica Carlson's neck (and cleavage) with two band-aids over her jugular vein, and the caption, "Dracula has risen from the grave . . . obviously!"

On March 26, 1969, the film opened in New York, where critic Howard Thompson wrote in the *New York Times*, "*Dracula Has Risen from the Grave*. Yes, again. And judging by this junky British film in color—asplatter with catchup or paint or whatever, to simulate the Count's favorite color—he can descend again."

Trading on his Dracula image, Christopher Lee appeared in red-lined cape and black bowtie as "the ship's vampire" in the 1969 psychedelic comedy *The Magic Christian*, starring Peter Sellers and Ringo Starr. Lee maintained that he didn't play Dracula, since he didn't wear his gray wig and since, instead of Dracula's black coat, he wore a tuxedo and bow-tie. He also had a cameo in 1970's *One More Time*, starring Sammy Davis Jr. and Peter Lawford. In this Jerry Lewis–directed sequel to *Salt & Pepper* (1968), Sammy Davis Jr. enters a dungeon and encounters Dracula (Lee), Baron Frankenstein (played by Peter Cushing) a hunchback, and Frankenstein's Monster.

Lee played Dracula again in 1970, but not for Hammer. *El Conde Dracula*, or *Count Dracula*, was a Spanish/Italian/English/West German co-production produced by Harry Alan Towers (who had produced five films featuring Christopher Lee as Sax Rohmer's Asian supervillain Fu Manchu) and directed by Jess Franco. Filmed in Barcelona, with some castle shots lensed in France, the film featured Herbert Lom as Van Helsing (a role originally meant for Vincent Price, who was unavailable), and Klaus Kinski as Renfield. It was intended to be a more authentic version of Bram Stoker's novel, but despite the filmmakers' good intentions, the production was undercut by budget limitations and director Jesús Franco's love of the zoom lens. Nonetheless, Lee was content that he finally had a chance to portray the character as written, as an old man who becomes progressively younger as the film unspools.

Taste the Blood of Dracula

With *Dracula Has Risen from the Grave* a success, Hammer immediately began work on the next film in their series. Again scripted by "John Elder" (Anthony Hinds), *Taste the Blood of Dracula* had the vampire revived by a London disciple played by Ralph Bates. Indeed, when it appeared that Lee wouldn't do the film, the script was rewritten to make Bates's Lord Courtley the vampire of the story. The distributors, Warner Bros., weren't interested in a Dracula film without Lee, so Hammer had to talk their reluctant star into returning. In the end, they resorted to emotional blackmail. Michael Carreras, now managing director of Hammer, called Lee at home, and told him that the company already

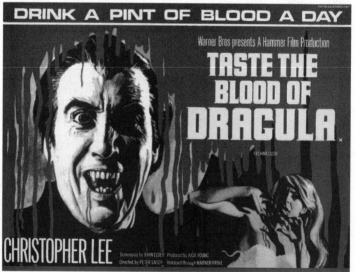

The poster campaigns for both 1968's *Dracula Has Risen from the Grave* and 1970's *Taste the Blood of Dracula* employ a cheeky humor completely out of keeping with the tone of the films themselves; this one satirizes the tag line from a then-popular "drink milk" public service ad campaign.

Author's collection

had a deal with Warner Bros. and if Lee didn't do the film it would put a great many people out of work. The tactic worked on both the new film and the ones that followed it.

The film was directed by Peter Sasdy, a Hungarian-born director of British television, making his feature-film debut. Shooting commenced at Elstree Studios on October 27, 1969. "We had the best cast of any of the Dracula films," Lee told *Starlog* magazine's Bill Kelley. "When actors like Geoffrey Keen, Roy Kinnear, Peter Sallis and Gwen Watford are prepared to be in the movie, who am I to say no?" The film was released in the UK on May 7, 1970.

Hammer produced *Taste the Blood of Dracula* for Warner Bros. to distribute worldwide, with the entire $480,000 production cost underwritten by Warner Bros. Hammer, however, received half the profits. The film appeared in America in September 1970, playing on a double bill with *Trog*, a film about a revived caveman starring Joan Crawford in her final role.

Christopher Lee bares his fangs for 1970's *Scars of Dracula*. On his pinky is a replica of the "Dracula crest" ring worn by Bela Lugosi, given to Lee by Forrest J Ackerman, editor of *Famous Monsters of Filmland*, visually linking Lee to his predecessor.
© *1970 Hammer Film Productions and EMI Films. Author's collection.*

Scars of Dracula

The next entry in the Hammer series, *Scars of Dracula*, attempted to put the character of Dracula back into the center of the film. With Anthony Hinds again scripting as "John Elder," it went into production on May 11, 1970, just four days after the UK release of *Taste the Blood of Dracula*. The new entry gave Christopher Lee more screen time and dialogue than any of his other Hammer Dracula films. There was also a token attempt to return to the spirit of Bram Stoker's character, with a shot of Dracula scaling the castle wall as in Stoker's novel, the first time this had ever been depicted on-screen. Lee's Dracula was at his most sadistic and savage in this film, which also featured the topless nudity that was becoming a staple of horror films in the more permissive 1970s. Its UK release came on October 8, 1970, just five months after *Taste the Blood of Dracula*.

Released by Continental in the U.S., *Scars of Dracula* made its way into theaters at year's end, opening on a double bill with *Horror of Frankenstein*, with Ralph Bates taking over the role of the Doctor previously played by Peter Cushing. The double bill made it to New York in mid-June 1971. Howard Thompson, of the *New York Times*, was put off by it, writing, "Avoid *Dracula* like the plague. It's garish, gory junk."

Dracula A.D. 1972

Warner Bros. backed the next Dracula project, tentatively titled "Dracula Chelsea '72." Produced by Josephine Douglas and directed by Alan Gibson, it went before the cameras on September 27, 1971. The script by Don Houghton, written as "Dracula Today," sought to take the vampire out of the nineteenth century and bring him into the present day, presumably in an attempt to make the character more modern and relevant. Christopher Lee had his doubts, stating publicly that he felt it was totally and completely wrong to take Dracula out of the gothic period, and put him in modern times.

The film featured yet another Dracula disciple, this time named Johnny Alucard, resurrecting the vampire in swinging Chelsea, though Dracula remained in the environs of a decrepit church which suggested a more gothic era. The film also returned Peter Cushing to the role of Van Helsing, first in a nineteenth-century prologue (in which he is called Lawrence Van

A British poster for *Dracula A.D. 1972*, done in action-movie style, complete with cool car.

Author's collection

Helsing, not Abraham), then as Van Helsing's twentieth-century grandson, Lorrimer Van Helsing.

During filming, Lee inserted a line of dialogue from Stoker's novel: "You would play your brains against mine . . . against me, who has commanded nations!" The actor told Donald Glut, author of *The Dracula Book*, "I did so deliberately, in a desperate attempt at putting in one line from the original Stoker book as a tribute to the author to show him that, as far as I was concerned, his original characterization is very much alive to me. . . . It was my tribute to the author as a desperate cry from the heart that at least I'm trying to get something original into this."

Unlike the previous Dracula films, which were superbly scored in a classical style by James Bernard (except for *The Brides of Dracula*, which was scored by Malcolm Williamson), *Dracula A.D. 1972* suffered from a modern score, provided by Mike Vickers, a former member of the Manfred Mann band who conducted the orchestra for the Beatles' famous worldwide-by-satellite TV performance of "All You Need Is Love." His music for

The sins of the forebears are visited upon the granddaughter in *Dracula A.D. 1972*, when the vampire (Christopher Lee) gets his revenge on Van Helsing by threatening the vampire hunter's modern-day descendant, Jessica Van Helsing (Stephanie Beacham).
© 1970 Hammer Film Productions/ Warner Bros.
Courtesy of Del Valle Archives.

Dracula A.D. 1972 sounded more appropriate for a TV cop show of the 1970s. On the other hand, since part of the plot centered on Police Inspector Murray (Michael Coles) investigating the mysterious murders of Johnny Alucard's acolytes, perhaps the music was fitting; after all, the film played like a police procedural with Dracula shoe-horned in.

Dracula A.D. 1972 was promoted with two unusual featurettes. One showed a bit of behind-the-scenes footage of the filming of the prologue. The other, called *Horror Ritual*, had Barry Atwater, fresh from his success as the vampire of TV's *The Night Stalker*, playing Count Dracula leading moviegoers into a pledge to initiate them into the Count Dracula Society. Atwater was seen in a black widow's peak wig, fangs, and a pasty white face; he later admitted that he

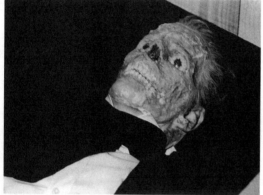

Dracula (Christopher Lee) in his coffin, and a dummy prepared for the vampire's demise at the finale of Jesus Franco's 1970 film *Count Dracula.*

*© 1970 Variety Communications.
Courtesy of Del Valle Archives.*

thought the makeup was atrocious, and he didn't enjoy doing the promo, but he did enjoy the money he was paid.

Dracula A.D. 1972 was released in the UK on October 1, 1972. In the U.S., it was paired with *Crescendo* (1969), director Alan Gibson's first film, comprising a double bill that opened in New York on Wednesday, November 29, 1972. Roger Greenspun, reviewing the films for the *New York Times,* wrote, "Gibson, who started weak, seems to be going downhill."

At the end of May 1973, a more modest vampire film opened at New York's Film Forum Theater. *Vampir,* a film by Pedro Portabella, was a behind-the-scenes look at the filming of Jess Franco's *Count Dracula* that was a languid, experimental meditation on both vampirism and filmmaking.

Satanic Rites

The next entry in the series bore the working title "Dracula is Dead . . . and Well and Living in London." Again directed by Alan Gibson, it began filming on November 13, 1972. The new film had Van Helsing once again teaming with Inspector Murray (Michael Coles) to expose a plot by a once-again revived Count Dracula, now masquerading as the head of a corporation and plotting to destroy mankind with a viral plague (a plot similar to 1971's James Bond film *Diamonds Are Forever,* in which 007's arch-villain, Ernst Stavro Blofeld, has taken the place of a Howard Hughes–type aerospace tycoon). The film once again starred Peter Cushing and, in his final appearance in a Hammer Dracula film, Christopher Lee, who had become more and more disenchanted with the treatment of the character.

"Dracula is Dead . . . and Well and Living in London" completed filming at Elstree Studios on January 3, 1973, fifteen years to the day since Lee's first

Dracula wrapped at Bray Studios. Before its release, the film's title was changed to *The Satanic Rites of Dracula.* It hit UK theaters in January 1974, but didn't receive an American release until 1978, under the title *Count Dracula and His Vampire Bride.*

After appearing in seven Dracula films for Hammer, Christopher Lee decided to hang up his cape.

Lee did, however, make a record for Hammer/EMI in 1974 in which he narrated a truncated version of *Dracula*, adapted by Don Houghton and scored by James Bernard. Though honored to be called a great horror film star, which he felt put him in distinguished company with Bela Lugosi, Boris Karloff, Peter Cushing, Vincent Price, Lon Chaney Jr., and others, he nonetheless regarded many of his own films as rubbish. As the 1970s progressed, he sought more "straight" roles, such as the English blacksmith in the Raquel Welch Western *Hannie Caulder* (1971), or Rochefort in *The Three Musketeers* (1973) and *The Four Musketeers* (1974), or Scaramanga in the James Bond film *The Man With the Golden Gun* (1974).

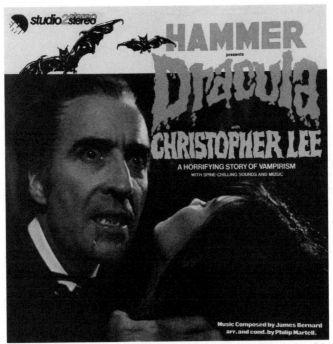

Christopher Lee narrated a shortened version of *Dracula* for this Hammer/EMI recording in 1974. In recent years, Lee has released recordings of heavy metal music. His Christmas song, "Jingle Hell," entered the *Billboard* Hot 100 chart at number twenty-two, making Lee, then ninety-one years old, the oldest performer to ever enter the charts. *Author's collection*

Dracula and the Seven Golden Vampires

Still pushing to make a Dracula film every year, Hammer next hit upon the idea of combining Dracula with the then-popular genre of martial arts movies. In collaboration with Hong Kong producer Run Run Shaw, the company made *The Legend of the Seven Golden Vampires*, also known as *Dracula and the Seven Golden Vampires* or *The Seven Brothers and Their One Sister Meet Dracula*. Under any title, it's a disappointing film, with Van Helsing (Peter Cushing's swan song in the role) traveling through China in the early 1900s and finding that the spirit of Dracula (played by John Forbes-Robertson) has possessed a Chinese cult leader. Directed by Roy Ward Baker from a screenplay by Don Houghton, who also produced, *The Legend of the Seven Golden Vampires* proved that gothic vampires mix with martial arts about as well as they do with garlic and holy water.

As *The Legend of the Seven Golden Vampires* was winding down, Hammer announced that the next in the series would be "Kali: Devil Bride of Dracula," based on an Indian religious cult. The film was never made. *The Legend of the Seven Golden Vampires* didn't receive a UK release until nearly a year after it was completed, on October 6, 1974. By then, even Peter Cushing had had enough; *The Legend of the Seven Golden Vampires* was his final Hammer horror film. The vampire/martial arts hybrid didn't receive a U.S. release until September 1979.

Despite his public vow not to play Dracula again, Christopher Lee was seen briefly as the vampire count in the documentary *In Search of Dracula*. In Calvin Floyd's 1975 film adaptation of the book by Raymond McNally and Radu Florescu, Lee also appeared as Vlad III and served as the film's host and narrator. The documentary opened in New York on Wednesday, May 15, 1975. The *New York Times*' A. H. Weiler noted that it was "more scholarly than chilling and hardly a competitor of the late Bela Lugosi and other ersatz Draculas."

On March 16, 1976, Lee appeared at Studios de Billancourt in Paris to begin work on a comedy for director Edouard Molinaro, in which the actor would once again play a vampire. Based on Claude Klotz's novel *Paris-Vampire*, the movie was a droll sendup of vampire conventions. After siring a son, from which he is eventually separated, Lee's character ends up in modern-day London, becoming a film star noted for playing vampires—a character not unlike Christopher Lee. The actor believed the film would be called "Pére et Fils"; he fought against the eventual title of *Dracula Pére et Fils (Dracula Father and Son)*, since his character is never referred to as Dracula. "It is totally misleading," he told an interviewer for *Cinefantastique* magazine. "I do not play the part of Dracula in the picture. . . . The reason I did it was not to parody myself, which I do not do, but because by doing this I can close the door very firmly on the vampire." Indeed, the film did mark Lee's final appearance as a screen bloodsucker, though he appeared on WNYC-AM's *Panorama of the Lively Arts* radio program on November 13, 1977, to discuss his role in the now-titled *Dracula and Son*.

In America, the Hammer horror films were often screened on television in the 1970s on the *CBS Late Movie*, where they scared up a whole new generation of fans. They hit the videocassette market in 1985, with the early October release of *The Curse of Frankenstein, The Mummy*, and *Horror of Dracula*. Many other releases of Lee's Dracula films followed on videotape, DVD, and Blu-ray, culminating with the three-disc release of the restored *Dracula (Horror of Dracula)* in the UK in 2013.

On Tuesday, December 2, 1997, London's Museum of the Moving Image held a tribute to Hammer Films, with attractions such as Dracula's coffin, Frankenstein's Monster, and a replica of Christopher Lee as the Mummy on display. Lee's Dracula cloak was also displayed at the British Film Institute in the late summer and fall of 2013, when the BFI screened *Horror of Dracula* as part of their series *Gothic: The Dark Heart of Film*.

With roles in popular film series like Star Wars and The Lord of the Rings and cameos in several films directed by Tim Burton, Christopher Lee continued to be a busy actor well into the twenty-first century. It seemed that, like Dracula, he had found the secret to immortality, until he was felled by pneumonia at the age of ninety-three on June 7, 2015.

After two divergent interpretations of Dracula, one by Bela Lugosi, who embodied the character in the 1930s and 1940s, and the other by Christopher Lee, who carried the legacy from the 1950s into the 1970s, it might have seemed that there was nothing new to say about Dracula. But the vampire was poised for yet another rebirth; shortly after Christopher Lee bid Dracula *adieu*, the character rebounded, more popular than ever.

12

The Byronic Bloodsucker

Frank Langella

From Broadway to Blighty

A lmost the moment it opened at the Martin Beck Theater on October 20, 1977, the revival of the Hamilton Deane–John L. Balderston version of *Dracula*, the play that had made Bela Lugosi famous fifty years earlier, became a sensation, catapulting Frank Langella into the limelight. By mid-November, Meta-Philm Associates began talks with Langella about starring in a film version of the story. But they weren't the only ones in the running—Walter Mirisch had also seen the play.

Mirisch was one of Hollywood's most prolific producers. With his brothers Marvin and Harold, he formed The Mirisch Company, which got its start in 1947 with the crime thriller *Fall Guy*, starring *King Kong*'s Robert Armstrong. Two years later, he produced the first in a series of *Bomba, The Jungle Boy* adventures starring Johnny Sheffield, who graduated to the starring role after a decade as "Boy" in the Johnny Weissmuller *Tarzan* series. By the 1960s, Mirisch hit his stride producing *The Magnificent Seven*, *The Great Escape*, and the *Pink Panther* series, and won an Academy Award for *In the Heat of the Night*. In 1971, he produced the film version of the stage musical *Fiddler on the Roof*, which collected three Academy Awards. He was a filmmaker with eclectic interests; by the 1970s, his films ranged from the Charles Bronson action thriller *Mr. Majestyk* (1974) to war epic *Midway* (1976) to the Peter Sellers comedy *The Prisoner of Zenda* (1978). Mirisch became a rarity in Hollywood—a man with the power and connections to turn a concept into a major film. Then, on a trip to New York, he took his wife to see the new hit play *Dracula*.

From the moment he saw *Dracula* on stage, Mirisch decided he wanted to make it as a film. He was so impressed by the power and originality of Frank Langella's stage performance that he was convinced that a new film version would only be commercially viable if Langella played the title role. With backing from Universal Pictures, who owned the rights to remake the 1931 *Dracula*, Mirisch began negotiating with the actor. In March 1978, they came to terms.

Mirisch had also chosen a director for the project: John Badham. Born in Luton, England, the son of a U.S. Army general, Badham grew up in Mountain Brook, Alabama, near Birmingham. As a young boy, he read EC horror comics such as *Vault of Horror* and developed an interest in horror films, including Hammer Films' *The Curse of Frankenstein.*

He went on to receive two degrees from Yale, moved to California, got a job in the mailroom at Universal, and rose up to the casting department, finding actors for shows like *Chrysler Theater* and *Run for Your Life.* A producer with whom he worked took him on as an assistant, and Badham eventually became an associate producer of Rod Serling's *Night Gallery*, which was shot at Universal. There, he met Steven Spielberg, who was just beginning his career and directed one of the segments in the show's pilot. Badham began shooting in-

Director John Badham and Frank Langella on the set of *Dracula.* Langella first played Dracula in 1967, at the Berkshire Playhouse in Massachusetts.
© *1979 Universal Pictures. Author's collection.*

serts and pickups for the show to gain directing experience, and then directed six episodes of the series. He also directed an episode of *The Senator* that won him an Emmy nomination. Moving on to TV movies, he directed *Isn't It Shocking?*, and *The Law*, which brought him his second Emmy nomination. After his first feature, *The Bingo Long Traveling All-Stars & Motor Kings* (1976), his next film was *Saturday Night Fever* (1977), an exploration of New York's disco culture that made a film star of TV sitcom heartthrob John Travolta.

Walter Mirisch had been trying to find a project to do with Badham for a few years, and had offered the director *Midway* and *Gray Lady Down*, but neither excited him. After *Saturday Night Fever* made him a hot commodity, Badham spent several months reading scripts, looking for his next project, when Mirisch approached him about *Dracula.* Intrigued, Badham went to New York and saw the play. He was excited by Langella's take on the character, but not so much by the production itself. Nonetheless, he immediately got in touch with Mirisch and agreed to do it.

Since Universal already owned the rights to the Deane-Balderston play, as well as rights to their 1931 film adaptation, it was accepted that the new film would essentially be a remake of the earlier classic. To update it for a 1970s audience, Badham and Mirisch talked to several writers, including playwrights from New York, before Badham turned to screenwriter W. D. Richter, who had just scored critical plaudits for his modern adaptation of *Invasion of the Body Snatchers*. Badham was aware that Richter, known as Rick to his friends, was a horror movie fan who would treat the material with respect. The filmmakers decided early on to eschew the stylized sets of Edward Gorey and go for a more naturalistic approach.

Badham and Richter screened about a dozen of what they thought were the best *Dracula* movies, including the Hammer films, the Bela Lugosi version, Murnau's *Nosferatu*, and *Andy Warhol's Dracula*, examining them to see if they contained any good ideas and also to learn what to avoid. They also read up on all the vampire legends and writings they could get their hands on, as well as Bram Stoker's novel.

Richter made copious notes, organizing them into categories like "Great Quotes from Stoker," and "Great Quotes from Deane and Balderston." He wrote on cards the scenes he thought would be interesting, arranged them into a story, met with Badham to get his input, and then the pair took the story to Walter and Marvin Mirisch. When the producers gave their approval, Richter began writing the screenplay.

Dracula Takes Shape

Badham and Richter stuck to the broad outlines of the play, beginning their story with Dracula's arrival in England rather than having Harker go to the vampire's castle in Transylvania. As in the play, Richter made Lucy—not Mina—Dracula's primary victim. The scriptwriter's biggest change was making Mina the daughter of Van Helsing, who, in this version, is not a professional vampire hunter, but simply a doctor whose daughter is destroyed. Badham felt, naturally, that the first person Dr. Seward would call upon Mina's death would be her father, and making that person Van Helsing gave the character an emotional motivation for wanting Dracula destroyed. Badham and Richter also sought to retain from the play Langella's interpretation of Dracula as an erotic, Byronesque figure. The scriptwriting process took approximately seven months. When the scenario was completed, Universal budgeted the film at $8 million.

As the script took shape, the other featured roles were cast. At the end of May 1978, Laurence Olivier was announced for the role of Van Helsing. Roderick Mann of the *Los Angeles Times* noted that many were surprised that Olivier, known as one of the world's greatest actors, would take on a horror film role. Though it was widely rumored that Olivier was basically taking any part offered him to leave a financial legacy for his family, Mann reported that the actor, in fact, had no money worries. Instead, with his health in decline, he was unable to perform on the stage, and since he couldn't stand being idle, he relished film roles. In any event, *Dracula* proved to be lucrative for him; Olivier was paid eight hundred thousand dollars.

For the co-starring role of Lucy, Canadian-born actress Kate Nelligan, fresh from starring in *Plenty* at London's National Theater, was chosen. Veteran character actor Donald Pleasence, who had just scored a horror film hit with his role as Dr. Loomis in John Carpenter's *Halloween* (1978), was tapped to play Dr. Seward. Up-and-coming British actor Trevor Eve was given the role of Jonathan Harker, and Sylvester McCoy, who would win fame nearly a decade later as TV's *Doctor Who*, had a small role as an asylum attendant.

On July 1st of 1978, Badham and Richter flew to London and began looking for castles and lunatic asylums. Shooting was set to begin on October 1, 1978, with location filming in County Cornwall, where St. Michael's Mount became Dracula's castle and the seaside village of Mevagissey was used for the harbor

at the climax. Camelot Castle Hotel in Tintagel, the birthplace of King Arthur, was used for exteriors of Dr. Seward's asylum. The location shooting was followed by work on four soundstages at Shepperton Studios and two soundstages at Twickenham Studios.

Badham originally wanted to make the film in black and white, so he kept the costumes and sets, as much as possible, in shades of black, white, and gray. Still, the film had richly saturated skin tones when it was released to theaters, but when it was transferred to DVD three decades later, Badham asked that the print be desaturated to make it even more monochrome.

Lensing Langella

In October 1978, just twenty-four hours after his last performance in *Dracula* on Broadway, Langella arrived in Cornwall to begin work on the film. The actor told Peter Travers of the

Lucy (Kate Nelligan) shares a coffin with Dracula (Frank Langella).   © *1979 Universal Pictures. Courtesy of Del Valle Archive.*

New York Times, "It was like jumping into an ice cold bath. I went from a stage production in which I had as much control as any actor can have, into a situation in which I had none at all."

Langella had very definite ideas of how to play Dracula, having done the role on Broadway for so long, but Badham knew some of the mannerisms wouldn't translate well to film, so modifications needed to be made. In some instances, Langella would do a few takes of the scene as he thought it should be played, then he would tone it down for a few takes for Badham, and then the two would compromise with a few "what the hell" takes just to see if any interesting moments came out of the experimentation. As the weeks went by, Langella grew to trust Badham's judgment, so that during the last half of the filming, Badham felt he didn't have to direct Langella at all; the actor had it under control.

During the filming, the crew jokingly referred to seventy-one-year-old Lord Laurence Olivier as "the good Lord." Olivier refused to let Langella call him anything but Larry. In return, the elder actor called his co-star "Sir Langella."

At day's end, Langella and Olivier repaired to their drafty hotel in Tintagel, Cornwall, where they had connecting suites. They began every morning reading newspapers, reminiscing, and trading insider gossip, and dined together at night. In his autobiography, *Dropped Names,* Langella recalled that as Olivier grew more comfortable in his presence, his language became more ribald and he teased his co-star about his "naughty bits." One morning, as Olivier sat reading in Langella's room, Langella streaked stark naked to the bathroom, turning at the door to say to Olivier, "Oh professor, see anything you like?" Olivier howled with laughter, exclaiming "Bravo, dear boy!"

But Olivier would not relent from his regal standing during a photo shoot, where the photographer wanted him to turn his head and look at Langella. "No," snipped Olivier. The photographer then asked Langella to turn and look at Olivier. "No," said Langella. When the photo shoot was finished, Olivier grabbed Langella's arm and said, "You know, Frankie, dear, you're a monster. So am I. It's what you need to be a star."

As shooting progressed, whenever Langella was asked to pose for still photographers, they wanted to light him with red and green gels and asked him to glare and hold his hands out like Bela Lugosi. As time went by, there was also pressure for him to be seen with fangs. But Langella refused such overtures, seeing Dracula as a noble seducer, a man concerned with a certain manner and protocol that was dying in society, not a monster. Badham supported Langella's choice, agreeing that the actor's romantic approach would be undercut by such gimmicks. There were fangs in the picture, very subtly on Lucy and more pronounced on Mina, but none on Dracula.

As filming wore on, there were other disappointments for Langella. He told Gene Siskel of the *Chicago Tribune* that a scene had been dropped from the final cut, in which the vampire and his adversary, Prof. Van Helsing, talk about the problem of being a creature of the night. "It was a very sad and beautiful scene," Langella said. "But it had to go. I think the studio wanted more action."

Langella was also not totally sold on the idea of juicing up Dracula and Lucy's love scene with laser effects. The laser was borrowed from the rock band the Who, letting the production use it on a Sunday. The final sequence, with the lasers and fog augmented by superimposed bats, was designed by Maurice Binder, best known for creating the silhouettes-of-naked-ladies titles of the James Bond films.

In the late 1970s, Olivier endured much ill health—prostate cancer, thrombosis, kidney trouble, and dermatomyositis, which made his skin oversensitve. The seventy-one-year-old actor's frailty sometimes posed problems when it came to filming Van Helsing's more strenuous scenes. For shots of Van Helsing running and leaping, and a brief shot in the climax when he is harpooned by Dracula, Olivier was doubled by his stand-in, Harry, who closely resembled the actor.

Badham was impressed with the work of his special-effects supervisor, Roy Arbogast. For the scene in which Mina was impaled by Van Helsing, Arbogast asked the director if he would like the stake to be seen going in the front and coming out the back in a single, uncut shot. He achieved the effect by making a stake in two separate pieces. The first, a telescoping stake that pushed inward on itself as it was shoved against Mina's stomach, and the second, attached to her back, that was a deflated, collapsible rubber stake that instantly inflated with compressed air at the push of a button. With the timing just right, the two "stakes" worked in tandem to produce a chilling effect.

For the shot of Dracula diving through the window and coming out a wolf, Badham used a split-screen effect, with the right half of the screen being a shot of Langella diving out the window, and the left side being a shot of a wolf leaping out. Filmed separately, the two shots were joined together to produce a seamless shot, but achieving it became a nightmare when the wolf

Dracula meets his end . . . or does he?
© 1979 Universal Pictures. Author's collection.

refused to cooperate and kept wanting to pad his paws down the outside of the building instead of making a mighty jump. As Badham told Roderick Mann of the *Los Angeles Times*, his main headache on the film was "finding wolves that can stare straight into the camera."

Dracula's disintegration at the climax was achieved by simpler means, with Langella made up in four stages of disintegration and cutaways to solar flare footage. Each time the camera cut back to the actor, the makeup was more extreme. In fact, it was filmed with Dracula disintegrating to the point of his skull being exposed and bursting into flames.

The film was slated for a July 1979 release, on Friday the 13th. John Williams, one of the most esteemed composers working in film, was engaged to provide the music. The result was one of the composer's most lush and stunning scores, playing up the romanticism of the movie rather than the horror and suspense.

When the film was previewed at the Academy of Motion Pictures Arts and Science's eleven-hundred-seat theater, the venue was so packed that nearly fifty people were left standing. Originally, the film was to end with Dracula hoisted into the sunlight and burning to a crisp, but at the preview, Sid Sheinberg, the president of MCA, told Badham he had gone too far, killing the star so totally that he couldn't take the next step, which was that maybe he got away. Badham agreed, and decided not to destroy Dracula so completely. The ending was recut with Dracula's cape popping loose and flying away, a more ambiguous ending that raised questions in the audience's collective mind: Was Dracula dead? Was Lucy carrying his child?

Taking Flight

At the end of June 1979, Langella spent two days in Chicago to hype the movie, almost a month in advance of its opening. The film had a preview at the Carnegie Theater in Chicago, and Langella quietly slipped into the theater after it began to see the finished product for the first time. He was shocked that there was less character development than he had hoped, and more horror elements involving Mina. He told Roderick Mann of the *Los Angeles Times*, "I fought for what I believed until a few weeks before the first showing. . . . But the truth is if I'd known how *Dracula* would turn out, I wouldn't have done it. . . . Understand, I did not wish to repeat my stage performance. But I didn't want to be in a horror film, either. They wanted a good deal of horror and violence in the movie, whereas in the play there was none."

Hot off his Broadway success and with the *Dracula* film under his belt, Langella had already lined up another project—*Those Lips, Those Eyes*. Walter Mirsich tried to goad him into signing a three-picture contract, and playwright John Guare was fashioning a new Broadway play for him, *Lydie Breeze*. He was offered more than $1 million to do commercials as Dracula, endorsing everything from candy bars to cars; he turned them down. He embarked on a ten-day national promotion tour, with rounds of constant interviews, which he refused to attend in his Dracula costume, as one of Universal's publicity executives wanted. Langella was adamant about not commercializing his *Dracula*. "It really isn't my philosophy to dress up in costume to sell chewing gum," he told the *Los Angeles Times'* Ellen Farley.

Dracula opened on Friday the 13th of July 1979 on 450 screens. The posters for the film featured a woman reclining on her back, neck bared, with Dracula looming in the clouds over her. A billboard of the poster looked out over Times Square, stretching two city blocks, prompting Langella to quip to Peter Travers of the *New York Times*, "Do you realize that if the film bombs, some guy with a big brush is going to be up on that billboard to wipe off my face?"

Reviews were mixed, with most critics finding the romanticism of Langella's performance and the gore of the horror scenes an uneasy mix. Gene Siskel of the *Chicago Tribune* felt the film was fatally undercut by the casting of the elderly, visibly feeble Laurence Olivier as Van Helsing, which offered too little of a

As with the Bela Lugosi *Dracula* film forty-eight years earlier, posters for 1979's *Dracula* accentuated the romantic aspects of the film as well as the supernatural.   *Author's collection*

challenge to the vampire. "Give us a credible Von Helsing [*sic*]," wrote Siskel, "and this *Dracula* might have been something special."

After playing Dracula, Langella was deluged with offers to repeat the role, all of which he refused. John Badham also turned down all overtures to do a follow-up, telling Steve Mitchell of *Fantastic Films*, "I don't do sequels."

When the Academy of Science Fiction, Fantasy and Horror Films held its seventh annual Science Fiction Film Awards at Metromedia Studios in July of 1980, the three thousand members bestowed Best Horror Film honors on *Dracula*. But Langella lost for Best Actor; that award went to George Hamilton for *Love at First Bite*. Langella shrugged it off. The last thing he wanted was to be forever associated with *Dracula*. He told *Us* magazine's Jean Cox Penn and Jill Barber, "Mr. Lugosi went on and played it the rest of his life. He died in 1956 at seventy-three, and his last words were: 'I blame it all on *Dracula*.' It won't be that way with me."

13

A Feast of Blood

Francis Ford Coppola's *Dracula*

Hart of Dracula

In 1977, screenwriter James V. Hart, having given up producing low-budget films in favor of writing his own scripts, began working on a new screenplay: *Dracula*. Anne Rice's *Interview with the Vampire* had just come out the year before, and Hart decided to pick up Bram Stoker's novel to see where it all started. The version he picked up was *The Annotated Dracula*, with copious notes by *Dracula* scholar Leonard Wolf. Hart took particular notice of the novel's ending, which explained that Mina had taken her son back to where the vampire was destroyed years earlier by Jonathan Harker, Van Helsing, and Lucy's suitors. This seemed inexplicable to Hart, leading him to theorize that perhaps the boy was Dracula's son. He combined that idea with a supposedly true story about a woman whom the historical Dracula, Vlad III, had loved. According to legend, while Vlad was fighting the Turks on the battlefield, his lover received a message that he had been killed. Heartbroken, she threw herself off the battlements, falling to her death. Combining those two ideas with Stoker's novel excited Hart. He felt it pointed a way toward a film that had never been made, and should be.

Hart wanted to tell *Dracula* more from a woman's point of view than a man's, making it Mina's story instead of Jonathan Harker's or Dracula's. Hart noted that most Dracula films were based not on the novel but rather on the Deane-Balderston play. The original novel, he discovered, was not only erotic, but had a great action-adventure story. "Dracula was not just this campy blood-sucking monster," Hart told Ryan Murphy of the *Los Angeles Times*. "The story was about how this great character came to London to establish this new race and find real love again."

Hart recalled that every couple of months or so, his agents would call and ask him what he wanted to do next. Whenever he answered *Dracula*, they'd say, "It's been done." Despite a vampire revival, one that saw several other vampire scripts go into development, no one wanted to bother with that old chestnut.

On October 20, 1977, Hart attended the opening night of the play *Dracula* starring Frank Langella. Like his screenplay, it put the emphasis on the erotic

Director Francis Ford Coppola is pictured giving advice to an impeccably attired Gary Oldman for 1992's *Bram Stoker's Dracula*.

© 1992 Columbia Pictures Corporation.
Courtesy of Del Valle Archive

aspects of the character, further piquing Hart's interest. There was a busload of women sitting in front of him, and when Langella's Dracula threw Lucy on the bed and took her, one of the women said out loud, "I'd rather spend one night with Dracula dead than the rest of my life alive with my husband." Hart thought that erotic aspect needed to come to the screen. But when the stage play was made into a film, and George Hamilton spoofed the character in *Love at First Bite*, it was a death knell to Hart's script . . . for a while. As any Dracula fan knows, you can't keep a good Count down.

In the 1980s, Hart spent a lot of time in "development hell" with various projects, but from time to time he returned to his *Dracula* screenplay. After writing *Hook*, a modern take on Peter Pan (later made by director Steven Spielberg), he decided to dive into *Dracula* once more. At that time, producer/director Michael Apted (best known for his *7-Up* series of documentaries) and his Osiris Films partner, Robert O'Connor, came on board and helped search for a studio to produce the script. All they got were rejections.

The only production company to show any interest was Wilshire Court, known for making small, low-budget made-for-TV movies, most of them airing on the USA cable network. The project was set up there in July of 1990. However, even the executives at Wilshire Court had their reservations. They felt Hart's script, as written, would be too expensive to produce. It was full of special-effects scenes, including six transformations for Dracula. They gave Hart six months to see if he could set it up elsewhere. If not, they would start paring it down to make it a TV movie. Wilshire Court's projected budget was a mere $3.5 million; it was thought that Steven Bauer or Roddy McDowall might play Dracula and Van Helsing, respectively.

Ryder to the Rescue

On a fall weekend in 1990, Winona Ryder sat down and began leafing through a stack of ten scripts. Having made her first film, *Lucas* (1986), at age fifteen, Ryder had moved into the ranks of A-list stars, with roles in *Beetlejuice* (1988), *Heathers* (1988), and *Edward Scissorhands* (1990). While making the latter film, she began a romance with her co-star, Johnny Depp.

She was supposed to have played the part of Michael Corleone's daughter, Mary, in director Francis Ford Coppola's *The Godfather, Part III* in 1990. But having just made two films back-to-back, *Mermaids* and *Welcome Home, Roxy Carmichael*, the exhausted actress developed flu-like symptons and had to drop out after one day of shooting. The director replaced Ryder with his own daugh-

ter, Sofia, a move that was roundly criticized. Coppola didn't want Ryder to feel responsible; he let her know that he still wanted to work with her, and invited her to bring him potential screenplays.

Now she picked up a script and, as she recalled when interviewed by Denise Barricklow of the *St. Petersburg Times*, "When I saw the title *Dracula*, I thought, 'No way.' But then when I read it, I found it to be this really emotional love story." Ryder later confessed to Alex Patterson of the *Toronto Globe and Mail* that although she'd read Stoker's novel growing up and liked it, she'd never seen a Dracula movie, except for a little of the original *Nosferatu*.

Dracula particularly intrigued Ryder because now, at age nineteen, she wanted to play more adult roles. The sexually awakening Mina of Hart's script would allow her to make an onscreen transition from girlhood to womanhood. To help assuage her guilt over dropping out of *The Godfather*,

Mina (Winona Ryder) is wooed by Prince Vlad (Gary Oldman) in 1992's *Bram Stoker's Dracula*.
© *1992 Columbia Pictures Corporation.*
Author's collection.

Part III, she sent the script to Francis Ford Coppola, seeking his advice on whether it was a role she should do. Coppola called Ryder and told her she was absolutely right for the part. He then asked who was going to direct. Three days later, he was attached to the project, and with his commitment it instantly went from TV movie to feature film status.

Coppola was attracted to Hart's script because of its faithfulness to Bram Stoker's original book, but his reasons for becoming involved were as practical as they were artistic. Since the one-two punch of *The Godfather* (1972) and *The Godfather, Part II* (1974), both Academy Award winners, Coppola was regarded as one of Hollywood's most enigmatic directors. His childhood was similar to Bram Stoker's, marked by closeness to a mother who filled his imagination with stories, and a crippling childhood disease. In Coppola's case, it was polio, which he contracted at age ten. He had to stay home for a year, during which he talked mostly to his sister. He became interested in puppets, building a puppet theater; the only time he saw people was when the family came together for parties. Food came out, everyone laughed, and there was a sense of serenity he spent much of his adult life trying to recapture; it resonates through the scenes of family gatherings in the *Godfather* saga and many of his other films.

He won critical accolades for *The Conversation* (1974), and then spent the next five years on his Vietnam-themed adaptation of Joseph Conrad's *Heart of Darkness*, 1979's *Apocalypse Now*, a film so intense that during its 238 days of filming in the Philippine jungles, star Martin Sheen suffered a heart attack. Coppola produced *Apocalypse Now* through his own company, American Zoetrope, investing his own money into it. He was nearly ruined making the film, but when it was released, it earned $150 million, salvaging American Zoetrope.

Back on his feet, he took the plunge again and self-financed his next film, a musical set in Las Vegas called *One from the Heart* (1982). This time the gamble didn't pay off. American Zoetrope went under, taking Coppola with it. The next decade, said the director, was "financial terror," during which he often went to bed in his Napa Valley house not knowing if it would still be his the next day.

After the spotty performances of films like *Gardens of Stone* (1987), *Tucker: The Man and His Dreams* (1988), and *New York Stories* (1989), Coppola needed to make a film that would connect with a mass audience to put him back in favor with the studios. After years of resisting appeals to do a second sequel to *The Godfather*, he finally relented and made *The Godfather, Part III*.

His earnings from the film—$5 million plus 15 percent of the gross—allowed Coppola to put aside some savings, which he said was a first, and to bail American Zoetrope out of bankruptcy. Now out of debt, he decided to start pursuing a strategy of partnering with studios rather than taking all the risk himself.

American Zoetrope's partner on *Dracula* would be Columbia Pictures, whose chairman, Frank Price, greenlighted the script and put up a budget of $40 million. Coppola pitched it to Columbia as a *Dracula* with youth appeal, a vision which Price felt would be very commercial.

Isolating the Team

The director originally wanted to make *Dracula* on a smaller, more experimental scale, using fewer expensive sets, more darkness, more projections, and costing $10 million less. The studio pushed for something more mainstream. "Trying to make a big-budget film is like trying to draw with a five-hundred-foot-long pencil," Coppola said in an interview with Jay Carr of the *Boston Globe*. "You sit there and you try to control it and do it, but you end up drawing a simple Mickey Mouse because you can't draw anything more complex."

Coppola's peers questioned why such a distinguished director would take on such pulpy material. His response was that although it had been made about fifty times, it had never been made like the Stoker book. To signal that his vision would be a return to the novel, he insisted on including the author's name in the film's title: *Bram Stoker's Dracula*.

The director had a personal connection to the story. When he was in his teens, he was the drama counselor at a summer camp in upstate New York. Since he wasn't allowed to visit his girlfriend at another camp until the eight-year-old boys he was minding went to sleep, he read to them at night, and the book he read was *Dracula*. They would listen, get scared, and go to sleep.

Coppola wasn't entirely a horror novice. In his youth, he enjoyed Universal Pictures' monster movies, particularly *House of Dracula* (1945) with John Carradine, and one of the first films he directed was an ultra-low-budget horror film for producer Roger Corman, 1963's *Dementia 13*.

Although he insisted on calling it *Bram Stoker's Dracula*, Coppola set about reshaping Hart's script to reinterpret it as Francis Ford Coppola's *Dracula*—a kind of lush visual opera, an erotic nightmare both campy and terrifying, modern yet nostalgic.

Coppola was particularly interested in the fact that the story was set in 1898, around the time of the dawn of cinema. He thought it would be interesting if, at a time when computer-generated imaging was the new standard in visual effects, he returned to the style of the early cinema and had all the special effects done optically in the camera, with double exposures, reverse motion, and mirrors.

In early 1991, Coppola began to assemble his team. Already on board was American Zoetrope's research director, Anahid Nazarian, who operated out of a hundred-year-old carriage house on Coppola's Napa Valley vineyard. Nazarian immersed herself in the minutia of the nineteenth century, creating over two hundred clip files brimming with articles and illustrations on everything from early typewriters to asylum practices to syphilis. Her "Harem" file contained information on Turkish and Persian art which would inspire the design of the boudoir where Jonathan Harker is seduced by three vampire women.

He also reached out to Jim Steranko, a comic-book artist and painter who was then the editor and publisher of *Prevue* magazine, to brainstorm ideas for freshening up Dracula's look. To design the costumes, the director turned to Eiko Ishioka, with whom he had previously collaborated for a segment of

Shelley Duvall's *Faerie Tale Theatre*. As Ishioka set to work, she contacted Zoetrope research director Nazarian to request photos of insects, exotic flowers, dragons, African tribal masks, and human sperm.

Coppola brought scriptwriter James V. Hart, Steranko, Ishioka, and others who were joining the creative team to the American Zoetrope headquarters in San Francisco, fostering the collegial atmosphere that would continue throughout the filming.

Coppola's son Roman (named after director Roman Polanski), who was to serve as both second-unit director and visual effects director, said that inspirations for the film's images came from such diverse sources as Renaissance genius Botticelli (for the scenes in fifteenth-century Transylvania) to pre-Raphaelite poet/artist Dante Rosetti and nineteenth- and twentieth-century painter/designer Gustav Klimt (for scenes set in the London of Bram Stoker). The movie was infused with Symbolist images—the peacock, the clock, the obelisk, the nude woman, the griffin. The film also reflected a fascination with early technology, such as the typewriter, Edison's phonograph, and motion pictures.

Hart and Coppola continued toiling on the screenplay, which eventually went through fifty rewrites. Coppola pushed to find ways of transferring Stoker's epistolary text into a visual experience. The director struggled with how to take a horrible bloodsucking monster and make him sympathetic by the film's finale, bringing unique visual transitions to the storytelling to create the equivalent of a literary experience on film, where the mind daydreams and the thoughts come to life.

As the script took shape, Coppola put it on its feet to see how it played, bringing in a group of theatrical actors from San Francisco and having them do a dinner theater–style run-through. The first performance took about two hours and fifteen minutes, with Coppola's team making notes throughout about scenes, how they worked, what the audience responded to, what evoked laughter, what bored them, and what put them on the edges of their seats.

When Coppola was finally satisfied with the script and the designs by Ishioka and the others were approved, Steranko prepared elaborate storyboards for every scene in the film, effectively creating a comic book of the entire movie. Coppola then filmed the storyboards, a technique common in animated movies and known as "pre-visualization." As with the theater performance, this allowed Coppola to see what worked and what was still problematic before filming began.

The director called the pre-visualization "The Score" of *Bram Stoker's Dracula*. When shooting began, he would replace the filmed storyboards with actual footage, assembling the film as he went. He also brought in high-definition video cameras developed by Japanese electronics firms for instant playback of scenes and for shooting screen tests; it was one of the first uses of high-definition video cameras in filmmaking. The extensive planning and use of new technology paid off; rather than the 120 days a movie on the scale of *Bram Stoker's Dracula* would normally have taken, Coppola scheduled his film for a tight sixty-nine days.

To ensure good box office, Coppola assembled a cast of mostly young British and American actors. Ryder, of course, was already set as Mina. For her friend Lucy, Coppola cast British actress Sadie Frost who, like Ryder, had been acting since her early teens. By the time she signed on for *Bram Stoker's Dracula*, she had already appeared in several British films, including *The Krays* (which starred her husband, former Spandau Ballet guitarist and songwriter Gary Kemp), and had recurring roles on three TV series, *Gentlemen and Players*, *Les Girls*, and *Press Gang*.

Lucy's suitors were played by Cary Elwes, Bill Campbell, and Richard E. Grant. All had previously delved into fantasy: Elwes starred in *The Princess Bride* (1987); Campbell had just essayed the title role in *The Rocketeer* (1991); and Grant had played a witch hunter in *Warlock* (1989).

Anthony Hopkins, fresh from his Best Actor Oscar win for *The Silence of the Lambs* (1991), took the role of Van Helsing. The actor brought a touch of Hannibal Lecter with him, playing the vampire hunter as someone who was heroic but slightly sinister.

Casting the lead role proved more difficult. Daniel Day-Lewis was considered, but had a scheduling conflict, having already signed on for *The Last of the Mohicans*. Next, Coppola thought of Jeremy Irons to play the vampire, but casting Irons as Dracula went counter to the director's notion of having a youthful cast. Once before, Coppola had found himself in the position of having difficulty casting a major role. With *The Godfather*, after having looked at a number of Italian actors, and not having found anyone with the charisma to embody Don Corleone, Coppola asked, Why not just hire the greatest actor in the world? At the time, that meant either Laurence Olivier or Marlon Brando. Now, Coppola was in the same spot with *Dracula*—if audiences didn't buy the actor in the lead role, the whole film would fall apart. Whoever played Dracula needed to be handsome, able to play the vampire as both young and old, be able to pull off a Romanian accent, and be amenable to wearing outrageous makeup, including a full man-bat costume. So, Coppola decided to think "outside the box," and just go for the best actor with the most originality and emotion.

With that in mind, he sent the script to Gary Oldman, who had made a splash as Sid Vicious in *Sid and Nancy* (1986) and as British playwright Joe Orton in *Prick Up Your Ears* (1987), two films in which he played difficult characters in unattractive circumstances yet made them relatable and sympathetic.

When he received the offer for *Dracula*, Oldman was skeptical. There had been so many Draculas already, he didn't see the pressing need for another. But then he heard that Francis Ford Coppola was directing, and he knew the idiosyncratic director would approach the material in a new and original way.

Oldman read Hart's screenplay in a trailer in New Orleans, between takes on the set of Oliver Stone's *JFK*, in which he was playing Lee Harvey Oswald. Sitting with a friend at lunchtime, he read a piece from the script to her, and she started to cry. Oldman told her, "Yeah, it's pretty good, isn't it? I'm going to get this part." And he did.

Coppola's most controversial decision came in his choice of all-American Keanu Reeves as staid British solicitor Jonathan Harker. Though he was an accomplished actor who had already appeared in a period drama, 1988's *Dangerous Liaisons*, Reeves's public persona was cemented by his engaging performance as Ted Logan in *Bill and Ted's Excellent Adventure* (1989), which spawned an animated series and a sequel, 1991's *Bill and Ted's Bogus Journey*. Coppola had a practical reason for casting Reeves; he didn't think Jonathan Harker was such a great role, so he wanted to elevate it by hiring an actor with a matinee idol quality. As he told Janet Maslin of the *New York Times*, "If we all were to go to the airport with Winona and Gary Oldman and I and anyone shy of Tom Cruise, Keanu is the one that the girls would just besiege."

"You know, it was a story of passion and hot, red blood," Coppola told Steven Rea of the *Philadelphia Inquirer*. "All this blood is a symbol of passion, and that Winona had the hots for Keanu, and Lucy had the hots for those three guys, and Van Helsing had the hots for Lucy. Everybody has a crush on everyone. My idea was that the vampires can only prey on healthy, young blood. It attracts them."

With the roles cast, Coppola brought his principal actors to his seventeen-hundred-acre Napa Valley winery and estate for a week of improvisations and exercises. The actors read the novel aloud, went through the script, and sat down for communal dinners. The idea was to break down barriers and establish relationships that would translate to the film.

The summer-camp atmosphere extended to all the principal actors except Oldman. The director instructed Elwes, Campbell, and Grant to go horseback-riding and hot-air ballooning together, getting to know each other and their characters better, and sent Ryder and Frost off to do things together while Oldman was kept isolated. Oldman didn't mind; he felt research was overused by actors, becoming a kind of security blanket. He preferred to rely on skill and technique.

Everything Old Is New Again

In November 1991, the cast and crew relocated to Los Angeles, where *Bram Stoker's Dracula* began filming on the same Columbia Pictures soundstages that had just been vacated by Steven Spielberg's *Hook*. Coppola decided to make the entire film on sound stages, eschewing location shooting, to eliminate possible weather delays. After wild rumors that had plagued Coppola productions like *Apocalypse Now* and *One from the Heart*, the director was concerned about showing that he would bring a film in on time and on budget, without excessive over-runs. To that end, he sent weekly reports on his progress to Columbia Pictures chairman Mark Canton to assure him that all was going as planned.

Coppola put more money into the costumes than into the sets, to best show off his young cast. There was little money left for special effects, so instead of utilizing expensive computer-generated imaging, visual effects director Roman Coppola decided to use old-fashioned techniques like trap doors, mirrors, reverse images and double-exposures, a style that enhanced the film, making it an homage to early cinematography.

Roman Coppola reached back to techniques pioneered by early special-effects pioneers like Georges Méliès, the turn-of-the-century French magician and filmmaker renowned for his fantasy films, particularly 1902's *Le Voyage Dans La Lune* (*A Trip to the Moon*). Roman Coppola also studied books of magic and made lists of effects that could be adapted for the film.

For one scene, in which Prince Vlad meets with Mina on the streets of London, Coppola found an old Pathé hand-cranked camera from the period and loaded it with color stock, giving the scene the twitchy, soft-focus look of primitive films.

The innovative approach extended into the various transformations Dracula undergoes in the script. In previous films, Dracula had changed into mist, into a wolf, and into a literal, tiny bat. Coppola asked scriptwriter James V. Hart if they could have him turn into a bat. Hart felt modern audiences would laugh at such a clichéd transformation. So, Coppola asked: What if he's a *big* bat? The result was Dracula as a human-sized creature, half bat and half man, trapped somewhere in-between. Hart liked the idea, feeling it would be a visual personification of the curse under which the vampire existed.

The bat costume was created by special makeup-effects man Greg Cannom, who also transformed Oldman into a part-human wolf. For the actor, turning into monsters and aging into an old man was taxing; for the elderly Dracula, he spent nearly seven hours in the makeup chair, then after ten hours on the set, spent another hour-and-a-half having it removed.

As the fourteen-week shoot progressed, there were rumors that Oldman was having an affair with Winona Ryder, despite her involvement with actor Johnny Depp and Oldman's own marriage to actress Uma Thurman. The rumors began after one day on the set when Ryder asked Oldman if he'd heard Bauhaus perform "Bela Lugosi's Dead." Oldman hadn't, so Ryder took him to Tower Records on Sunset Boulevard to buy the tape. The next day, newspapers reported that the two had been spotted together and inferred that they were having a love affair—all because of Bauhaus.

By early April 1992, the film was ready for a test screening. Scriptwriter James Hart was thrilled with the movie, telling a reporter that it was like watching *Gone With the Wind* with sex and violence. In September, with all the editing completed, Wojciech Kilar, a Polish composer who was a newcomer to American films but who nevertheless had an extensive film career in Europe, began recording the score. When all was said and done, *Bram Stoker's Dracula* came in at $45 million—on budget and on time.

Coppola wouldn't have long to bask in his accomplishment, however. After early test screenings, rumors began to circulate that the film was not for the faint of heart, that it was too bloody, too erotic, and too violent, even gorier than the director's *Godfather* films.

Many pundits in the entertainment industry predicted the film would turn out to be an expensive flop, like the recent big-screen version of Tom Wolfe's novel *The Bonfire of the Vanities*; they were calling Coppola's movie *Bonfire of the Vampires*.

It didn't help that on Thursday, November 5, 1992, at a press and industry preview in Westwood, the audience clearly felt Keanu Reeves was miscast, laughing at him when he appeared in the beginning of the film, and hissing his name in the final credits, although they applauded the film as a whole.

Steadying himself for the worst, Coppola and his cast attended the official world premiere at Mann's Chinese Theater on Hollywood Boulevard on Tuesday, November 10, 1992. Three days later, the film opened in twenty-four-hundred theaters nationwide, on Friday the 13th. It would prove to be a lucky day for Coppola.

Dracula's Reception

Reviews were generally favorable, with critics saluting the dizzying energy of the film, calling it a feverish, extravagant, visual tour-de-force with gorgeous sets and hallucinogenic special effects. Others found it too campy and impressionistic, quasi-pornographic, and with an undercooked plot and characters. The *Boston Globe*'s Jay Carr called Coppola's approach "wrong-headed."

Kenneth Turan in the *Los Angeles Times* even derided Coppola's young cast, writing that "almost none of these people look comfortable in their period costumes or sound at ease in their earnest accents, the result tends to feel like a $40-million high-school play." Particular scorn was heaped upon Keanu Reeves and his attempt at an English accent.

But on the Monday after the film's opening, all those who predicted its failure were eating crow. The film played to unexpected crowds, with theaters in New York, Los Angeles, and other cities selling out in advance on Friday and Saturday nights. By Monday morning, it had grossed a whopping $32 million. At the time, it was the seventh-highest opening weekend on record. Columbia Pictures chairman Mark Canton pronounced it "thrilling"; John N. Krier, the president of Exhibitor Relations Company Inc., a company that monitored box-office grosses, said it was one of the biggest fall openings in history.

Bram Stoker's Dracula had the third-biggest opening of the year, after *Batman Returns* (first weekend gross, $42.7 million) and *Lethal Weapon 3* (first weekend gross, $33.2 million). Those films, however, were sequels that opened in the peak filmgoing season. *Bram Stoker's Dracula* opened strongly in the winter months, after receiving mixed reviews, with some critics roundly denouncing it.

To maximize the box-office receipts, Columbia Pictures had moved the film up from its planned Thanksgiving release, when it would have competed with *Home Alone 2* and *Malcolm X*, and initiated a marketing campaign that emphasized both its horror aspects and its sexuality. They positioned the film as a scary, fun, romantic event.

When the dust settled and the numbers were adjusted, the *New York Times* reported that after one week, *Bram Stoker's Dracula* had pulled in $30.5 million on 2,491 screens, making it the country's number-one film. After five weeks in release, it pulled in $78.1 million. It was still in the Top Ten, placing at number eight on 1,602 screens, with a fifth week gross of $1.6 million.

Analyzing the popularity of *Bram Stoker's Dracula*, the *New York Times*' Frank Rich compared it to Orson Welles's 1938 *War of the Worlds* broadcast, which tapped into Americans' subliminal fear of the coming war in Europe. "Is there any doubt which foreign invasion Americans are fearing this time?" wrote Rich. "The audience that turns out for *Bram Stoker's Dracula* smells blood even more literally than Welles's audience did. And Mr. Coppola gives it to them, in a movie that both frightens and arouses by playing off the unchecked fear of further

The poster for 1992's *Bram Stoker's Dracula* again plays up the romantic aspects of the story as well as the horrific. *Author's collection*

AIDS invasions of the national bloodstream. *Bram Stoker's Dracula* is an orgy of bloodsucking, bloodletting and blood poisoning. It's beyond Grand Guignol: it's opera for the new blood culture."

Columbia Pictures spent $10 million in marketing *Bram Stoker's Dracula*. Just before the film opened, the windows of Macy's West 34th Street store in New York were filled with mannequins wearing Eiko Isioka's jaw-dropping outfits from the film. Complementing them were five Dracula-inspired evening outfits from other fashion designers, including Byron Lar, who created what Anne-Marie Schiro of the *New York Times* called a "coffin-like bustier complete with bronze handles on the hips." Coviello & Erickson provided a black dress adorned with crosses for a mannequin draped over a baptismal font, displayed along with Dracula's gray suit and top hat. Other designers featured were Van Buren, Zang Toi, and Anna Sui.

By Christmastime, there were about a hundred licensed products available, including a fifteen-hundred-dollar bustier from Macy's, shirts inscribed with the word "Beware," a man's tie with a wolf symbol, red lace underpants with rosebud appliqué, boxer shorts, bat and spider brooches, Vampire-red lipstick, a five-hundred-dollar lipstick holder shaped like a coffin and covered in jewels, removable fang-bite tattoos, a *Dracula* hologram, pewter figurines, a role-playing game, trading cards, and a Virgin Air promotion that promised the winner a trip to Romania.

There were also four official tie-in books on bookstore shelves. Two were published by Signet, including a paperback edition of Stoker's novel, promoted as "the original classic" and containing eight pages of photos from the Coppola film, and a paperback adaptation of the film's script by author Fred Saberhagen, which also featured photos from the movie as well as an afterword by Coppola. Collins Publishers did the most lavish celebration of the film, *Coppola and Eiko on Bram Stoker's Dracula*, which focused mostly on the wardrobe designed for the film. For behind-the-scenes details on the film's production, readers could pick up Newmarket Press's *Bram Stoker's 'Dracula': The Film and the Legend*, which included the film's script, excerpts from Stoker's novel, and 160 photos.

The success of the film also put Bram Stoker back on the bestseller list. The Signet tie-in edition of *Dracula* reached number nine on the *New York Times* Paperback Best Sellers: Fiction. It remained there for two weeks.

At the sixty-fifth annual Academy Awards broadcast, *Bram Stoker's Dracula* took home the award for Best Costumes, and also won in two of the technical categories, for Make-Up and Sound Effects. To the dismay of many in Hollywood, the film once dismissed as *Bonfire of the Vampires* was now a three-time Academy Award winner.

Francis Ford Coppola took $9.5 million of his profits from *Bram Stoker's Dracula* and purchased a ninety-four-and-a-half-acre parcel of Napa Valley land from Heublein Inc., which included a large winery building. It adjoined the 1,560 acres of the Inglenook winery he had purchased twenty years earlier, using his profits from *The Godfather*. Now, he owned the largest contiguous-acreage vineyard in Napa Valley. Speaking to Denise Barricklow of the *St. Petersburg Times*, he said of *Bram Stoker's Dracula*, "I accept that I am not the kind of filmmaker that's gonna have a lot of kudos. But the positive thing is that maybe ten years from now, people are still going to be looking at this film."

14

Vamping for Laughs

Dracula Comedies

Old Dracula

By the early 1970s, Dracula was no longer a character to be either respected or feared. With the old films running on TV creature features and traditional vampires becoming the butt of jokes on programs like *The Munsters* or unintentional laughing stocks in films like *Billy the Kid vs. Dracula*, it was thought to be practically impossible to treat the character with anything other than ridicule.

So it was that in the summer of 1973, David Niven, an actor who was the very embodiment of British wit and sophistication, was looking forward to a relaxing vacation at Cap Ferrat, until his agent interrupted his water-skiing with the news that he'd secured a role for the actor in a film then called "Vampirella." Niven signed up for the role of Dracula in the film, which was to be shot in London beginning in July. By mid-August, he was completing his final scenes and preparing to go to America for a lecture tour.

When the film was released in the United States at the end of November 1975, it had undergone a title change to *Old Dracula*. Directed by Clive Donner from a script by

This French poster from 1974's *Old Dracula* features some, how should we say, provocatively posed ladies.

Author's collection

Jeremy Lloyd, the film had Count Dracula attempting to revive his dormant wife, who had turned black after eating "some poisoned peasant." The spoof ended with Dracula himself becoming black, a conceit that seemed rather daring in the post-Civil Rights era but is in rather bad taste in any era.

David Niven's legacy is hardly represented by a schlock film like *Old Dracula*. He had won an Oscar and the New York Critics best actor award for his dramatic appearance in *Separate Tables* (1958). An accomplished raconteur, he wrote two witty autobiographical volumes, *The Moon Is a Balloon* (1971) and *Bring on the Empty Horses* (1975). In 1985, two years after the actor's death, both volumes were republished under one cover, titled *Niven*.

Love at First Bite

A little more than a year later, while Frank Langella was putting the bite on Broadway, George Hamilton decided to approach Dracula from a different vein, after running into a screenwriter friend while in Mexico. Robert Kaufman, the screenwriter of *Freebie and the Bean*, *Getting Straight*, and *Divorce American Style*, was swimming with Hamilton in the pool of composer Leslie Bricusse's rented house in Acapulco. Clowning around, they began doing Dracula imitations to each other, and then thought, wouldn't it be funny if Dracula came to New York in the 1970s and instead of terrorizing New York, New York terrorized him?

By the 1970s, George Hamilton was beginning to feel the best years of his career were behind him. Born the son of a bandleader in Memphis, Tennessee, on August 12, 1939, Hamilton made his way to Hollywood and won a role in *Where the Boys Are* in 1960, for which he picked up the Golden Globe award as Most Promising Newcomer. Under contract to MGM, he appeared in a string of films in the 1960s, including the Hank Williams biopic *Your Cheatin' Heart* (1964).

In 1971, Hamilton both produced and starred in another biopic, *Evel Knievel*, in which he played the infamous motorcycle daredevil. Although the film did well, Hamilton's career went into a slide; after twenty years in the business, he was no longer getting offered leading parts in movies. He had become a tabloid figure, the playboy with the perpetual tan whose marriage to Alana Collins disintegrated after she was seen spending nights on the town with rocker Rod Stewart. In 1978, Hamilton taped a pilot for a TV series called *George and Alana*, which was to feature he and his wife as a divorced couple surviving in Beverly Hills. When their real-life divorce was finalized (she later married Stewart), Hamilton moved to a 430-acre plantation he had just purchased in Mississippi.

He now decided that instead of continuing as a dramatic leading man, the time was ripe to reinvent himself as a comedic actor, a modern-day equivalent of Cary Grant—by way of Bela Lugosi. Working with Robert Kaufman, they took their birthed-in-a-swimming-pool idea and fleshed it out into a fish-out-of-water comedy, which they called *Love at First Bite*.

Since other producers wouldn't hire Hamilton for comedic roles, he decided to produce his Dracula spoof on his own and hire himself. With Kaufman co-producing, they first took the project to Columbia Pictures, which agreed to back it only if another actor played Dracula. Hamilton refused, and the studio turned the project down. When the same offer was made to Melvin Simon Productions, that company said they would put up $2.9 million to finance the project only if Hamilton *did* play Dracula. A deal was set.

Kaufman continued hashing out the script, receiving input from Hamilton. They developed a story in which a love-struck Dracula is forced out of his home country and goes to New York in search of a cover-girl model with whom he's become infatuated. Hamilton pushed for making Dracula a man out of time, a very old-fashioned romantic living in a world where people no longer have manners. Kaufman was paid fifty thousand dollars for his screenplay, and he and Hamilton split a one-hundred-thousand-dollar fee as executive producers; all of those fees were deferred to keep the budget within reasonable limits.

To direct the film, Hamilton chose a New York–based filmmaker, Stan Dragoti, who helmed the popular "I Love New York" TV commercials, which won Dragoti a special Tony Award citation. Dragoti was no stranger to the film-making industry; he had previously directed the 1972 feature *Dirty Little Billy*, a gritty look at the early years of Billy the Kid (played by Michael J. Pollard), and an episode of Tony Curtis's 1976 TV series *McCoy*. By April 1978, newspapers were reporting that there was a new *Dracula* film on the horizon.

Susan Saint James, who endeared herself to TV audiences as the female half of NBC's *McMillan & Wife* from 1971 to 1976, was cast as Cindy Sondheim, the fashion model—not much of a stretch for Saint James, who had been a model in her youth. For *Love at First Bite*, the actress bleached her hair blonde. Afterwards, she noticed she was getting more attention from random men on the street and decided that yes, blondes do have more fun. Saint James enjoyed working with George Hamilton, and even dated him during filming.

Dracula (George Hamilton) rises from his coffin in 1979's *Love at First Bite*.

© 1979 American International Pictures.
Courtesy of Del Valle Archives.

To outfit himself as a vampire, Hamilton went to Dunhill Tailors, a clothing company frequented by the likes of New York's Governor Hugh Carey and actor Paul Newman. Dunhill also made Gregory Peck's wardrobe for *The Man in the Gray Flannel Suit* (1956). The clothier provided a black cape that required over eight yards of woolen fabric and was lined, at Hamilton's insistence, with white silk, which the actor felt was "more elegant" than red. They also made classic 1930s-style tailcoats, a quilted black velvet robe and two "at home" outfits, one single-breasted and one double-breasted, both in black velvet. Why did Hamilton choose Dunhill's? Because for several years he had been having his own personal wardrobe made by them. Hamilton decided early on that one thing he would not wear as Dracula would be fangs. As he kept reminding people, neither did Bela Lugosi.

Shooting got underway on location in New York City in June of 1978. Wearing lots of white makeup to tone down his trademark tan, Hamilton made an interesting discovery. "Women find a pale-looking man rather sexy," he told Roderick Mann of the *Los Angeles Times*, "probably because it looks as if he spends most of his time in bed."

In mid-July, hyping of the film got an early start when invitations were sent out for a celebration on the castle lot of MGM in Hollywood in honor of Dracula's 710th birthday. "Come as you are or as you want to go," read the invites. "No gifts please. However, the Count will appreciate a donation to your local blood bank in his name. He would like to think of it as your investment in his future." When guests dialed the phone number to RSVP, they heard a recording of Hamilton as Dracula saying, "I'm not in at the moment but please leave your reply after the scream."

Taking a Bite from the Box Office

After filming wrapped, Hamilton felt confident that *Love at First Bite*, whose total cost was $3.3 million, would be a big hit. "It's kind of a 1930s, Capraesque film with a Mel Brooks flavor," he told Elaine Markoutsas of the *Chicago Tribune*. "Dracula has lived 712 years and is very sophisticated. . . . He's a romantic who believes it's better to be dead in a world without romance."

Preparing the film for release, American International Pictures conducted market research into how to blend comic overtones into the Dracula image. As a result, newspaper ads carried such taglines as, "Your favorite pain in the neck is about to bite your funny bone."

By the time Hamilton finished the film, he was again a hot property. He soon landed a role in the TV movie *The Users*, and by the end of January 1979, as the film was opening in theaters, he was starring in the play *Count Dracula* at the Drury Lane Martinique near Chicago, Illinois.

The film hit theaters on April 13, 1979, and immediately caught on with audiences and critics alike. In the *Los Angeles Times*, Frank Taylor wrote that *Love at First Bite* was "a whimsical, 'fresh' look at the perennial Count Dracula, but as audiences have never seen the old lecher before. . . . George Hamilton who we have long been familiar with in the past couple of decades as a film star, makes a nice parody of himself and the Count."

Janet Maslin, writing for the *New York Times,* said, "Quite unexpectedly, George Hamilton's Dracula turns out to be—pardon the expression—a scream. Mr. Hamilton's knack for comedy has been a well-kept secret until now, but he's certainly funny in *Love at First Bite,* a coarse, delightful little movie with a bang-up cast and no pretensions at all."

However, one who did not enjoy *Love at First Bite* was the *Chicago Tribune'*s critic Gene Siskel, who wrote, "[George] Hamilton, who has never been mistaken for an actor, has no idea how to play comedy. . . . Hamilton's character winks at us throughout his Dracula portrayal. It's a smug performance in a film full of tired jokes and some of the most cruel racial stereotyping you'll ever see."

A couple of weeks into the film's release, George Hamilton participated in an audacious publicity stunt. Dressed in full Dracula attire and makeup, he arrived via horse-drawn hearse to the location of Bela Lugosi's star on the Hollywood Walk of Fame, where he deposited a wreath of white lilies and drank a toast to Lugosi of a red liquid, quipping, "I told them to make it body temperature." He then kissed a fan on the neck. "Women seem to have a preconceived image of Dracula as being very sexy," Hamilton told Martin Rossman of the *Los Angeles Times.* "They don't come up and say hello, how are you—they ask me to bite them."

In a time when feminism was at the forefront, Hamilton ruffled feathers with statements like the ones he made to a staffer from the *Chicago Tribune,* when he said, "I know what women want and don't want. And so did the count. Aside from his strange thirst for blood, he is exactly what every woman wants in a man—strength, aggression, and protectiveness. Every woman fantasizes about a dark stranger who manacles her. Dracula represents the ultimate romantic figure. Women don't have fantasies about marching with Vanessa Redgrave."

In interview after interview, Hamilton claimed that women secretly yearned for a man with old-fashioned values and manners instead of an "Alan Alda type" who wore his emotions on his sleeve; in other words, he felt women wanted a man with the courtly Old World values of a Bela Lugosi—never mind that it was precisely those values, with expectations of a wife's subservience to her husband, that had driven a stake in practically all of Lugosi's marriages.

American International Pictures decided to promote the movie with old-style ballyhoo, like films from the 1940s and '50s. Hamilton appeared on just about every talk show—*Tonight, Today, Merv Griffin, Mike Douglas*—and also local TV shows, as well as personal appearances at theaters and shopping centers. In his talk show appearances, Hamilton drank tomato juice. At shopping malls, he bit young ladies on the neck.

He participated in another horse-and-hearse stunt in New York City that drew media attention, and when the film's soundtrack was released, it was celebrated with a party staged at a New York disco. There was also a beauty contest

George Hamilton, seen here with Susan Saint James, pulled out all the stops to promote *Love at First Bite*, including leaving a wreath at Bela Lugosi's star on the Hollywood Walk of Fame and toasting his predecessor with a glass of "blood."   *Photofest*

in which the winner won a night on the town with Dracula (Hamilton, not a stand-in), and a Dracula look-alike contest wherein the winners received round-trip tickets to visit Dracula's castle in Transylvania.

It was hard work for Hamilton, who was up at 6:00 a.m. to get into his Dracula makeup and outfit before spending a day signing autographs at movie theaters and doing eight to twelve interviews. But he didn't complain, especially since—as one of the film's producers—his publicity efforts increased the box-office take. The results spoke for themselves; after twenty-four days in release, the film raked in $8.3 million on seven hundred screens nationwide. After scaring up audiences in America, Hamilton next traveled to Europe and Australia.

When *Love at First Bite* became a hit, director Stan Dragoti, suddenly a hot commodity, revealed that he, Hamilton, and Kaufman had considered following it up with *Divorce, Vampire Style*, but decided they should wait, lest audiences overdose on Dracula.

By the middle of May, publicity for the film shifted to the Cannes Film Festival, where Hamilton was seen on the beach in his Dracula regalia before a screening of *Love at First Bite* at the Play Girl disco. Afterwards, Karen Black, Joan Collins, and Stuart Whitman hit the dance floor. Dragoti was absent from these festivities; on his way to Cannes, he was arrested at the Frankfurt airport on charges of cocaine possession. Dragoti spent two months in a West German jail before, on the Fourth of July, a judge heard his case and suspended his sentence, saying that though he committed a criminal act, he was not a criminal.

For Hamilton, the success of the film was a vindication. For years, he had been trying to persuade producers to let him take on a comic role. Now that he had, in a film he co-produced, he'd had one of the biggest hits of his career. He was deluged with offers, and his salary quote jumped from a hundred thousand dollars to $1 million, plus 10 percent of the gross. For his next project, he planned a comedic take on Zorro—*Zorro, The Gay Blade.*

By January of 1980, *Love at First Bite* had earned a staggering $46 million. As a result, producer and scriptwriter Robert Kaufman signed a nine-picture deal with the film's distributor, American International Pictures-Filmways. The nine films were to be completed within five years, each budgeted at no less than $4 million.

At the Academy of Science Fiction, Fantasy and Horror Films' seventh annual Science Fiction Film Awards ceremony, on July 26, 1980, *Love at First Bite* collected honors for George Hamilton for Best Actor and Arte Johnson (who played Renfield) for Best Supporting Actor.

After playing Dracula and Zorro, Hamilton found that he'd reached a whole new audience. Fifteen-year-old girls with crushes were now writing to him, calling him a fox.

A sequel to the Dracula film, "Love at Second Bite," was supposed to have followed *Zorro, the Gay Blade*, but by the time that film was released, the actor found himself at odds with his former collaborators. "Bob Kaufman and I fought and Stan Dragoti and I fought and so we all went our separate ways," Hamilton said in a 1985 interview with Roderick Mann of the *Los Angeles Times.* "But that's all over now. Now the movie will definitely be made. And it's even funnier than the other film." Script issues delayed the sequel, which was rescheduled for 1986. Eventually, the financing fell through and Hamilton moved on to other projects. By 1988, George Schlatter, best known as the producer of TV's *Rowan and Martin's Laugh-In*, came onboard and worked with Robert Kaufman and Hamilton to nail down a final shooting script and get the project rolling. According to reports, the plot would follow Dracula and his mate, Cindy Sondheim, as they married and moved to Hollywood. Before Kaufman completed the script, the Writer's Guild went on strike, delaying the project yet again. It was the final nail in the coffin for "Love at Second Bite"; the project eventually died of indifference.

Dracula: Dead and Loving It

George Hamilton wasn't the only Hollywood fixture who thought a comedic take on Dracula could give his career a transfusion of fresh blood. As Mel Brooks sat in a theater in 1992 watching Francis Ford Coppola's *Bram Stoker's Dracula*, he got an idea. In an interview with Ian Spelling in *The Denver Post*, he said, "I loved Coppola's film and as I sat there I thought, 'This is almost a Mel Brooks spoof.' I thought a Dracula spoof would be the perfect film for me to do next."

The director was just completing his latest genre spoof, *Robin Hood: Men in Tights*, which cost $18 million to produce. When it was released in 1993, despite taking a critical drubbing, it earned $40 million at the domestic box office and nearly $100 million worldwide.

At that point in his career, Brooks was a celebrated veteran of both television and movies. The son of Russian Jewish immigrants, Melvin James Kaminsky went from being a performer in the Catskills to writing for Sid Caesar's *Your Show of Shows* (1950–54), where he rubbed shoulders with other budding talents, such as Neil Simon and Carl Reiner. With Reiner, Brooks wrote and performed a series of skits called "The 2,000-Year-Old Man," which they recorded on comedy albums in the early 1960s. Brooks scored a bigger hit in 1968, writing and directing the film *The Producers*, which brought him an Oscar for Best Original Screenplay. But it was his third film, 1974's *Blazing Saddles*, with its anarchic cowboys farting around the campfire scene, which made him a household name. That same year, he produced a comedic love letter to the Universal horror films he'd loved in his youth, *Young Frankenstein*. By the end of the decade, he'd formed his own company, Brooksfilms, to produce more serious fare. Besides his own films, the company produced hits including *The Elephant Man* (1980), *My Favorite Year* (1982), *Frances* (1982), *The Fly* (1986), and *84 Charing Cross Road* (1987).

Now that he knew what he wanted to do next, his first concern was whom to cast in the title role. He didn't think any of the big, established comic names would work, and he started to be concerned. Then, the day after seeing Coppola's *Dracula*, he turned on his TV and found the answer. *Naked Gun 2½* was on cable, starring Leslie Nielsen. "I thought, deadpan, arrogant, stupid and debonair, and one of the few funnymen around who could wear a cape and get away with it," Brooks recalled to Ian Spelling of *The Denver Post*. It didn't hurt that Nielsen was a marquee name with a huge following.

At sixty-nine, Canadian-born Leslie Nielsen was nearing the end of a career that stretched back to 1948, when he made his first television appearance with Charlton Heston on an episode of *Studio One*. After dozens of live TV performances, Nielsen entered films in 1956 with a part in *The Vagabond King*. He next auditioned for and won the leading role in the science-fiction classic *Forbidden Planet*, resulting in a contract with MGM. Through the 1960s and '70s, he made hundreds of film and TV appearances, often playing villainous roles. Then, in 1980, he accepted a role in the comedy *Airplane!* When that film became a hit, it rejuvenated his career, leading to the short-lived TV series *Police Squad* and the resultant film series, *The Naked Gun*. After years of dramatic roles, Nielsen was now a bona-fide comedy icon. Having become famous for a film with cowboys farting, Mel Brooks clicked with Nielsen, who often amused himself by squeezing a Whoopie Cushion while riding in elevators.

Working with writers Rudy DeLuca and Steve Haberman, Brooks created a script that retained the basics of Bram Stoker's plot while spoofing a variety of its interpreters. He felt the new film was a companion piece to his 1974 horror spoof, *Young Frankenstein*. But unlike that black-and-white comedy, *Dracula: Dead and Loving It* was filmed in color. Though the production design was an homage to Bela Lugosi's 1931 *Dracula*, filming it in color was reminiscent of the Hammer Dracula films with Christopher Lee.

Co-produced with Gaumont and Castle Rock Entertainment, *Dracula: Dead and Loving It* was budgeted at $30 million. The film began photography in May 1995. Rounding out the cast were Steven Weber (of the TV series *Wings*), Amy Yasbeck (*Robin Hood: Men in Tights*), and Peter MacNicol (*Ghostbusters II*). As Dr. Seward, Harvey Korman made his fourth appearance in a Brooks movie, having been in *Blazing Saddles*, *High Anxiety*, and *History of the World, Part I*. Korman based his performance on British actor Nigel Bruce, who was Dr. Watson in several Sherlock Holmes films with Basil Rathbone, but he prepared for the movie by watching older vampire films.

Leslie Nielsen as Dracula in Mel Brooks's *Dracula: Dead and Loving It* (1995). The title was inspired by the TV spy spoof *Get Smart* (1965–1970), created by Brooks and Buck Henry. In *Get Smart*, one of the catchphrases of Maxwell Smart, played by Don Adams, was ". . . and loving it."

Courtesy of Del Valle Archives

Brooks put himself in the role of Dracula's nemesis, Dr. Van Helsing, a specialist in bizarre diseases, gynecology, and vampire slaying. In a case of art imitating life, Van Helsing barks orders and directs the actions of the other characters much as Brooks directed the actors in the film. His wife, Anne Bancroft, who won the Academy Award for Best Actress for 1962's *The Miracle Worker*, was given a cameo as a gypsy woman, Madame Ouspenskaya.

Brooks instructed Leslie Nielsen to approach his role with all the seriousness he brought to his early dramatic performances in *Playhouse 90*; the director felt the scenes were already absurd enough, and would be funnier if played straight. Nielsen did, however, adopt a faux Bela Lugosi accent. Brooks said Nielsen was so funny in the part that the director often had to stuff a handkerchief in his mouth to keep from laughing during takes.

One typical Brooksian comic moment comes in the ballroom scene that reverses an idea from Roman Polanski's *The Fearless Vampire Killers*: Nielsen's Dracula thinks everyone is impressed with his great dancing ability, but instead they're aghast because he has no reflection in the mirror. "That's the definition of farce," he told Steve Persall of the *St. Petersburg Times*. "The audience knows, and the characters don't."

Brooks began testing *Dracula: Dead and Loving It* at sneak previews in August 1995. He considered it one of his best films in years. At the film's preview, the gory blood-drenching staking scene hit a nerve with audiences—the one in their funny bone. Brooks said preview audiences literally fell out of their seats, laughing; he hadn't seen a reaction like it since the breaking-wind scene in *Blazing Saddles*.

The film would have been a natural for a Halloween release, but for some inexplicable reason, it hit theaters three days before Christmas, on December 22, 1995. Brooks shrugged it off, telling Rob Salem of the *Toronto Star*, "There are a lot of other movies opening (at the same time), but we're not worried about dying, because we're immortal. We're gonna take 'em all." *Dracula: Dead and Loving It* faced competition from the animated film *Balto*, Oliver Stone's *Nixon*, *Waiting to Exhale*, *Cutthroat Island*, and *Grumpier Old Men*. Critics, never in a holiday mood, were harsh, with most taking the opportunity to comment on how the director's abilities seemed to fade more with each successive film. The critics also indulged in their own lame jokes: *Dracula* sucked, it was hard to "B positive" about it, Brooks's career was down for the "count," etc.

Among the few favorable notices was one from Janet Maslin of the *New York Times*, who proclaimed that while *Dracula: Dead and Loving It* was thin-blooded, "its better moments redeem a lot of dead air. It's hard to resist a vampire film in which someone says, 'Yes, we have Nosferatu. We have Nosferatu today.'"

In the *St. Petersburg Times*, Stever Persall wrote, "One of the most reassuring times I've spent in a theater lately was watching Mel Brooks prove he's still got it in *Dracula, Dead and Loving It*. Brooks punctures our memories of Tod Browning and Francis Ford Coppola's bloodsuckers, with a dose of Hammer Films harpooning for good measure."

In its opening week, *Dracula: Dead and Loving It* was number ten at the box office, grossing only $2.7 million. However, it was Christmas week, not the traditional time to release a horror film or a movie that spoofs them. It fared better during New Year's week, pulling in $3.4 million. But faced with more bad reviews than good, the film performed miserably, bringing in less than $11 million at the domestic box office.

In March 1996, *Dracula, Dead and Loving It*, along with *Congo*, were chosen as the most boring movies of 1995 by the Boring Institute, a New Jersey organization so dull it had only one member, Alan Caruba.

15

The Dead, the Bad, and the Ugly

Other Dracula Movies

Atom Age Vampires

From the time Universal produced *Dracula* with Bela Lugosi in 1931 until he reprised the role in the studio's *Bud Abbott and Lou Costello Meet Frankenstein* in 1948, no other studio made films with Bram Stoker's immortal vampire until the 1950s.

One of the first, released in the fall of 1957 on a double bill with *I Was a Teenage Frankenstein*, was *Blood of Dracula*, whose press release touted that it would "give you nightmares forever." *Blood of Dracula* involved a teenage schoolgirl (Sandra Harrison) who becomes a vampiric killer after coming under the influence of an evil chemistry teacher.

Blood of Dracula was produced by Herman Cohen, who cornered the market in teen horror in the late 1950s with films such as *I Was a Teenage Werewolf* (1957), *I Was a Teenage Frankenstein* (1957), *How to Make a Monster* (1958), and *Horrors of the Black Museum* (1959). Cohen's formula was simple—low budgets, high grosses. He claimed to have made as much as $2 million on a $150,000 investment. In fact, it was the success of *I Was a Teenage Werewolf* that led to the others. When it opened in Texas on Labor Day, it did so well that the head of the Interstate Theater circuit told Cohen that if he could deliver another picture like it, he'd exhibit it at Thanksgiving. Cohen decided to make *I Was a Teenage Frankenstein*, and Jim Nicholson, head of American International Pictures, suggested Cohen make another feature so AIP wouldn't have to share the booking with another company. So, Cohen came up with *Blood of Dracula*, and shot the two films back-to-back, delivering them in time to make the Thanksgiving booking.

While some considered his films an abuse of artistic freedom, Cohen felt he was providing an uplifting service. Young people were generally the protagonists of his films, with adults as the antagonists. The teens in his movies didn't drink, smoke, or take drugs, and while they may have been turned into werewolves,

Baron Meinster (David Peel) throttles Van Helsing (Peter Cushing) before putting the bite on him in *The Brides of Dracula* (1960).   *© Hammer Film Productions / Universal Pictures. Courtesy of Del Valle Archives.*

vampires, or teenage Frankenstein Monsters, they were never portrayed as juvenile delinquents. With that template, Cohen profited by targeting the 70 percent of the moviegoing audience between twelve and twenty-five years of age. Cohen wanted the teenage audience, and, making movies designed for teenagers, he got them.

Cohen wasn't the only one profiting from the teen horror boom. Another vampire film, *The Return of Dracula*, hit theaters at the end of April 1958, playing in various cities through the summer, sometimes on a double bill with *The Flame Barrier*. By the end of the year, it was on the drive-in circuit, along with *Rodan* and *The Mysterians*.

Produced by Arthur Gardner and Jules Levy and directed by Paul Landres, *The Return of Dracula* transplanted Stoker's vampire king to the American heartland, where Dracula masquerades as a family's long-absent uncle and has designs on their teenage daughter until he ends up staked at the bottom of a mine shaft. Czech-born actor Francis Lederer starred as a sublimely cunning Dracula, with curly, jet-black hair combed forward and, instead of the usual opera cape, a black overcoat draped over his shoulders. Born Frantisek (Franz) Lederer on November 6, 1899, the handsome actor played Romeo in Berlin for stage impresario Max Reinhardt and starred opposite Louise Brooks in *Pandora's Box* (1929) for director G. W. Pabst before coming to Hollywood in the early 1930s, where his good looks typed him as a heartthrob. By 1958, he was nearing the end of his film career; his last film appearance was in 1959's *Terror Is a Man*, though he made TV appearances for the next dozen years, his final one being as Dracula in the 1971 *Night Gallery* segment "The Devil is Not Mocked," in which Nazi soldiers descend upon a remote castle not realizing the identity of its occupant. He died on May 25, 2000, at the age of one hundred.

Swinging '60s Vampires

Pop artist Andy Warhol made his first Dracula film in 1964, when he produced the black-and-white *Batman Dracula*. More a collage of images than a narrative film, the 120-minute production starring a black-bearded Jack Smith as Dracula was only shown at Warhol's art exhibitions.

After Hammer Films released *Horror of Dracula* in 1958, no American producers dared to compete with them until 1965, when Embassy Pictures financed two films produced by Circle Productions which they described as "adventure-shock" films: *Jesse James Meets Frankenstein's Daughter* and *Billy the Kid vs. Dracula*.

Both movies were scripted by Carl Hittleman and directed by William "One Shot" Beaudine. Beaudine began directing in 1922 and had 175 films under his belt, ending his lengthy and prolific career with the two quickie horror pictures. For *Billy the Kid vs. Dracula*, John Carradine dusted off his black top hat and cloak, playing a goateed Dracula. The director boasted that he filmed both Western/horror hybrids in sixteen days; assistant director Howard W. Koch said the filming of *Billy the Kid vs. Dracula* took only five. The storyline was not unlike *The Return of Dracula*, with the vampire assuming the identity of another person to insinuate himself into the family of a silver mine heiress. In August of 1967, both *Billy the Kid vs. Dracula* and *Jesse James Meets Frankenstein's Daughter* were offered as pay-per-view movies in Hartford, Connecticut, site of an early experiment in subscription television.

French poster from *The Brides of Dracula* (1960), highlighting several of Baron Meinster's victims—including Van Helsing. *Author's collection*

Twenty-one years after *House of Dracula*, John Carradine returned to the role for the quickie Western-horror hybrid, *Billy the Kid vs. Dracula.*

© 1966 Circle Productions Inc./Embassy Pictures. Courtesy of Del Valle Archives.

Following in the footsteps of Andy Warhol, Filipino filmmaker Leody M. Diaz directed 1967's *Batman Fights Dracula*, written by Bert R. Mendoza. Now considered lost, the Eastmancolor feature was the third of six unauthorized Batman films made in the Philippines between 1965 and 1973. Dante Rivero played Dracula, with Jing Abalos as Batman/Bruce Wayne.

Now that monster movies that once frightened adults were considered late-night kiddie fare, and "monsters" like Herman Munster were lighting up TV screens, producer Arthur Rankin Jr. and director Jules Bass decided to make a comedy feature with animated puppets, called *Mad Monster Party?* (1967). Produced by Avco-Embassy, the good-natured film featured the voices of Boris Karloff and comedienne Phyllis Diller, with Allen Swift voicing Dracula. The film received positive reviews upon its release.

Interviewed by Jane Boylan of the *New York Times* in 1969, critic Rex Reed, who became as much of a celebrity as his subjects, said, "Andy Warhol has asked me to be in the first all-nude musical horror film, which he's calling *Dracula's Baby*. It's set in Brooklyn Heights, and it has a very interesting rock score which Edith Sitwell wrote before she died. But the book needs work." Like others, that particular film never came to fruition.

But 1969 was not without a new Dracula film. Crown International released the low-budget *Blood of Dracula's Castle*, directed by B-movie maestro Al Adamson, who also produced along with the scriptwriter, Rex Carlton. The film relocated Dracula to Southern California, and incorporated a concept from *Mystery of the Wax Museum*, that some of the figures of movie stars in the Movieland Wax Museum were, in fact, the actual stars (in some cities, the film played on a double bill with *Nightmare in Wax*). Alex D'Arcy played Dracula, living in a stone mansion in the desert with his companion, Countess Townsend

(Paula Raymond), remaining youthful by drinking Bloody Marys made with real blood, obtained from young women in the dungeon. The castle staff included a butler named George (John Carradine), a quasi-werewolf named Johnny (Robert Dix), and a hulking, deformed mute named Mango (Ray Young). Kevin Thomas of the *Los Angeles Times* dismissed the R-rated thriller with, "[I]t's all pretty rotten, but at least it's played tongue-in-cheek."

In the 1930s, a Jalisco tax collector, Salvador Lutteroth Gonzales, took money he won in the National Lottery and built Mexico's first wrestling arena. By the 1960s, Mexican wrestling, also known as *lucha libre*, had spawned a litany of masked wrestlers who were seen as heroes by the

Poster from 1966's *Billy the Kid vs. Dracula*, a film that presents Billy the Kid as an okay guy, at least compared to Dracula. *Author's collection*

public, especially after they began starring in movies. In a forty-four-year career, El Santo (Rodolfo Guzmán Huerta), fought fifteen thousand matches and made fifty-three movies, including 1969's *Santo en el Tesoro de Dracula* (*Santo and Dracula's Treasure*), with Aldo Monti as Count Dracula, who reprised the role in 1973's *Santo y Blue Demon vs. Dracula y el Hombre Lobo* (*Santo and the Blue Demon vs. Dracula and the Wolf Man*).

Disco Draculas

Laurence Merrick, proprietor of Merrick's Academy of Dramatic Arts, wrote, produced, and directed the 1970 low-budget *Guess What Happened to Count Dracula?* The answer? He was hosting drug-filled parties in his Hollywood disco, and making an indecent proposal to an aspiring actor, promising him stardom in return for his girlfriend. Des Roberts played the bloodsucker. Two years later, Merrick made an Academy Award-nominated documentary, *Manson*, about the Manson murders (Sharon Tate, a victim of the Manson gang, had been one of Merrick's acting students). On January 26, 1977, he was leaving the parking lot and entering the school around noon when he was shot once in the lower back by an unidentified man in his twenties, who escaped. Merrick called out, "I've been shot," collapsed in his office and was carried to Hollywood Presbyterian Hospital, where he died an hour after the shooting.

Originally titled *Count Downe*, 1974's *Son of Dracula* was produced by former Beatle Ringo Starr, who played Merlin the Magician in the film. Ringo previously co-starred with Peter Sellers in the 1969 film *The Magic Christian*, in which Christopher Lee appeared as "the ship's vampire."   *Author's collection*

In the spring of 1973, an even more offbeat Dracula film emerged. *Son of Dracula*, starring rock musician Harry Nilsson as Count Downe and former Beatle Ringo Starr (who also produced the film) as his mentor, Merlin the Magician, had nothing to do with the 1943 Lon Chaney Jr. film of the same name. Apple Films, a production company that had the Beatles as managing directors, produced the film, which went into production under the title "Count Downe." Starr told Rex Reed of the *Chicago Tribune*: "I know we'll get our money back. If anyone said to me it will be a flop, I'd give them a personal check and sign it and tell them to fill it in for whatever money we lost. I'm that confident."

Lucky for Ringo, he never actually handed out those blank checks. With a title change to *Son of Dracula*, the film had a sneak preview at Phoenix's University Theater in May 1973. Ringo Starr did not attend; he was in Los Angeles working on an album with his former bandmate George Harrison. But Harry Nilsson and a chartered jet full of friends did fly to the screening. According to Joyce Haber of the *Los Angeles Times*, by the time it concluded, some audience members wanted to strangle the singer. *Son of Dracula* officially premiered in Atlanta, Georgia, on April 19, 1974. According to Ringo Starr, it was the first film to premiere in the Southern capital since *Gone With the Wind*. By October of 1974, it was being seen in theaters featuring midnight screenings.

A Japanese film, *Lake of Dracula*, executive produced by Fumio Tanaka, directed by Michio Yamamoto and starring Midori Fujita and Choei Takahashi, was screened at the Elgin Theater in New York in July of 1973. The Toho

Company production featured a great-grandson of Dracula settling in Japan in the middle of Lake Fujimi, called the Lake of Dracula.

At the end of 1973 came the low-budget entry *Dracula vs. Frankenstein*, another product of director Al Adamson, in which Dracula (Zandor Vorkov) and a mad scientist (J. Carrol Naish, in his final film appearance) resuscitate the Frankenstein Monster (John Bloom), who looks as though he's spent a few years too many in the sulfur pits. The film also featured Lon Chaney Jr. and had an appearance by Forrest J Ackerman. It was supposedly Ackerman who suggested that Roger Engel, a former stockbroker, use the stage name Zandor Vorkov. The film was completed in 1971, but not released in New York until December of 1973, on a double bill with *Frankenstein's Bloody Terror*, starring Paul Naschy.

In the summer of 1974, *Andy Warhol's Dracula*, also known as *Blood for Dracula*, hit theaters. The film was directed by Paul Morrissey as a follow-up to his adaptation of *Frankenstein*. With an emaciated-looking Udo Kier as Dracula, the film has the vampire count on the prowl for virgins (he becomes violently ill if he drinks any blood other than virgin blood). He ends up in a castle with four young maidens; unfortunately, Warhol discovery Joe Dallesandro is there, also, deflowering the ladies before Dracula bites them.

Both *Frankenstein* and *Dracula*, the first Andy Warhol films to be shot in 35mm, were made back-to-back with $700,000 raised by London producer Andrew Braunsberg from Italy's Carlo Ponti, Germany's Cinerama, and France's Jean Pierre Rassam. Once completed, Bryanston Pictures purchased rights to exploit the films in the U.S. and Canada. Prior to its August 16 release in the U.S., *Andy Warhol's Dracula* was selected for official entry into the Atlanta Film Festival.

Andy Warhol's Dracula featured famed Italian director Vittorio DeSica among its cast,

Servant Maro Balato (Joe Dallesandro) foils the plans of Dracula (Udo Kier) to acquire virgin blood in 1974's *Andy Warhol's Dracula*.   © *1974 Bryanston Distributing. Courtesy of Del Valle Archives.*

and a cameo by director Roman Polanski. It also featured enough gore to earn it an X rating. Joyce Haber of the *Los Angeles Times* put *Andy Warhol's Dracula* on her list of Ten Best Films of 1974. However, in the *Chicago Tribune*, critic Gene Siskel wrote, "The four daughters are sexy; Dallesandro's Bronx accent is hilarious; and Morrissey directs the chase scenes with solid energy. But then it's ghoulie time. The film concludes with protracted scenes of dismemberment, scenes that make you feel dirty just watching them. If Morrissey had omitted the blood and stumps, and earlier in the film had eliminated Dracula spitting up blood all over his chest, the film might have held a little interest. As it now plays, however, it's repulsive." The film didn't open in New York until February of 1975, playing through May.

The same year *Andy Warhol's Dracula* hit theaters, French director Pierre Grunstein made *Tendre Dracula* (U.S. title: *Tender Dracula, or Confessions of a Blood Drinker*), with Peter Cushing taking a walk on the wild side, turning in his Van Helsing crosses and stakes for Dracula's black cloak and fangs. The plot involves two scriptwriters and two actresses visiting the castle of a vampire who has been posing as an actor, and who wants to switch from making horror films to romantic ones. The film is distinguished, if that's the right word, by a few offbeat musical interludes and the requisite 1970s female nudity.

Orsatti Productions, Inc., announced in April of 1976 that they were going to produce an animated version of *Dracula*, based closely on Stoker's novel and using character designs by famed illustrator Frank Frazetta. George Greer penned the screenplay and was expected to be one of the directors, along with Andrew Chiaramonte. The film, budgeted at $3 million, never happened.

When 1978 saw George Hamilton preparing *Love at First Bite* and Frank Langella planning to star in Universal's *Dracula*, British director Ken Russell announced he was doing his own adaptation of *Dracula*, and acclaimed French director Roger Vadim was said to be preparing yet another version of the Dracula story. Vadim's former flame, Catherine Deneuve, agreed to be in the film, but as with many proposed Dracula projects, these two never took flight.

One that did was 1978's *Doctor Dracula*, Al Adamson's final journey into Dracula-dom. As with other Adamson films, it was like two disparate movies unevenly joined together—which it was. Adamson and producer Sam Sherman acquired a half-finished satanic-sacrifice film from director Paul Aratow and filmed new sequences to flesh it out, bringing in John Carradine to add an air of horror film legitimacy. Geoffrey Land played Dracula, posing as psychiatrist Anatole Gregorio.

Filmmaker Al Adamson eventually came to a grisly end. In August of 1995, police discovered his body buried beneath his house in Indio, 150 miles southeast of Los Angeles. Fred Fulford, an independent contractor who had been living in Adamson's house while remodeling it, was convicted of the murder and sentenced to twenty-five years to life in prison.

Dracula's Dog, also known as *Zoltan, the Hound of Hell*, also hit theaters in 1978. A rather ridiculous exercise scripted by Frank Ray Perilli and directed by Albert Band, the film begins with Russian soldiers unknowingly releasing Zoltan, the hound of the Dracula family, as well as a Renfield-like creature named Veidt Smith (Reggie Nalder) from their tombs. Needing a master, the pair travels to America to find the last remaining member of the Dracula family, now living under the name Michael Drake (Michael Pataki).

John Carradine literally dusted off the cape and tuxedo he'd worn in his Dracula appearances for Universal Pictures in the 1940s for his role in 1979's *Nocturna*, in which he and Yvonne de Carlo (Lily, from *The Munsters*) played an aging vampire couple. (This was Carradine's final portrayal of the Count; he died, in Milan, Lombardy, Italy, on November 22, 1988, at the age of eighty-two.) Nai Bonet, a dancer-turned-actor, not only starred in the film but also came up with the storyline and executive produced the movie.

The year 1979 also saw the release of the porn film *Dracula Sucks*, starring Jamie Gillis as a bearded vampire count. Adult film star Annette Haven played Mina, with Serena as Lucy, and John Holmes as "John Stoker." For budgetary reasons, the film took place in one location, a Northern California castle that was also a sanitarium. Dracula bites his female victims on their breasts, and a male victim is bitten on his penis. The film climaxes, as it were, with Dracula deflowering the virgin Mina, until Van Helsing enters, opens a door, and floods the room with sunlight.

Taking Flight in the '80s

Louise Fletcher, who won an Academy Award for 1975's *One Flew Over the Cuckoo's Nest*, made a stab at vamping in the lead role of 1980's *Mama Dracula*. Produced, directed, and co-written by Boris Szulzinger, the film was produced in Belgium and co-starred Maria Schneider. Based on the legend of Countess Elisabeth Bàthory, the film has Mama Dracula looking for virgin blood in which to bathe and finding it in short supply in the modern era.

Dracula was away from movie screens for awhile, but popped up again in 1985 in the Italian horror-comedy *Fraccia contro Dracula* (*Who Is Afraid of Dracula?*), directed by Neri Perenti and starring Edmund Purdom as Dracula. The story concerns a shy estate agent and a severely nearsighted accountant going to Transylvania to sell Dracula's castle. They encounter not only Dracula but also the vampire's sister, who romances the estate agent to keep from being wed to the Frankenstein Monster.

Two years later, in August of 1987, the immortal Count returned in *The Monster Squad*, directed by Fred Dekker from a script by Dekker and Shane Black. The film centered on a group of kids who call themselves The Monster Squad; they decide to band together to stop a plot by Count Dracula (Duncan Regehr), who has brought together the Frankenstein Monster (Tom Noonan), the Wolf Man (Carl Thibault), the Gill-Man (or Creature from the Black Lagoon, played by Tom Woodruff Jr.), and the Mummy (Michael MacKay). An attempt at mixing a modern-day *Our Gang* comedy with classic monsters, the film scared up few good reviews. When the film was released on home video in 1988, Dennis Hunt of the *Los Angeles Times* called it "a minor league *Ghostbusters.*"

Also in 1987, DeLaurentiis Entertainment Group produced *Dracula's Widow*, starring Sylvia Kristel, best known for the 1974 French soft-porn classic *Emmanuelle*, in the title role. Before the film was released, however, DEG went through a bankruptcy restructuring, which held up the movie's release until the following year. The film was directed by Christopher Coppola, whose brother Nicolas Cage starred in the film *Vampire's Kiss* that same year; four years later, their uncle Francis Ford Coppola made *Bram Stoker's Dracula.*

Waxwork, released in June 1988, involved a group of college students entering a wax museum where they are drawn into exhibits based on horror film characters that come to life, including Dracula (Miles O'Keefe) and his brides. Produced by Vestron on a budget of $1.5 million, the film earned only $808,114 at the box office but took in an additional $2 million when it was released on home video.

The 1990s

In 1990, a year after Romanian dictator Nicolae Ceauşescu was deposed, Charles and Albert Band's Full Moon Productions established a thirty-acre studio in Bucharest. The idea was to churn out low-budget horror movies in the Transylvania region, for extra added authenticity. In 1997, they released *The Creeps*, a film in which a mad scientist brings back Dracula, Frankenstein's Monster, a werewolf, and a mummy by tossing the books of Bram Stoker and Mary Shelly into a machine along with the essence of a naked virgin. When the virgin turns out to be not as advertised, the monsters emerge—just three feet tall. Ooops!

Among the more unusual vampire films that didn't get made was one by Rudolph Grey, a one-time associate of *Plan 9 from Outer Space* director Ed Wood. In the early 1990s, Grey co-wrote a screenplay with film critic Cole Gagne called *Dracula vs. Hitler*. The story concerned Nazis taking a supernatural book from Dracula's castle library to learn the secrets of ultimate power. The ending, said Grey, lived up to the promise of the premise: Dracula did actually fight Hitler.

Nadja (1995), written and directed by Michael Almereyda, featured Elina Löwensohn in the title role, and Peter Fonda as both Dr. Van Helsing and Dracula. The stylish black-and-white film transplanted Dracula's family to modern-day New York and Carpathia.

Bobby "Boris" Pickett's 1962 novelty song "Monster Mash," along with the 1967 stage musical *I'm Sorry the Bridge Is Out, You'll Have to Spend the Night*, became the basis for the 1995 direct-to-video release *Monster Mash: The Movie*. Pickett himself appeared as Dr. Frankenstein, with Anthony Crivello as Dracula, and Sarah Douglas as Countess Natasha ("Nasty") Dracula. The film includes several musical numbers, including—of course—"Monster Mash."

Modern Vampires (1998) was one of the stranger Dracula tales of recent years, with Dracula (Robert Pastorelli) running the club scene in Los Angeles, and Dr. Frederick Van Helsing (Rod Steiger) enlisting the aid of the Crips street gang to take him down.

Dracula 2000 and Beyond

Director Patrick Lussier began a horror trilogy with a film that was called *Dracula 2000* in the U.S., where it was released December 22, 2000, and *Dracula 2001* in other countries, where it was released the following year. Produced by horror master Wes Craven, the film starred Gerard Butler as Dracula, with Christopher Plummer as his nemesis, Abraham Van Helsing. It was Plummer's second time as Van Helsing, having played the role in 1986's *Nosferatu in Venice*. In *Dracula 2000*, Plummer's Van Helsing was almost as old as Dracula, having been kept alive through the years by feeding off a sample of Dracula's blood. The film explained Dracula's vampirism as being a sentence put upon him by Christ, cursing him to live forever in agony. The modern-day story was partly filmed in New Orleans, leading producer Wes Craven to tell Chris Rose of the *New Orleans Times-Picayune*, "New Orleans has that sense of Old European culture, a touch of the exotic, the spiritual, a taste of danger and sexiness. It has the attitude Dracula himself has—of beauty, and a sense of death. Both Dracula and New Orleans love cemeteries."

Though the film was a critical disappointment, it did well enough at the box office to spawn two direct-to-video sequels. *Dracula II: Ascension*, released to video on June 7, 2003, was filmed entirely in Romania, and had Stephen Billington taking up the Dracula role, pursued by Jason Scott Lee as a Vatican vampire hunter. Two years later, on July 12, 2005, *Dracula III: Legacy* was released to video, with Jason Scott Lee reprising his role, and Rutger Hauer taking over as Dracula.

The 2004 TV film *Dracula 3000*, also known as *Dracula 3000: Infinite Darkness*, was a hybrid of Stoker's *Dracula* and the 1979 film *Alien*. Directed by Darrell Roodt, the film had a space crew salvaging a derelict ship, *Demeter*, only to find that it was infested with vampires. It featured Casper Van Dien as Capt. Abraham Van Helsing, and Langley Kirkwood as Orlock, a name derived from F. W. Murnau's 1922 *Nosferatu*.

Van Helsing (2004) revived Universal's famous movie monsters—Dracula (Richard Roxburgh), Frankenstein's Monster (Shuler Hensley), and the Wolf Man (Will Kemp)—in a special-effects extravaganza. Hugh Jackman played the vampire hunter in writer/director Stephen Sommers's epic display of computer-generated action.

Sommers had previously scored hits with *The Mummy* (1999) and *The Mummy Returns* (2001), which reinvented a Universal horror character from the 1930s and '40s by combining it with the whirlwind action and period milieu of 1981's *Raiders of the Lost Ark*. Part of the charm of the old Universal thrillers, however, is that they were limited by what was technically possible to achieve given the state of film advancement at the time and, after the 1930s, their relatively meager budgets. By the time Sommers made *Van Helsing*, he had all the benefits of computer-generated imaging and a budget of $160 million. With virtually no limit on what he could show, Sommers threw in everything, leaving nothing to viewers' imaginations. The result was a film plotted with breakneck speed that didn't give the characters, or the audience, adequate time to breathe, and was coldly uninvolving. The overabundance of computer effects and whiplash camera movements make the film look like a video game and keep the viewer distanced, so that watching it is about as much fun as watching someone else play a video game.

It certainly wasn't your great-grandfather's Van Helsing. Instead of the studied meticulousness of Edward Van Sloan's 1931 interpretation of the kindly, but calculating, Dutch doctor, Sommers's film reinvented Van Helsing as an action hero, with a wide-brimmed hat and duster that would have been at home in a Clint Eastwood Western. And like a Western, the story takes place in the 1880s, though rather than the windswept American plains the setting is Transylvania, where Van Helsing is dispatched by the Knights of the Holy Order to do away with Count Dracula after the vampire revives Frankenstein's Monster. Along the way, Van Helsing meets Anna Valerious, whose brother Velkan has become a werewolf. Anna and Velkan help Van Helsing defeat Dracula, but by the end both have sacrificed their lives to do so. The film ends with Van Helsing setting off for new adventures.

Hugh Jackman, in the title role, lacked the emotional resonance he brought to the *X-Men* franchise, while Richard Roxburgh gave a Lugosi-ish interpretation to his long-haired Dracula, but ultimately came across as being more annoying than terrifying, as did the rest of the film.

Despite its shortcomings, the film was a hit with audiences. After it opened on May 7, 2004, it became the weekend's number-one movie, and eventually took in over $300 million at the international box office. Fittingly, it spawned a casino slot machine game and a *Van Helsing* video game with the character voiced by Jackman. In May 2012, Universal announced that the film would be remade, with Tom Cruise starring.

Two mysterious caped figures of the night confronted each other in the 2005 direct-to-video animated movie *The Batman vs. Dracula.* The film made its debut on the Cartoon Network on October 15, 2005, before being released on home video three days later. Rino Romano provided the voice of Batman, with Peter Stormare voicing Dracula. The plot had the Penguin unleashing Dracula in Gotham City, then becoming the vampire's minion. Batman soon finds himself dealing with the disease of vampirism, leading to a climactic showdown with the vampire king. Guess who wins?

Dracula's Curse, written and directed by Leigh Scott, had a team of vampire hunters led by Rufus King (Thomas Downey) and Jacob Van Helsing (Rhett Giles) battling a group of vampires in a modern metropolis led by Countess Bathorly (Christina Rosenberg). The film, which owed more to *Blade* and *Underworld* than Stoker, was released on DVD on April 25, 2006.

Patrick McManus made his feature film directing debut with 2012's *Dracula Reborn*, with Stuart Rigby as Dracula in yet another modern-day retelling of Stoker's story, this time set in Los Angeles.

That same year, Italian horror director Dario Argento served up *Dracula 3-D*, also known an *Argento's Dracula*, an Italian-French-Spanish co-production starring Thomas Kretschmann as Dracula, and Rutger Hauer, who had played Dracula seven years earlier, doing an about-face as Van Helsing (after his turn as the king vampire, Kretschmann also changed sides and played Abraham Van Helsing in the 2013–14 NBC-TV series *Dracula*). Fans of Argento's horror films consider *Dracula 3D* to be one of his worst, with only one truly original idea: in one brief scene, Dracula turns into a giant computer-generated praying mantis.

Argento's Dracula 3-D (2012): you'll believe Dracula can turn into a giant praying mantis.   *Author's collection*

Yet another 3-D Dracula film, *Dracula 2012*, was released in India on February 8. Directed by Vinayan, it starred Sudheer Sukumaran as Count Dracula. Portions of the film were shot at Bran Castle in Romania, where the historical Vlad III was once held captive.

Not to be outdone, in 2014, Universal Pictures, the studio that started it all, released *Dracula Untold* in 3-D, with Luke Evans as Vlad Tepeş, who becomes a vampire to protect his people. The studio hoped the film would reboot their monsters franchise. Whether it does or not, one thing is certain: after appearing in over two hundred films in the past century, Dracula will return . . .

16

Bad-Ass Bloodsuckers

Blacula and *Blade*

Blacula

T he 1950s and '60s were a time of racial turmoil in America, culminating with the Civil Rights movement that led to the passage of the Civil Rights Act in 1964. Many white communities were resistant to implementing integration, leading to rising tensions in the nation and an eventual split in the movement between the non-violent ideas of leaders like Martin Luther King and the more radical proposals of leaders like Malcolm X and the Black Power advocates who pushed for change "by any means necessary." In any event, the consciousness of the nation was raised, and as the 1960s progressed, blacks were seen on TV in roles other than Pullman porters and maids; by 1965, Bill Cosby was co-starring with Robert Culp in *I Spy,* and the following year saw Nichelle Nichols as a communications officer on *Star Trek.* There was also a push for blacks to establish their own social identity, one tied more to African culture than White Anglo-Saxon Protestant culture.

It was against this backdrop that, in the early 1970s, Dimension Productions and Meier-Murray announced plans to film "Black Dracula," to be directed by Paul Norbert. "Black Dracula" never materialized, but Power Productions began developing *Blacula.* According to horror historian Donald F. Glut, in the original script, the main character was named Andrew Brown, after one of the title characters in the radio and TV series *Amos 'n' Andy.* Chills and laughs ensue when Brown stumbles upon Dracula's castle in Transylvania.

Producer Joseph T. Naar set about interviewing black athletes for the title role, but couldn't find anyone suitable. He then approached distinguished black actor Raymond St. Jacques, who was not interested.

Meanwhile, William Crain, a young black filmmaker fresh out of UCLA's School of Theater, Film and Television who had directed some television episodes (including a superior episode of *The Mod Squad*), went to Screen Gems looking for a job and met Leonard Goldberg, the company's head of production. Crain hoped to get a job directing *Bewitched;* Goldberg suggested

Actor William Marshall fought to keep some dignity in the character of *Blacula* (1972).

© *1972 American International Pictures. Courtesy of Del Valle Archives.*

that he meet producer Samuel Arkoff of American International Pictures, who was looking for a good, reliable, efficient director. Crain duly went to AIP and met with Arkoff, who talked with him for a few minutes, and then offered him *Blacula.*

Crain would have preferred his first feature film to be one he had written. He went to his mother and told her AIP seemed to have their own concept of the story, and maybe he could just skate through it and wait for a better opportunity to show off his skills later. She advised him to take the job, and then do the best to make it *his* movie.

According to Crain, AIP originally wanted to call the film "Count Brown's In Town," and they had their own ideas about who should play the vampire; Harry Belafonte's name was mentioned. Ultimately, the part went to six-foot-five-inch Shakespearean actor William Marshall. After spending months auditioning actors, Crain said Marshall, whom he had seen on an episode of *The Man from U.N.C.L.E.*, had exactly the right persona.

As a proud black man wary of perpetuating harmful stereotypes, Marshall was determined to steer the project in a different direction. He insisted on being involved in a rewrite of the script, changing the lead character from "Andrew Brown" to the African Prince Mamuwalde, who goes to Dracula's castle in 1780 to convince the Count to help him put an end to the slave trade, unaware that his host is a vampire. AIP was nervous about introducing slavery into the script, but, at Marshall's insistence, it remained. Marshall also suggested the idea that in the modern-day scenes, the woman Blacula becomes involved with is the reincarnation of his long-lost wife.

The son of a dentist and a schoolteacher, William Marshall, who was born in Gary, Indiana, in 1924, recalled that it was a backstage visit to the original production of *The Green Pastures* when he was eight years old that inspired him to become an actor. Growing into a handsome, baritone-voiced young man, he seemed destined for film and theater. After fighting in World War II, he trained with the American Theater Wing in New York and received operatic training. One of his first Broadway roles was in a revival of the play that originally inspired him, playing De Lawd in *The Green Pastures* in 1951. He went on to perform in Europe and America, landing the title roles in *Oedipus Rex*, *Othello*, and a play about Paul Robeson. After moving to California, he taught acting at California State University at Northridge, won roles in films like *Lydia Bailey* (1952) and *Demetrius and the Gladiators* (1954), and eventually distinguished himself on television, with guest-starring parts on such 1960s TV series as *Rawhide*, *The Man from U.N.C.L.E.*, *Star Trek*, and *Tarzan*. With a voice made for Shakespeare, he also starred in numerous stage productions: Harold Hobson, a critic for the *Times of London*, called Marshall "the best Othello of our time."

When he was asked to star in *Blacula*, Marshall initially balked. He had been frightened by horror films as a child, but he saw Blacula as a tragic hero rather than a monster. Playing the role wouldn't make Marshall rich; he was paid two thousand dollars per week, for four-and-a-half weeks of shooting, ending up with nine thousand dollars before income taxes.

William Crain sought to make not just a good blaxploitation film but a good horror film, one that would reach beyond its target black audience. He cast Canadian actor Gordon Pinsent as the police lieutenant; Thalmus Rasulala as the Van Helsing character, Dr. Gordon Thomas; and Denise Nicholas, with whom he had previously worked on *Room 222* when he was the show's dialogue coach. Vonetta McGee, who was getting a lot of attention in Hollywood at the time, was cast in the dual role of Mamuwalde's wife, Luva, and her modern-day reincarnation, Tina. Charles Macauley portrayed a white-haired, dandified Count Dracula. Reportedly, half the crew of *Blacula* was black, including assistant director Charles Walker.

Crain fought against some of the more conventional ideas AIP tried to foist on him. Rather than the lining of Blacula's cape being blood red, he insisted on making it steel gray, which he thought looked cooler on film.

One of *Blacula*'s most famous scenes has a female vampire cabbie running in slow-motion down a hospital corridor toward character actor Elisha Cook Jr., playing a morgue attendant. He shot that scene on the third day of filming, using a high-speed camera. He had to put up a fight to get AIP to arrange for the camera, but it was worth the struggle; the terrifying slow-motion shot became one of the film's iconic images.

The film ends tragically, with Blacula, having lost the woman he loves, destroying himself out of grief. The finale was Marshall's idea—he felt it was important that Blacula not be staked, but that he chooses to walk into the sunlight. After shooting at locations all around Los Angeles, the production wrapped after twenty-eight days.

Blacula reached theaters at the end of July 1972. It benefited from a word-of-mouth publicity campaign organized by Samuel Arkoff through black fraternal magazines and journals. In both Los Angeles and San Francisco, gala premieres of *Blacula* were held in the black communities. The *Los Angeles Sentinel*, a black newspaper, ran a two-page photo spread of the event.

To ensure the film's success, Marshall embarked on an extensive cross-country publicity tour, stopping in twenty cities. Consequently, *Blacula* became one of American International's all-time top earners, leading the distributor to take out ads in *Variety* proclaiming: "He's *Blacula*, He's Beautiful, He's Box-office!" By April of 1973, the film had grossed $13 million, making it the highest-grossing film in AIP's nearly twenty-year history. The film also made William Crain the first black filmmaker out of a major film school to have substantial mainstream success; it did not, however, immediately lead to better offers. Crain returned to television, directing episodes of *Starsky & Hutch*, *S.W.A.T.*, *The Rookies*, and the groundbreaking *Roots* before closing out the blaxploitation era with another horror entry, *Dr. Black and Mr. Hyde*.

Scream, Blacula, Scream

A year after *Blacula*'s release, Marshall was back in *Scream, Blacula, Scream*. Rather than William Crain, AIP turned to Robert Kelljan to direct the sequel. Kelljan had made a minor success of another low-budget vampire film, *Count Yorga, Vampire* (1970). The script for the second *Blacula* film, again written by Joan Torres and Raymond Koenig along with Maurice Jules, put more emphasis on humor, diminishing the menacing quality of the title character. The plot had Blacula seeking out a voodoo queen played by cult favorite—and AIP's top female star—Pam Grier, in search of a cure for his vampirism.

The *Chicago Defender*, a black newspaper, was one of the first to carry mention of the sequel, reporting on March 6, 1973, that character actor Bernie Hamilton had been cast as voodoo priest Ragman in "Blacula II."

Marshall felt uncomfortable returning for the sequel, feeling there was a sense of sliding downhill, though he did look forward to working with Pam Grier.

Poster for 1973's *Scream, Blacula, Scream*. Before the film was released, employees of American International Pictures were asked to submit possible titles.   *Author's collection*

On Friday, June 29, 1973, *Scream, Blacula, Scream* opened at the Michael Todd Theater in Chicago, with Pam Grier in attendance. It opened in New York on July 18, 1973, not quite a year after its predecessor. In his *New York Times* review, Roger Greenspun chided director Robert Kelljan for having an insufficiently developed plot, writing, "In William Marshall (Mamuwalde) and Pam Grier (Lisa) he has two good performers—powerful, ironic, potentially rather complicated. But he hasn't enough for them to do. It is as if the movie had completed filming without there ever having developed the shooting script."

In Whittier, California, a double feature of *Blacula* and *Scream, Blacula, Scream* was screened on January 24, 1974, at a fundraiser for the Society for the Development of Black Heritage Drama and Whittier Area Fair Housing Legal Defense Group. Four months later, Marshall was honored by the members of the Count Dracula Society with the Cinema Award for his two films as Blacula. In addition, Marshall won the first annual award of the Academy of Science Fiction, Fantasy and Horror Films.

Plans were afoot for a third *Blacula* movie, and William Marshall was to co-star with Robert Quarry and Vincent Price in a third film in Price's *Dr. Phibes* series, but those projects never came to fruition. AIP also approached Marshall about making a cameo as Blacula in *Blackenstein* (1973). The actor declined. Marshall was also supposed to have co-starred with Peter Cushing in Amicus Productions' *The Beast Must Die* (1974), but was prevented from doing so because his AIP contract wouldn't allow him to do a horror film for another company. Instead, he played an exorcist in AIP's *Abbey* (1974), a blaxploitation version of *The Exorcist.*

Vampire in Brooklyn

After *Blacula*, it would be nearly two decades before a black vampire would again headline a horror movie. Finally, on October 18, 1992, Ryan Murphy of the *Los Angeles Times* announced that Eddie Murphy was preparing a vampire film for Paramount Pictures to be called *Vampire in Brooklyn*, due to start filming in 1993. Originally, Murphy did not intend to star in the movie, but planned to appear in several cameo parts, similar to *Coming to America* (1988), in which he played several different roles. He did plan, however, to direct the film. Paramount persuaded Murphy to take only $4 million up front for his services, instead of his normal $12 million fee, in return for a percentage of the gross.

Murphy was deeply involved in the project. The idea for the story came from Murphy's brother, Vernon Lynch Jr. The script was written by Murphy and his older brother, Charlie Murphy. Murphy's cousin Ray Murphy Jr. was a co-producer.

By March of 1993, Murphy had changed his mind about directing, and Robert Townsend was attached. Townsend eventually dropped out, and a director known more for horror than comedy stepped in: Wes Craven, director of *The Hills Have Eyes* (1977) and *A Nightmare on Elm Street* (1984).

In interviews, Craven said that it wouldn't be the usual Eddie Murphy comedy, explaining that it would instead be the ultimate fish-out-of-water story. Although known as a comedian, Murphy played the role relatively straight, leaving the comedy to Kadeem Hardison and John Witherspoon, as a nephew and uncle who get swept up in the vampire's plans. Angela Bassett signed on to play the love interest.

Soon after filming began, tragedy struck. On the night of November 3, 1994, the crew was filming a scene in downtown Los Angeles which involved a woman falling backwards off a building. Twenty-six-year-old stuntwoman Sonya Davis invited her family to come to the set and watch the filming. When it was time for Davis to do the stunt, she fell backwards and plummeted to the ground, forty two feet below, where an airbag was supposed to break her fall. Whether the air bag was improperly inflated, out of position, or both, remains unclear. What is certain is that Davis only partially landed on a corner of the air bag and the rest of her body struck the cement, leaving her critically injured; she died thirteen days later. Davis's family retained famed attorney Melvin Belli, who sued Eddie Murphy and Paramount Pictures for $50 million, citing shoddy work by the film crew (nine crew members were also named in the suit). The suit maintained that Davis should have been provided with a safety cord and that an ambulance should have been on standby when the stunt was filmed.

Patrons who went to see *Scream, Blacula, Scream* at the Michael Todd Theater in Chicago on June 28 and 29, 1973, also got to see Pam Grier in person.

Author's collection

The movie was in rough-cut form by June of 1995. Craven said that Murphy was pleased with the result, watching it over and over, sometimes twice or three times a day. To create buzz for the film, Paramount scheduled a screening prior to the film's official premiere, when Wes Craven appeared at *Fangoria*'s Weekend of Horrors convention at Manhattan's Park Central Hotel at the end of August 1995 and introduced the film to an audience of horror-film aficionados.

Vampire in Brooklyn arrived in theaters on October 27, just before Halloween. It received mostly negative reviews, with critics finding it an uneasy mix of laughs and chills. The *Boston Globe*'s Jay Carr wrote, "Murphy looks good in his dandified vampire duds and flowing hair. But he never comes close to capturing the grand romantic sweep and seductiveness of the great movie vampires. He isn't even very scary. And he's got a too-obvious wig line. There's nothing primal about his Nosferatu, nothing noble, poignant, resonant, dangerously sexy. . . . *Vampire in Brooklyn* is no *Blacula*." In the *Chicago Tribune*, Gene Siskel wrote that *Vampire in Brooklyn* "will drive another nail in the coffin of Eddie Murphy's film career."

Not all critics were so dismissive, however. Michael Wilmington of the *Chicago Tribune* called it, "A gaudy, bawdy, amusingly gory and sometimes spectacular horror comedy about a Carpathian-African vampire prowling modern Brooklyn in search of his mate, *Vampire* hands Murphy the kind of showcase he hasn't had for years."

On its opening weekend, *Vampire in Brooklyn* was in second place at the box office, pulling in $7 million, behind *Get Shorty*, which had $10.5 million in its second weekend. It ended its run grossing $19 million in the U.S.

In an interview with Brian Hiatt of *Rolling Stone*, Eddie Murphy said he made *Vampire in Brooklyn* to get out of his deal with Paramount Pictures so he could move on to Universal and make *The Nutty Professor* (1996). Summing up *Vampire in Brooklyn,* he told Hiatt, "You know what ruined that movie? The wig. I walked out in that longhaired wig and people said, 'Oh, get . . . out of here! What the hell is this?' It's those little things."

Blade

In 1973, the year that *Blacula* came to cinema screens, another black vampire made his debut, this one in the comics. Blade, a depiction of a part-human vampire hunter as action hero, was introduced as a supporting character in Marvel Comics' *Tomb of Dracula* #10. It took twenty-one years for Blade to get his own comic book, *Blade: The Vampire Hunter,* which lasted for only ten issues, published from July 1994 to April 1995.

One of the readers of those 1970s *Tomb of Dracula* comics was Wesley Snipes, who twenty years later would take Hollywood by storm. For the Bronx-born actor, success came relatively quickly. After appearing in the video for Michael Jackson's *Bad* in 1987, he moved into film roles, winning notice for playing Willie Mays Hayes in *Major League* (1989). He was then signed by one of Hollywood's biggest agencies, Creative Artists. His then-agent, Donna Chavous, was impressed by his charisma, his martial art abilities, and his discipline. Snipes, she said, knew what he wanted and what he needed.

What Snipes wanted was to be a superstar, but his former manager, Dolores Robinson, said studio executives told her Snipes's skin was too dark and compared him unfavorably to Denzel Washington, saying they would never hire anyone "darker than Denzel." Snipes persevered, landing leading roles in *New Jack City, Jungle Fever* (both 1991), *White Men Can't Jump, Passenger 57* (both 1992), *Demolition Man,* and *Rising Sun* (both 1993). Despite what the studios believed Middle America would accept as a hero, he succeeded as a dark-skinned black man who defined a whole new type of sex appeal. At that point in his career, Snipes was receiving $10 million per picture, with 10 percent gross profit participation.

After those early hits, however, Snipes began to make headlines for such escapades as being found with a concealed weapon at a traffic stop, and leading police on a 30-mile, 120-miles per hour chase until he crashed his motorcycle. Unlike other black celebrities, he did not make a point of showing up to black-themed events, and alienated black women by appearing in the film *One Night Stand* (1997), in which his character—like the character he played in *Jungle Fever*—becomes involved with a white woman. He then admitted in an interview that he preferred Asian women; he had two children with his wife, Nikki Park, a painter of Korean ancestry. There were also ongoing legal troubles, with Snipes being sued, or suing, former bodyguards, managers, publicists, and agents.

Snipes's career went into a slump, with one mediocre film after another, and the actor was all too aware that his fans were feeling let down. Having established his own production company, Amen Ra Films (Afrakhan Minds Engaged N Royal Affairs), Snipes decided to produce a starring vehicle for himself.

He remembered how inspiring it had been for him, as a child, to see a black hero in the comics. Now, he would bring that hero to the screen. Snipes was attached to a proposed film version of the comic book *The Black Panther*, a character created by Stan Lee and Jack Kirby. Due to legal issues with Marvel Comics, that project stalled. Meanwhile, *Blade* began to pick up steam at New Line Productions. By the time Snipes was approached, they already had a working script, by David S. Goyer, who broke into the industry with his 1989 script for the Jean-Claude Van Damme action vehicle *Death Warrant*. Snipes's managers and agents all thought he was out of his mind for wanting to do it. He was, they said, a classically trained actor. Why play a vampire from a comic book? But Snipes was excited by the script, the opportunity it would give him to show off his martial arts skills, as well as the promise of a potential franchise, and the offer of an $8 million salary. Snipes was soon involved in the script, the casting, and the production; he wanted to have his hands in it as much as possible.

The *Blade* script involved half-human/half-vampire Blade seeking to eradicate other vampires with his mentor and helper, Abraham Whistler, played by country music singer/songwriter and Rhodes scholar Kris Kristofferson. Blade and Whistler are opposed by Deacon Frost (Stephen Dorff), whose goal is to bring about a bloody vampire apocalypse called "The Blood Tide." Caught in the middle is Dr. Karen Jansen (N'Bushe Wright), a hematologist who may have found a cure for vampirism.

As originally conceived in the 1970s *Tomb of Dracula* comics by Marv Wolfman and Gene Colan, Blade was one of a band of vampire hunters who assembled to confront Count Dracula. In updating the character for the '90s, the producers made some changes. They decided not to deal with Dracula at all, saving him for a later entry. Both Whistler and Frost were new characters created for the film, to give Blade an ally and a formidable antagonist.

After having given an over-the-top, scenery-chewing performance in *Demolition Man*, Snipes took a more restrained approached to *Blade*, making him more controlled and determined. "He gets his fun out of his intervention with the vampires and the fight, the hunt," Snipes told *Starlog* magazine's Ian Spelling. "These things thrill him. But he has a morality as well, which I like."

Snipes enjoyed making the film, which, despite the fact that the main character was half-vampire, he didn't classify as a horror film, but as a suspense-action movie with a lot of humor and elements of drama.

Upon its release on August 19, 1998, the film received effusive reviews. Roger Ebert gave the film three out of four stars, writing, "Wesley Snipes understands the material from the inside out and makes an effective Blade because he knows that the key ingredient in any interesting superhero is not omnipotence, but vulnerability. . . . By embodying those feelings, Snipes as Blade gives the movie that edge of emotion without which it would simply be special effects."

Carlton Jackson Jr., in the black newspaper the *New York Amsterdam News*, wrote that *Blade* was "a movie comparable to any Hollywood summer action film, and better than most. Buyers beware—*Blade* is a vampire film, not a Black vampire film. See it and enjoy the mixed blessing of progress."

Blade II

Blade earned $70 million at the U.S. box office and almost as much overseas. It also did good business on home video. Its success ensured that there would be a sequel, but it was four years before the vampire hunter returned. Producer and star Wesley Snipes said he held off until he could get everything right and make it, as he told Terry Lawson of *Knight Ridder Tribune News Service*, "the baddest, hippest, most daring comic-book movie we can make."

Co-executive producer David S. Goyer once again penned the screenplay, and—wanting a strong visual style for the film—turned to Guillermo del Toro to direct. Del Toro was not the usual journeyman director; he put his heart and soul into every film he made. As he told Jonathan Romney of London's the *Independent on Sunday*, "*Blade II* has one of the most offensively simplistic storylines in the history of film, but I view it like a musical. You go to a Gene Kelly movie and what do you want to see? Gene Kelly dancing. What, you want the movie to stop and Blade recite Keats?" Del Toro wanted to give the film a certain freshness, and infused the action scenes with the purely escapist and sometimes funny and outlandish violence of Japanese anime.

Budgeted at $48 million, *Blade II* was filmed in the Czech capital of Prague in 2001. It was a long shoot, lasting five months. To add more pizzazz to the fight scenes, Snipes brought in Donnie Yen, the fight coordinator of the Hong Kong action film *Iron Monkey*, to choreograph the martial arts action.

The climactic fight in *Blade II* lasts four minutes on screen, but took days to capture on film. At one point during filming, despite practicing the scene, Luke Goss missed a cue and clipped Snipes. Snipes shrugged it off, telling Goss that when he was making *Demolition Man*, he accidentally landed one on Sylvester Stallone. By the time he finished making *Blade II*, Snipes had been stabbed through the hand, had torn a meniscus cartilage in his knee, and received a cut on his nose.

Blade II had its premiere at Mann's Chinese Theater on March 21, 2002. The film's stars, including Snipes, Goss, Kristofferson, Ron Perlman, Leonor Varela, and Norman Reedus were in attendance, along with director Guillermo del Toro and screenwriter/executive producer David S. Goyer. Invited guests included Magic Johnson, Carl Lewis, Eriq LaSalle, Cedric the Entertainer, and Kate Beckinsale.

The film opened nationwide the following day, released to 2,707 theaters. In its first weekend, it was the number-one movie in America, grossing $33.1 million over three days, twice as much as the first film did on its initial weekend. In the end, the film became Guillermo del Toro's biggest hit, earning $82.3 million in 2002.

Despite its box-office success, the film was met with mostly negative reviews. It didn't matter; by the time of its theatrical release, screenwriter David S. Goyer was already at work on a third instalment.

Blade: Trinity

After wrapping *Blade II*, screenwriter/executive producer David S. Goyer and Guillermo del Toro began tossing around ideas for "Blade III." They were thinking it might take place twenty-five years in the future. After being out of sight for a decade, Blade has become a mythic figure. Meanwhile, vampires have overrun the world, enslaving humans. Blade eventually emerges and leads a rebellion. Del Toro called it a "*Spartacus* with vampires."

With the success of *Blade II*, Guillermo del Toro was offered a job directing *Hellboy*. He took it, which made him unavailable to direct "Blade III." He encouraged David S. Goyer to take the reins. Goyer had previously directed Wesley Snipes in the 2002 film *Zigzag*, and had done some assistant directing on the first two Blade movies, as well as producing the second one, during which he spent a lot of time with Guillermo del Toro, learning the ropes.

When Snipes voiced doubt about the "*Spartacus* with vampires" script, it was replaced with one a bit less epic, pitting Blade, assisted by Hannibal King and Abigail Whistler (leaders of the vampire-hunting Nightstalkers), against the king vampire of them all, Dracula. Dominic Purcell, an Australian TV star who had more recently played the title role in the American TV series *John Doe*, took on the role of Dracula, who is also called Drake in Goyer's action-packed screenplay. Jessica Biel, star of TV's *7th Heaven*, came on board as Abigail, and Ryan Reynolds, who had starred in the comedy *Van Wilder*, took the role of wisecracking Hannibal King.

Having tried to write a script with more wit and character than your average comic-book movie, Goyer also sent the screenplay to Parker Posey, an actress known primarily for her work in quirky independent films. "I tried not to act shocked when she called to say she wanted to do it, but I was," he told Terry Lawson of Knight Ridder Tribune News Service.

By the time he made *Blade: Trinity*, Snipes was able to command a larger paycheck; he earned $12 million for his third outing as the vampire hunter. The film was budgeted at $65 million and was originally planned to be filmed in Prague, but production began September 21, 2003, in Vancouver, Canada.

Goyer prepared by having storyboard artists sketch three different scenarios for every shot, and in the action scenes he had extra cameramen who had no fixed-shot assignments, free to spontaneously shoot anything interesting that happened. He also surrounded himself with skilled, experienced craftspeople and technicians.

Despite his preparation, filming did not go off entirely without a hitch. Goyer enrolled Biel, Posey, and Reynolds in a training program to prepare them for the physical challenges of making the movie and to acquaint them with bows and firearms. While filming one scene, Biel accidentally shot an arrow straight into the lens of a camera. Goyer was told the camera lens cost three hundred thousand dollars.

Later in the shoot, an onset fight over a T-shirt escalated until Snipes reportedly tried to strangle Goyer. Goyer then hired bouncers from a strip club to be his security detail. Snipes spent the rest of the shoot communicating with his director only through Post-it notes. "There has always been a little bit of drama on the *Blade* sets," Goyer told Lorenzo Munoz of the *Los Angeles Times*. "It became clear to me that Wesley is a very Method actor. When he is doing a *Blade* movie he is Blade and he acts like Blade. Blade is edgy and bristly."

Part of Snipes's unease was his feeling that his Blade character was being sidelined in favor of the younger

Poster for 2004's *Blade Trinity*. A TV ad for the film was pulled after its first day of airing because it misidentified actress Jessica Biel as Jessica Alba.   *Author's collection*

vampire hunters, played by Jessica Biel and Ryan Reynolds. The actor's relationship with Goyer became so contentious that when the film wrapped, Snipes wrote a five-page letter to New Line Cinema co-chairman and founder Robert Shaye detailing his grievances.

Blade: Trinity was originally set for an August opening, but its release was moved to avoid competing with *Alien vs. Predator*. Instead, New Line shifted it into a December slot, opening *Blade: Trinity* in 2,912 theaters on Wednesday, December 8. The R-rated film did an estimated $5.5-million on its opening day.

The third instalment of the franchise received the worst notices of the series. In the *Boston Globe*, Ty Burr called it "an unholy mess: underlit, overedited, with a glum star and about three too many story lines."

After his behind-the-scenes battles with David Goyer, Wesley Snipes wasn't surprised when the film performed poorly, telling Tim Robey of the *London*

Sunday Telegraph, "I wouldn't call it a disappointment, more of an expectation. . . . Bad ingredients going in, bad cake coming out. If you've got sour milk going in your cake, you're going to get sour cake."

Blade: The Series

After *Blade: Trinity*, there was talk of a possible Blade TV series for Showtime to star Wesley Snipes. Those plans evaporated when Snipes sued New Line over profits from the films.

The cable network Spike TV later stepped in and ordered a pilot based on the *Blade* movies, which kicked off with a two-hour telefilm premiere on June 28, 2006. *Blade: The Series* had music star Kirk Jones, who used the stage name Sticky Fingaz as part of the rap group Onyx, taking over the role of the half-human vampire hunter. The thirty-two-year-old actor relished playing the action role, especially since, for the show, Blade was given a cool motorcycle.

Jones, like Wesley Snipes, was from New York. A physically fit five feet ten, he started as a barber while in his early teens. As a favor, he joined his cousin Fredo Starr's hip-hop group, Onxy. The group was signed by Jam Master Jay of Run-DMC and, at age seventeen, Jones was in the recording studio. Onyx's first album went platinum, producing the hit single, "Slam." Jones began acting in films in 1995, with roles in *Clockers*, *Dead Presidents*, and the TV series *Over There*.

For the series, Blade was given a new colleague, Krista Starr, an ex-soldier played by Jill Wagner. Neil Jackson took on the role of villain Marcus Van Sciver, oozing continental elegance.

David S. Goyer, who developed the series, brought in Geoff Johns, his co-writer on the *Justice Society of America* comics, to produce the show. The series was set in Detroit, largely because both Goyer and Johns were from Michigan: Goyer grew up in Ann Arbor; Johns, in Clarkston. The series was actually filmed, however, in Vancouver. The two-hour pilot performed well enough for Spike TV to order eleven episodes of the series. The final one was broadcast on September 13, 2006.

Nearly two years later, on April 24, 2008, Wesley Snipes was convicted of willfully failing to file tax returns and sentenced to three years in Pennsylvania's McKean Federal Correctional Institution; he was released on April 2, 2013.

One could argue that the *Blade* films, beginning in 1998, helped point the way to just how profitable a comic-book-based franchise could be. The three *Blade* films piled up worldwide grosses of $286 million, with an additional $250 million in domestic DVD sales. Altogether, the three films brought in over $1.5 billion in worldwide grosses.

While promoting 2014's *Expendables 3*, Wesley Snipes let it be known that he would like to return to the *Blade* franchise. Not surprisingly, it was soon announced that he had signed on for *Blade 4*.

17

Louis and Lestat

The Vampire Chronicles

A Novel Idea

Anne Rice's novel *Interview with the Vampire* hit the ground running. By the time it was published by Alfred A. Knopf in April of 1976, the motion picture rights had already been sold to Paramount Pictures, the Book-of-the-Month Club listed it as an alternate selection, and it had immediately high sales in paperback.

The novel is constructed as a kind of memoir, with vampire Louis telling his story to an investigative journalist in a seedy San Francisco apartment. Louis's tale begins with his initiation in 1791, when a vampire named Lestat turns him into a vampire. The reader then follows Louis's progress as he learns to kill, feels revulsion for what he's become, and ultimately learns that in order to accept his separateness, he must be divorced from his human emotions. But it's not simply the plot that kept readers turning the pages—it was the lush, elegant prose of its author, Anne Rice.

As a young girl, Rice lived with her family in a white clapboard house on St. Charles Street in New Orleans and attended Holy Name of Jesus School, where the Sisters of Mercy nuns considered her a bit of an odd one. Speaking to Stewart Kellerman of the *New York Times*, Rice said, "I was a misfit at Holy Name. . . . I was an oddball and a dreamer, just as I am now."

She also, at an early age, began to rebel against the strict Catholicism of Holy Name of Jesus. "I'll never entirely get over the damage done to me by the Catholic attitude toward sex. The hatred of sex, the loathing of it and the denial of the loathing of it," she told Carolyn Kellogg of the *Los Angeles Times*. As a child, living in a city redolent of voodoo and Old World culture, she was fascinated by stories about haunted houses. At the local public library, she looked for horror stories, but the two books that most chilled her were *Great Expectations* and *Jane Eyre*.

Her alcoholic mother died when she was fifteen, and her father took his four daughters to Texas. While a student at North Texas State University in Denton, Texas, Rice turned her back on the Catholic Church. Soon after, she married her high-school sweetheart, Stan Rice, and the couple moved to San Francisco.

Embarking upon a writing career, she wrote erotic novels under the pen name Anne Rampling, and then, as A.N. Roquelaure, penned three books that, according to the *New York Times*' Kellerman, turned "the *Sleeping Beauty* fairy tale into three books of sadomasochistic pornography." Her steamy novels stemmed not from real life but from her fertile imagination, as she told Kellerman. "I've been married for 28 years and my life is really that of a mother," she said. "I'm a totally conservative person. In the middle of Haight-Ashbury in the 60's [*sic*], I was typing away while everybody around me was dropping acid and smoking grass. I was known as my own square."

Then one day in the late 1960s, she began writing a short story about an interview with a vampire named Louis. She worked at it on and off into the early '70s as she got a master's degree in English and creative writing from San Francisco State University, where her husband taught creative writing.

The Rices had a child, Michelle, born in 1966. Sadly, just a month before her sixth birthday in 1972, she died from leukemia. Rice channeled her grief into her vampire story. As the story evolved into a novel, a new character emerged: Claudia, a child who became a vampire at the same age Michelle died.

Most notable of the characters modeled after Rice's family members was Lestat, whose physical description, tall and blonde, was similar to her husband, Stan. She chose the name "Lestat" because she thought it was an old Louisiana name. When she later investigated, she discovered the name was actually "Lestan."

Interview with the Vampire

In the spring of 1976, Paramount Pictures optioned the film rights to *Interview with the Vampire*. After John Travolta became a cinema sensation with *Saturday Night Fever*, it was felt that the vampire story would be a perfect fit for him. The novel passed through several producers and was even considered as a possible mini-series, with a diverse array of scriptwriters attempting to adapt it, from Frank DeFelitta, who penned the script to the supernatural horror film *Audrey Rose*, to Pulitzer Prize–winning playwright Michael Cristofer. After balking about versions of the story where one of the male vampires was altered to be a woman (Cher, considered for the role, wrote a song with Shirley Eikhard for the proposed film, "Lovers Forever," which eventually appeared on her 2013 album, *Closer to the Truth*), or scripts that dropped the Claudia character altogether because she was considered "pornographic," the author herself tried her hand at adapting her own book, writing scripts in 1977, 1988, and 1992.

The rights passed from Paramount to Lorimar, which acquired film rights to the first three Vampire Chronicles novels as well as rights to Rice's Mayfair Witches trilogy. Then, in 1988, Warner Bros. acquired Lorimar Productions, and with them the film rights to Rice's books. The studio struck a deal with music impresario David Geffen to take up the producing chores on *Interview with the Vampire*. Geffen felt the problems in adapting the book were due to its

Louis (Brad Pitt) is introduced to the ways of the vampire by Lestat (Tom Cruise) in 1994's *Interview with the Vampire.*   © *1994 Geffen Pictures/Warner Bros. Courtesy of Del Valle Archives.*

"vast canvas," though he told Pat H. Broeske of the *New York Times* in 1992, "I can only assure you that we're making progress."

Rice envisioned British actor Julian Sands for the role of Lestat, but it was felt that he was too much of an unknown in the U.S., except for art film aficionados who had seen *A Room with a View* (1985). When the role was given to Tom Cruise, Rice was taken aback, saying he was no more her vampire Lestat than Edward G. Robinson was Rhett Butler. She changed her mind after seeing the film, saying on her website, "[F]rom the moment he appeared, Tom was Lestat for me."

Brad Pitt, who was cast as Louis, later said that making *Interview with the Vampire* was one of the worst experiences of his life. Aoife Bannon of London's the *Sun* reported Pitt as saying, "Six months in the . . . dark, contact lenses, make-up, I'm playing the bitch role. . . . Now I'd be able to say, 'This is a problem, we fix this, or I'm outta here.'" At the time, he became so fed up that he went to David Geffen and asked what it would take to get out of the picture. Geffen calmly responded, "Forty million dollars."

River Phoenix was originally cast as the interviewer, Daniel, but four weeks before filming was due to begin, on Halloween morning 1993, he overdosed and died outside The Viper Room, a Sunset Strip nightclub partly owned by Johnny Depp. Christian Slater took the role, donating his entire salary to

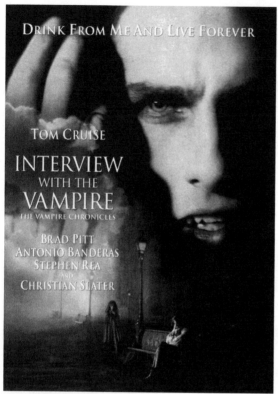

When *Interview with the Vampire* was released, Tom Cruise was a bigger box-office draw than any of his co-stars, hence his face dominates the poster.   *Author's collection*

Phoenix's favorite charities. The film concludes with a dedication to Phoenix after the end credit roll.

Though lushly produced on a budget of $60 million, *Interview with the Vampire* struggled to cram a lot of story into a too-short running time. Nonetheless, it was the number-one film the weekend after it opened on November 11, 1994, taking in $36.4 million. Its eventual worldwide box-office was $224 million, with $105 million being earned in the U.S.

The Vampire Lestat

Published in 1985, Rice's second novel in The Vampire Chronicles series, *The Vampire Lestat*, took the focus off Louis and told Lestat's story, from how he was turned in ancient Rome to eighteenth-century France to the modern-day 1980s, when he becomes a rock star whose music literally wakes the dead. After breaching vampire etiquette by revealing to the masses that he is a literal bloodsucker, the dead descend on his concert at the novel's climax to banish Lestat once and for all. The cliffhanger ending sets the stage for the next novel, *Queen of the Damned*.

A film adaptation of *The Vampire Lestat* was meant to follow *Interview with the Vampire*. The rights to the Rice novels became entangled in legalities as David Geffen went off to start his own studio, Dreamworks SKG, with Steven Spielberg and Jeffrey Katzenberg. But the books remained tied to Warner Bros., who inherited them from Lorimar Pictures when Warners bought them out.

In the late 1980s, Rice moved back to New Orleans. She continued writing, working in an uncluttered corner of her upstairs bedroom. She completed the third book of The Vampire Chronicles in 1988. *Queen of the Damned* picked up where *The Vampire Lestat* left off, with Lestat, the self-proclaimed "James Bond of vampires," explaining how he escaped his supposed demise in the previous book. He also told how his re-emergence threatens the six-thousand-year-old underworld of vampires, the origin of which stretches back to pre-dynastic Egypt. There was also a subplot that involved Armand, coven-master of the Theater of Vampires from *The Vampire Lestat*, pursuing and seducing Daniel, the naïve young man who conducted the interview with Louis in *Interview with the Vampire*.

In reviewing the book for the *Chicago Tribune*, Richard Panek broke down the "satisfying formula" of Rice's novels. First, eroticism, or more specifically, homoeroticism. "Where Rice raises the stakes, so to speak, is by creating an original metaphor for gay society—an underworld of the undead that functions within society, yet, of necessity, outside of it." Second: perversions of Christianity. "Once again," said Panek, "Rice is relying on a solid foundation from vampire legends, which first arose partly as a reaction to the cannibalistic symbolism of Christianity. In *Queen of the Damned*, Rice goes so far as to send the world a modern vision of the Virgin Mary." Third: the decadence of modern life, symbolized in past novels by eighteenth-century Paris and nineteenth-century New Orleans, but in *Queen of the Damned* it is modern-day Miami, described as a "vampire's city—hot, teeming and embracingly beautiful," and "a parody of both heaven and hell." And, of course, the struggle between good and evil, with Lestat claiming, "I wanted to be a symbol of evil in a century that didn't have a place for the literal evil that I am."

"If all this sounds a little like *Dark Shadows* on an epic scale, it is," said Panek. "Yet for all their flippancy, for all their sheer silliness, the *Vampire Chronicles* represent sophisticated storytelling. Anne Rice has constructed a legend that, like many an omnipotent religious presence, seemingly has no beginning and conceivably has no end."

Queen of the Damned

The film rights in Rice's novels were due to revert back to her at the end of 2000. In 1997, Rice began talking with a director who was very excited in pursuing a film of *The Vampire Lestat*. She claimed that she begged studio executives to let her write a script for union scale and a deferred payment that wouldn't be due until the release of the picture. They weren't interested.

The following year, story meetings began regarding adapting one or both of the other Vampire Chronicles novels. Early on, it was decided that *The Vampire Lestat* was too broad and episodic for a two-hour feature, so the plan was to base most of the movie on the third book, *Queen of the Damned*, rewriting much of the plot. Lesat's career as a rock star from the second novel would provide the basis for the plot. Rice was put out by the studio's treatment of her, saying they hadn't been receptive to her or her ideas at all.

In 1999, the project was developed by screenwriters Scott Abbott and Michael Petroni. Australian Michael Rymer was chosen to direct. After considering Jenna Dewan and Foxy Brown, singer Aaliyah, having made an impressive debut in *Romeo Must Die*, was chosen for the role of Akasha, Queen of the

Aaliyah receives instructions from director Michael Rymer during the filming of 2002's *Queen of the Damned.*   © *2002 Warner Bros. Courtesy of Del Valle Archives.*

Damned. Wes Bentley, Heath Ledger, and Josh Hartnett were considered for the role of Lestat, which eventually went to Stuart Townsend. Matthew Newton appeared as Armand, a character played by Antonio Banderas in the previous film. Principal photography began on October 2, 2000, in Melbourne, Australia, just before the rights would have reverted back to Rice.

During pre-production, Rice pleaded with the studio not to make the film, thinking her fans would want *The Vampire Lestat* to be filmed first. Initially refusing to cooperate with the filmmakers, by July 2001, she was feeling more optimistic, saying, "Everything I hear about the movie is good. . . . I met Stuart Townsend, the young man who is playing Lestat and he was absolutely charming. He had Lestat's excellent speaking voice and his feline grace. I cannot wait to see him in the film."

Six months before the release of the film, Aaliyah went to the Bahamas to film a video for her song "Rock the Boat." When shooting ended early, she and her crew boarded a plane to fly to Florida. The twin-engine Cessna crashed almost immediately after takeoff, killing all eight people on board. The film *Queen of the Damned* is dedicated to her memory.

Anne Rice saw the completed film in late 2001, agreeing to let the studio use her name on promotional materials. But ultimately, she became disillusioned about *Queen of the Damned* and dismissed it, saying she was hurt to see her work "mutilated" in such a way.

Released on February 22, 2002, *Queen of the Damned*—budgeted at $35 million—was considered a bomb, taking in just $45.5 million worldwide. The film was back in the headlines in December 2002, when Allan Menzies from West Lothian, Scotland, murdered one of his friends, claiming he was compelled to do so by Akasha, Queen of the Damned.

The Body Thief and Beyond

The fourth novel in The Vampire Chronicles, *The Tale of the Body Thief*, featured Lestat in a new adventure after his fling with vampire queen Akasha. It was published in the fall of 1992.

Most reviewers found the new book wanting. In his critique for the *New York Times*, Walter Kendrick wrote, "The chief pleasure of *Interview* and *Lestat* came from the unfashionable gorgeousness of Ms. Rice's prose. Reading those novels was like glutting oneself on some overrich, sinful dish, just as her vampires did. Gorgeousness dropped off sharply in *Queen* and is practically absent from *Body Thief*. Lestat claims to lapse in to 18th-century French, but he writes brain-dead 1992 American. 'The Vampire Lestat here,' he begins. 'I have a story to tell you. It's about something that happened to me.' He drones on in that dull vein for more than 400 pages."

The death of Rice's father informed some of the writing in the novel. When her father was dying, Rice wished that she could make him young again so she wouldn't lose him. In *The Tale of the Body Thief*, Lestat switches bodies with a young rascal, Raglan James. But having been a vampire for two centuries, Lestat has trouble readjusting to being human.

Three years later came *Memnoch the Devil*, a novel which borrowed some themes from Charles Maturin's nineteenth-century gothic novel *Melmoth the Wanderer*. In this novel, Lestat meets the devil, who calls himself Memnoch, and claims that he is merely working for God by ushering lost souls to Heaven.

Over the next four years, Rice wrote four more entries in The Vampire Chronicles: *The Vampire Armand* (1998), *Merrick* (2000), *Blood and Gold* (2001), and *Blackwood Farm* (2002). Then, in 2002, Stan, her husband of forty-one years, died of a brain tumor at age sixty.

Rice's next book, *Blood Canticle*, was intended to conclude the story of the vampire Lestat. After it was published in 2003, Rice took an eleven-year break, enjoying other people's vampire stories. "I came to realize we all make our own cosmology, and there are certain traits that are common to all of the fiction in this area," she told Carolyn Kellogg of the *Los Angeles Times*.

Feeling lonely in a big house without her husband, Rice left New Orleans in 2005, eventually settling in Rancho Mirage, California, to be near her son who lived in Los Angeles. But Lestat would not let her be. On October 28, 2014, Rice revived The Vampire Chronicles with the publication of *Prince Lestat*.

Despite the failure of *Queen of the Damned*, Hollywood continued to be interested in Rice's vampires. In 2009, talks were underway to revive the Vampire Chronicles film series, with *The Vampire Lestat* said to be first up, with Robert Downey Jr. in talks for the lead role. The actor dismissed the rumors.

Imagine Entertainment, a production company operated by producer Brian Grazer and director Ron Howard, announced in February 2012 that they had begun development of a film version of *The Tale of the Body Thief*, with Lee Patterson writing the script. They intended to proceed as if audiences had not yet been introduced to Lestat. Rice's own son, Christopher, also did a screenplay adaptation, but by April 2013 the project had collapsed due to creative differences. In August of 2014, Universal Pictures acquired the film rights to the entire Vampire Chronicles canon. Alex Kurtzman and Roberto Orci were named as producers.

As of 2014, Anne Rice's books had sold over 100 million copies worldwide. The impact of her vampire fiction cannot be overstated. Prior to the publication of her first novel, vampires had descended into figures of camp, almost always shown in the Bela Lugosi mold with black cape and Transylvanian accent. Rice totally reimagined vampires, explaining their powers and abilities and, most importantly, their yearnings and profound loneliness. She gave vampires something they weren't to supposed to possess—souls. She pumped new blood into an old formula, and launched a whole new genre—the paranormal romance. Without Anne Rice, it's fair to say there would have been no *Twilight*, no *True Blood*, no *Vampire Diaries*.

"The vampire is hyper-romantic, a Byronic hero—a larger-than-life, extremely strong, mysterious, tragic personality," Rice told Carolyn Kellogg of the *Los Angeles Times*. "Basically the vampire is untamed mystery, and that's what men seem to women. It's a deep, deep metaphor for sexual difference. Every man's a vampire to us, in a way." Rice is now at work on a follow-up to *Prince Lestat*, to be called "Blood Paradise."

18

A Bright, Shining Success

The Twilight Saga

The Dawn of *Twilight*

T he scars of high school linger forever," author Stephenie Meyer said to Denise Lythgoe of Salt Lake City's the *Deseret News.*

Twilight, Meyer's first novel, centers on Isabella "Bella" Swan, a typical high-school student, who comes from sunny Phoenix to dreary Forks, Washington, to live with her father, the town policeman. She's attracted to Edward Cullen, whose secretive nature hides the fact that he and his foster brothers and sisters are a group of vampires who have come together to help each other resist feeding on human blood.

Edward and Bella face the usual high-school issues, not sure if their feelings are reciprocated, dealing with family objections to their heart's desires, and unsure of their future. It is, in effect, a teen romance, albeit one with vampires and werewolves.

Author Stephenie Meyer said in an interview with Amanda Craig of the *Times of London,* "I think the attraction vampires hold for us humans has to do with their dual natures. . . . They have attributes we envy: they are beautiful, they are forever young, they are intelligent and well-spoken, they often wear tuxedos and live in castles. We want what they have, even as we fear what they want."

Meyer graduated from Brigham Young University, having majored in English. She made her home with her husband and three small children in Glendale, Arizona. As with Bram Stoker, who claimed that *Dracula* came to him in a nightmare, Meyer got her idea for *Twilight* from a dream, at age twenty-nine. "I saw two characters talking about the fact that they were in love. He was telling her that his problem was that he wanted to kill her because she smelled so tasty," Meyer told Jeffrey A. Trachtenberg of the *Wall Street Journal.* "I have no idea where the vampires came from. . . . But I had an early-morning dream about a boy and a girl in a meadow with bright sunlight. The boy was sparkly and he was a vampire. It was such a vivid dream that I didn't want to forget it, so I wrote it down. I wondered what would happen next, so I kept writing. It became chapter 13 of *Twilight*, then I had to write the 12 chapters before chapter 13."

Meyer had no outline, no plot, and no agent, and she didn't tell her husband what she was up to. When her sister, who hadn't heard from Meyer in weeks, called to check on her, Meyer admitted she was writing a book, though she was embarrassed that it was a vampire story. Prior to writing *Twilight*, she had read only one vampire tale, by Anne Rice, and she didn't watch scary movies.

Her sister read the draft and convinced Meyer she should try and have it published. After three months, Meyer's book, which she called "Forks," was finished. Then she spent a month writing query letters to fifteen agents. She received ten responses, nine of them rejections. Only Writers House in New York was interested, so Meyer signed with their agent Jodi Reamer, who suggested they come up with a new title. They settled on *Twilight*. Reamer submitted the final manuscript to nine editors. Megan Tingley of Little, Brown was the first to reply. They offered three hundred thousand dollars for a three-book contract. Reamer turned it down, a move that scared Meyer to death. Reamer then asked for $1 million, eventually settling for three-quarters of a million for a three-book series. When the young adult novel was published in October of 2005, it quickly became a bestseller, with more than one hundred thousand copies in print.

In *Twilight*, Edward Cullen's family is sworn to abstinence, feeding only on animals or on criminals. And Edward can't consummate his relationship with Bella as long as she remains human, so the tension in the series becomes when she will relent and "turn"; it's vampirism as a metaphor for sexual abstinence, which the novels promote. There's also tension from Bella being targeted by more predatory vampires, and her attraction to a friend who turns out to be a werewolf. Meyer was taken aback when some reviewers commented that the storyline between Bella and Edward exhibited sexual tension; she saw it as an innocent romance.

Meyer's vampires have some of the usual vampire abilities, such as supernatural strength, and telepathic abilities, but they aren't affected by garlic or crucifixes, and instead of smoking or burning to a crisp in the sunlight, they sparkle.

Critic Laura Miller argued that Meyer's vampires were "high school's aristocracy, the coolest kids on campus, the clique that everyone wants to get into." She saw *Twilight* as "the 21st century's version of the humble governess who captures the heart of the lord of the manor."

Eclipsing Harry Potter

After Meyer finished *Twilight*, she wrote an epilogue so long that she could tell a sequel was imminent. Five months later she had completed it; called *New Moon*, it was finished before *Twilight* was published.

In *New Moon*, Edward leaves Bella, sacrificing his lover for her own personal safety. Once Edward is gone, a despondent Bella receives consolation from her friend Jacob Black, who she discovers is actually a werewolf. When a miscommunication leads Edward to believe that Bella is dead, he goes to Italy to the vampire authority, the Volturi, to commit suicide. Thankfully, Bella arrives in Italy just in time to stop him, but the Volturi tell Edward that Bella must be either turned into a vampire herself or killed to protect the secret of their existence. This puts Edward in a difficult position; upon returning to Forks, he is told by Jacob that the tenuous détente between the werewolves and the Cullens will be broken if the Cullens bite a human. Deborah Morris, in New Zealand's *Dominion Post,* called it, "heart-wrenchingly written, a vampire *Romeo and Juliet* with fangs."

New Moon was published September 6, 2006, with an initial print run of one hundred thousand copies. Like its predecessor, it quickly became a bestseller. At book-

As a young boy, before becoming an actor, Taylor Lautner won three gold medals in the twelve-years-and-under division of the World Karate Association.   *Vera Anderson/ Getty Images*

release parties held in bookstores across the nation, buttons were distributed so the hard-core fans, known as "Twi-hards," could show their preference for whom they thought Bella should choose: Edward or Jacob. The buttons identified the wearer as being on "Team Edward" or "Team Jacob."

While on the surface the books were romances in a supernatural milieu, they explored themes important to teenagers. Edward and the Cullens represented a welcoming family, and if Bella chose to be with Edward, she would become a vampire, losing both her virginity and her mortal life. On the other hand, while Jacob offers promise of a human life, he has anger-control issues, turning into a wolf when he loses his temper, and is terribly possessive and protective of Bella. One imagines that life with Jacob would be life with a suffocating and controlling husband. On the plus side, choosing either one offered Bella a mate with terrific hair and great abs. Although the books were written primarily for an audience of teenage girls, they established a sizable fan base among an older demographic, as well. Mothers who picked up their daughters' books found they couldn't put them down.

By 2007, *Twilight* and *New Moon* had 1.6 million copies in print nationwide. A third novel was published in August of 2007. Titled *Eclipse*, it picked up where *Twilight* and *New Moon* left off, with Bella hunted by vampires and forced to choose between vampire Edward or werewolf Jacob. Publishers Little, Brown were hopeful it would sell 40,000 on its first day. They were amazed when eager fans snapped up 150,000 copies. The book immediately became the week's number-one bestseller at Barnes & Noble, Inc, pushing the J. K. Rowling book *Harry Potter and the Deathly Hallows* into second position. "I've been in this business for 20 years, and I've never seen anything like this," said Megan Tingley of Little, Brown.

Eclipse had a first printing of one million copies. Tingley noted that since the books didn't include sexually provocative material or graphic language, it was an easier sell for parents. Meyer told Jeffrey A. Trachtenberg of the *Wall Street Journal*, "I don't think teens need to read about gratuitous sex."

In the fourth book in the series, *Breaking Dawn*, Bella and Edward finally marry and Bella soon finds herself pregnant with a half-human, half-vampire child. She becomes a vampire and must protect herself and her child from Edward and his family, who advise her to abort it for her own safety. She and the child also face danger from werewolves who seek to destroy them, fearing what the child will become. Jacob becomes the child's protector, and when the Volturi descend on Forks, it precipitates a union between the shapeshifters and vampires in defiance of the vampire authority. *Breaking Dawn* had an initial print run of 3.7 million copies, and sold 1.3 million on the day it was released.

Meyer began a fifth book, *Midnight Sun*, which retold the *Twilight* story from Edward's perspective instead of Bella's. After twelve chapters, the work-in-progress was leaked to the Internet. Meyer then posted the completed chapters on her website, but lost interest in finalizing the book.

The Twilight Film Saga

Paramount Pictures initially acquired the film rights to *Twilight*, and spent three years developing a script through their MTV Films. Their script differed greatly from the novel, changing Bella into a star high-school athlete. In April 2007, Summit Entertainment acquired the film rights to the Twilight series and vowed they would start over, remaining faithful to the novels. Catherine Hardwicke was hired to direct, and Melissa Rosenberg collaborated closely with her in writing the screenplay. Though they combined some characters and dropped some minor characters, they strove to remain faithful to the novel's plot and character arcs.

In 2010, researchers from Ancestry.com claimed that Robert Pattinson was a distant relative of Vlad III, due to his lineage to British royalty; he is also a distant cousin of Princes William and Harry. *Jason Kempin/Getty Images*

The lead roles were quickly filled by Kristen Stewart, Robert Pattinson, and Taylor Lautner, and filming began in Oregon in March 2008, with a week of rehearsals followed by a forty-four-day shoot. Filming ended May 2, 2008, and the film was released on November 21, 2008, pulling in $7 million in ticket sales from midnight shows. *Twilight* ended up grossing over $192 million in the U.S., and almost $200 million internationally.

The following March, filming began on the sequel, *New Moon*, in Vancouver, Canada, and Montepulciano, Italy, aiming for a release date of November 20, 2009. Though Melissa Rosenberg continued as screenwriter, Catherine Hardwicke stepped aside as director, with Chris Weitz coming aboard. Weitz, in an interview on the DVD of the film, said directing the sequel was "very daunting, because there are so many fans who have high expectations for this film. Half the time I'm nervous that I'm going to be hunted down and killed by a pack of teenage girls."

Upon its release, Mark Kermode of London's the *Observer* said of *New Moon*, "[F]or the most part this is a proper old-fashioned gothic romance, defined by absence, separation, longing and (most importantly) loss. No wonder the fans love it so." *The Twilight Saga: New Moon* set records as the biggest midnight opening in United States and Canada box-office history, with $26.3 million. Its ultimate domestic box-office gross was over $296 million, with another $413 million internationally.

The third film in the series, *The Twilight Saga: Eclipse*, began principal photography in August 2009. Since Chris Weitz had been busy with post-production of *New Moon* as *Eclipse* was going into pre-production, another director, David Slade, was brought in to helm the third Twilight film. The new film was shot in Vancouver, Canada, wrapping at the end of October.

The Twilight Saga: Eclipse hit cinemas on July 9, 2010, and grossed over $300 million in the U.S. and $393 million overseas. Besides burning up the box office, the films helped generate interest in the books. By November 2011, the Twilight books had sold more than 120 million copies worldwide and had been translated into at least thirty-eight languages. When a special edition of *The Twilight Saga: Eclipse* was released on DVD in 2008, it contained iron-ons, reading "Team Edward" and "Team Jacob."

The final novel to be filmed was *Breaking Dawn*, which, due to its length, was split into two movies. Melissa Rosenberg again did the script adaptation. To direct, the producers approached Sofia Coppola, Gus Van Sant, and Bill Condon, ultimately choosing the latter. Although they would be released a year apart, both *Breaking Dawn* films were shot back-to-back. Filming began November 1, 2010, in Brazil, before moving at the end of the month to Baton Rouge, Louisiana. In February and March, the crew moved to Vancouver, Canada, and Squamish, British Columbia. Filming wrapped in April 2011, after the wedding scene was filmed under extremely tight security.

The Twilight Saga: Breaking Dawn, Part 1, in which Bella and Edward finally marry, much to Jacob's dismay, hit theaters on November 18, 2011. David Edwards of London's the *Daily Mirror* wrote, "The Twilight films have always worked best when focusing on themes of teenage sexual anguish, the sheer silliness of the premise offset by the seeming impossibility of Ed and Bella's romance. But, as the pair finally get[s] what they want, we're confronted with a film that feels merely daft. The couple's woodland wedding is just one example as they exchange vows before a congregation comprised of the living and a pack of grey-skinned vampires. . . . For all that, things pick up dramatically in the last 40 minutes in a plot twist that cribs from *Rosemary's Baby* and *It's Alive!* Despite being about creatures of the night, it's the first time the series has moved into traditional horror territory, making for a creepily effective third act." Edwards summed up the Twilight canon by saying they had a "formula of torsos plus longing-stares times teenage angst."

Peter Howell of the *Toronto Star* said, "For a series so heavily freighted with messages of abstinence, you'd think birth control would have crossed somebody's mind—before the spectre of a feared human/vampire hybrid would arrive to turn both mortals and bloodsuckers a whiter shade of pale."

The birth scene was accompanied by colorful flashes of red, black, and white light that had an unanticipated result: they triggered a wave of seizures in cinemas across America. An epilepsy specialist said the scene might have had an adverse effect on anyone susceptible to photosensitive epilepsy, which is triggered by flashes of light.

The Twilight Saga: Breaking Dawn, Part 1 ended its run, grossing over $281 million in North America and over $430 million internationally.

The final film in the series, *The Twilight Saga: Breaking Dawn, Part 2*, was released November 16, 2012. It brought an end to the story of Bella and Edward, now with a child, Renesmee, whom they have to protect from the Volturi. It clicked with fans eager for a resolution to the saga, racking up more than $292 million in domestic box office and over $537 million overseas. When the box-office receipts for all the films in the series was combined, they brought in over $3.3 billion worldwide.

The Twilight saga may have seemed like just a teen love story with vampires and werewolves, but it was, at heart, a modern morality fable, with Bella and Edward as a Goth

Actress Kristen Stewart wore dark contact lenses in the Twilight films to make her naturally green eyes a closer match to costar Robert Pattinson's.

Dominique Charriau/Getty Images

Romeo and Juliet, caught between feuding factions—Bella's human family, the vampire Cullens, the shapeshifting clan of Jacob Black, and the Volturi. In an interview with Alison Rowat of the *Glasgow Herald*, Wyck Godfrey, who was a producer on all the Twilight films, summed up the series thusly: "The first film is about new love, the second about loss, the third about choice, the fourth about the challenges of marriage and family, and this last film is about protecting that family."

Screenwriter Melissa Rosenberg, who adapted all of the Twilight books into film scripts, said the films helped break a glass ceiling in the movie industry, where it was felt that in order to have a blockbuster success, a film had to have a male protagonist and be made for a primarily male audience. "This series has been really eye-opening for the industry in terms of audience," she told Rowat.

"Women are coming out in droves and they're seeing it repeatedly. You can have a female lead drive a successful movie. Women can make a number-one box office, multi-billion-dollar franchise."

The Twilight films propelled their young stars—Robert Pattinson, Kristen Stewart, and Taylor Lautner—to global stardom. On November 3, 2011, the trio had their hands and feet imprinted in cement in front of Mann's Chinese Theater, as Twilight fans and author Stephenie Meyer looked on. For Meyer, a young author who, like Bram Stoker, was inspired to write a novel based on a nighttime vision, it was truly a dream come true.

19

From Beyond the Grave

Vampire Cinema Through the Decades

Early Vamps

During the silent film era, the word "vampire" (or, more commonly, "vamp") suggested a young, seductive woman who took sexual and/or financial advantage of a usually much older, wealthy man. Although not the first female vampire of the screen (that distinction belongs to Alice Hollister), the actress most closely identified with the role was born Theodosia Goodman, a Jewish tailor's daughter from Cincinnati, Ohio, who took the exotic stage name Theda Bara, as it was an anagram for "Arab Death." Bara became a sensation in her role of "The Vampire" in the 1915 Fox film *A Fool There Was*. To essay the role, Theda wore Kohl-rimmed eye makeup, which served to emphasize her ghostly complexion. Her publicity photographs (many of which she personally staged) show her posing with symbols of death, including a human skeleton and a raven. Thus, many silent films that have "vampire" in the title are about flappers, not bloodsuckers. But there were some notable exceptions . . .

Many consider 1896's *Le Manoi du diable* (*Manor of the Devil*) to be the first actual vampire film. The two-minute film depicted a bat that metamorphosed into Mephistopheles. A cavalier then arrives with a cross and holds it up to the demon, which disappears in a puff of smoke. Over the next two decades, there would be several dozen more vampire films, from 1909's *Vampire of the Coast* to 1927's *London After Midnight*, a silent mystery starring Lon Chaney in dual roles as a Scotland Yard detective who is also a hypnotist and as a pointy-toothed, top-hatted vampire. By the film's end, it was revealed that the vampire was not real but actually an actor being used to flush out a murderer. Director Tod Browning remade the film in 1935, with Bela Lugosi in the role of the vampire and Lionel Barrymore as the detective, and the title changed to the less evocative *Mark of the Vampire*. Unfortunately, the original *London After Midnight*, like most of the early silent vampire movies, has been lost to time.

The 1930s

Nineteen thirty-two brought Danish filmmaker Carl Theodor Dreyer's *Vampyr*, a German-French film based on J. Sheridan Le Fanu's *In a Glass Darkly*, a book of five short stories, including "Carmilla." The film's financier, Nicolas de Gunzberg, under the stage name Julian West, starred as Allan Grey, a student of the occult who travels to a village that is under a vampire's curse. Dreyer and his cinematographer Rudolph Maté filmed on location in Courtempierre, France, with various scenes filmed through gauze to give the images a ghostly, dreamy look.

After starring together in two horror movies for Warner Bros. and their subsidiary First National (*Doctor X* in 1932 and *Mystery of the Wax Museum* in 1933) Majestic Pictures, a Poverty Row production company known for its low-budget quickies, nabbed Lionel Atwill and Fay Wray to star in their own horror production, *The Vampire Bat*. With Dwight Frye in a small role and sets leased from Universal Studios, it was another story in which the "vampire" of the title turned out to be just a mad scientist (Atwill) conducting macabre experiments.

Warner Bros. trod similar ground with 1939's *The Return of Doctor X*, less a sequel to their earlier thriller than a mystery featuring a miscast Humphrey Bogart (who consider this, his only attempt at a horror role, to be one of his absolute worst) as a once-dead scientist who, when reanimated, needs human blood to remain active.

The 1940s and '50s

In October 1943, RKO Studios, having scored successes with Val Lewton's *The Cat People* and *The Leopard Man*, decided to try their hand at a vampire story. Edwin Schallert of the *Los Angeles Times* revealed that the studio was preparing an adaptation of J. Sheridan LeFanu's 1872 story *Carmilla*. RKO's Josef Mischel was preparing the film for producer Val Lewton, whose low-key scares had made hits of the other RKO horror films.

The RKO film never went into production, so ten years later, Universal-International announced they were adapting the story. Thomas M. Pryor of the *New York Times* reported that the studio was looking for an actress to play a vampiress in the feature, which they were considering filming in 3-D. DeWitt Bodeen went to work on the screenplay, with Ross Hunter producing, but like the RKO project, it never came to fruition.

During the 1930s and '40s, when the Fascists were in power in Italy, horror films were banned. In 1957, with the ban lifted, filmmakers Riccardo Freda and Mario Bava set out to make the country's first sound horror film, *I vampiri*, or *The Vampires*. The plot involved a female vampire maintaining her youthful looks with injections of a serum derived from virgin blood. Gianna Maria Canale starred, and Mario Bava photographed the film, taking over the directing reins when Riccardo Freda left the project before it was completed.

The 1957 Mexican film *El Vampiro*, or *The Vampire*, is believed to be the first vampire film in which the predator had visible fangs, unlike the bloodsuckers of the Universal Studios shockers. The film, starring Germán Robles as Count Karol de Lavud (Duval), was directed by Fernando Mendez. It spawned a sequel the following year, *El ataúd del Vampiro*, or *The Vampire's Coffin*.

The 1960s

One of the most stylish of vampire films was 1960's *Et mourir de plaisir* (*Le sang et la rose*), or *Blood and Roses*, French director Roger Vadim's adaptation of J. Sheridan LeFanu's *Carmilla*, changing the location from nineteenth-century Styria to twentieth-century Italy. The film presented Annette Vadim as a woman possessed by the spirit of a vampire on the eve of her wedding. It was shot in the plush setting of a sumptuous villa near Rome built by Emperor Hadrian (whose reign occurred in the second century) and in the village of San Vittorino. The moody color cinematography highlighted the gorgeous costumes and settings. Co-starring Mel Ferrer and Elsa Martinelli, the film was one of the first to deal explicitly with lesbianism.

Boris Karloff played a vampire for the only time in his long screen career in 1963's *Black Sabbath*. Directed by Mario Bava, the film told a trio of horror tales, the last of which was based on Alexei Tolstoy's 1839 vampire story, *The Family of the Vourdalak*, about a family patriarch who returns home as a vampire.

That same year, Hammer released *The Kiss of the Vampire*. Directed by Don Sharp from a script by John Elder (the pen name of producer Anthony Hinds), the story involved a honeymooning couple (Edward de Souza

When their car breaks down, Gerand and Marianne Harcourt (Edward de Souza and Jennifer Daniel) are invited to the castle of Dr. Ravna (Noel Willman); they learn too late that he's the leader of a vampire cult in the Hammer Films production *The Kiss of the Vampire* (1963).   *Author's collection* and Jennifer Daniel) who become stranded in a Bavarian village. They accept help from the aristocratic Dr. Ravna (Noel Willman), unaware that he is the head of a vampire cult. The film concludes with the Van Helsing-esque Professor Zimmer (Clifford Evans) releasing a swarm of bats from hell to destroy the cult. The film was originally planned as the third entry in the studio's Dracula series, continuing the idea begun in *Brides of Dracula* that although Dracula had been destroyed, he still had disciples spreading the plague of vampirism. Indeed, the film's ending had been the original ending of *Brides of Dracula*, which was scrapped when Peter Cushing protested that Van Helsing would not resort to black magic to destroy Baron Meinster.

Meanwhile, though he refused to return to the Dracula role, Christopher Lee starred in the Italian film *La cripta e l'incubo* (*Crypt of the Vampire*), directed by Camillo Mastrocinque. The rather slow-moving tale was yet another adaptation of J. Sheridan Le Fanu's *Carmilla*, with Lee as Count Ludwig Karnstein, whose daughter Laura (Audry Amber), believes the spirit of her dead ancestor Carmilla is forcing her to murder those around her.

In 1967, Polish filmmaker Roman Polanski produced *Dance of the Vampires*. On the surface, it appears to be a spoof of the Hammer vampire films, yet Polanski's film is even more atmospheric and more overtly sexual. Polanski introducing a couple of new twists into the genre, including Jewish vampires who aren't afraid of crosses (one chuckles, when a potential victim thrusts a cross in his face, "Oy vey, have you got the wrong vampire!"), and a young male vampire who is flagrantly homosexual.

The protagonists are a vampire hunter, Professor Abronsius (Jack MacGowran, looking like Albert Einstein), and his naive young assistant, Alfred (played by Polanski). They arrive at an inn in snow-shrouded Transylvania, where Alfred falls in love with the innkeeper's daughter, Sarah (Sharon Tate). Sarah is kidnapped by Count von Krolock (Ferdy Mayne) and taken to his castle, where other vampires are amassing for a vampire's ball, and Professor Abronsius and Alfred go to rescue her.

Polanski had intended for Jill St. John to play Sarah, but she dropped out shortly before filming began. Producer Martin Ransohoff suggested Sharon Tate to replace her. During filming, Tate and Polanski began a romance; they married in London in 1968. Tragically, Tate was among the victims of the Manson family, who brutally murdered her on the night of August 9, 1969. She was eight-and-a-half months pregnant.

Before Roman Polanski's *Dance of the Vampires* was released in the United States, producer Martin Ransohoff had it trimmed from 108 minutes to ninety-eight; added exaggerated "comical" sound effects; changed the voice of the somber narrator (Ferdy Mayne) to one more cartoonish; eliminated most scenes featuring a Jewish vampire; redubbed some of the actors (including Polanski); and retitled it *The Fearless Vampire Killers, or Pardon Me, But Your Teeth Are in My Neck*.

In 1988, Polanski's original 108-minute version was shown on cable TV's Z Channel. It was later released on DVD, albeit still under the title of *The Fearless Vampire Killers*. With its sly comedy and production design that out-Hammers the Hammer films, it has since come to be regarded as one of the classics of the genre.

A Taste of Blood (1967), also known as *The Secret of Dr. Alucard*, was a sort of low-budget *Dracula* update from director Herschell Gordon Lewis, who considered it his masterpiece. The story involved Miami businessman John Stone (Bill Rogers), who receives two bottles of brandy from a recently deceased ancestor. Upon drinking them, Stone becomes a vampire, putting his wife in a trance while he goes to England to avenge for the death of Count Dracula by killing the descendants of Abraham Van Helsing. The vampire hunter's relative, Howard Helsing (Otto Schlessinger), eventually catches up to Stone.

Jean Rollin made his directorial debut with 1968's *Le Viol du Vampire* (*Rape of the Vampire*), which was a film in two parts, *The Rape of the Vampire* and *The Vampire Woman/Queen of the Vampires*. Rollin filmed the second segment to stretch the film out to feature length. The film mixed explicit eroticism with vampirism, a stew that many viewers and critics found hard to swallow. Rollin made sixty films over the next forty-two years, most of them surreal, poetic vampire porn, with titles like *La Vampire Nue* (*The Nude Vampire*), *La nuit des étoiles filantes* (*A Virgin Among the Living Dead*), *Suce moi vampire* (*Suck Me Vampire*), and *La fiancée de Dracula* (*The Fiancée of Dracula*).

The 1970s

In 1971, Boris Sagal directed *The Omega Man*, scripted by John William and Joyce H. Corrington, with Charlton Heston as one of the last humans alive in a post-apocalyptic city filled with vampire-like scavengers. *The Omega Man* was the second time Richard Matheson's story *I Am Legend* was filmed; in 1964, it was adapted as *The Last Man on Earth*, starring Vincent Price. In 1994, Matheson told Albert J. Parisi of the *New York Times*, "As a teen-ager I saw the movie *Dracula*, and it occurred to me that if one vampire was scary, a whole world populated by vampires would be really scary."

Valerie and Her Week of Wonders, a 1970 Czechoslovakian film by director and co-writer Jaromil Jires, looked at vampirism through the eyes of a thirteen-year-old girl, played by Jaroslava Schallerova. The film was not released in the U.S. until 1974, with Howard Thompson of the *New York Times* calling it, a "weird exercise, striking out boldly in the paths of Bergman, Fellini and Buñuel with characters in something of a clutter who shift into evil incarnate or plain tooth-chomping vampires."

In 1970, producer Michael Macready and writer-director Bob Kelljan decided to make a low-budget, soft-core horror porn film, "The Loves of Count Iorga." They asked actor Robert Quarry to star in it, and he agreed so long as they dropped the sexually explicit scenes and simply made it a straight horror

Count Yorga (Robert Quarry) goes in for the kill in 1970's *Count Yorga, Vampire.*
© *1970 American International Pictures. Courtesy of Del Valle Archives.*

film. When filming began, Quarry was already under contract to act in *WUSA*
with Paul Newman, filming at the same time. Unavailable for filming during
the day, most of his work was relegated to nights and weekends. With location
shots filmed by a skeleton crew—often just four people high on marijuana and
plum wine—the film was completed for less than one hundred thousand dollars. American International Pictures purchased the film and changed the title
to *Count Yorga, Vampire.* When it was released in the United States on June 10,
1970, it made millions at the box office, ensuring that there would be a sequel,
and unleashing one of the first modern-era vampires. Quarry's own dentist
made his fangs, which he sported on his lower as well as upper teeth.

Quarry snapped the fangs back on for the following year's *The Return of
Count Yorga* (1971), with Mariette Hartley co-starring and a young Craig T.
Nelson appearing as a police detective. For Quarry, the most difficult part of
the two films was doing the coffin scenes, as he was claustrophobic.

With his newfound status as a horror star, Quarry produced a horror film of
his own, *The Deathmaster* (1973), from an idea he had previously: what if Charles
Manson were a vampire? Quarry played Khorda, a vampire leading a hippie cult.
He hoped to make a third Count Yorga film, but by then director Bob Kelljan
had died and the rights fell to Michael Macready, with whom Quarry didn't
want to continue working.

In the 1970s, an influx of films from Europe in the UK and American
markets showed that mainstream audiences would pay to see films that featured
explicit nudity and violence, once considered the realms of pornographic and
exploitation films.

The new permissiveness in society—brought on by a combination of factors ranging from the introduction of birth control to the popularity of mainstream men's magazines like *Playboy* to the sexual revolution that came along with the youth rebellion movement—was now reflected in films. With their Dracula series losing steam, Hammer decided to take advantage of these conditions to juice up their vampire tales. And what better vehicle for exploring sexuality than J. Sheridan Le Fanu's *Carmilla*, a story whose lesbian overtones were apparent to any reader?

Screenwriter Tudor Gates was hired to script Hammer's *Carmilla* adaptation, called *The Vampire Lovers*, with Roy Ward Baker directing. Polish-born actress Ingrid Pitt starred as Carmilla/Marcilla/Mircalla Karnstein, spending a great deal of screen time sans clothes.

The blatant full-frontal nudity of the Hammer films, and the mixture of sex and blood, was shocking for its time, but since horror films were meant to shock, the films caused little concern among the censors. After 1970's *The Vampire Lovers*, Hammer made two more films inspired by *Carmilla* and featuring lesbian vampires: *Lust for a Vampire* (1971), directed by Jimmy Sangster, and *Twins of Evil* (1971), directed by John Hough.

Following in the footsteps of Jean Rollin, Jesús Franco co-wrote and directed the 1971 West German-Spanish film *Vampyros Lesbos*, with Ewa Stroemberg as a woman having erotic dreams about a vampire woman who seduces her before drinking her blood. Soledad Miranda, who had appeared in Franco's *Count Dracula* (1970), played the vampiress. Sadly, after appearing in six films for the director, Miranda was killed in a car accident in Portugal in August 1970. In a similar vein was 1971's *Le Rouge aux lévres* (*Daughters of Darkness*), yet another film in the vampire lesbian genre, with a storyline inspired by the story of Countess Erzsebét (Elizabeth) Báthory de Ecsed, played here by Delphine Seyrig.

Ingrid Pitt as Carmilla Karnstein, haunting Laura (Pippa Steele) in 1970's *The Vampire Lovers*, a film version of J. Sheridan Le Fanu's *Carmilla*.
© *1970 Hammer Film Productions/American International Pictures. Courtesy of Del Valle Archives.*

The art in this poster for the Hammer film *The Vampire Lovers* evokes
the style of black-and-white horror comic magazines of the era.
Author's collection

The blaxploitation film *Ganja & Hess* (1972), written and directed by Bill
Gunn, featured Duane Jones, best known for his leading role as Ben in George
A. Romero's 1968 shocker, *Night of the Living Dead*, in his only other starring role,
this time as an archaeologist who becomes a vampire after being stabbed with
an ancient dagger with a curse on it.

Serious vampire fans sank their teeth into a Hammer Films double bill,
Vampire Circus and *Countess Dracula*, released together in October of 1972.
Vampire Circus, whose title pretty much sums it up, was directed by Robert Young
and scripted by Judson Kinberg. Anthony Corlan, who played the lead vampire,
had previously appeared in Hammer's *Taste the Blood of Dracula* (1970); he later
changed his name to Anthony Higgins and played Professor Rathe/Moriarty
in *Young Sherlock Holmes* (1985) and Sherlock Holmes himself in the 1993 TV
movie *Sherlock Holmes Returns*.

Countess Dracula, directed by Peter Sasdy and scripted by Jeremy Paul, was
yet another film based on the life of Elizabeth Báthory. The film (which, despite
its title, has nothing whatever to do with Dracula) starred Ingrid Pitt as the aged
Countess Elisabeth Nádasdy, who discovers that bathing in the blood of young
virgin women causes her to appear youthful . . . albeit temporarily.

Writer/director Hans W. Gessendorfer's 1972 film *Jonathan* looked at
Dracula from the perspective of Jonathan Harker. Released to art house cin-
emas in 1972 after having first been screened at the Museum of Modern Art's
New German Cinema show, the film was billed "as the first anti-Fascist film of

its kind." Writing in the *New York Times*, Roger Greenspun stated, "The whole film is invested with a kind of solemnity that is sometimes terrifying (though never cheaply shocking) and sometimes silly, but that, on balance, makes it the most beautiful-looking vampire movie I have seen." Count Dracula was played by Paul Albert Krumm.

The mid- to late-1970s were a good time for vampires, with a plethora of new vampires in cinemas and drive-ins. Many of the films were R-rated mixtures of eroticism and gore, like 1975's *Vampyres: Daughters of Darkness*, starring Marianne Morris and Anulka.

A variant on the vampire theme came with *Deafula*, a Signscope Production written and directed by Peter Wechsberg, who also played Deafula. It was the first full-length feature film made in sign language for the 24 million deaf and hard-of-hearing people in the U.S., although the film did feature music and sound effects for the benefit of hearing audiences. *Deafula* used the Dracula legend to parable the difficulties deaf people encounter in the course of their daily lives.

In 1976's *Rabid*, David Cronenberg presented vampirism as a virus. The plot involved a scientific breakthrough that goes wrong, turning a young woman into a blood-craving killer. Each of her victims is infected with the same hunger, spreading the vampiric disease throughout Montreal. The film, which starred former porn queen Marilyn Chambers, was produced by Ivan Reitman, who would later become the director of *Ghostbusters* (1984).

In July of 1976, the New Yorker theater in New York City began what would become a decades-long tradition by screening *The Rocky Horror Picture Show*, a film version of the stage

Mike Raven as Count Karnstein hopes to resurrect his daughter, Mircalla, in the 1970 Hammer film, *Lust for a Vampire*, yet another film based on J. Sheridan Le Fanu's *Carmilla*. © *1970 Hammer Film Producitons/ EMI Film Productions Ltd. Courtesy of Del Valle Archives.*

French actress Catherine Deneuve brought a touch of class to *The Hunger*,
a stylish tale of modern-day vampires in Manhattan.
© 1983 MGM/UA Entertainment Company. Courtesy of Del Valle Archives.

musical, starring Tim Curry as transvestite vampire Dr. Frank N. Furter. The film
began playing midnight shows in Austin, Texas, the previous April, and a year
later the screenings were still ongoing.

Producer Lou Adler saw the film's success as being tied to its marketing,
telling Greg Kilday of the *Los Angeles Times*, "In some cities, it opened too strong.
We tried to sell it and its following turned away. We discovered that if you
opened it small, it would attract a smaller, hip audience, and as the film became
a hip attraction, a broader audience followed."

In 1978, in between George Hamilton and Frank Langella's disparate takes
on Dracula, director George A. Romero released *Martin*, a film about a teenager
who claims to be an eighty-four-year-old vampire. Unlike the supernatural
creatures generally seen in films, Martin cut his victims with razor blades and
drank their blood, so the film might be considered more of a serial killer film
than a vampire film.

Australian Rod Hardy directed 1979's *Thirst*, yet another film inspired by
the Elizabeth Báthory story, in which a woman descended from Báthory is
abducted by a shadowy organization called "The Brotherhood," who initiate
her into their blood cult.

The 1980s

Vincent Price, having played a vampire hunter in 1964's *The Last Man on Earth*, switched sides for 1980's *The Monster Club*, playing Erasmus, a vampire who takes a writer to the monster club, where Erasmus introduces a trio of stories about his fellow members, who are supernatural creatures. One tale, "The Vampires," features Richard Johnson as a bloodsucker on the run from vampire hunters led by Donald Pleasence. The film, in which Price made his only appearance as a vampire (although he was mistaken for one in a 1967 episode of the ABC-TV sitcom *F-Troop*), also featured horror icon John Carradine as the writer.

One of the most stylish horror films of the 1980s was *The Hunger* (1983), a vampire tale that was the first feature directed by Tony Scott. The film starred David Bowie and Catherine Deneuve as Eurotrash vampires in modern-day New York preying on Susan Sarandon, as a doctor who specializes in sleep and aging research. Its lesbian vampire seduction scene, accompanied by "The Flower Duet" from Leo Delibes's *Lakmé*, was considered controversial at the time, at least by general audiences who had bypassed all the European vampire lesbian films of the 1970s.

Nineteen eighty-five's *Fright Night*, directed and written by Tom Holland, brought vampires to the suburbs, with Chris Sarandon as Jerry Dandrige, a Dracula-esque vampire who moves next door to a monster-crazed teen, Charley (William Ragsdale), who quickly discerns that his mysterious new neighbor is literally out for blood. The teen enlists the aid of Peter Vincent (a fitting *homage* to Peter Cushing and Vincent Price, played by Roddy McDowall), a former horror star turned TV monster movie host, to defeat the vampire.

Ragsdale and McDowall reprised their roles for *Fright Night II*, a 1988 sequel directed by Tommy Lee Wallace, in which Charley, now a college student, is pursued by a female vampire (Julie Carmen) and her entourage.

Director Craig Gillespie remade *Fright Night* in 3-D in 2011, with Anton Yelchin as Charley, Colin Farrell as the vampire, and David Tennant as vampire expert Peter Vincent, who, in this version, is a Las Vegas magician. Two years later, *Fright Night 2: New Blood*, a direct-to-video reboot, retold the stories of the 1985 and 2011 *Fright Night* films. The story was now set in Romania, with Charley (Will Payne) and his friends as exchange students, and the vampire a woman, Gerri Dandridge (Jaime Murray), a reincarnation of Elisabeth Báthory. Sean Power played Peter Vincent, and Eduardo Rodriguez directed.

The Goldwyn Company released *Once Bitten* in 1985, with Lauren Hutton as a four-hundred-year-old vampire searching for the blood of a virgin teenage American boy. In a Hollywood nightclub, she finds a naïve teenager (Jim Carrey, in his first starring role in a motion picture).

Director Tobe Hooper's *Lifeforce* (1985), written by Dan O'Bannon and Don Jakoby, was based on Colin Wilson's 1976 novel, *Space Vampires*. Mathilda May, as "space girl," a shape-shifting humanoid who drains the "life force" out of

Horror host Peter Vincent (Roddy McDowall) fends off a vampire in 1985's *Fright Night.*
© 1985 Columbia Pictures. Courtesy of Del Valle Archives.

people, leaving a desiccated corpse, goes through nearly the entire film naked; apparently, the future has no clothes.

New World Pictures released 1985's *TRansylvania 6-5000*, which featured Jeff Goldblum and Ed Begley Jr. as tabloid reporters traveling to Transylvania, where they encounter an odd assortment of ghouls, including a mad scientist, a sexy vampire, a Frankenstein Monster, a mummy, and a hunchback. A relentlessly unfunny comedy, it received deservedly scathing reviews.

Even worse was 1986's *Vamp*, with three college students (Chris Makepeace, Robert Rusler, and Gedde Watanabe) seeking to hire a stripper for a college fraternity party. They end up hiring surreal stripper Queen Katrina, a vampire played by singer Grace Jones.

With those two films scraping the bottom of the barrel, there was nowhere to go but up for director Joel Schumacher, who teamed with scriptwriters Janice Fischer, James Jeremias, and Jeffrey Boam to unleash *The Lost Boys* in 1987. The moody serio-comic film centers on a family that moves into a coastal California community overrun by a band of youthful vampires, led by a menacing young man known as David (Kiefer Sutherland). Caryn James, in her review for the *New York Times,* called it "timely, sardonic and shrewd."

Nearly twenty years after the original, the film spawned two sequels, 2008's *Lost Boys: The Tribe* and 2010's direct-to-video *Lost Boys: The Thirst,* with Corey Feldman reprising his role as vampire killer Edgar Frog in both films.

Kathryn Bigelow's *Near Dark,* another film of a renegade vampire troupe, this time traveling through the American Midwest, arrived in 1987. Bigelow, who co-wrote the script with Eric Red, made a deliberate choice not to mention the word "vampire" in the film. She saw her roving band of bloodsuckers as nocturnal modern-day cowboys. After stripping away elements of traditional gothic vampire lore, the filmmakers then added in motifs of the Western, ending with a climactic showdown.

In the late 1970s, there were reports that Ken Russell planned to do an adaptation of Bram Stoker's *Dracula.* That project fizzled, but Russell did end up adapting a Stoker novel, when he made 1988's *The Lair of the White Worm.* Typical of latter-day Russell films, it was a goofball mix of horror and overt phallic symbolism, starring Amanda Donohoe as a supernatural snake-woman attempting to free a huge dragon-snake that lives underneath her Scottish estate.

Nicolas Cage and Jennifer Beals starred in 1989's *Vampire's Kiss,* a satire scripted by Joe Minion and directed by Robert Bierman, in which Cage is bitten by a bat and is convinced that he is turning into a vampire. Cage told Ellen Pall of the *New York Times* that he was so aghast after seeing that he'd made a sweet romantic movie with *Moonstruck* that he had to go and do *Vampire's Kiss* right after.

The 1990s

Writer Allan Moyle and director David Blyth's *Red-Blooded American Girl* (1990) concerned a young woman who is changed into a vampire by a virus. That same year, Dean Cameron was vampire Ralph LaVie in director Luca Bercovici's *Rockula,* with Toni Basil as Ralph's mom, Thomas Dolby as the villain, and Bo Diddley in a small role. The plot has Ralph losing his girlfriend every twenty-two years; she is reincarnated until Ralph can figure out how to save her, making it a kind of vampire precursor to the 1993 comedy *Groundhog Day.*

Director Ted Nicolaou made the first of his five-film *Subspecies* series in 1991. The direct-to-video films, shot in Romania, chronicled the exploits of vampire Radu Vladislas in his quest to turn a beautiful girl named Lillian (Michelle Morgan) into his companion. Anders Hove played Radu in the first four films, including sequels *Bloodstone: Subspecies II* (1993), *Bloodlust: Subspecies III* (1994), and the final film *Subspecies 4: Bloodstorm* (1998). The penultimate film, 1997's *Vampire Journals,* featured Jonathon Morris as the vampire, Ash.

Prolific horror master Stephen King provided an original script for 1992's *Sleepwalkers,* directed by Mick Garris, about an incestuous mother-son duo of energy vampires who drain the life force of virgin women.

Besides Francis Ford Coppola's *Bram Stoker's Dracula,* 1992 brought a number of other undead entries. French actress Anne Parillaud starred in *Innocent Blood* as a vampiress who only kills bad guys, teamed with an undercover cop on the trail of a mobster. Directed by John Landis, the Warner Bros. production was written by Michael Wolk, a novelist and playwright from New York, and mixed comedy and romance with gory horror.

Rubel Kuzui directed screenwriter Joss Whedon's *Buffy the Vampire Slayer* for 20th Century-Fox, in which a Valley Girl cheerleader (Kristy Swanson) discovers that she is destined to become a vampire killer. The film eventually spawned a popular long-running (1997–2003) TV series.

The 1992 comedy *Love Bites* was writer/director Malcolm Marmostein's adaptation of his own off-off-Broadway play *The Reluctant Vampire*. Singer Adam Ant stars as a vampire who tries to re-humanize himself after falling in love. Marmostein came to the project with good credentials; he created the character of Barnabas Collins for the TV series *Dark Shadows*.

One of the more eccentric vampire entries was 1995's *The Addiction*, from filmmaker Abel Ferrara. Lili Taylor starred as Kathleen, a philosophy student bitten by an aggressive vampire (Annabella Sciorra). Kathleen's bloodsucking is out of control until she runs into another, more experienced vampire (Christopher Walken) who has learned to control his urges through fasting and meditation. The film used vampirism as a metaphor for AIDS.

Martin Kemp was a vampire haunting the dreams of a girl named Charlotte (Alyssa Milano) in 1995's *Embrace of the Vampire*, an erotic film that mixed elements of vampires and *A Nightmare on Elm Street*. A direct-to-video remake appeared in 2013, with Sharon Hinnendael as the dreamer, and Victor Webster as the vampire.

From Dusk Till Dawn (1996), written by Quentin Tarantino and directed by Robert Rodriguez, starred George Clooney and Tarantino as bank robbers on the run who cross the Mexican border and end up in a strip club atop an ancient Mayan temple run by vampires. In a clever twist on the vampires-being-killed-by-sunlight trope, Tarantino and Rodriguez have vampires being killed by sunlight reflected from the club's mirrored disco ball. The film spawned a direct-to-video sequel, *From Dusk Till Dawn 2: Texas Blood Money* (1999), and a prequel, *From Dusk Till Dawn 3: The Hangman's Daughter* (2000) both produced by Tarantino and Rodriguez along with Lawrence Bender but directed by others (Scott Spiegel and P. J. Pesce, respectively). The film also spawned a TV series that premiered March 11, 2014, on Rodriguez's cable channel, El Rey, which was renewed for a second season.

A similar setting was explored in the 1996 *Tales from the Crypt* film, *Bordello of Blood*, in 1996. Directed by Gilbert Adler, the comedy-horror film featured Dennis Miller as a private investigator looking for a young man who disappeared in a brothel disguised as a funeral home where all the prostitutes, led by a recently reanimated Lilith (Angie Everhart), are vampires.

Another vampire named Lilith shows up in the 1998 British indie film *Razor Blade Smile*, written and directed by Jake West and filmed on a budget of just £20,000. The film featured Eileen Daly as Lilith, portrayed as a kind of white, female *Blade*, on the hunt for Sethane (Christopher Adamson), the vampire who turned her.

More vampire hunters were seen in director *John Carpenter's Vampires* (1998), with James Woods on the hunt for vampire Valek, played by Thomas Ian Griffith. With a story set in the American Southwest, Carpenter saw it as his chance to do a Howard Hawks–style Western, only disguised as a horror film. The film spawned one sequel produced by Carpenter, 2002's *Vampires: Los Muertos*, written and directed by Tommy Lee Wallace and starring rocker Jon Bon Jovi, and another in which Carpenter was not involved, 2005's *Vampires: The Turning*, directed by Marty Weiss and starring Stephanie Chao as a vampire terrorizing a couple vacationing in Thailand.

The 2000s

The vampires in Michael Oblowitz's 2001 film *The Breed* are at war with humans who don't want to live with them in a dystopian future. They are led by Orlock (the name of the vampire in Murnau's *Nosferatu*) and include a bloodsucker named Lucy Westenra (Bai Ling). Among those plotting against the vampires is a character named Seward (Lo Ming). Adrian Paul and Bokeem Woodbine star as detectives, one a vampire, one a human, both caught up in the conflict.

Underworld, a 2003 film dealing with the ongoing conflict between vampires and Lycans (werewolves), scripted by Danny McBride and directed by Len Wiseman, introduced vampire Lycan hunter Selene (Kate Beckinsale), whose saga continued in three sequels (or more accurately, two sequels and a prequel), *Underworld: Evolution* (2006, also directed by Wiseman), *Underworld: Rise of the Lycans* (2009, directed by Patrick Tatopoulos), and *Underworld: Awakening* (2012, directed by Måns Mårlind). As of this writing, "Underworld: Next Generation" is in production.

After making films based on the video games *House of the Dead* and *Alone in the Dark*, director Uwe Boll next turned his attention to the Majesco/Terminal Reality game *Bloodrayne*. The main character, Rayne (Kristanna Loken), is a Dhampir, a vampire who does not have a thirst for human blood and is not affected by crucifixes. She's the daughter of a vampire king, Kagan (Ben Kingsley), who has gathered an army of both vampires and humans dedicated to wiping out the human race. The diverse cast included former Dracula Udo Kier, rocker Meat Loaf, Michael Madsen, and Billy Zane. The film, shot in the Carpathian mountains of Romania, spawned a direct-to-DVD sequel, *BloodRayne 2: Deliverance* (2007, also directed by Boll) starring Natassia Malthe as Rayne in a tale set in 1880s America that had vampire Billy the Kid taking over the West. Another direct-to-video sequel followed, *BloodRayne: The Third Reich* (2011), again directed by Boll and starring Malthe, with Rayne opposing Nazis in World War II.

In a similar vein, Milla Jovovich was *UltraViolet* in the 2006 Chinese-American co-production of the same name. Directed by Kurt Wimmer, the film took place in a future dystopia in which a female martial arts specialist, infected by a vampire-like disease, seeks to overthrow a government that sentences anyone with the disease to death.

Sweden produced its first vampire film in 2006 with *Frostbiten* (*Frostbite*), set in World War II, with an SS officer heading a vampire clan in northern Sweden in midwinter, when there is no sunlight for months. A similar film came in 2007, *30 Days of Night*. Based on the comic-book series of the same name, the film starred Josh Hartnett as Sheriff Eben Oleson, who must sacrifice himself to save his town of Barrow, Alaska, from vampires led by Marlow (Danny Huston) during the winter's month-long polar night. Directed by David Slade and budgeted at $30 million, the film made over $102 million, including DVD sales. A direct-to-video sequel, *30 Days of Night: Dark Days* (2010), directed by Ben Ketai, picked up the story of Oleson's ex-wife, Stella (Kiele Sanchez, replacing the earlier film's Melissa George) one year later, on the hunt for queen vampire Lillith (Mia Kirshner).

New Zealand's first vampire film, *Perfect Creatures* (2007), was another film in which vampires and humans work together to ferret out an evil vampire. The "good" vampires are part of The Brotherhood, a collection of vampires organized rather like the Catholic Church. Saffron Burrows starred as the human police detective alongside Dougray Scott, who played the "good" vampire, helping her in her quest to apprehend the evil Edgar (Leo Gregory). Jonathan Rhys-Meyers was originally cast as Edgar, but had to leave the production due to other commitments. However, he eventually played a more iconic vampire, starring in NBC-TV's *Dracula*.

The third feature film version of Richard Matheson's *I Am Legend*, and the only one to use the original novel's title, came in 2007, starring Will Smith as a man in a post-apocalyptic city where he appears to be the last human not infected with a virus that turns people into vampires. Scripted by Mark Protosevich and Akiva Goldsman and directed by Francis Lawrence, the film was a long time coming; it had begun development in 1995, with Ridley Scott attached to direct and names such as Tom Cruise, Mel Gibson, Michael Douglas and even Arnold Schwarzenegger attached to star. It was worth the wait; *I Am Legend* was the seventh-highest-grossing film of 2007, earning $585 million worldwide. In 2014, Warner Bros. purchased a spec script from Gary Graham titled "A Garden at the End of the World," which was described as a post-apocalyptic variant of John Ford's classic 1956 Western, *The Searchers*. Deciding it was too similar to *I Am Legend*, the studio asked Graham to rewrite it as a reboot of the earlier film, in hopes of creating a new franchise.

Having come late to the vampire game, Sweden produced a bona-fide classic of the genre with 2008's *Låt den Rätte Komma In* (*Let the Right One In*). Directed by Tomas Alfredson from a script by John Ajvide Lindqvist, based on his novel, the film takes place in the 1980s and has a bullied boy from a Stockholm suburb (Kåre Hedebrant) developing a friendship with a vampire child (Lina Leandersson). Britain's Hammer Films acquired the rights for an English-language remake, which was released in 2010. Directed by Matt Reeves and starring Kodi Smit-McPhee and Chloë Grace Moretz, the remake was set in 1980s Los Alamos, New Mexico. A stage play adaptation of the story opened to critical acclaim at London's Apollo Theatre on March 26, 2014.

Cirque Du Freak: The Vampire's Assistant (2009) tells the story of a young man (Chris Massogilia) who becomes the assistant to a vampire (John C. Reilly) who runs a traveling circus. The young man's name is Darren Shan, which is also the name of the author of the twelve-part young adult book series on which the film is based, *The Saga of Darren Shan*, published between 2000 and 2004. Darren Shan is actually the pen name of Irish author Darren O'Shaughnessy. The film, directed by Paul Weitz, cost $40 million to produce and brought in just under that amount at the box-office, quashing the studio's hoped-for *Harry Potter*–style franchise.

Australian filmmakers Michael and Peter Spierig released *Daybreakers* in 2009. The film takes place ten years after a plague was unleashed that turned 95 percent of the world's population into vampires. Edward Dalton (Ethan Hawke), a hematologist working for a corporation trying to develop a human blood substitute, meets a former vampire, Lionel "Elvis" Cormac (Willem Dafoe) who has found a way to reverse the process and make vampires human.

Six-foot-three-inch Benjamin Walker portrayed America's sixteenth president as an action hero in 2012's *Abraham Lincoln: Vampire Hunter.*   *Author's collection*

Students of American history may have been surprised to learn that Abraham Lincoln was an anti-vampire crusader, but so he was in 2012's *Abraham Lincoln: Vampire Hunter*, produced by Tim Burton and directed by Timur Bekmanbetov from a script by Seth Grahame-Smith, who also wrote the novel on which the film is based. Juilliard-trained stage veteran Benjamin Walker, who played

Tilda Swinton and Tom Hiddleston as vampires Adam and Eve in Jim Jarmusch's
2013 film, *Only Lovers Left Alive.*   *© 2013 Recorded Picture Company/*
Sony Pictures Home Entertainment. Author's collection.

another U.S. president as the star of the 2010 Broadway play *Bloody Bloody Andrew
Jackson*, beat out Adrien Brody and Josh Lucas to play Abe Lincoln from age
nineteen until his death.

The Abraham Lincoln Presidential Library and Museum in Springfield,
Illinois, gave the film its seal of approval, but the movie was filmed in New
Orleans, where the producers received a bigger tax credit than they would have
in the Land of Lincoln.

In one of the most unusual press junkets for *Abraham Lincoln: Vampire Hunter*,
reporters were invited to the actual tomb of the actual Abraham Lincoln at Oak
Ridge Cemetery in Springfield, Illinois, where they were given private tours
of the Lincoln family crypts, normally off-limits to the public. While inside
the tomb, one of the junket members, a radio personality from Los Angeles,
tweeted: "Chillin with Abraham @ Abraham Lincoln Tomb." The film opened
June 22, 2012, to mixed reviews.

Soon after came the British-Irish thriller *Byzantium* (2012), directed by Neil
Jordan and starring Gemma Arterton and Saoirse Ronan as a mother-daughter
vampire duo hiding out from other vampires in a rundown hotel.

In director Amy Heckerling's *Vamps* (2012), two female vampires decide
to become humans again, which they can only achieve by killing Ciccerus, the
vampire who turned them, after one becomes pregnant by the son of Dr. Van
Helsing. The vampires were played by Alicia Silverstone and Krysten Ritter, with

Dan Stevens as Joey Van Helsing, Wallace Shawn as Dr. Van Helsing, Sigourney Weaver as Ciccerus, and Malcolm McDowall as Vlad Tepeș.

Based on Richelle Mead's 2007 novel, *Vampire Academy*, followed the mysterious goings-on at St. Vladimir's Academy, a school for vampires. Scripted by Daniel Waters and directed by his brother, Mark Waters, the film was panned as a feeble mashup of the Twilight and Harry Potter franchises. When the film failed to take flight, a Kickstarter campaign was begun to raise funds to make the sequel. Fans chipped in $272,882, but the campaign failed to reach its goal and sequel plans were canceled.

Jim Jarmusch turned his laconic eye to the vampire genre with his 2014 film *Only Lovers Left Alive*, chronicling the love story of a dissolute vampire named Adam (Tom Hiddleston) living in Detroit, a city whose urban decay matches his own spiritual decay, and Eve (Tilda Swinton), a vampire in hiding in the Middle East. Eve comes to Detroit to rescue Adam from his malaise, and trouble ensues when a younger, more impulsive vampire (Mia Wasikowska) crashes the party. In the *Boston Globe*, Ty Burr wrote, "*Only Lovers Left Alive* is disarmingly direct and charmingly directed; it's a bona fide love story, if an exhausted and occasionally thin one."

20

At Home with the Count

Shock Theater

By the late 1950s, most Hollywood studios had begun mining their film libraries for the new medium of television. The two last holdouts were Universal and Paramount, and in the fall of 1957, Universal succumbed, turning over six hundred of its pre-1948 films to Screen Gems for TV broadcast. The first of the studio's films to make it to TV were their famous horror films. Fifty-two of them were packaged together and released under the title *Shock!*

In New York, WABC-TV leased the *Shock!* package at a price reported to be more than $750,000. The films were presented on *The Night Show* beginning September 30, 1957. In Los Angeles, the first of the features broadcast on KTLA was *Frankenstein*, followed in subsequent weeks by *Dracula, Bride of Frankenstein,* and *The Wolf Man. Dracula* was presented on *Shock!* in New York City on October 3, 4, and 5, 1957.

The *Shock!* package began to be shown on Chicago television station WBKB on Saturday nights at ten, beginning December 7, 1957. Screen Gems did some inventive publicity to ballyhoo the show. Just before the films began airing, three men dressed as, respectively, the Frankenstein Monster (in a rather goofy-looking rubber mask), Dracula, and the Wolf Man came into the offices of the *Chicago Daily Tribune* and gave TV columnist Larry Wolters a shrunken head.

Once considered adults-only fare, the classic horror films were now viewed as appropriate entertainment for children of the baby boom, hardened as they were by the real-life possibility of nuclear war and worries about Communist infiltration, *Sputnik,* and foreign wars, not to mention the influences of rock-and-roll and violent gangster dramas and Westerns on television.

By the autumn of 1958, a new phenomenon had swept the land: the horror host, or "monster of ceremonies," local actors in extreme, ghoulish makeup, who hosted the showings of the films in the *Shock!* package, usually after-hours, on Saturday nights. While the films were particularly popular with children, adults also got in on the fun, hosting "shocktail" parties.

The monster mania soon crept into mainstream TV. On an instalment of Steve Allen's comedy program broadcast November 30, 1959, Tony Randall and Gabe Dell (the latter a former member of the East Side Kids) did a musical version of *Dracula*, with Dell doing his impersonation of Bela Lugosi.

The Munsters

TV executives took note of the popularity of the monster programs, and soon were planning a new hybrid: the situation horror/comedy program. Set to debut in 1964 were *The Munsters, The Addams Family,* and the witchcraft comedy *Bewitched,* plus the sci-fi-tinged *The Living Doll,* with Julie Newmar as a robot. *The Munsters* featured a family unit consisting of Herman Munster (a lovable Frankenstein's creature, played by Fred Gwynne); his wife, Lily (a vampire, played by former starlet Yvonne de Carlo); their son, Eddy (a junior were-wolf, played by Butch Patrick); and Lily's father, Grandpa (also known as Sam Dracula, and played to the hilt by vaudevillian Al Lewis); the joke was that their niece, Marilyn (first played by Beverley Owen, and then Pat Priest), was a beautiful, normal human—and they considered her a freak. In its warped way, the show revolved around the theme of intolerance—though they were decent, good-hearted people, the Munsters were considered outcasts simply because of how they looked.

Fred Gwynne and Al Lewis had worked together previously in the TV comedy *Car 54, Where Are You?,* in which Gwynne played patrolman Francis Muldoon, and Lewis was officer Leo Schnauser.

Lewis, who was born in Brooklyn as Albert Meister on April 30, 1923, had been a sailor and schoolteacher before becoming an actor. He appeared in burlesque and vaudeville, then acted in dramas on Broadway before moving into television. He enjoyed the role of Grandpa Munster, but not so much the time it took him to get ready. He was in the makeup chair for two hours having it put on every morning and an hour and a half having it taken off at night.

In the summer of 1966, *The Munsters* were featured in a theatrical film released on a double bill with the drama *Johnny Tiger. Munster, Go Home!* gave fans of the show a chance to see the characters in nonliving color. The plot involved the Munsters going to England, where they have inherited a home in Shroudshire. Once they arrive, Cousin Grace (Jeanne Arnold), Freddie (Terry-Thomas) and Lady Effigie (Hermione Gingold) scheme to scare them out of the home, which of course only makes the Munsters enjoy it more. The film ends with Herman entering an auto race, in which he drives Grandpa's custom car, the Drag-u-la, a dragster that resembles a coffin. The Drag-u-la was designed by George Barris, best known for having designed the Batmobile for the *Batman* TV series. The film was written by George Tibbles, Joe Connelly, and Bob Mosher and directed by veteran sitcom helmer Earl Bellamy.

Al Lewis as Grandpa, the Borscht belt Dracula, in the 1964–66 TV series *The Munsters*.

© *1964 CBS Television Network/Kayro-Vue Productions. Courtesy of Del Valle Archives.*

In 1981, it was announced that *The Munsters* was returning to television as a TV movie for NBC. The result was the *The Munsters' Revenge*, with Fred Gwynne, Al Lewis and Yvonne De Carlo recreating their original roles. The plot had a wax museum proprietor using his robot duplicates of Herman and Grandpa to pull a jewel heist. The Munsters then have to prove their innocence and get their titular revenge on the museum owner.

The Munsters returned in the fall of 1989, in a new series called *The Munsters Today*. Produced for syndication instead of a network run, the series featured John Schuck as Herman, Lee Meriwether as Lily, and Howard Morton as Grandpa. Unlike the original, which was a filmed series, *The Munsters Today* was videotaped before a live audience at Universal Studios. The series lasted for three seasons, ending in 1991.

Robert Morse next played Grandpa Munster in the TV movie *Here Come the Munsters*, which featured Edward Herrmann as Herman, and Veronica Hamel as Lily. Aired on Halloween 1995, this telefilm begins with the Munsters being chased out of their European castle and coming to America, where Herman's brother-in-law Norman Hyde (Max Grodénchik) has become congressional candidate Brent Jekyll (Jeff Trachta).

The wacky family was back for *The Munsters' Scary Little Christmas*, which aired December 17, 1996. Sam McMurray now took the role of Herman, with Sandy Baron as Grandpa, in a tale that had the family trying to bring some Christmas cheer to a melancholy Eddie Munster (Bug Hall).

Producer/director Bryan Singer (*X Men, Superman Returns*) made a final attempt to return *The Munsters* to television with *Mockingbird Lane*, a TV movie with British comedian Eddie Izzard as red-robed Grandpa Sam Dracula, and Jerry O'Connell as a much more human-appearing Herman (with just a few visible scars, not the green skin and Karloff-inspired flat head and neck bolts). The TV film aired October 26, 2012; it never went to series.

1970s Televamps

Needless to say, *The Munsters* was not the only evidence of Dracula on television. In 1972, Rankin/Bass Productions made an animated prequel to their 1967 stop-motion feature *Mad Monster Party?* The prequel, *Mad, Mad, Mad Monsters*, aired on September 23, 1972 as part of *The ABC Saturday Superstar Movie. MAD* magazine artist Paul Coker provided the characters designs, with Dr. Frankenstein based on Boris Karloff and Dracula done in an exaggerated Bela Lugosi style. Many of the characters and plot elements from the previous film are referenced in William Keenan and Lou Silverman's script, which involves Dr. Frankenstein creating a mate for his monster and inviting other monsters to the wedding. The voice of Dracula—as well as most of the other creatures—was provided by Allen Swift.

In August of 1976, NBC announced their slate of upcoming Saturday morning programs for children, including *The Monster Squad*, an adventure-comedy about a teenager who works in a wax museum where figures of classic monsters—including Dracula (Henry Polic II), the Wolf Man (Buck Kartalian) and Frankenstein's Monster (Michael Lane)—come to life. The show was a kiddie version of the popular *The Mod Squad*, with the monsters fighting crime to make up for their past misdeeds.

In 1978, NBC began developing a series called *Cliffhangers*, with the idea being that each one-hour show would feature three separate continuing twenty-minute serials, each of which ended every week with a cliffhanger. One of the three continuing stories was to be *Dracula Is Dead and Living on the Coast*, in which the vampire king hid in plain sight as a professor of East European History at Southbay College in San Francisco. Dracula was being hunted by Kurt von Helsing (Stephen Johns), grandson of Abraham Van Helsing, and Mary Gibbons (Carol Baxter), who blamed Dracula for the death of her mother. Michael Nouri, an actor who had appeared in the daytime soap opera *Search for Tomorrow*, was chosen to play Dracula in the episodes, the segments of which were retitled *The Curse of Dracula*. The program debuted to low ratings. It was canceled after ten weeks; in the final aired episode, the young Van Helsing succeeds in firing a shaft from a crossbow into Dracula's heart. NBC later edited the ten chapters into a made-for-TV movie also called *The Curse of Dracula*, and created a second telefilm from the footage called *The World of Dracula* that was issued as a package of Universal TV movies in 1986.

Before *Cliffhangers* debuted, NBC was thinking of taking the Dracula segment and spinning it off into a stand-alone one-hour series for the 1979–80 season. When the ratings of *Cliffhangers* plunged, the idea was dropped.

Us magazine reported that Jason (*The Exorcist*) Miller would play Dracula in an ABC-TV movie scheduled for fall 1979, but it was never produced. A CBS sitcom pilot, "The Reluctant Vampire," also failed to make the airwaves.

ABC had another Dracula in the works, with Judd Hirsch playing the Count in *The Halloween That Almost Wasn't*, for broadcast in late October 1979. The half-hour special also featured Mariette Hartley as a witch, Henry Gibson as Igor, John Schuck as Frankenstein's Monster, Jack Riley as the Wolf Man, Bob Fitch as the Mummy, and Josip Elic as a zombie, from a script by Coleman Jacoby and directed by Bruce Bilson. The half-hour comedy had the Halloween Witch threatening to strike unless Dracula meets her demands, which include having her picture on all Transylvania T-shirts, and disco dancing every night. At an emergency meeting of monsters, Dracula complains they are losing their ability to frighten, noting that the Wolf Man is doing razor-blade commercials.

The 1980s

In 1980, CBS did a kind of revamp of the Saturday morning live-action program *The Monster Squad* with an animated series called *The Drak Pack*, in which teenage descendants of Dracula, Frankenstein's Monster, and the Wolf Man battle crime to atone for the sins of their ancestors.

A show that was set to premiere on ABC in September of 1980 but was taken off the schedule was *Mr. and Mrs. Dracula*, a comedy starring Dick Shawn as Count Dracula and Carol Lawrence as the Mrs., who are forced to flee Transylvania and resettle in the Bronx with their family and must learn the customs of the new country in a classic fish-out-of-water scenario. When an actors' strike postponed the new TV season, the networks began airing unsold pilots to fill up the airtime, so *Mr. and Mrs. Dracula* was shown on September 5, 1980. The show's humor went from the obvious—the daughter wants to go to a rock concert because it's headlined by the Grateful Dead—to the downright offensive, as when Dracula bites a black hustler in a Village bar and speaks "jive," saying, "Ah nevah had such soul food before."

Dracula Series

Another syndicated Dracula arrived in 1990. *Dracula: The Series* starred Geordie Johnson as the vampire, now seeking global domination through his conglomerate empire. It was an updating of the story that fit the go-go '90s—*Dracula* as *Dallas*. This particular Dracula had found a way, through modern innovation, to move about in the day, though he had no vampiric powers until nightfall.

The series featured two American teenagers visiting Europe with their mother, who suspects that all is not as it seems with Alexander Lucard. Their Uncle Gustav, descendant of a vampire hunter, aids them. The half-hour episodes, filmed in Luxembourg, were intended for a family audience. *Dracula: The Series* sold to 113 U.S. TV stations, but ultimately only twenty-one episodes were produced and aired.

In 2012, with vampire shows geared for teens and young adults like *True Blood* and *The Vampire Diaries* doing well in the ratings, and having scored a success of their own with the supernatural series *Grimm*, NBC decided to go back to the source, *Dracula*. The show was written by Cole Haddon, author of the graphic novel *The Strange Case of Mr. Hyde,* who pitched the new idea to the network as having themes of "reason versus faith, science versus religion."

In an interview with Danielle Turchiano of the *Los Angeles Examiner,* Haddon said, "I wanted the bad guys to be fundamentalists. It was about fundamentalism to me, and they were technically Christians, and so that can be a scary thing to say to a network out loud—that your villains are going to be fundamentalist Christians." Surprisingly, the network told him to "go for it" in his scripts.

Looking more to Vlad the Impaler than Bram Stoker, Haddon said, the writer approached Dracula as a hero rather than a villain. In the process, he created a bigger antagonist—the Order of the Dragon, a chivalric order for selected nobility founded in 1408 by Hungary's King Sigismund. In the show, the order's mission is to fight enemies

Michael Nouri, seen here with Carol Baxter, was a modern-day Dracula in San Francisco in "The Curse of Dracula" segment of the 1979 NBC series *Cliffhangers.* © *1979 Universal Televison/ NBC Television. Author's collection.*

of Christianity, and toward that end, it has its own vampire huntress. Dracula holds the group responsible for the death of his wife.

In Haddon's concept, Dracula encounters a woman who is a dead ringer for his wife, Mina Murray, played by Jessica De Gouw; once again, we have the "reincarnation of a lost love" plot that became an integral part of several Dracula productions after being introduced in William Crain's 1972 film, *Blacula,* and Dan Curtis's 1974 TV movie, *Bram Stoker's Dracula.* But the show also borrowed from other popular vampire programs, introducing a "Buffy the vampire slayer"–type character, Lady Jayne Wetherby (Victoria Smurfit); Jonathan Harker, played by Oliver Jackson-Cohen, was now a journalist instead of a solicitor; and Renfield was reimagined as a black valet and bodyguard, played by *Game of Throne*'s Nonso Anozie as a sort of Cato to Dracula's Green Hornet. Dracula's nemesis, Van Helsing, also underwent a facelift; in the new show, played by Thomas Kretschmann, he was a medical school professor and Dracula's ally. But the biggest change was in Dracula himself. Now masquerading as American industrialist Alexander Grayson, he comes to London with plans to bring electric light to high society; he's introducing a new form of clean energy to destroy petroleum-based energy, in which the Order of the Dragon has heavily invested. Haddon patterned Dracula's persona of Alexander Grayson on Apple Inc. co-founder Steve Jobs and Tesla Motors Inc. founder Elon Musk.

NBC was excited enough about the pitch that they ordered it directly to series, not bothering to make a pilot. NBC Universal signed on to co-produce the series with Carnival Films, the producer of *Downton Abbey*. It was also the first time the network co-produced a series with British entertainment company Sky Living, a partnership made necessary by the cost of the show, which was reportedly more than $2 million per episode.

As had become the custom with popular British series, the first season of *Dracula* was to consist of ten episodes, versus the twenty-two episodes more common in the U.S. The show was executive-produced by former president of HBO Films and Emmy winner Colin Callender (*The Life and Adventures of Nicholas Nickleby*), Tony Krantz (*24*, *Sports Night*) and Gareth Neame (*Downton Abbey*). Dan Knauf, the creator of the HBO series *Carnivale* (2003–05), was hired as show runner and executive producer.

Robert Greenblatt, then chairman of NBC Entertainment, had been head of Showtime when Jonathan Rhys Meyers was cast in the pay-cable network's *The Tudors*, and felt the actor would be perfect for Dracula. Rhys Meyers told Mark Jefferies of the *London Daily Mirror* that his "shoulders drooped" when he was first offered the part because he "didn't want something supernatural." But then he was convinced that *Dracula* would be different than the sparkling vampires of *Twilight*; the new show would take the Dracula story and merge it with elements of *The Da Vinci Code*, giving it a financial and political side. Plus there would be a bit of sex.

Rhys Meyers grew up in Ireland with a musician father who wasn't around much. Taking up acting at a young age, he landed a part in a commercial at age sixteen and made his first film two years later. He won critical plaudits for roles in such indie films as *Velvet Goldmine* (1998), and later for playing Elvis Presley in a 2005 CBS TV movie. Then came a long stint as Henry VIII on *The Tudors* (2007–10).

Along the way, Rhys Meyers made headlines as an often out-of-control bad boy. He was arrested in 2007 in Dublin Airport for being drunk and disorderly. Two years later, he was again arrested at Paris's Charles de Gaulle airport after assaulting a barman who refused to pour him a drink, then attempted to resist three officers trying to arrest him and threatened to kill both them and their families. Rhys Meyers has been checked into rehab half a dozen times and, in 2012, was rushed to the hospital in an ambulance after a suspected suicide attempt with pills. Hugo Boss, for whom he had been advertising since 2006, dropped him as their spokesmodel.

Now, seven years later, Rhys Meyers had sought help for his addictions and put the brakes on his self-destructive behavior. Still, this troubled past gave the actor something to draw upon in his portrayal of Dracula. "I can convey conflict because I'm a guy who lives in conflict a lot of the time," he told Sarah Hughes of the *London Independent*. He also drew upon his substance abuse, telling Hughes that he saw Dracula "as somebody affected with a terrible illness that has no cure. I absolutely believe it's a metaphor for addiction."

Playing Mina was Irish actress Katie McGrath, who previously worked with Rhys Meyers on *The Tudors*, and from there went on to the BBC's *Merlin*, where she played the evil character Morgana for five years. The actress had once been rumored to have been in a relationship with Rhys Meyers.

Dracula began filming in Budapest, Hungary, in March 2013. The network feared that Rhys Meyers's struggles with alcoholism might hold up work. They provided a sober companion to accompany him to the set, and withheld part of his $100,000-per-episode fee until the first ten-episode season was completed. When shooting began, Rhys Meyers claimed he'd given up alcohol and had been treated for depression. Those on the set claimed he was heavily committed to the project.

The actor admitted he wasn't the best company during filming of the show, since he stayed pretty much in character for seven months. But the filming wasn't easy; sadly, both his best friend and his grandfather died while he was on location in Budapest.

After 120 days of filming, *Dracula* wrapped in July 2013. The network began marketing in July, erecting a tent filled with Dracula's coffin, costumes, and props from the series across from the 2013 San Diego Comic-Con. The goal, said NBC marketing chief Len Fogge to Alexandra Cheney of the *Wall Street Journal*, was to "get the horror-genre audience excited and aware. . . . This is not your grandfather's *Dracula*."

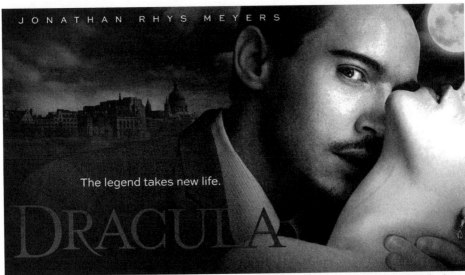

Dracula (Jonathan Rhys Meyers) was presented as a Victorian-era Steve Jobs in NBC-TV's short-lived *Dracula* series. *Author's collection*

The show premiered on NBC on October 25, 2013. Reviewing it for the *Washington Post,* Hank Stuever wrote that it found "an undiscovered sweet spot between *Downton Abbey* and Bela Lugosi."

Robert Bianco in *USA Today* wrote, "If the title leads you to think the show is hewing to Stoker's original vision, think again. Inexplicably, NBC's approach owes far more to two recent film flops, blending the Victorian steampunk aesthetic of *The League of Extraordinary Gentlemen* with the camp and gore of *Van Helsing* into an unpalatable, impenetrable stew that is uniquely and foolishly its own."

Jasper Rees, in London's the *Daily Telegraph,* said, "Here comes Jonathan Rhys Meyers in a version of *Dracula* . . . that would have Stoker plunging a stake through the hearts of all involved. . . . Waging economic warfare is not what vampires do."

Rhys Meyers said he was signed up with *Dracula* "for years," but after it finished its initial run, *Dracula* was canceled by NBC. The final episode aired January 24, 2014.

21

Death in the Afternoon

Dark Shadows

A Nightmare in Daytime

Just as Bram Stoker sometimes claimed that he got the idea for *Dracula* from a nightmare, so also did Dan Curtis claim that *Dark Shadows* was inspired by a dream. As he told *Los Angeles Times* reporter Cecil Smith, "I put my nightmares on film."

Curtis, who started out as a sales executive for NBC and MCA, first rose to prominence in television by producing golf programs, including *Arnold Palmer–Gary Player Challenge Golf* and *CBS Golf Classic.* He produced golf shows for ten years, working six months out of the year. Finally, another opportunity presented itself. A friend at ABC suggested he try developing a daytime show, and Curtis said he'd consider it, but, as he told the *Los Angeles Times'* Burt Prelutsky: "I had no ideas. However, the night before our meeting was scheduled to take place, I had a dream. In my dream, a girl was sitting on a train, reading a letter, going up the New England coast to a job. She was a governess. She got off the train track at a dark, deserted railway station. Then I woke up. At first it seemed intriguing, but after I took a shower I decided it was a lousy idea. But that morning I mentioned it to ABC—and within four days we had a deal. And that's how *Dark Shadows* came to be."

The show premiered June 27, 1966. Although it was set in present day, the daytime serial had gothic elements, with the stories taking place mostly at night and involving a manor house hiding generations of family secrets. Each episode was videotaped like a live play, in real time in one half-hour chunk, on a per-episode budget of about eighteen thousand dollars. Curtis was told to keep the storylines slow-moving, for the sake of busy housewives. But housewives didn't make up the core audience; since ABC broadcast it in the late afternoon at 4:00 p.m. Eastern/3:00 p.m. Central—about the time most kids got home from school—it soon began attracting an avid juvenile audience.

The matriarch of the Collins family, Elizabeth Collins Stoddard, was played by fifty-six-year-old movie legend Joan Bennett, who thirty-three years earlier had co-starred with Katharine Hepburn in *Little Women*. In the 1940s, she starred in film noir thrillers like Fritz Lang's *Scarlet Street* (1945), and five years later played Elizabeth Taylor's mother in *Father of the Bride* (1950). For a while, Bennett's own life played out like a soap opera. At the end of 1951, she was the subject of scandal when her husband, producer Walter Wanger, suspected she was having an affair with agent Jennings Lang, and shot Lang in the groin. Bennett denied that she was having an affair, Lang recovered from his wounds, Wanger pleaded insanity and served a four-month sentence, and the marriage survived for another fourteen years.

The role of governess Victoria Winters, whose arrival in Collinwood initiates the series, was played by Swedish-born actress Alexandra Moltke. She wed Philip Isles in 1967 and left the show a year later after becoming pregnant; her role was briefly filled by actresses Betsy Durkin and Carolyn Groves before the character of Victoria was written out of the show completely. In the early 1970s, Moltke began an affair with Claus von Bülow. Some years later, police investigating von Bülow, who had been accused of trying to murder his heiress wife, Sunny, with an insulin injection that sent her into a coma, interviewed *Dark Shadows* writers about whether the show had ever included an insulin plotline. At von Bülow's trial, Moltke was twice called to testify; in one of the appearances, she admitted that she had given von Bülow an ultimatum to leave his wife a few months before Sunny fell into a coma.

Rounding out the cast were Louis Edmonds as Elizabeth's brother, Roger, Nancy Barrett as Elizabeth's daughter, Carolyn Stoddard, and David Henesy as Roger's troubled son, David. The early shows explored the family dynamics and featured murder and blackmail plots; though there was conversation about locked rooms and some howling in the towers, there was never anything overtly supernatural. Ratings quickly fell off, and the show looked as though it was headed for a quick end. But then Curtis's young children suggested that if it was going to be canceled anyway, why not make it scary? Nearing the end of its twenty-six-week run, Curtis introduced a ghost on the stairs. When the ratings immediately jumped up, he decided to see how far they could push the horror element.

Enter Barnabas

Having been scared by movie vampires as a kid, Curtis decided to put one on the show, reasoning that if they could get away with a vampire, they could get away with anything. Consequently, in episode 202, when a character went rummaging in the family crypt for hidden treasures, he mistakenly released vampire Barnabas Collins, and also unleashed considerably higher ratings.

The character of the 175-year-old vampire was developed by writer Malcolm Marmorstein. The name "Barnabas Collins" came from producer Robert Costello, who saw it on a tombstone in Flushing, New York. To play the role of the Dracula-like vampire, the producers chose velvet-voiced actor Jonathan Frid.

The son of a construction company executive, John Herbert Frid was born in Hamilton, Ontario, on December 2, 1924. After serving in the Royal Canadian Navy towards the end of the Second World War, he studied at McMaster University, Hamilton, at the Royal Academy of Dramatic Art in London, and at Yale University's School of Drama. He then spent many years working in theater, appearing in a wide range of classical roles, including Shakespeare. The actor had just moved from Canada to California when his agent called to say he had landed the part of Barnabas Collins. This necessitated a move to New York, where the show was taped at ABC's Studio 16 in Manhattan.

Frid, who was of Scottish ancestry, seemed destined to find fame as a supernatural character. As he told Helen McArdle of Glasgow's the *Sunday Herald*, "In the 11th century, the name Frid was related to names like Frith, Firth, and so on, and there was a surname at that time that was related to it: Freak. And there was a surname, Fright. So I say I came

Jonathan Frid as TV's original vampire, Barnabas Collins, in the 1966–71 TV serial, *Dark Shadows*.
© *1966 Dan Curtis Productions/ABC Television.*
Courtesy of Del Valle Archives.

by my reputation honestly. Then we found another book in which the word Frid was a kind of prehistoric animal up in the highlands of Scotland and they were called Frideans. They were kind of half-human, half-animal." In Celtic legend, the "fride" is a Scottish goblin that lives under rocks, luring travelers to their deaths unless given treats of bread and milk.

Though supposed to have only a limited run in the dying daytime serial, instead of draining the life out of the series, Barnabas pumped new blood into it. Curtis originally planned to kill off the vampire shortly after introducing him, but the character was such an immediate sensation, generating five thousand fan letters a week and attracting millions of viewers, that he and his writers now had to find a way to make the character heroic. They settled on making him a reluctant vampire.

Frid infused the courtly Barnabas with elements of his own personality, attempting "to play all the subtle, psychological problems that come from being a vampire." He told Mary Daniels of the *Chicago Tribune*, "A vampire's got something going for him. At least Barnabas does. He's dignified and has a lot of Old World charm, which is what women like, but he has this terrible affliction which takes over, and then he becomes thoroughly unpredictable."

Once awakened, Barnabas becomes attracted to Maggie Evans (Kathryn Leigh Scott), whom he believes to be a reincarnation of his long-dead true love, Josette du Pres. Maggie's admittance to a sanitarium leads to the introduction of another character who continued through the run of the series, Julia Hoffman (Grayson Hall). The wife of series writer Sam Hall, Grayson Hall had been nominated for both a Golden Globe award and an Academy Award for her performance in John Huston's 1964 film of the Tennessee Williams play, *The Night of the Iguana*.

When Barnabas caught on, the producers decided to introduce other supernatural characters into the show, including witches and werewolves and mad Frankenstein-like doctors. When Curtis was told he couldn't bring back actors whose characters had been killed off in new parts, he created parallel universes or brought them back as ghosts. When he decided to send the whole cast back to the past, the network executives thought he was crazy, but audiences tuned in to find out how Barnabas became a vampire.

The answer was that he had been cursed by the witch Angelique Bouchard, a character introduced into the show on November 22, 1967. Angelique was played by Lara Parker, who had just arrived in New York when she went for an on-camera audition with Jonathan Frid. As she told Craig Hamrick of *Dark Shadows Online*, "I didn't realize the part was a witch. I thought it was a simple little lady's maid who had been jilted by the master of the house. Jonathan told me she was a witch and I turned and stared into the camera. I thought to myself, 'Hell hath no fury like a woman scorned.' Then I zapped the camera with my eyes and put a spell on the lens." She won the role, and began bewitching viewers for the next four seasons.

Once she was on the show, Parker was let in on a secret. Like many female viewers of the program, she had connected with the look of mournful yearning in Barnabas's eyes, thinking it communicated the suffering of his soul. Now she realized how Frid achieved that look—he was actually looking for the teleprompter.

Along with the game show *Let's Make a Deal*, *Dark Shadows* became one of the earliest daytime hits for ABC. At its peak, the show had an audience of twenty million. With five episodes churned out every week, *Dark Shadows* racked up 1,245 episodes from 1966 to 1971. Along the way, it helped launch the acting careers of Kate Jackson (*Charlie's Angels*), David Selby (*Falcon Crest*), and John Karlen (*Cagney & Lacey*). It was also a hit South of the border; in Central and South America, dubbed into Spanish, it was retitled *Sombras Tenebrosas*.

Dark Shadows generated a cryptful of merchandise tie-ins, including comic books, a paperback novel series, bubblegum cards, puzzles, and a board game. Bob Cobert's music for the show was released as a soundtrack album in 1969 that made it onto Billboard's Top Twenty albums chart. The Charles Randolph Green Sound recorded a cut from the album, "Shadows of the Night (Quentin's Theme)," as an instrumental single that reached number thirteen on Billboard's pop chart and number three on the easy-listening list.

But even with its devoted fan base, *Dark Shadows* was not invulnerable to the whims of television network executives. During the recession of 1971, when ABC hit a ratings slump, the network's executives decided to cancel *Dark Shadows* on the premise that its primary viewership was too young to influence household purchases and, consequently, weren't very desirable to advertisers. Besides, game shows and talk shows were cheaper to produce.

When the show ended, Jonathan Frid found other roles difficult to come by, having been typecast as a TV vampire. He played Thomas Becket in an off-Broadway production of *Murder in the Cathedral* in 1971, appeared with Shelley Winters in the 1973 TV movie *The Devil's Daughter* and was a horror writer whose characters come to life and terrorize him in Oliver Stone's directorial debut, *Seizure* (1974). From 1986 to 1987, he toured in *Arsenic and Old Lace*.

Lingering Shadows

The original series continued to be popular through the decades. It spawned a fan club, World of Dark Shadows, and a *Dark Shadows* catalog for collectors, "Inside the Old House," published by Dale Clark. As the digital age dawned, so did several *Dark Shadows* websites, including www.Collinwood.net. The show sold six hundred thousand copies within a year of its release on home video in 1989, and reached a new generation of viewers in early 1991, when it was shown on the newly launched Sci-Fi Channel.

As the series was winding down, it spun off two movies, *House of Dark Shadows* (1970) and *Night of Dark Shadows* (1971), only the former of which included Barnabas Collins. A kind of retelling of several seasons of the TV show in ninety-seven minutes, in *House of Dark Shadows* Barnabas is released from his coffin and meets a young woman whom he believes to be the reincarnation of a lost love. He undergoes treatments to release him from his vampire curse, which temporarily backfires, causing Barnabas to age significantly before he meets his end.

House of Dark Shadows hit theaters in October of 1970. Filmed on a miniscule budget, the MGM release grossed $5 million at the box office. In Britain, the *Monthly Film Bulletin* critic Tony Rayns hailed *House of Dark Shadows* as the best horror film in years, but it had a limited impact on a British public who weren't familiar with the TV series.

When *Dark Shadows* was canceled, Dan Curtis wasn't entirely bereft. After five years of doing a daily show, he was totally drained of ideas. Throughout the rest of the 1970s and '80s, Curtis brought adaptations of *The Picture of Dorian Gray*,

Dracula, The Turn of the Screw, and *Frankenstein* to television. He also produced *The Night Stalker,* and began to veer away from horror subjects with the gangster telefilm *Melvin Purvis G-Man,* the nostalgic *When Every Day Was the Fourth of July,* and his masterpiece, the epic World War II miniseries *The Winds of War* (1983) and *War and Remembrance* (1988–89), which at the time were the most expensive mini-series ever made for television.

At the end of September 1988, *Dark Shadows* was resurrected by the experimental Via Theater ensemble at Dance Theater Workshop/Economy Tires Theater in New York, where the performance began each night at eleven o'clock and ran past midnight. Adapted and directed by Brian Jucha, the play began with a séance and transported theatergoers back to 1975 to reveal the secrets of Barnabas Collins's origin. The part of Barnabas Collins was played by Julian Stone.

Return to Collinwood

At the same time the play was running, Curtis was contemplating resurrecting the TV series. Over the years, he turned down several offers to bring it back, but Brandon Tartikoff, head of NBC, was persistent. In 1988, the Writer's Guild of America went on strike. With no new scripts in the pipeline, Tartikoff began looking for previously produced scripts that could be dusted off for broadcast with a minimum of tinkering. He thought of *Dark Shadows* and was making plans to put it into production, but when the strike ended soon after, the revival went back on the shelf. By 1990, when good shows were hard to find, Tartikoff again turned to *Dark Shadows,* hoping it would deliver to them the same audience that had made ABC's *Twin Peaks* a surprise hit.

In a post-Anne Rice, post-AIDS era, *Dark Shadows* seemed quaintly old-fashioned. Instead of picking up where the old series left off, the new series retold the old serial's storylines, though they were considerably condensed; plotlines that once took months were now covered in a single episode.

Ben Cross starred as Barnabas Collins. Best known for his role in the Academy Award–winning film *Chariots of Fire,* Cross had previously played a vampire in the USA Network film *Nightlife.* Before auditioning for the role of Barnabas, he had never heard of the original *Dark Shadows.* The actor told Greg Quill of the *Toronto Star* that what happened to Barnabas was "a cautionary tale for married men—he has a fling with the wrong person, then regrets it too late. He becomes a vampire, but as much a victim of his own condition as the people he finds himself biting."

British actress Jean Simmons, best remembered for her work in Michael Powell and Emeric Pressburger's *Black Narcissus* (1947) and Laurence Olivier's *Hamlet* (1948) before winning starring roles in Hollywood productions like *Guys and Dolls* (1955) and *Elmer Gantry* (1960), was cast as Elizabeth Stoddard, the role previously played by Joan Bennett. As her film career dwindled in the 1970s, the actress turned to TV movies and miniseries, winning an Emmy for her role in *The Thorn Birds* (1983). "I have been saying this for years now that I would love to play head madam vampire of a whorehouse, but nobody took me seriously," Simmons told Susan King of the *Los Angeles Times*. "So *Dark Shadows* will be the closest I have come."

The role of Julia Hoffman, previously played by Grayson Hall, went to another Englishwoman, Barbara Steele, the former star of 1960s horror films *Black Sunday* (1960) and *The Pit and the Pendulum* (1961), among others. In the 1980s, she turned to producing, working on Curtis's *The Winds of War* and *War and Remembrance*.

Rounding out the cast were Joanna Going as Victoria Winters, Jim Fyfe chewing the scenery as the Renfield-like Willie Loomis, Roy Thinnes as Roger Collins, Lysette Anthony as Angelique, and a very young Joseph Gordon-Levitt as David.

Production of the new *Dark Shadows* began March 19, 1990, with locations at Warner Hollywood Studios and Greystone mansion in Beverly Hills, which became Collinwood. Instead of a half-hour show five days a week, the new series had one-hour episodes, once a week, each budgeted at $1.2 million.

NBC prepared the new *Dark Shadows* for a mid-season launch. The series was to begin with a two-part opener, with each segment running two hours, including commercials. By the first week of December 1990, *Dark Shadows* wrapped production of its initial run of twelve episodes. Curtis was hopeful it would be extended; the actors had been signed to five-year contracts.

In anticipation of the *Dark Shadows* premiere, NBC began a four-week promotional campaign on December 16, 1990, backed by financial support from the show's sponsor, Domino's Pizza. Two-minute promotional trailers were shown in 175 nationwide Circuit City stores. In addition, highlight clips and promotional spots were run in over two hundred United Artists movie theaters across the country. There was also a radio promotion contest sponsored by Domino's called "Don't Be Afraid of the Dark." Winners of call-in *Dark Shadows* trivia contests earned prizes ranging from videocassettes to their own vampire slumber party at

Ben Cross takes up the role of Barnabas Collins for the 1991 revival of *Dark Shadows*, meant to be NBC's answer to the popular ABC series, *Twin Peaks*.

© *1991 Dan Curtis Productions/NBC Television.*
Courtesy of Del Valle Archives.

Greystone Manor, where a press party for the TV critics of the nation's newspapers was held. The series was also advertised on MTV, Nick at Nite, the USA Network, radio stations, and with print ads in *TV Guide*, *People*, *Us*, and *Rolling Stone* magazines, not to mention a multitude of advertisements on NBC. All told, the network spent about $750,000 on promotion, with the rest of the multimillion-dollar campaign paid for by Domino's.

After its four-hour debut miniseries aired January 13 and 14, the one-hour episodes of *Dark Shadows* began airing on Fridays at 9:00 p.m., beginning January 18, 1991.

The critical response was mixed. David Zurawik of the *Baltimore Sun* wrote, "Barnabas is a steamy vampire. You don't have to be Masters and Johnson to understand that the bite-on-the-neck scenes are being played as orgasm in *Dark Shadows*. . . . Cross makes for one great romantic hero. If the show can figure out its tone, sharpen its focus and home in on Barnabas as the tortured sinner-saint, Collinwood could become a Southfork of the 1990s."

Matt Roush, in *USA Today*, also felt the series began promisingly, writing, "Ripe with fruity dialogue, played with clench-jawed earnestness by an impossibly gorgeous cast with oh-so-vulnerable necks, this resurrection of the cult supernatural soap is junky, clunky and altogether irresistible."

In the *Los Angeles Times*, critic Howard Rosenberg called it "wonderful dumb fun. From ABC came *Twin Peaks*, now from NBC *Twin Teeth*, as Barnabas Collins, the vampire from daytime TV past, shows up in prime time almost as if—Ooooooh!—rising from the dead."

But not everyone was won over. In the *Orlando Sentinel*, Greg Dawson wrote, "It's odd that the vampire (Ben Cross) in *Dark Shadows* would hang out in a town like Collinsport, Maine. I mean, most of the characters in this NBC miniseries have already had the life sucked out of them by the time Cross puts the bite on them." In the *Toronto Star*, Greg Quill called it, "*Phantom of the Opera* without the songs."

The January 13 premiere of *Dark Shadows* tied with the newsmagazine program *20/20* for thirtieth place in the Nielsens. After the first show, viewership plummeted over the remainder of its eight-week run, hovering between sixtieth and seventieth place, with fewer than 7.8 million viewers weekly. By the end of February, it was finishing third in its 9:00 p.m. Friday time slot, and eightieth out of ninety-eight shows. The show aired its final episode on March 22, 1991.

NBC wouldn't say if the show was going to be canceled, so in mid-May its fans organized and rallied at eighteen affiliates nationwide. Eleven hundred fans of the show gathered in Winter Park, Florida, at station WESH-Ch. 2. Fifty people gathered at Philadelphia's KYW-TV. Rallies were also held in New York, Chicago, Boston, and other major cities. Actor Roy Thinnes joined cast members at the Burbank, California, rally, but the activism of the fans was all for naught. At the end of May 1991, NBC officially canceled *Dark Shadows*.

Dark Whispers

Still, *Dark Shadows* lived on. In the 1990s, Lara Parker, who played the witch Angelique on the original series, having attained a master's degree in creative writing, decided to revisit Collinwood and create new stories in the *Dark Shadows* universe. Her first novel, *Dark Shadows: Angelique's Legacy*, was published in 1998. Two more novels followed, *Dark Shadows: The Salem Branch* (2006), focusing on how Angelique became a witch, and *Dark Shadows: Wolf Moon Rising* (2013).

Also, members of the original cast reunited to record audio dramas based on the series. The first, *Return to Collinwood*, was based on a stage play performed by members of the original TV cast at a *Dark Shadows* convention on August 31, 2003. The following day, the cast reassembled at a Manhattan studio to record the play for release on CD.

The year 2004 saw another attempt to bring *Dark Shadows* back to television, with Warner Bros. producing a pilot for a potential new series. The roles were written to be much younger than in previous incarnations, to attract a youthful demographic. Alec Newman played Barnabas Collins, with Blair Brown taking the role of Elizabeth Collins Stoddard. Dr. Julia Hoffman was played by Kelly Hu, Marley Shelton was Victoria Winters, and Ivana Milicevic was Angelique. Dan Curtis executive produced, along with Jim Pierson, Mark Verheiden, and John Wells.

Rob Bowman, who directed two episodes of the 1991 *Dark Shadows* series and thirty-three episodes of *The X-Files*, was assigned to direct the pilot, but had to pull out to do the feature film, *Elektra*. He was replaced by Australian writer/director P. J. Hogan, who had previously helmed *My Best Friend's Wedding* (1997) and *Peter Pan* (2003). Filmed on a budget of $6 million, the pilot failed to generate enthusiasm from the WB, which chose not to proceed with a series. The unaired pilot was first exhibited at a *Dark Shadows* Festival in Los Angeles in July 2005.

In 2006, Big Fish Productions, under license from Dan Curtis Productions, Inc., began producing a new series of audio dramas with the original cast. Two CDs were launched at the *Dark Shadows* 40th Anniversary Celebration in Brooklyn, New York, in August 2006. Sadly, series creator Dan Curtis passed away on March 27 of that year. Jim Pierson, marketing director of Dan Curtis Productions, said, "It is bittersweet that, on this 40th anniversary of *Dark Shadows*, we have just lost the mastermind behind Collinwood and its characters, creator-producer Dan Curtis. Dan knew that his legacy of gothic mystery and magic would live on. He greatly loved his original group of actors and it is truly fitting that they are helping to continue his *Dark Shadows* dream." As of 2013, thirty-eight recorded dramas have been produced and made available for purchase on CD and digital download from www.DarkShadowsReborn.com.

The first inkling of a new *Dark Shadows* feature film came in July of 1993, when it was reported that Dan Curtis was preparing a third one, which he planned to direct, using the cast from the 1991 series. Though that sounded promising, it would be another twenty years before a new *Dark Shadows* film would haunt the multiplexes. And for many die-hard fans, they'd rather it hadn't.

Barnabas Sinks to a New Depp

When Tim Burton was a young boy, he rushed home from school every day to catch the tail-end of *Dark Shadows*. "It was something that affected me," he said in an interview with Kevin Maher of the *Times of London*, "and gave me a really strange feeling when I was at that awkward age of 13, 14 and 15, when I just felt like a real weirdo. I felt like I didn't fit into the world, so this kind of weird vampire, this weird, out-of-place person, had an impact on me."

Released in 2012, the feature film adaptation of *Dark Shadows* was Tim Burton's eighth collaboration with actor Johnny Depp, who is making a career playing off-kilter, larger-than-life characters. Barnabas Collins was a part the actor had yearned to play since he was a little boy, when, like Burton, he was mesmerized by the original series.

Burton's *Dark Shadows* was much more of a Tim Burton movie than a *Dark Shadows* movie. Instead of a serious retelling of the 1960s TV series, Burton reimagined it as a satirical spoof of the 1970s, with Depp playing a variation of the fish-out-of-water type he perfected in Burton's 1990 *Edward Scissorhands*. Much of the film's humor came from Barnabas Collins, reawakened after two hundred years, being baffled by the wonders of 1970s America, such as record players, television, and fast food.

The task of condensing over a thousand half-hour soap-opera episodes into a coherent two-hour film fell to thirty-six-year-old screenwriter and novelist Seth Grahame-Smith, author of the bestselling novels *Pride and Prejudice and Zombies* and *Abraham Lincoln, Vampire Hunter*. "Our fascination with renewing ourselves, being more powerful and living longer—these are very human qualities," Grahame-Smith told Maher. "And as long as we have those qualities within ourselves

Johnny Depp, looking like a cartoon character come to life in his extreme white-face makeup, takes a comedic approach to Barnabas Collins in director Tim Burton's 2012 film version of *Dark Shadows*.   *Photofest*

I don't think that vampire mythology is going anywhere." For *Dark Shadows*, Grahame-Smith boiled the plot down to a central theme—"blood is thicker than water." In the film, Barnabas helps bring the disparate members of the modern Collins family back together.

Depp explained his take on Barnabas Collins by saying it was a reaction against the sparkly teen vampires of *Twilight*, the PVC-clad vampires of *Underworld*, and the plethora of vampires on TV. "Over the years, these vampire movies have come out, and vampire TV shows, and you go, 'Well, nobody looks like a vampire, man! What happened?'" Depp told Maher. "I adored *Dracula*, and still do, from Bela Lugosi to Christopher Lee. And *Nosferatu*, with Max Schreck. I adore all those wonderful horror films. So *Dark Shadows* was an opportunity to go into what really doesn't exist anymore—classic monster make-up and a classic monster character."

But though Depp's Barnabas Collins was a monster, the actor played him for laughs. He told Aakanksha Naval-Shetye of Mumbai's *Daily News & Analysis*, "What I wanted to come across with Barnabas is . . . the idea of this very elegant, upper echelon, sort of well-schooled kind of gentleman who's cursed in the 18th century and is brought back to probably the most surreal era of our times, the 1970s."

Production began on May 18, 2011, with much of the filming occurring in England at Pinewood Studios. Burton invited a handful of actors from the original 1960s series—Jonathan Frid, Kathryn Leigh Scott, Lara Parker, and David Selby—to appear in cameos; they're glimpsed briefly entering the Collins mansion during a party near the film's end. It was Jonathan Frid's final film appearance; he died in the early hours of April 14, 2012, at the age of eighty-seven.

When the film was released on May 11, 2012, it left some viewers and critics baffled. In Washington, D.C.'s *McClatchy-Tribune Business News*, Kathi Scrizzi Driscoll wrote, "My apologies if it sounds disrespectful, but one of my first thoughts when I heard that actor Jonathan Frid had died recently was that now he could roll over in his grave at what movie director Tim Burton had done to the TV series *Dark Shadows*."

Kenneth Turan of the *Los Angeles Time* concurred, writing, "This film has much more to do with what goes on inside director Tim Burton's head than with any TV show, no matter how beloved. In fact, *Dark Shadows* is as good an example as any of what might be called the Way of Tim, a style of making films that, like the drinking of blood, is very much an acquired taste and, unless you're a vampire, not worth the effort."

In one of the most equivocal reviews ever written, for London's *Guardian*, Peter Bradshaw opined, "The new film from Tim Burton does something that is rarer than you might think. It whelms you. Its effect is whelming. The film delivers precisely the satisfaction a sympathetic audience could expect from its director, not one degree above or below. The audience is whelmed. It's a whelmer. . . . This really is a reasonably, moderately, whelmingly good film."

Despite the mixed reviews, the $150 million film grossed over $245 million worldwide. Though those would be good numbers for most directors, they were disappointing for a Tim Burton movie; the director's previous film, *Alice in Wonderland*, took in $1 billion at the global box office. Speaking to Kevin Maher of the *Times of London*, Burton shrugged it off, saying, "Studios don't like to hear me say this, but it's all a bit of an experiment. It's like, is *Dark Shadows* a comedy? Is it a dark Gothic drama? Is it both? I've never thought about it in those terms. Because it's more about trying to get a vibe right. Trying to get a feeling right in a weird, melodramatic, soap opera-y way. I've made something that I can't quite categorize."

Neither, apparently, could audiences.

22

Blood on the Tube

Dracula Telefilms

Matinee Theater

On November 23, 1956, John Carradine appeared on television's *Matinee Theater* in a presentation of *Dracula*, the Deane-Balderston play, in which he was then touring. "John Carradine, an old hand at this sort of thing, is properly repulsive as the vampire, and the climax in a creepy castle is designed for shudders," said the *Chicago Daily Tribune*. According to a *New York Times* TV listing, the one-hour presentation was presented in color. This presentation is now as much a phantom as the vampire himself—no recordings of it are known to exist.

Dracula 1968

Thames Television produced the first British TV version of Bram Stoker's *Dracula* in 1968, starring Denholm Elliott in the title role. The TV movie aired on the ITV series *Mystery and Imagination*, as episode three of season four. The black-and-white teleplay begins with Dracula already in Seward's home, playing Beethoven's "Moonlight Sonata" on a piano. With his Van Dyke beard and retro smoked eyeglasses (the same type of eyeglasses later worn by Gary Oldman in *Bram Stoker's Dracula*), Elliott seems not so much like a vampire from the past, awakened in the nineteenth century, but rather a Mod aesthete sent back in time. With limited sets, the videotaped production condenses Stoker's story, making Harker (Corin Redgrave) the lunatic in Seward's asylum and omitting all scenes in Transylvania.

Denholm Mitchell Elliot, CBE (Commander of the Order of the British Empire), was born on May 31, 1922, in Ealing, London, in the United Kingdom. After receiving his training at the Royal Academy of Dramatic Arts in London, he went on to have a long and distinguished career, with more than 120 film and television credits, including his stint as Dracula. He died of tuberculosis (caused by AIDS) on October 6, 1992. He was seventy.

Bram Stoker's Dracula—1974

When *Dark Shadows* became a hit, it gave Dan Curtis the leverage to go to the TV networks and propose adaptations of horror classics. Over the next eight years, he produced a series of TV movies based on gothic literature: *Strange Case of Dr. Jekyll and Mr. Hyde* (1968), *The Picture of Dorian Gray* (1973), *Frankenstein* (1974), and *Bram Stoker's Dracula* (1974). "Make 'em good enough and horror shows will never go out of vogue," Curtis told Cecil Smith of the *Los Angeles Times*. "The trouble is that material of this kind is very difficult to do well." While Curtis's other gothic telefilms aired on ABC-TV, *Bram Stoker's Dracula* was snatched up by the more prestigious CBS, known as the "Tiffany Network."

Curtis, a man of strong convictions, told Smith, "There are only two great classic horror stories, *Frankenstein* and *Dracula*. And *Frankenstein* has been done well, several times. But not *Dracula*. The 1931 Bela Lugosi *Dracula* is unwatchable, except as camp. The 1958 Christopher Lee *Dracula* is one of the worst movies ever made."

By 1974, Curtis had also produced *The Night Stalker* (1972), which became the highest-rated TV movie ever aired when it was broadcast, and was followed up with a sequel the following year, *The Night Strangler*. Both of those telefilms were written by Richard Matheson, who had gained fame with some of the most revered episodes of *The Twilight Zone*, including "The Invaders" and "Nightmare at 20,000 Feet."

Working with Matheson to adapt *Dracula*, Curtis claimed he ripped himself off, taking the Barnabas Collins–Josette Du Pres love story from *Dark Shadows* and putting it into Stoker's story, giving the vampire a stronger motivation to go to England than simply to find more fruitful hunting grounds. In Matheson and Curtis's *Dracula*, when Harker arrives at Dracula's castle, he discovers there a newspaper clipping of a wedding announcement that includes a photo in which he is seen with Mina Murray, Arthur Holmwood, and Lucy Westenra; Lucy's face is encircled, suggesting Dracula's premeditation in bringing Harker to Transylvania.

Harker then steps to a painting labeled "Vlad Tepeș, Prince of Wallachia, 1475," which shows Dracula on a rearing horse, with sword drawn, and a woman standing behind him who looks suspiciously like Lucy. This painting, seen in both the first and last acts of the telefilm, makes *Bram Stoker's Dracula* the first film or TV adaptation of the story to draw upon the research in Raymond T. McNally and Radu Florescu's book *In Search of Dracula*, establishing a definite link between Stoker's fictional vampire count and the warlord of history.

Bram Stoker's Dracula was originally scheduled for a three-hour time slot. When CBS decided to go for a more conventional two-hour runtime, Matheson had to greatly condense the events of the novel, while still infusing the new historical and romantic elements that Curtis insisted upon, believing that the secret to a good horror story was for the viewer to feel some sympathy for the monster.

Casting for the telefilm began in April, when it was announced that Simon Ward, a British actor who had just appeared as Winston Churchill in *Young Winston,* was signed for the role of Arthur Holmwood. Other British actors cast included Nigel Davenport as Van Helsing, Penelope Horner as Mina, Pamela Brown as Mrs. Westenra, Fiona Lewis as Lucy, and Murray Brown as Jonathan Harker. To play the vampire count, Curtis turned to an actor with whom he'd worked previously on *Strange Case of Dr. Jekyll and Mr. Hyde,* Jack Palance.

Palance, born Volodymyr Palahniuk on February 18, 1919, was one of six children of Ukrainian immigrants who settled in the Lattimer Mines section of Hazle Township, Pennsylvania. As a child, he worked with his father in the coal mines. He played football in high school and fought as a professional boxer under the

In Bram Stoker's novel, Dracula claims the blood of Attila flows through his veins. How appropriate, then, that Jack Palance, who played Attila the Hun in 1954's *Sign of the Pagan,* should star as *Bram Stoker's Dracula,* in Dan Curtis's 1974 TV movie.
© *1974 Dan Curtis Productions/CBS Television.*
Author's collection.

name Jack Brazzo in the 1930s. When World War II began, he enlisted in the U.S. Army Air Forces. After being discharged in 1944, he attended Stanford University, but left—one credit shy of graduating—to pursue acting. Changing his name to Jack Palance, he became Marlon Brando's understudy in the stage version of *A Streetcar Named Desire,* eventually taking over the role of Stanley Kowalksi and making his Broadway debut in 1947. In the 1950s, he entered movies and gained critical notice for his role as gunfighter Jack Wilson in *Shane* (1951). He also shone on the small screen, starring in Rod Serling's *Requiem for a Heavyweight* in 1957, resulting in his winning an Emmy award for Best Actor.

Palance had already appeared as Dracula, in a sense. In 1971, when Marvel Comics introduced their *Tomb of Dracula* comic-book series, artist Gene Colan made a pitch to be the artist, drawing up a sketch of a mustachioed Dracula, using Jack Palance as his inspiration. He won the job.

Though he had played villains before, Palance found Dracula an interesting challenge. "It was kind of a strange attitude," said the actor when he was interviewed for the DVD release of the telefilm. "I think it was the only character I have ever played that frightened me. Even in the doing of it, I had a feeling of perhaps on occasion, becoming too near to Dracula—too much the character. I used to walk away from the set hoping that the entire production would end [as] soon as possible. I didn't really want to *become* Dracula, y'know." But become Dracula he did. In a remembrance of her career in London's *Observer*, Fiona Lewis recalled that Palance was "a method actor of such devotion that when he bit my neck, I was immediately taken to hospital."

"Jack was extraordinary," said producer/director Dan Curtis. "Jack is the best Dracula there ever was. He was the most frightening Dracula that ever put on that cape. . . . He could grab you by the throat and pick you up off the floor. He was terrifying. And an extraordinary actor."

Perhaps playing the lovelorn vampire helped put Palance in touch with his sensitive side; during the shooting, the actor—a journalism major in college—finished a novel which he placed with the W. H. Allen publishing company, who also took an option on a book of his poetry.

Bram Stoker's Dracula began filming on location in Yugoslavia in the summer of 1973. Trakoscan Castle in Croatia was used for long shots of Dracula's castle. By July, the production had moved to England, where Oakley Court was used for scenes taking place in Carfax Abbey.

CBS scheduled the telefilm for the evening of October 12, just before Halloween. On the day it was scheduled to air, Howard Thompson of the *New York Times* weighed in with a review, saying, "Even with a good color production and chilling portions, tonight's made-for-TV *Dracula* can't touch the old Hollywood tingler, a home-screen perennial, or England's *Horror of Dracula*, best of the theater follow-ups. And Jack Palance, gritting his fangs in agony and occasionally roaring like King Kong, is no Bela Lugosi or Christopher Lee."

Cecil Smith of the *Los Angeles Times* had a more favorable view, writing that the telefilm would "chill the bones of a plaster saint. It's as flesh-crawling an experience as you've ever had. Don't watch it with the lights off." After Smith called Jack Palance the definitive Dracula, Bela Lugosi Jr. defended his father's reputation with a letter to the newspaper saying, "It might be believable if you said that Jack Palance was the 'definitive' anything else but Dracula, because Jack Palance is an excellent, effective and very professional actor, and I have always liked him."

But viewers who were primed to watch Palance's take on Dracula were in for a bitter disappointment. On the Friday of the broadcast, President Nixon decided at the last minute to make an address to the nation to inform the public of his choice of Gerald Ford to succeed Spiro Agnew as his vice-president. Rather than wait for the speech to end and cut into *Bram Stoker's Dracula* already in progress, CBS decided to pre-empt the telefilm altogether.

A flurry of complaints were lodged at CBS, particularly since the president's address was rather brief and viewers thought that *Dracula* could still have been aired afterwards, in a later time slot. Fred Silverman, then program chief for CBS, decided it would be improper to air what he considered to be a high-quality film in a late-night slot usually reserved for talk shows and used-car commercials. Instead, he promised that it would air in the spring of the following year.

The movie was finally broadcast in the winter, on February 8, following the debut of a new CBS series, *Good Times*. Interviewed a few days before the airdate, Dan Curtis told Cecil Smith of the *Los Angeles Times*, "I was furious when they jerked the film last October, particularly after those great reviews appeared. But if they'd shown it, it would be long gone already. Now I still have it to look forward to." After the publicity build-up, many people assumed it had already aired, and after reading about it, felt they'd already seen it, so when it did actually air months later, the ratings were less than spectacular.

After its television broadcast, *Bram Stoker's Dracula* was shown in theaters in Europe, distributed by London-based distribution company Anglo-EMI. Palance's performance earned kudos from one former Dracula. In the 1996 British TV special *In Search of Dracula with Jonathan Ross*, Christopher Lee said of the actor, "The moment Palance appears on the screen, you can't take your eyes off him."

In his interview for the DVD release, Palance said, "I've been offered Dracula several more times, and I didn't want to do it anymore. I think once was enough. It's good to see what somebody else does with it, how they approach it and what they accomplish."

Jack Palance went on to have a prolific career, and was nominated for three Academy Awards, all in the Best Actor in a Supporting Role category. He finally won an Oscar in 1992 for his role as a tough cowboy, Curly Washburn, in the comedy hit *City Slickers*. During his acceptance speech, he showed the world just how hale he was at seventy-three by dropping to the floor and performing some one-armed push-ups. He died of natural causes, at the age of eighty-seven, on November 10, 2006.

Dracula, with a French Twist

The British were next to do a televised *Dracula*, when the BBC produced a three-hour adaptation of Stoker's novel. *Count Dracula* was adapted by Gerald Savory, a writer and producer who, early in his career, provided the script for Alfred Hitchcock's 1937 film *Young and Innocent*. The director was Philip Saville, an actor-turned-director who was known for telefilms that featured technical innovations and trippy effects. For *Count Dracula*, he often showed the vampire in a garish negative image, à la *Nosferatu*, and used music and sound effects in a hypnotic, surrealistic fashion.

Count Dracula (Louis Jourdan) makes his point, in Philip Saville's *Count Dracula* (1977).
© 1977 British Broadcasting Corporation. Courtesy of Del Valle Archives.

To play the vampire count, the producers chose distinguished French actor Louis Jourdan. Born Louis Robert Gendre on June 19, 1921, in Marseille, he was educated in France, Turkey, and the UK, and studied acting at the École Dramatique. His first movie role was in the French production of *Le Corsaire*, in which he was cast opposite Charles Boyer. After serving in the Resistance during World War II, Jourdan received an invitation from American producer David O. Selznick, who wanted him for a role in *The Paradine Case*, a 1947 film directed by Alfred Hitchcock. Jourdan remained in Hollywood, starring in *Gigi*, his best-known film, in 1958. The actor was pleased with the script for the new *Dracula*. "People will be expecting blood and fangs and they will have all that," he said. "But . . . our version is based on Bram Stoker's book." Jourdan underplayed the part, instilling his Dracula with an air of quiet menace. "I've tried to make him as attractive as possible," said the actor. "Like so many evil people, Dracula really believes he is doing good. He claims that he gives his victims eternal life."

Count Dracula had its first airing in the UK on BBC 2 on December 22, 1977, shown in its 155-minute entirety. For subsequent BBC broadcasts, it was cut into either three or two parts. The telefilm was broadcast in the U.S. in three parts over PBS's *Great Performances* series. As with *Bram Stoker's Dracula*, the film aired in winter, this time debuting on March 1, 1978.

For some critics, *Count Dracula* was a mixed bag. It was more faithful to the source novel than any other version of the story, though some changes were made (like making Lucy and Mina sisters); it had good production values, including filming on location in Whitby; and the acting, overall, was sincere and effective. But the telecast was marred by video effects that, while they may have given it a surreal feel in its original broadcast, seem dated and cheesy by modern standards, though critic Michael Church in the *Times of London* didn't mind the electronic flourishes, writing, "In purely technical terms *Count Dracula* was a *tour de force*. The soundtrack . . . underlined the camera's deft pinpointing of detail, a lengthening canine, a suddenly red eye. Sometimes, with a swift lurch into negative colour, the screen itself seemed to go mad, and then back we would be in pretty Whitby—graves, clouds and the sea."

The casting of the very Gallic Louis Jourdan as Dracula was also divisive, resulting in a vampire who, despite his hairy palms and predilection for biting the necks of young ladies, seemed somehow lacking in menace. As Nancy Banks-Smith wrote in London's *Guardian*, Jourdan "emphasised the lover at the expense of the demon. It makes a change. Though, I would say, for the worst."

However, other critics were won over by Jourdan. Reviewing the production for the *Los Angeles Times*, Cecil Smith wrote, "Louis Jourdan plays Bram Stoker's vampire king with the sort of suave elegance he displayed as a Parisian boulevardier. Don't let it fool you. . . . He seems more to the manor born, the ultimate aristocrat, than other Draculas we've had, including the great Bela Lugosi."

In the *New York Times*, John J. O'Connor wrote, "Dressed in black and properly pale, Mr. Jourdan portrays the Count as a rather reasonable fellow who just happens to have a few peculiar habits . . . some of the special effects, particularly the electronic device of negative images, are merely jarring in the context of a costume production set in 1890. But, overall, the thing works to a remarkably chilling turn and, once again, Dracula proves a phenomenon of almost puzzling endurance."

The members of The Count Dracula Society in America applauded Louis Jourdan's performance, presenting the actor with an award in April of 1978.

At midnight of March 17, 1978, all three hours of the production were presented back-to-back on PBS. The airing of the BBC production had an unexpected consequence in Altamont, New York, where nearly two hundred communion wafers and the ciborium that contained them went missing from St. Lucy's Catholic Church. Police surmised that the theft might be linked to the broadcast of *Count Dracula*, in which Van Helsing was seen breaking communion wafers and sprinkling pieces over vampires' graves.

Louis Jourdan retired in the 1990s to spend more time at home in Beverly Hills, California, although he briefly returned to France, where he was made a Chevalier de la Legion d'honneur. He died, on February 14, 2015, at the age of ninety-three.

Dracula in the 2000s

Patrick Bergin played Vladislav Tepeş, a.k.a Dracula, in a two-part Italian miniseries called *Il bacio di Dracula* that hewed fairly closely to Stoker's tale, though updating it to modern times and setting it in Budapest instead of Whitby and London, and renaming Van Helsing (Giancarlo Giannini), Dr. Enrico Valenzi. Roger Young directed from a script he co-authored with Eric Lerner. The telefilm aired May 29, 2002, in Italy, and was released on DVD in the U.S. as *Dracula's Curse.*

A new BBC version of *Dracula* arrived in 2006, produced by Granada Television. Bill Eagles directed from a script by Stewart Harcourt, who reimagined the story, with Dracula summoned to London by Arthur Holmwood, soon to be wed to Lucy, because Holmwood hopes the Count can cure him of his syphilis. Before writing his script, Harcourt re-read Stoker's novel. As he wrote in an article he penned for the *London Sunday Telegraph,* he discovered "there are lots of unexplained plot developments—why on earth does Dracula go to Whitby?—and there are too many poorly drawn characters. It became clear to me that *Dracula* was no *Bleak House* or *Pride and Prejudice*—it is not a perfect work written by a genius. Rather, it's an inspired and messy piece of gothic imagination."

Even before Harcourt delivered his first draft script, there was a buzz about the production. At one point, executive producer Damien Timmer found himself in an elevator at Granada Television with David Suchet, star of the *Poirot* mystery series, who said that whenever they filmed *Dracula,* he wanted to play Van Helsing. Six months later, Suchet was on the set, enacting the role of the vampire hunter.

The role of Arthur Holmwood went to Dan Stevens, while Dracula was played by Marc Warren. The slight, young Warren realized he wasn't quite what people pictured when they thought of the vampire. He told Nancy Durrant of the *Times of London,* "When you do something like this, it's so iconic, so many people have done it, there's just a great fear of messing it up. Fear that people have trusted you with something. I'm just getting on with it and trying to do it the best I can, really."

The TV film aired on BBC in the UK on December 28, 2006, and on PBS in the U.S., where it was called *Bram Stoker's Dracula,* on February 11, 2007. It received generally favorable reviews.

23

Vamping for Ratings

The Night Stalker

When *Night Gallery* and *Sixth Sense* were canceled, it seemed audiences were becoming fed up with the supernatural on TV. But Dan Curtis didn't believe so; he had just produced the film *Night of Dark Shadows* when ABC's Barry Diller called him about producing and directing *The Night Stalker*.

Having finally made the leap from television to the movies, Curtis wasn't interested, until Diller told him the script was by Richard Matheson. Curtis considered Matheson the master of the supernatural teleplay, and liked the idea of putting a vampire in a familiar American locale—Las Vegas. He agreed to produce the TV movie, but with a feature film commitment at MGM, he had to relinquish the directing duties. John Llewelyn Moxey, who directed episodes of several British TV series, including *The Saint*, before coming to America and directing episodes of *Hawaii Five-O* and *Mission: Impossible*, took up the reins.

With a superb cast headed by Darren McGavin as down-on-his-luck reporter Carl Kolchak, Simon Oakland as his crusty bureau chief, and Barry Atwater as vampire Janos Skorzeny, on the loose in Las Vegas where—as director Moxey observed—*everyone* is a vampire, the film delivered the perfect combination of thrills, chills, and humor; little wonder that it became the most popular television movie ever made up to that time. The following year, Curtis produced a sequel, *The Night Strangler*, which aired on ABC's *Movie of the Week* on January 16, 1973.

In the 1974–75 TV season, *Kolchak: The Night Stalker* became a weekly supernatural series on ABC, with Darren McGavin continuing in the role he played in the two TV movies: wisecracking wire service reporter Carl Kolchak, whose chief (Oakland) keeps squelching his stories of vampires, zombies, witches, and other supernatural creatures. The fourth episode, a sequel to the original telefilm, pitted him against a female vampire, a former victim of Janos Skorzeny. The series ran for twenty episodes, ending on March 28, 1975.

In one of TV's highest-rated TV movies, reporter Carl Kolchak (Darren McGavin) uncovers vampire Janos Skorzeny (Barry Atwater) in Las Vegas.
© *1972 Dan Curtis Productions/ABC Television. Courtesy of Del Valle Archives.*

Salem's Lot and Other Delights

In the 1970s, even *Sesame Street* introduced a vampire Muppet, Count von Count, to teach children basic math skills. Joining the show in its fourth season (1972–73), the Count, modeled on Bela Lugosi's Dracula, loved to count, and counted anything, from the number of times a phone rang to the hairs in someone's mustache. On one show, his car was shown, with a license plate that read Transylvania 6-5000.

NBC's cowboy detective *McCloud* (Dennis Weaver) investigated a supposed vampire in New York in the April 17, 1977, episode of the mystery series entitled, "McCloud Meets Dracula." John Carradine guest-starred in the episode as Loren Belasco, an eccentric actor who once starred in Dracula films; some would call that typecasting.

In November of 1979, CBS broadcast a two-part TV miniseries that extended the Halloween chills into the Thanksgiving season. Directed by Tobe Hooper, *Salem's Lot* starred David Soul as Ben Mears, a writer who returns to his home town to work on a novel and finds that a vampire has moved into an abandoned house nearby. The telefilm was based on the second published novel from Stephen King, who got the idea while teaching a high-school Fantasy and Science Fiction course at Maine's Hampden Academy. One of the books covered in the class was Bram Stoker's *Dracula*, leading King to speculate what would happen if Dracula came back to twentieth-century America. If he showed up in New York, thought King, he'd probably be hit by a cab and killed. But if he showed up in a small town . . .

King's 439-page book was published in October 1975. A year later, New American Library/Signet released a paperback version that sold two million copies in its first month, hitting number two on the *New York Times* Mass Market Paperback Best Seller list on September 19, 1976. It remained in the top ten through November 28. Warner Bros. purchased the film rights, and several writers (including Larry Cohen and Stirling Silliphant) took a crack at distilling the plot into a two-hour theatrical feature. Then Richard Kobritz, a TV production executive at Warners, thought perhaps the project could be better served as a TV movie, where it could stretch over three or more hours. Paul Monash wrote a 190-page script (as opposed to the 120 pages common for a theatrical film), and Kobritz began searching for a director. *Halloween*'s John Carpenter was approached, but was busy prepping his next feature, *The Fog*. Kobritz then turned to Tobe Hooper, best known for his low-budget horror film *The Texas Chainsaw Massacre* (1974).

The TV executives wanted either David Janssen or James Garner to play writer Ben Mears, but Kobritz wanted a younger actor and offered the role to David Soul, whose action series *Starsky & Hutch* had just ended its four-year run.

Kobritz then signed iconic actor James Mason for the malevolent Richard K. Straker, and also found a role for Mason's wife, Clarissa Kaye; she would play Marjorie Glick. For the role of vampire Kurt Barlow, Kobritz cast character actor Reggie Nalder and had him made up to resemble *Nosferatu*'s Max Schreck. This was a departure from King's book, whose Barlow was a more traditionally elegant vampire.

The resulting telefilm was very well received and later re-edited for airing in one three-hour instalment. It was also released as a feature film overseas, with more graphic violence and horror.

The BBC adapted King's book into a seven-part radio series in 1995, and then in June 2004 TNT produced a cable television remake, with Mikael Salomon directing from a script

Salem's Lot (1979). Richard K. Straker (James Mason) and Kurt Barlow (Reggie Nalder) have just moved into an old house in Salem's Lot, Maine. As they say: there goes the neighborhood . . .

© 1979 Warner Bros. Television. Courtesy of Del Valle Archives.

adapted by Peter Filardi. This time, Rob Lowe played writer Ben Mears, with Donald Sutherland as Straker and Rutger Hauer as Barlow, portrayed more as King perceived him, a sophisticated gentleman with a slightly anachronistic way of dressing. Just as with the CBS mini-series, it was broadcast over two evenings.

Der Kleine Vampir and Der Vampyr

Angela Sommer-Bodenburg's book series *The Little Vampire* (*Der kleine Vampir*) was adapted as a Canadian-German children's TV series in 1986. The series involved a lonely ten-year-old, Anton, who befriends another young boy who turns out to be a 146-year-old vampire. Fourteen years later, Uli Edel directed a film adaptation of Sommer-Bodenburg's books, *The Little Vampire*, in 2000. Changing the names of the characters, the comedy involved a young boy, Tony Thomson (Jonathan Lipnicki), who befriends child vampires searching for a magical stone that will make them human.

On December 2, 1992, as *Bram Stoker's Dracula* was released in the UK and the British Isles succumbed to the vampire mania that was washing over America, the BBC aired *The Vampyr: A Soap Opera*. It was an updated version of Heinrich Marschner's Romantic opera of 1820, *Der Vampyr* (itself based on John Polidori's *The Vampyre*), relocated to contemporary London. John Rockwell of the *New York Times* described it as "a soap opera complete with ample frontal nudity and lustily simulated sexual couplings. All of which were performed by opera singers without doubles, singing the score pretty much as Marschner composed it, albeit with updated lyrics by a sometime collaborator of Andrew Lloyd Webber, Charles Hart."

Vampires in the City

On August 20, 1989, CBS aired the TV movie *Nick Knight*, starring Rick Springfield as the title character, a Los Angeles detective who is really a centuries-old vampire, searching for a killer who drains bodies of blood. The pilot was not picked up by the network, but a few years later, CBS revamped it, so to speak, as *Forever Knight*, with the role now played by Geraint Wyn Davies. The location was switched to Toronto, where the series was filmed, and the original TV movie was reshot as the first two episodes of the new series. The episodes aired in CBS's "Crimetime After Primetime" slot, following the ten o'clock local news (or eleven, depending on the time zone). The series ran for three seasons, from May 1992 to May 1996, comprising seventy episodes.

Prolific TV producer Aaron Spelling, who brought American viewers *Charlie's Angels, The Love Boat, Fantasy Island, Dynasty, Beverly Hills 90210,* and *Melrose Place,* introduced his own vampire series in 1996. *Kindred: The Embraced* has five clans of gorgeous-looking vampires living in San Francisco, where they are locked in a turf war. The most powerful clan is led by Julian Luna

(Mark Frankel); one clan is composed of young biker vampires, another—the Brujah—of muscle-bound bodybuilder vampires. Yet another clan is led by a mini-skirted nightclub owner named Lillie Langtry—*the* Lillie Langtry, and finally there are the Nosferatus, who—like Murnau's silent screen vampire—are hairless and pointy-toothed.

The show developed its own vampire vocabulary. To be "embraced" was to become a vampire, one of the "kindred." The "masquerade" was the vampire's term for passing as humans. The series premiered on April 2, 1996, on the FOX network. After just eight episodes, it was canceled, its final broadcast occurring on May 9. All eight of the produced episodes were later released on home video.

Another TV vampire, Crispian Grimes (Greg Wise), turned up in 1997's two-part telefilm *House of Frankenstein*. Millionaire Grimes runs a nightclub called House of Frankenstein, which is a secret haven for vampires; he is also a serial killer, known to the police as "the Midnight Raptor." Police detective Vernon Coyle (Adrian Pasdar) is hot on his trail, a mission that becomes complicated when his girlfriend, Grace Dawkins (Teri Polo), is bitten by a werewolf and later kidnapped by Grimes. Produced by NBC, the telefilm was meant as a revival of Universal Studios' classic monsters: the vampire, werewolf, and Frankenstein's Monster (Peter Crombie).

The six-episode 1998 UK series *Ultraviolet* has a detective investigating the disappearance of a friend drawn into a covert war between humans and vampires. In 2000, the FOX network produced a pilot that was a remake of the show for American audiences, but it was never aired.

Buffy, Teenagers, and Bloodsuckers

Five years after its moderate success as a movie, *Buffy the Vampire Slayer* came to television. Originally telecast on The WB network, the show was created by Joss Whedon, who wrote the screenplay for the 1992 feature film. The series follows the high-school exploits of vampire slayer Buffy Summers (Sarah Michelle Gellar), who, aided by Rupert Giles (Anthony Stewart Head) and friends Willow (Alyson Hannigan) and Xander (Nicholas Brendon), opposes vampires and other creatures of darkness. Giles is Buffy's Watcher, a member of The Watchers Council, which trains and assists slayers. While Xander has no supernatural abilities, Willow is eventually revealed to be a witch.

With Whedon as executive producer of the series and show runner for the first five seasons, the show became a hit, attracting a large teen following with stories that used supernatural events as metaphors for teenage anxieties; Whedon saw the show's central theme as "high school as a horror movie." It racked up 144 episodes from March 1997 to May 2003, and spun off the series *Angel*, starring David Boreanaz as Buffy's one-time love interest, relocated to Los Angeles and working as a (what else?) private detective. *Angel* ran for five seasons, from October 1999 to May 2004, with 110 episodes. Unlike *Buffy*, *Angel*

The Master (Mark Metcalf) menaces Buffy Summers (Sarah Michelle Gellar) in the WB's 1997–2003 series, *Buffy the Vampire Slayer*. The program was ranked #2 on *Empire* magazine's list of the "50 Greatest TV Shows of All Time." *Courtesy of Del Valle Archives*

had more action and was more of a "guy's show."

The Disney Channel TV movie *Mom's Got a Date with a Vampire* (2000) has grounded teens arranging a date for their divorced mother (Caroline Rhea) and then realizing that Dimitri (Charles Shaughnessy), the mysterious stranger she is dating, is a vampire. They enlist the aid of vampire hunter Malachi Van Helsing (Robert Carradine), who helps them defeat Dimitri and seal him in his coffin. The Disney Channel repeated the film every October through 2009.

The 2001–02 Canadian series *Vampire High* has a group of vampire students attending a private boarding school with human teens in an attempt to civilize the vampires. Twenty-six half-hour episodes were produced.

What happens when your father is Count Dracula and you just want to be a normal teen? That was the question posed by the British TV series *Young Dracula*, with Gerran Howell as Vlad, and Clare Thomas as Ingrid, the children of Count Dracula (Keith-Lee Castle), who has relocated from Transylvania to Stokely Wales, where his children attend Stokely Grammar School. The woodwork teacher, Eric Van Helsing (Terence Maynard), turns out to be a vampire hunter, naturally. The first series of fourteen episodes aired on the CBBC Channel from September to December 2006. Four more seasons of thirteen episodes each followed, airing in 2007–08, 2011, 2012, and 2014. The show, based on Michael Lawrence's children's book, *Young Dracula and Young Monsters*, won the Royal Television Society Award for Best Children's Drama in 2007.

Vampires on the Beat

Similar to *Forever Knight*, the Lifetime network's 2007 series *Blood Ties* has Vicki Nelson (Christina Cox), a Toronto policewoman turned private investigator, solving crimes with the aid of 470-year-old vampire Henry Fitzroy (Kyle Schmid), the illegitimate son of Henry VIII. Although two seasons of eleven episodes each were filmed, all twenty-two episodes were broadcast in 2007.

CBS's *Moonlight* (2007–08) has Alex O'Loughlin as Mick St. John, a vampire working as—you guessed it!—a detective, struggling with his feelings for human Beth Turner (Sophia Myles) while solving crimes involving vampires in Los Angeles. The series was originally titled *Twilight*, but the title was changed when Warner Bros. purchased the film rights to Stephenie Meyer's Twilight novels; Warner Bros. Television and Silver Pictures Television produced *Moonlight*.

True Bloodsuckers

Pay cable network Home Box Office (HBO) entered the vampire business with the premiere of *True Blood* in 2008. *True Blood* shows that vampires can be more than just gothic—they can be Southern gothic. Based on Charlaine Harris's *The Southern Vampire Mysteries* novels, the series centers on the adventures of telepathic waitress Sookie Stackhouse (Anna Paquin), who meets and falls in love with a 173-year-old vampire named Bill Compton (Stephen Moyer) in Bon Temps, Louisiana.

The series was predicated on the notion that vampires had come "out of the coffin" when a synthetic blood, called True Blood, was developed, so that they no longer had to feed on humans. But not all vampires were happy with the arrangement; the vampire community was now split into two camps, those who wanted to integrate peacefully with humans, and those who were militantly against it. Similarly, the humans were of two minds about the vampires. Many viewed the series as being a metaphor for the struggle for gay rights, especially when the show introduced a group of ultra-conservative vampire haters who adopted the slogan, "God hates fangs," a take-off on the real-life protest slogan, "God hates fags."

As the series progressed, it unveiled other supernatural creatures besides just vampires. Sookie's employer, Sam Merlotte (Sam Trammell) is actually a shapeshifter, and Sookie herself eventually learns that she is a faerie. And then there are the werewolves, and the witches, and Lilith . . .

Much of the humor of the series comes from the matter-of-fact approach it takes to the humans, who are often not-very-bright, undereducated "white trash" types, as well as the vampires, who are a far cry from the usual portrayal of bloodsuckers as well-heeled aristocrats.

True Blood producer Alan Ball had previously overseen the popular *Six Feet Under* series for HBO. When that show ended, he signed a two-year deal to develop new projects for the cable network. Sometime afterward, he arrived early for a dentist appointment and went into a bookstore, where he picked up a copy of *Dead Until Dark*, the first book in Charlaine Harris's series of Sookie Stackhouse Southern Vampires novels. He then read the rest of the books in the series, met with Harris, and convinced her to let him go forward with a TV adaptation.

The series was noted not only for its violence but for its sexuality. Every episode contains nudity and sex acts, often accompanied with vampiric bites and bloodletting. In that regard, it is rather a throwback to the Hammer films of the 1970s, which mixed sex and the supernatural and often featured naked female breasts splattered with bright red blood. The cocktail of sex, vampires, and Southern accents caught on with viewers, who made *True Blood* one of HBO's highest-rated series. The onscreen sparks also led to an offscreen union: Anna Paquin and Stephen Moyer married on August 21, 2010. The show ran for seven seasons, with the final episode airing on August 24, 2014.

Being Human

The BBC series *Being Human* also features supernatural beings trying to blend in with humans. Created and written by Toby Whithouse, it features a vampire, Guy Flanagan (Aidan Turner); Annie Sawyer, a ghost (Lenora Crichlow); and George Sands, a werewolf (Russell Tovey). The three unlikely flatmates do their best to blend in with the humans around them. The third and fourth seasons added two more werewolves, Nina Pickering and Tom McNair (Sinead Keenan and Michael Socha) and another vampire, Hal (Damien Molony), while the fifth season added a ghost, Alex Millar (Kate Bracken). The show ran from February 2008 to March 2013. The efforts of the characters to sublimate their supernatural abilities and live among humans are often threatened by their own natures and by the efforts of other supernaturals to expose them. Stephen Armstrong of the *Guardian* wrote that the appeal of the show was that it dealt "more with the horror of living in modern Britain than the horror of the undead."

The series was remade for American audiences, with Sam Witwer as the vampire, Aidan Waite; Meaghan Rath as the ghost, Sally Malik; and Sam Huntington as Josh Levison, the werewolf; and the locale shifted from Bristol to Boston. Broadcast on the Syfy Channel, it ran for fifty-two hour-long episodes over four seasons, from January 2011 to April 2014.

Another British series, *Demons*, created by Johnny Capps and Julian Murphy, borrowed a page from *Buffy the Vampire Slayer* with London teenager Luke Rutherford (Christian Cooke) meeting his godfather, Rupert Galvin (Philip Glenister), who informs Luke that he is the descendant of Van Helsing, and his destiny is to save the world from demons. He is assisted by Mina Harker (Zoë Tapper), whose infection by Dracula's vampire blood has kept her alive for more than a century. Among the vampires Luke has to vanquish are Quincey (Ciarán McMenamin), the son of Mina and Jonathan Harker, and Gladiolus Thrip (Mackenzie Crook), a demon vampire of unusual strength and speed. The six episodes aired from January 3 to February 7, 2009.

The Vampire Diaries

A year after *True Blood* appeared on HBO, *The Vampire Diaries* debuted on The CW. Airing on free television and subject to censorship, the show was similar to *True Blood* in that it centered on a young female who lives in a small community (in this instance, Mystic Falls, Virginia) and becomes enamored of a vampire. Elena Gilbert (Nina Dobrov) is the high-school teenager who falls for Stefan Salvatore (Paul Wesley), a 163-year-old vampire, who is attracted to Elena because she is the spitting image of Katherine Pierce, Elena's ancestor and once the love interest of Stefan and his impulsive brother Damon (Ian Somerhalder).

Kevin Williamson and Julie Plec developed the series, based on the young adult books *The Vampire Diaries*, which L. J. Smith began publishing in 1991. The TV series has several characters dealing with addictions; some of the humans struggle with their thirst for alcohol, while the vampires struggle with their thirst for blood. Addiction is the show's running theme, and addiction is what it creates in its viewers. As of this writing, the show is in its sixth season and still going strong. After more than 120 episodes, the twists in the plotline have seen Elena becoming a vampire and getting romantically involved with Damon. A spin-off series, *The Originals*, premiered in 2013, focusing on a family that became the original vampires from which all subsequent vampires were propagated. *The Originals* premiered October 3, 2013, and, as of this writing, is in its second season.

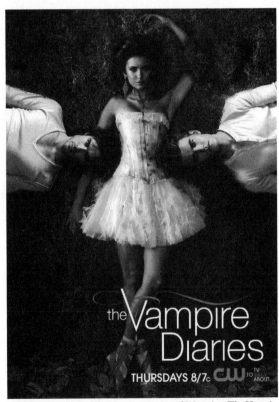

ABC TV introduced its own short-lived series featuring vampires, werewolves, and witches on June 20, 2010. *The Gates* has a family moving to an upscale neighborhood where the patriarch, Nick Monohan (Frank Grillo), was to become chief of police. One of the inhabitants of the community, Dylan Radcliff (Luke Mably), is a vampire. After an initial run of thirteen episodes, the series was canceled.

The young stars of the long-running CW series *The Vampire Diaries*: Ian Somerhalder, Nina Dobrev, and Paul Wesley. The show's pilot, broadcast September 10, 2009, had the largest audience of any series premiere in the network's three-year history.   *Author's collection*

The Strain

Among the latest prime-time vampire series is *The Strain*, created by Guillermo del Toro and Chuck Hogan. The show began July 13, 2014, on the cable channel FX. Del Toro originally pitched the TV series in 2006, but when FOX Broadcasting asked him to make it a comedy, he decided to write it as a novel series instead, with the help of Chuck Hogan. Three novels were eventually written: *The Strain* (published in 2009), *The Fall* (2010), and *The Night Eternal* (2011). Once the books appeared, several networks began negotiations to adapt the story into a series. Del Toro decided to go with FX because they were willing to remain faithful to the novels and envisioned the series as being one that would end after three to five seasons.

The series centers on a team from the Center for Disease Control out to stop a vampire called the Master from creating a vampiric army through a worm-spread virus. Corey Stoll stars as Dr. Ephraim "Eph" Goodweather, head of the CDC team, while Robert Maillet plays the Master, voiced by Robin Atkin Downes. Thus far, two thirteen-episode seasons have been produced.

Penny Dreadful

A co-production of America's Showtime and the UK's Sky TV, *Penny Dreadful* premiered in the U.S. on May 11, 2014. Created and written by John Logan, the show is set in Victorian London and features characters from classic gothic literature, including Dorian Gray (Reeve Carney), Victor Frankenstein (Harry Treadaway), Caliban (Frankenstein's Monster, played by Rory Kinnear), Mina Harker (Olivia Llewellyn), Abraham Van Helsing (David Warner), and a vampire (Robert Nairne). Eight episodes were produced in the first season; the show was renewed for a second season of ten episodes.

24

Video Vixens

Vampira Versus Elvira

Vampira

When Cassandra Peterson's movie, *Elvira: Mistress of the Dark*, was released in 1988, she expected it would please the legions of fans who tuned in to her TV series and turned out to her personal appearances. What she didn't expect was that it would be the final straw for Maila Nurmi, formerly known as "Vampira," the original horror hostess from the 1950s, who filed suit against Peterson, claiming that "Elvira" had stolen her vampire woman characterization.

As Pat Broeske pointed out in the *Los Angeles Times*, the original vampire woman was Carroll Borland, whose appearance in the 1935 film *Mark of the Vampire* set the standard: tight dress (though Borland's was white and draped her entire body, not a form-fitting, cleavage-plunging black), long black hair, long black fingernails, pale face, and Clara Bow lips. Borland told Broeske that MGM makeup man William Tuttle believed her makeup should be similar to co-star Bela Lugosi's. "So I was given this pasty white face," said Borland, "which looked pretty strange when I walked around the lot—with dark, heightened eyes and dark red lips." The studio wanted her hair cut, curled, and bobbed, but Borland insisted on keeping her long tresses. A pop-culture image was born.

After that one film, Borland, who had previously toured with Lugosi in the stage play of *Dracula*, was pigeonholed as a horror actress. She eventually left showbiz and became a professor at Pasadena's Pacific Oaks College. Asked about the dispute between Petersen and Nurmi, she told Broeske, "I get a kick out of the fact that those two are fighting over my face!"

Charles Addams might have argued that the real prototype for the "vampire woman" look was his own creation, Morticia Addams, matriarch of the Addams Family. A cartoonist whose work frequently appeared in the *New Yorker* magazine, Addams created the Addams Family, a group of macabre, but wealthy, eccentrics, in 1938. Over the next fifty years, he drew some 150 single-panel cartoons featuring the characters, and saw them spin off into a TV series. After his death in 1988, the Addams Family was adapted to feature films and a Broadway musical. Depicted as a very slim woman with pale skin and long dark hair, Morticia

One of the originators of the "vampire woman" look, in a gown designed by Adrian, Carroll Borland had appeared in a stage production of *Dracula* with Bela Lugosi before landing the role of Luna, the daughter of Lugosi's Count Mora in 1935's *Mark of the Vampire*.   *Courtesy of Del Valle Archives*

was clad in a skin-tight hobble gown with a plunging neckline that accentuated her bosom and hourglass figure, with tendrils like an octopus at the bottom hem.

The look was co-opted by an aspiring actress named Maila Nurmi in 1953. When the thirty-two-year-old was invited to attend a masquerade ball in Hollywood, she decided to go as Morticia. She bound her bosoms to appear flat-chested, put on a long, dark wig, and painted her body with white pancake makeup, with a little lavender powder so that she would look as though she had just crawled out of a crypt. According to Nurmi, her costume was judged the best at the ball. Months later, when Los Angeles television station KABC decided to hire a host for their program of late-night horror films, a producer who had been at the ball remembered her and called her in. She got the job.

Previously, Nurmi had been a hat check girl, an engraver, a neck-tie artist and a lady bellhop. She joked that before being hired as a horror hostess, she had an off-the-shoulder billboard painted that read, "I'm neurotic and can't work. Please help."

Born Maila Syrjaniemi on December 11, 1922, in Petsamo, Finland, Nurmi immigrated to the United States when she was a toddler. By age seventeen, she took the surname of Paavo Nurmi, a world-class runner known as the "Flying Finn," whom she claimed was her uncle. Pursuing acting, she moved to New York and Los Angeles, along the way befriending Marilyn Monroe, Elvis Presley,

Orson Welles, and James Dean, with whom she had a close platonic relation-ship. She also picked up a husband, actor and writer Dean Reisner, who would later pen the script for 1971's *Dirty Harry*. Little came of Nurmi's efforts to land leading roles in theater or film, until she attended that masquerade ball.

As Vampira, Nurmi appeared with fishnet stockings, six-inch fingernails, a low-cut black gown, dramatically arched eyebrows, and the tiniest waist on live television, courtesy of a waist cincher that gave her measurements of 36B-21-35. In interviews, she claimed Vampira was part Morticia Adams, mixed with "cheesecake" and phallic symbols like the long cigarette holder, plus a bit of Greta Garbo, a touch of beatnik culture, and a healthy dose of *Sunset Boulevard*'s Norma Desmond. It has been written that she effectively pioneered Goth aesthetics and sensibilities long before they became fashionable.

After slinking through a fog-filled hallway up to the camera and screaming into it, she would introduce herself and the evening's horror film. During commercial breaks, she spiced up the proceedings by lounging on a couch and cracking jokes. In one show, she searched for the book *Tom Swift and His Electric Throat Slasher*. She talked of making a bad-will tour of America. Instead of a birthday, she spoke of having a "dead-day" party. She celebrated Thanksgiving with "young tom vulture." Christmas was the "cruel time" season, when she did her "Christmas chopping." When TV awards season came, she claimed she had been nominated for an "Enemy" award. She bathed in a boiling cauldron, played with her pet tarantula Rollo, and gave out recipes for vampire cocktails. She even promoted a beer with the slogan, "My bier is a dry bier."

The show was an instant hit, propelling Nurmi into the limelight, though Walter Ames in the *Los Angeles Times* reported that Nurmi's husband was slightly embarrassed by "all the notoriety his 'spook' wife" was getting; the couple divorced in 1954. Vampira was invited to appear along with Bela Lugosi on Red Skelton's show, made appearances on talk shows, and was invited to movie premieres.

Shortly after her debut, Vampira appeared in *Life* magazine, and soon fan clubs were organized around the world. "I was high-rolling in Hollywood, and I was quite full of myself," Nurmi said in a 1994 interview with *People* magazine. Her celebrity was such that when Sonia Henie gave a party at Ciro's with a "circus festival" theme and asked guests to come in costume, Zsa Zsa Gabor arrived dressed as the horror hostess.

Then, at the end of March 1955, Vampira's show was abruptly canceled. Even so, she continued to appear in character on other programs, such as *Juke Box Jury*, and appeared in Liberace's Las Vegas nightclub act, hypnotizing him.

On January 8, 1956, Nurmi was in New York when a "wiry little man" forced his way into her apartment. He grabbed Nurmi, beat her, choked her, and tore off her clothes. She struggled with the attacker for two hours before being able to escape. Police later arrested the attacker, Ellis Barber, alias "The Dip" and "The Vamp," when he attempted to re-enter her apartment building. He was held under ten-thousand-dollar bond.

The original mistress of the dark, Vampira (Maila Nurmi).
Author's collection

She returned to Los Angeles and horror hosting duties in May 1956, on station KHJ. She telegraphed columnist Walter Ames of the *Los Angeles Times* that she wanted viewers to think of her "as the average friendly neighbor they would expect to find living halfway up the next swamp," adding, "I've undergone a grave change. My motto now is 'home sweet homicide.'"

During the height of her career, she met director Ed Wood at a party and felt nothing but disdain, but when Wood approached her in 1956 and offered her two hundred dollars to appear in a movie with Bela Lugosi, she accepted. "I was scraping by on $13 a week," she told *People.* "I thought, 'Well, here I go. I'm going to commit professional suicide right now.'" The result, released in 1959, was *Plan 9 from Outer Space,* often cited as the worst film ever made. Nurmi appeared in a few more movies, including *The Big Operator* (1959), *I Passed for White* (1960), *Sex Kittens Go to College* (1960), and *The Magic Sword* (1962), but by 1961, Vampira was gone, and largely forgotten. Interviewed by Paul Coates of the *Los Angeles Times* in 1962, she said, "I'm in oblivion, and I'm very happy here. . . . I'm a lady linoleum-layer. And if things are slow in linoleum, I also do carpentry, make drapes or refinish furniture." Asked if she would reprise Vampira, she replied, "No. I just attracted a bunch of psychos. And besides, that waist-cincher I wore played hell with my breathing."

Elvira

In the 1970s, Maila Nurmi opened a Vampira antiques shop, but struggled to make ends meet. In 1980, she resurrected Vampira "from the cobwebs" to help raise money for organizations that provided aid to stray animals. Los Angeles TV station KHJ contacted her the next year, interested in doing a Vampira-type show and using the Vampira name. She told Christine Ziaya of the *Los Angeles Times* that after three months of negotiations, the station offered a contract that would have forced her to give up all rights to the Vampira character. She declined, and discussions ended. Walter Baker, KHJ vice president and program director, told the paper that the station negotiated with Nurmi to use the name Vampira, and to have Nurmi make occasional appearances on the show, but he maintained that "when negotiations ceased at her doing, we changed the show—the whole concept."

Well . . .

The show KHJ went with instead was called *Movie Macabre*, hosted by Elvira. In Vampira's 1950s show, she entered down a fog-shrouded hallway in a tight black dress that accentuated her bosom, settled onto a couch, and made risqué jokes about the films she presented. Elvira, on the other hand, entered down a fog-shrouded hallway in a tight black dress that accentuated her bosom, settled onto a couch, and made risqué jokes about the films she presented. Totally. Different. Concept.

As it happened, at the time Nurmi was in talks with KHJ about a Vampira revival, actress and comedienne Cassandra Peterson was negotiating with the station about playing the part of their new horror-hostess, Elvira.

Peterson was born in Kansas in 1951, but moved with her family to Colorado Springs when their home was flooded. After graduating from Palmer High School in 1969, she went to Las Vegas and became a chorus girl. While there, she was spotted by Elvis Presley, who encouraged her to persist with her career. She did, and in 1972, while in Italy, landed a small part in director Federico Fellini's *Roma*.

Returning to America, she settled in Los Angeles and joined The Groundlings, a Los Angeles Improv troupe that also included Paul Reubens, who would later find fame as Pee-Wee Herman. She left The Groundlings when she was offered the Elvira job, which paid a steady three hundred dollars a week.

Hiding her strawberry-blonde tresses beneath a black bouffant wig and squeezing into a tight-fitting, low-cut black dress, she joked her way through one cheesy horror film after another. In the beginning, she spoke slowly because, being nearsighted, she had trouble reading the cue cards. Later on, she had corrective vision surgery, considered experimental at the time. Now that she could see the cue cards, her speech became faster. As the years progressed, her black bouffant also became higher and higher.

Peterson worked with fellow comedian/writer and former Groundling John Paragon, who played Jambi on *Pee-Wee's Playhouse*, to come up with funny, teasing banter for Elvira. She based the character on a Valley Girl type she had played with The Groundlings. "I think of myself as a comedian," Peterson said in her interview with Wayne Bledsoe of the *McClatchy-Tribune Business News*. "Without the funny element, it's just another Goth character. . . . Without that I wouldn't be Elvira—I would be Vampira."

The show caught on with the public and was quickly syndicated, airing in sixty-three markets nationwide. Elvira's fan club grew to thirty-five thousand members. The best part for Peterson was that despite the character's popularity, she still had her anonymity; out of the extreme makeup, black wig, and costume, she was unrecognizable.

During *Movie Macabre*'s 1981 to 1986 run, Elvira lampooned such forgettable horror fare as *Count Dracula's Great Love*, *Maneater of Hydra*, and *The Werewolf of Washington*. In 1986, Miller-Coors made Elvira its Halloween marketing centerpiece. It became one of their most successful campaigns ever. She did three Coors commercials over three Halloween seasons, including one in which Coors called itself "The Official Beer of Halloween." Life-size cardboard Elvira/Coors standees were regularly stolen from convenience stores. She put the beer money into a new house.

Seeing how profitable it could be to market the Elvira image, she licensed a plethora of products. Before long, there were over four hundred Elvira items, including calendars, posters, Halloween costumes, greeting cards, makeup, perfume, plastic model kits, comic books, and porcelain collector's plates.

See You in Court

Peterson was laughing all the way to the bank. But Maila Nurmi didn't see the humor in it. "The character she is playing is 75–80 percent Vampira," Nurmi told Christine Ziaya of the *Los Angeles Times*. "Some parts are missing, some things have been added. They've taken a large part of Vampira and added these lowly commodities and given it a wider common denominator, but in so doing this, destroyed the character. I resent their taking my product and doing that to it." She resented it so much that she retained an attorney, Jan Goodman, and in September 1988 filed suit against Cassandra Peterson, KHJ-TV, NBC Productions, Panacea Entertainment and Elvira Merchandising, Inc., seeking $10 million in damages. The suit contended that Peterson infringed upon her trademark, public reputation, and ability to market her lucrative character.

Goodman argued that Elvira should compensate Vampira, who was then dependent upon Social Security, adding that Nurmi was "very mad." Goodman told Jack Jones of the *Los Angeles Times* that Nurmi "spent a good portion of her life coming up with a character and a show and used that for many years, and the character was ripped off. There is no Elvira. There is only a pirated Vampira."

Peterson was mystified by Nurmi's resentment, saying she'd like to be friendly with her and didn't understand her hostility, while also countering that the vampire woman was a stock pop-culture character and therefore in the public domain. "You can't claim copyright on that any more than you could on a cowboy," Peterson told Alex Patterson of *The Toronto Star*.

On February 27, 1989, U.S. District Judge Matthew Byrne dismissed part of the lawsuit, ruling that Nurmi could seek damages against Peterson and the other defendants for unfair competition, but not for violating her right to publicity. Byrne said an actor's right to publicity is not violated by a simulation of a character, since the actor's actual voice, face, or name must be used to sustain a violation of such right. "Both Vampira and Elvira, they're not focusing on the face particularly, as I see it," said the judge, prompting laughter in the court. In March, the case was dismissed.

In 1994, while Nurmi was making ends meet cleaning celebrities' houses for ninety-nine cents an hour (or so she told *Entertainment Weekly*), director Tim Burton's film *Ed Wood*, starring Johnny Depp and Martin Landau, introduced a new audience to Nurmi and Vampira (played in the film by actress Lisa Marie). With the revival of interest in her character, Nurmi began a website, www.VampirasAttic.com, and started creating Vampira drawings that she sold on the Internet. With a new following of fans, she became a cult figure and was featured in several documentaries. On January 10, 2008, she was found dead in her Hollywood home, at age eighty-five.

Elvira: Mistress of the Cineplex

While the lawsuit was ongoing, Elvira starred in her own feature film, 1988's *Elvira: Mistress of the Dark*. Since her show had gone into national syndication, Peterson and her managers, Eric Gardner and Mark Pierson, had gone around to various studios with different treatments for a feature film, but without success. The consensus was that although Elvira was well known on the West Coast, the rest of the country wasn't aware of her. As her fame grew, helped by the Coors promotions, she and writers Sam Egan and John Paragon wrote a new story.

Around this time, the NBC television network was seeking to expand into theatrical feature film production. NBC president Brandon Tartikoff thought Elvira, with her ready-made audience, would be a safe risk, and called Peterson in to pitch his idea for a feature film. Describing the meeting to Kyle Counts of *Cinefantastique* magazine, she said, "The weird thing was, our treatment was exactly what he was

Edie McClurg, who appears with Cassandra Peterson on the poster for 1988's *Elvira, Mistress of the Dark*, previously appeared with her as a fellow member of the Los Angeles improv group the Groundlings.
Author's collection

At a 2014 Fanboy Expo, Cassandra Peterson—sans her Elvira make-up—greets fans.

© 2014 Vanessa Way. Courtesy of Vanessa Way.

describing. I pulled it out of my bag—it was just two or three typewritten pages—and showed it to him. He was flabbergasted. They were so similar you would have thought some sort of eerie brain transference had occurred."

A deal was made, and the Elvira movie became the first theatrical effort for NBC Productions, in cooperation with Peterson's own Queen B production company and distributor New World Pictures. Budgeted at $7.5 million, the film featured Jeff Conaway, Susan Kellerman, Daniel Green, and former Groundling Edie McClurg. James Signorelli directed. The original title was "Elvira: The B-Movie," but NBC felt that would signal that it was a second-rate, low-budget knockoff, and suggested the title be changed to *Elvira: Mistress of the Dark.*

In the film, Elvira is fired from her job as a TV horror hostess and goes to the extremely conservative community of Falwell, Massachusetts, to collect an inheritance left by her recently deceased great aunt—Peterson told Counts it was "a macabre *Harper Valley PTA.*"

To sustain a ninety-minute film, an entire history had to be created to flesh out the character. "Elvira is slowly becoming a character like Dracula—one with her own legend," Peterson said in her interview with Counts. "Sure, she has something to do with Halloween, but what is she? People think she's a vampire, but she doesn't have fangs; or they assume she's a witch, but she's not really a witch, either. That's a major part of the movie: explaining why she looks the way she does and where she comes from."

After a seven-week shooting schedule, mostly at Raleigh Studios in Hollywood, New World released the film on September 30th, in advance of Elvira's favorite holiday—Halloween. The results were disappointing; it earned only $5.6 million at the U.S. box office. It also brought Peterson both a Saturn Award from the Academy of Science Fiction, Fantasy and Horror Films for Best Actress and a Golden Raspberry Award for Worst Actress. The film's home video release came on Valentine's Day, 1989.

Having co-financed the production, NBC received its first network broadcast, albeit in a tamer, re-edited form. Planning ahead, during the making of the movie, several scenes were shot twice: once for theaters and video, and once for TV. For instance, in the film, the license plate on Elvira's 1958 Thunderbird reads KICKASS, while in the TV version, it spells out 2MACABRE. Also, much of Elvira's risqué humor was toned down.

Peterson eventually released a second film, *Elvira's Haunted Hills*, in 2001. Self-financed with a budget of less than a million dollars, the feature was shot on location in Romania and screened at AIDS charity fundraisers throughout the U.S. before having an official premiere in Hollywood on July 5, 2002. It subsequently screened at the Cannes Film Festival in 2003.

The Return of Elvira

Peterson returned to TV in the 2010–11 season with a resurrected *Elvira's Movie Macabre*. Twenty-six episodes of the program, including several that never aired, were released in a thirteen-disc box set, *Elvira's Movie Macabre: The Coffin Collection*, from Entertainment One. The films she introduced were ones that had fallen into the public domain, including *The Satanic Rites of Dracula, Night of the Living Dead, Attack of the Giant Leeches*, and *Jesse James Meets Frankenstein's Daughter*.

Through the years, Peterson has continued making personal appearances as Elvira, including a yearly Halloween show at Buena Park, California's Knott's Berry Farm theme park, where she performs a Vegas-style variety show twice nightly in October. "I've made a career off of Halloween," Peterson said to *USA Today*'s Bruce Horovitz.

Unlike Maila Nurmi, who died in poverty, perpetuating and merchandising the vampire woman persona has made Cassandra Peterson a wealthy woman. Without giving exact figures, she claims that she's made more than $1 million a year for about half the years that she's been Elvira.

Part of her legacy is that she's helped turn Halloween into a more adult-focused holiday. "If ever there was a holiday that deserves to be commercialized, it's Halloween," she told Horovitz. "We haven't taken it away from kids. We've just expanded it so that the kid in adults can enjoy it, too."

25

License to Chill

Toys

Most toy manufacturers conformed to the Toy Advertising Guidelines drawn up by the Code Authority of the National Association of Broadcasters, which admonished them to "avoid dramatization of the toy which could frighten or scare children."

In the 1960s, millions of American families did their shopping from retail catalogs, and the Christmas catalogs from Sears, J. C. Penney, Spiegel, and Montgomery Ward were hotly anticipated items. In 1963, Ward mailed out six million copies of its Christmas catalog, which contained, among thousands of other items, models of Dracula, Frankenstein's Monster, and the Wolf Man for $2.69 each. Aurora Plastics Corporation made the model kits, which they promoted by sponsoring a Monster Maker Contest in partnership with Universal Pictures and *Famous Monsters of Filmland* magazine, with the winner given a trip to Hollywood and an opportunity to appear in a horror movie.

There were monster-shaped cocktail stirrers called "Mon-stirs," "I Scream Spoons" designed with monsters on the handle, and bubblegum spook cards produced in numbered series and distributed by companies such as Leaf Brands, Inc., and Bubbles, Inc. Some pictured black-and-white movie scenes from the Universal Pictures films, with humorous and silly dialogue printed under the scenes. The first series was distributed in 1953 by Leaf Brands, Inc., and consisted of seventy-two cards. The second series was distributed in 1964 and was called "Son of Spook" cards, numbered seventy-three to 144. There were also forty-eight different "Spook Stickers."

In 1964, Philip Shabecoff of the *New York Times* reported on the monster-mania among toymakers. He mentioned that Remco was producing dolls as tie-ins with the TV series *The Munsters* and *The Addams Family*. However, a Remco spokesman admitted, "Our monster toys aren't nearly the hot item that our Beatles dolls are."

The Munsters had their own lunch box in 1965, picturing the cast members, plus hand puppets of Herman, Lily, and Grandpa, and a *Munsters* Drag Race game. Other items from the '60s include gold-colored, metal-and-plastic rings

Talk about an eye-opener! Christopher Lee's vampire king, from
1958's *Horror of Dracula*, adorns a Hammer-licensed coffee mug.
© *2014 Bruce Scivally*

of monster faces with rhinestone eyes, by Elvin. There were also games, books,
and records based on *Dark Shadows*.

In 1980, Mattel introduced Gre-Gory, a vampire bat that hung upside down
while blood flowed through its see-through chest. Hasbro, meanwhile, had the
Loud Mouth line, including a green-faced plastic Dracula; it was an odd toy
that existed only to make a very loud noise if you put a newspaper strip in its
mouth and bopped it on the head. Sigma produced a Dracula teapot for sale at
Macy's that sold for $32.50. There was also an accompanying candy dish shaped
like a coffin.

Role Playing and Computer Games

Pacesetter Ltd. introduced the role-playing game *Vengeance of Dracula* in 1984,
for a mere six dollars. With an intermediate complexity level, the game required
a gamemaster and four to six players, and provided two to six hours of playing
time. The year 1990 saw a new role-playing game, *Vampires*, which retailed for
twelve dollars. It included a 128-page source book of descriptions and game
stats for ten vampire characters.

One of the first Dracula computer games was 1981's *The Count*, from
Adventure International, compatible with the Apple II Plus, Commodore 64,
Atari 400, and other systems. In 1986, CRL released *Dracula*, a text adventure
game for the Commodore 64, Amstrad CPC, and Spectrum home computer systems. The game included static graphics that were considered so gory it became
the first computer game to be rated by the British Board of Film Censors, which

gave it a "15" certificate, meaning it shouldn't be purchased by anyone under fifteen years of age.

Video games were becoming ubiquitous in 1990, and that year Konami introduced *Castlevania III: Dracula's Curse* for the Nintendo Entertainment System. The game took players through the Sunken City of Poltergeists, the Clock Tower of Untimely Death, and Curse Castle. Inside the box was an entry form for a chance to win a trip to Dracula's Castle in Transylvania for Halloween 1991.

Dracula the Undead was released for the Atari Lynx handheld system in 1991, featuring a storyline in which Jonathan Harker must escape Castle Dracula. Two years later, Viacom New Media introduced *Dracula Unleashed*, one of the first games to make extensive use of full-motion video as part of the gameplay.

Several versions of a *Bram Stoker's Dracula* video game were unveiled in 1993, one year after the release of the Francis Ford Coppola film on which it was based. The basic plot of the game was the same for each platform, with Jonathan Harker escaping Dracula's castle, but the level of complexity varied depending on whether one played the Nintendo Game Boy version, with backgrounds resembling *Super Mario Land*, or the Sega CD version that had digitized backgrounds and full-motion video cutscenes from the film.

Dracula also cropped up in the 1993 Sega video game *Night Trap*, in which a gang of vampires captures young girls and mayhem ensues. Critics called the game too violent for children. In response, Ellen Beth Van Buskirk of Sega, in an interview with Peter M. Nichols of the *New York Times*, described *Night Trap* as being like a "B Dracula flick on the level of a horror movie you would see on TV." Buskirk said, "*Night Trap* is the first example of why we need a rating system for video games," though with roughly 40 percent of their market being over eighteen, "they want narratives on adult themes."

In 2000, Dreamcatcher Interactive introduced the video game *Dracula Resurrection* for Windows 95, 98, and NT. The point-and-click horror/adventure game was set seven years after the events of Stoker's novel, with Jonathan Harker again opposing Count Dracula. Designed for players seventeen and older, Charles Herold of the *New York Times*

A ceramic Dracula refrigerator magnet, with full moon over his shoulder.   *© 2014 Bruce Scivally*

said that it could "be finished by any experienced gamer in 10 hours or so, hardly enough time to get bored," calling it "good-looking and unoriginal. The puzzles are unexceptional in design and ingenuity and are truly notable only for their remarkable lack of challenge." Herold said it had "a certain B-game charm. Much of the game feels like an old Dracula movie with Christopher Lee: fearful villagers, sinister demons, a damsel in distress. Every time you solve a puzzle, the game moves forward with a brief animated scene. It was as if a projectionist kept stopping the movie to ask you simple riddles, then showed you a little more once you had answered." Four sequels were released over the next thirteen years.

Count Chocula

In October of 1971, General Mills introduced two monster-themed cereals, Count Chocula and Franken-Berry. Count Chocula cereal consisted of chocolate-flavored corn cereal bits and

Vampires may never drink . . . wine, but the rest of us can enjoy Vampire Merlot and Witchcraft Sauvignon Blanc. Photographed in the window of Clarke's of Whitby.   © 2014 Bruce Scivally

marshmallows, while Franken-Berry consisted of strawberry-flavored corn cereal bits and marshmallows. Franken-Berry, because it was made with a pink dye, had the unusual side effect of turning the consumer's feces pink, a condition referred to as "Franken-Berry Stool." The cereals were advertised in commercials featuring animated versions of their spokesmonsters, a vampire who vaguely resembled Bela Lugosi (voiced in the commercials by Larry Kenney) and a pink Frankenstein's Monster that sounded like Boris Karloff (voiced by Bob McFadden). The cereals are still manufactured, but only during Halloween season.

General Mills caught some flack in 1987 when they introduced a new Count Chocula box that featured an image of Bela Lugosi as Dracula from the 1931 film. In the drawing, Dracula wore what some consumers and Jewish newspapers took to be a Star of David; in the actual film, Lugosi had worn a medallion that was a mixture of Ottoman "Order of Merit" elements and found objects. Four million boxes of the cereal arrived in stores, and within days the protests began. General Mills decided against doing a recall, since it wasn't a health issue, but changed the design to eliminate the medallion on subsequent boxes. William

Shaffer, manager of public relations for the cereal maker, issued an emphatic statement: "We are not anti-Semitic."

Action Figures

Mego released their "Mad Monsters" series of eight-inch action figures in 1973, including "The Monster Frankenstein," "The Human Wolfman," "The Horrible Mummy," and "Dreadful Dracula." And it was, indeed, a pretty dreadful generic Dracula, with white face, a severe widow's peak, black-rimmed eyes, and fangs protruding from blood-red lips. The dolls featured glow-in-the-dark eyes and hands.

Another set of monster figures, from Azrak-Hamway, International (AHI), was available on store shelves from 1973 to 1976. These eight-inch action figures included Frankenstein's Monster, the Mummy, the Wolf Man, the Creature from the Black Lagoon, and Dracula, with all but the latter being officially licensed from Universal Studios and bearing much closer likenesses to the monsters from the films. The Dracula figure was sculpted to resemble Bela Lugosi and was made in two styles, one with a traditional high-collared cape, and one with a cape that had a hood attached. AHI didn't stop with action figures; they also made monster squirt guns, wind-up walkers, wire bendies, flashlights, and rubber jigglers.

In 1974 and '75, Lincoln International released an unlicensed series of cheap knockoffs of the eight-inch monster action figures, featuring the usual line-up—Frankenstein's Monster, the Mummy, the Wolf Man, and Dracula—along with a Phantom of the Opera, Hunchback, and, strangest of all, "Mr. Rock," a knockoff of *Star Trek*'s Mr. Spock. The Dracula figure, done in a vaguely Lugosi-ish style, has an open mouth to better show off his fangs and his eyes outlined in light blue.

When the Museum of Holography opened in New York in 1979, one of the holograms offered for sale was an eighteen-inch "Dracula Sucking Blood from a Lady" hologram. Said Nancy Trachtenberg

TITAN MERCHANDISE
HAMMER HORROR
CHRISTOPHER LEE AS
COUNT DRACULA
8" PREMIUM MAXI-BUST
£59.99
BY TITAN MERCHANDISE, FEATURING
HAMMER HORRORS LEGENDARY STARS
FROM SOME OF THE MOST FAMOUS MOVIES
OF THE HORROR GENRE.

The Dracula Maxi Bust from Titan's Masterpiece Collection, made in the image of Christopher Lee, haunts the window of London's Forbidden Planet comics store.
© 2014 Bruce Scivally

in the *New York Times*, "[J]ust put the film ($75) in the display ($42.50), hang it up and turn it on."

Remco was back with more monster toys in 1980, with The Universal Monsters nine-inch action figures. Although the Dracula looked like a generic vampire, the packaging featured an image that looked suspiciously like Robert Quarry as Count Yorga. The following year, a three-and-three-quarter-inch version was introduced, with the Dracula packaging featuring an image of Bela Lugosi.

In the 2000s, baby boomers who watched the old *Shock Theater* programs in the 1950s and '60s, or who caught the Hammer Dracula films on the *CBS Late Movie* in the 1970s, were now professionals with big bucks to spend on collectibles. And now there was an even greater array of items to splurge on, including a twelve-inch Dracula figure with Bela Lugosi's likeness from Sideshow Collectibles; another twelve-inch Dracula figure from Product Enterprise in the image of Christopher Lee; a Lee Dracula bust from Titan; one-eighth-scale Lugosi models from Moebius; life-size busts of Lugosi; and re-releases of models and toys from the 1960s.

For vampire aficionados, it seems, childhood can last an eternity.

26

Blood Read

Dracula in the Comics

The 1950s

In the 1950s, Universal kept approaching comic-book companies about doing a comic adaptation of *Dracula*, but at a price. Publisher and editor L. B. Cole, who had his own Star Comics line, told John Wooley of *Starlog* magazine about Universal reps peddling the rights: "Once a day they would come by. They approached everybody, apparently—but they wanted their money up front, before the books were even printed, and nobody wanted to go with that. . . . *Dracula* would have been a wonderful property, if we could have paid them a royalty on copies sold—but not before we even printed the books."

Dracula was first adapted as a comic book in *Eerie* #12 (August 1953), published by Avon Periodicals. Though generally faithful to Stoker, it changed the ending to Van Helsing driving a stake in the vampire's heart, rather than the vampire being dispatched by knives wielded by Jonathan Harker and Quincey Morris. *Classics Illustrated* had thought of doing a comic-book adaptation of *Dracula*, but postponed their plans when the *Eerie* version appeared. *Eerie* #12 was converted to a 3-D book and reprinted by Ray Zone in 1992, with new front and back covers by Chuck Roblin.

The 1960s

In the early 1960s, the Comics Code Authority put limitations on comic books, prohibiting "scenes dealing with, or instruments associated with walking dead, torture, vampires, ghouls, cannibalism and werewolfism." With vampires banned by the Comics Code Authority, the bloodsuckers could only appear in comics produced by companies who didn't subscribe to the Code. One such company was Dell Comics, which produced a *Dracula* comic in October–December 1962. The story involved an artist who travels to Transylvania, meets a beautiful woman, and is turned into a vampire at Castle Dracula. His father comes searching for him with vampire hunter Janos Tesla, who confronts Dracula and narrowly escapes. Presumably, a series would have followed the Dracula–Tesla conflict, but there was no follow-up until the mid-1960s.

In 1964, *Famous Films* #2 featured photo-novella versions of Hammer's *Horror of Dracula* and *Curse of Frankenstein*, with word balloons pasted over movie stills. Publisher Jim Warren ran a seven-page adaptation of Hammer's *Horror of Dracula* (1958), by Russ Jones and former EC Comics artist Joe Orlando, in *Famous Monsters* magazine #32 (March 1965), which was reprinted in *Famous Monsters* #50 (July 1968).

In 1966, *Batman* had become a sensation on TV, so Dell re-thought *Dracula*. When issue #2 finally appeared, it had a descendant of Dracula deriving a serum from bats that gave him the ability to transform into the mammal. Developing his body to physical perfection, he donned a skin-tight purple suit with bat-ears to fight crime and to remove "the blight of history" on his ancestors. It was, simply put, as close a ripoff of *Batman* as one could get without inciting a lawsuit. Drawn by Tony Tallarico, the superhero Dracula, whose secret identity was Al U. Card and who operated out of a "secret cave," lasted for only three issues. The comics were reprinted in the 1970s, when other *Dracula* comics appeared. In 1974, Doug Murray, in an article in *The Monster Times*, called the superhero Dracula the "world's worst comic," saying the concept was "strenuously inane—even for a comic book."

Russ Jones prepared a paperback comic of *Dracula* in 1966, written by Otto Binder and Craig Tennis and illustrated by Alden McWilliams. A second paperback from Jones, *Christopher Lee's Treasury of Terror*, included an adaptation of "Dracula's Guest," adapted by E. Nelson Bridwell and drawn by Frank Bolle.

The 1970s

In the early '70s, *Vampirella* magazine serialized a Dracula adaptation by Spanish artist Esteban Maroto, which was later published as a color one-off 120-page comic. April 1972 brought Marvel Comics' *Tomb of Dracula* #1 in four colors. *Dracula Lives!* (1973) and *Giant-Size Dracula* (1974) followed. At one point in the '70s, all three titles were being published

Comic book artist Gene Colan used Jack Palance as a model for his interpretation of Dracula several years before Palance played the role on television.   *Photofest*

simultaneously, with art by Bernie Wrightson, Howard Chaykin, Rich Buckler, Steve Ditko, and Gene Colan. The last of the original Marvel *Dracula* titles finished printing in 1980.

In *The Monster Times* #1 (1972), Berni Wrightson did an adaptation of 1922's *Nosferatu*. Also in 1989, Dark Horse published a one-shot sci-fi vampire tale, *Nosferatu*, by French artist Druillet. Caliber/Tome comics released yet another comic-book version of Murnau's *Nosferatu*, this one in 1991. That same year, Millennium began a four-part series, *Nosferatu: Plague of Terror*, that was both a prequel and sequel to Murnau's film.

The *Now Age Illustrated* series from Pendulum Press did a *Dracula* adaptation written by Naunerie Farr and illustrated by Nestor Redondo in 1973, which is a fairly faithful retelling of Stoker's story.

On July 7, 1973, the Federal Censorship Service of Brazil banned nineteen horror comics and photo-novels, including the title *Count Dracula's Tomb*, on the ground that they exploited terror and the supernatural.

The 1980s

In 1986, editor Mark Wheatley and writer Rick Shanklin collaborated on the four-issue Apple Comics title *Blood of the Innocent*. The title was reissued as a graphic novel in 1992. The comic led to *Blood of Dracula*, which ran for nineteen issues. Most issues presented three different continuing storylines: early events in the Count's life were told in "Count Dracula"; "Death Dreams of Dracula" put him at the center of historical events; and "Dracula 2199" put the vampire in the future.

In 1987, Malibu Graphics produced *Scarlet in Gaslight*, written by Martin Powell and drawn by Seppo Makinen, pairing Dracula with Sherlock Holmes going up against Professor Moriarty.

In 1989, Eternity Comics began reprinting the old Skywald *Dracula* stories in *Vampyres*. They also created an adaptation of Stoker's novel in the four-issue *Dracula*. Both *Vampyres* and *Dracula* were reissued as one-volume trade paperbacks. Also in 1989, Pioneer Comics debuted *Vegas Knights*, which had Dracula battling ninjas.

That same year, with Tim Burton's *Batman* movie in theaters, Apple premiered *The Bat* #1, with a crime fighter who derived secret powers from Dracula's ring, but there was a side effect—it began to corrupt his soul.

The 1990s

In 1991, Marvel resurrected *Tomb of Dracula* as a four-issue limited series, written by Marv Wolfman and drawn by Gene Colan. "It's a somewhat darker world now," editor Terry Kavanagh told *Starlog* magazine's John Wooley. "It's a world better suited for Dracula. This is an age of computers, of worldwide networking. He's lived for centuries, but never through anything like this."

That year's five-issue *Ghosts of Dracula*, from the same team, had Dracula and Houdini together in one title, in which Dracula is revealed to be a reluctant Antichrist. Malibu also released a four-issue black-and-white adaptation of the Stoker novel and a one-shot of "Dracula's Guest," called *Dracula: Lady in the Tomb.*

Published in hardcover, DC Comics' *Red Rain* from writer Doug Moench and artists Kelly Jones and Malcolm Jones III (no relation) was released in time for Christmas in 1991. Pitting Batman against Dracula, it was an immediate sell-out.

Wheatley-Shanklin's studio, Insight, developed a couple of new titles for Apple, including the 1992 adults-only *Dracula in Hell*, from artists Neil Vokes and Ryan Kelly. The story had Vlad Tepeş, at age sixteen, being released by the Turks and going to the scholomance (Devil's Abbey) in the Carpathian mountains, where the devil himself teaches him deceit, treachery, and magic.

They also produced *Big Bad Blood of Dracula*, a one-shot written and drawn by Mike McCarthy, which pitted Dracula against punked-out Cadavera, a character built from the body of dead actresses.

Dracula: The Suicide Club, which appeared in August 1992, scripted by Steve Jones and drawn by John Ross, was published by Eternity's Adventure Comics. The storyline added Dracula to Robert Louis Stevenson's *The Suicide Club.*

Trading-card company Topps began a comic-book division in the 1990s, one of whose first titles was a comic-book adaptation of Francis Ford Coppola's *Bram Stoker's Dracula.* Roy Thomas wrote the adaptation, with art by Mike Mignola.

In 1992, besides the Coppola adaptation, Topps published a *Dracula: Vlad the Impaler* comic, the *Dracula Chronicles*, the *Frankenstein-Dracula War*, and *Dracula vs. Zorro.* Marvel, meanwhile, reprinted some *Tomb of Dracula* issues, and also printed *Savage Return of Dracula, Wedding of*

Apple Comics' *Dracula in Hell* was a two-issue story, published in January and March 1992.   *Author's collection*

Dracula, and *Requiem for Dracula*. The vampire also cropped up in *X-Men vs. Dracula*, a reprint of *X-Men Annual* #6.

The year 1993 saw Marvel's *Spider-Man vs. Dracula* (a reprint of *Giant-Size Spider-Man* #1) and *The Silver Surfer vs. Dracula* (a reprint of *Tomb of Dracula* #50). Dracula went on to oppose practically every hero in the Marvel Comics universe until Dr. Strange eradicated all vampires with the Montesi Formula. But Dracula returned, dropping the Victorian apparel for a more modern look of body armor and a blond ponytail. A 2006 comic pitted Dracula against Apocalypse; he later was resurrected by the X-Men to help them defeat Dracula's son, Xarus. Having accomplished that, the vampire king put a vampire colony on the moon, from which he entered a non-aggression pact with Doctor Doom and tried to take over Great Britain.

The original Bram Stoker novel received a fresh comic-book adaptation in 2009, when writers Leah Moore and John Reppion and artist Colton Worley adapted it into a limited-issue series for Dynamite Comics called *The Complete Dracula*. The adaptation was later issued in hardcover. They also adapted Stoker's short story, "Dracula's Guest." The following year, IDW presented *Bram Stoker's Death Ship*, retelling Dracula's voyage from Transylvania to England from the point-of-view of the sailors aboard the *Demeter*. The four-issue story was written by Gary Gerani and illustrated by Stuart Sayger. These recent adaptations prove that Stoker's original story still has a lot of bite.

27

Out of the Casket

Goth and Vampire Culture

What Is Goth?

In the late '70s and early '80s, an offshoot of the punk movement, combining punk attitudes and horror movie aesthetics, produced the Goth movement, a reaction to the sunny materialism of the Reagan era. Goths are identified by their black clothing, piercings, dyed hair (sometimes spiked), fishnet stockings for women, and a predilection for gothic literature of the eighteenth and nineteenth centuries, or modern novels like Anne Rice's *Vampire Chronicles* that draw on gothic literature for inspiration. They also tend to listen to brooding music with depressing lyrics, with Bauhaus being the band that set the tone for all the Goth music to follow. On the whole, they tend to be creative, cynical, and intellectual, as well as tolerant of other races, sexual orientations, and ideas.

The Goth Bible: A Compendium for the Darkly Inclined by Nancy Kilpatrick was published by St. Martin's Griffin in September 2004. Through hundreds of interviews with Goth adherents as well as through historical research, the author explored Goth culture from its historical origins as a Germanic tribe in the sixth century who fought alongside the Romans against the Huns to modern-day Goths, portrayed in the media as homicidal, suicidal, and sociopathic. An award-winning mystery novelist, Kirkpatrick writes, "Nobody knows what modern goth is about, but the simplest truth is this: Goth is a state of mind."

For current practitioners of the Goth aesthetic, the Whitby Goth Weekend is a twice-yearly event. It had its start in 1994 when Jo Hampshire of Top Mum Productions invited forty pen pals she'd met through New Musical Express to come to Whitby in north Yorkshire for a Goth music festival. The event was a success, and continued yearly until 1997, when it became a twice-yearly event, in April and October. Though billed as a "weekend," fringe events generally begin on Thursday and run through the following Monday, with the music festival itself at Whitby's Spa Pavillion hosting the main music attractions. A sort of Mardi Gras for Goths, who come from all over the world to attend, the event

The cobbled streets of Whitby play host to the annual Goth Weekend.
© 2013 Vanessa Way. Courtesy of Vanessa Way.

brings in over £1 million pounds per year to the local businesses. Whitby was chosen as the location for the twice-yearly Goth Weekends because of its affiliation with Bram Stoker and *Dracula.*

True Vampires

It is a mistake, however, to think of all Goths as vampires, or all vampires as Goths. Vampires sometimes dress in all black, but they could also be the guy or girl in the next cubicle at work. Whereas Goths are identified by their distinct clothing, hair styles, and music tastes, vampires are defined by one thing only—a taste for blood.

In 1996, Frank Bruni of the *New York Times* set out to interview a real vampire. He found twenty-year-old Ethan Gilchrist in an East Village sixth-floor walk-up with blood-red satin brocade drapes. Gilchrist assured Bruni that he didn't sleep in a coffin, but he did like to occasionally drink blood. Whenever a friend got a nick or cut, they would oblige Gilchrist with a taste, which he said was "like liquid electricity."

Gilchrist was part of small group of vampire enthusiasts in New York City who frequented an underground scene with its own wardrobe, music, and nightclubs. Vampires, like Gilchrist, who were not ashamed to flout their existence, were said to be "out of the casket."

Vampires in Manhattan had their own cable-access television show, broadcast Thursdays at 1:00 a.m., featuring conversations with out-of-the-casket vampires and vampire wannabes. Vampire bands with names like Nosferatu and Type O Negative also sprang up in the '90s.

Hal Gould, who owned an East Village club called the Bank where patrons could hear Goth rock, told Bruni, "The scene has really taken off in the last few years." Bruni noted that patrons of the Bank tended to dress in crushed velvet and wear pale makeup and Victorian jewelry. A Garment District club, Downtime, ran a promotion every Saturday called the Bat Cave, hoping to attract some of the Bank's clientele.

The website Good Goth began in 1996 (www.goodgoth.com), offering corsets, cosmetics, capes, boots, hair dye, jewelry, and apparel for Goth women. The site features specialty shops for Gothic Prom, Gothic wedding, and Steampunk.

Good Goth would have been the perfect place to shop for clothes to wear to a vampire ball, held on July 30, 1996, at The Limelight in Chelsea, with vampire bands like Jerico of the Angels performing. Jerico was noted for drinking his own blood onstage, and having simulated sex with a naked vampiress. Jerico, while identifying himself as a vampire, liked to think of vampirism as a metaphor for any human beings who fed off each other to exist, including emotional vampires.

Jerico admitted to once using a ceremonial knife to make a tiny cut above the heart of a consenting girlfriend. He then pressed his lips to her bleeding flesh and drank her blood. Recalling the incident for Bruni, he said, "It's an extremely powerful experience."

In a book called *Something in the Blood*, Jeff Guinn presented interviews with eight of the roughly eighty vampires he spoke to who admitted to drinking blood. Guinn said actual blood drinkers ran the gamut from the curious out for a one-time thrill, to habitual imbibers who drank blood for ceremonial purposes, or because of a psychological affliction, or as a sexual fetish—or all three combined. He said such die-hards only drank blood from consenting partners, whom they sometimes connected with through classified ads.

Vampire clubs were still going strong in New York as the new century dawned. In an article in the *New York Times* in November of 2000, reporters Margaret Mittelbach and Michael Crewdson visited a gathering called Long Black Veil, held every Thursday at a club in the Flatiron District, called True. They found three hundred "undead heads," dancing and drinking. A D. J. spun records from a band called Switchblade Symphony. A sexy vampiress in black, with a tattoo of a bat on her belly, danced while couples canoodled in the corners.

Since the mid-'90s, the popularity of the vampire watering holes had grown through the profusion of vampire TV shows and movies as well as Internet sites and chat rooms. At the clubs, only patrons who dressed in vampire garb were welcome. Those who just came to sit and gawk were turned away at the door. Many wore an Egyptian ankh to identify themselves as members of the

Revelers get their Goth on at the Whitby Goth Weekend, 2013.
© 2013 Vanessa Way. Courtesy of Vanessa Way.

Sanguinarium, a nationwide network of vampire clubs with their own initiation rites founded in 1995 by Father Sebastian Todd, True's promoter.

The bartender at True, Ms. Kaos, served drinks like Blood Bath, a cocktail made of three parts wine, one part Chambord liqueur, and a splash of cranberry juice, topped with a maraschino cherry. The patrons, with names like Shadow and Rapture, danced to music from bands such as Nosferatu, Sukkubus, Cruxshadows, and Inkubus. Some wore fake fangs and contact lenses to make their eyes appear red.

For those wishing to become appropriately tricked-out for a visit to a vampire club, a company called Sabretooth, Inc., marketed custom-made fangs which ran the gamut from dental acrylic fangs at forty dollars per pair to porcelain fangs for three hundred. They also had $250-per-pair contact lenses to give wearers feline eyes or red irises. Specialty boutiques such as the Transformatorium, located inside the Halloween Adventure Shop at Fourth Avenue and 11th Street in the East Village of New York, made custom-fitted fangs hand-carved out of dental acrylic for seventy-five to $350, depending on whether one went for the "Lost Boys" style or the "Nosferatu." The boutique also sold an array of contact lenses, including the all-black style popularized by Limp Bizkit guitarist Wes Borland.

Michael Laird, the founder and lead singer of the band Unto Ashes, told Mittelbach and Crewdson, "Vampires have an extreme obsession with beauty that takes the form of body worship and blood worship. They wear clothing that delights the eye—baroque styles but also PVC fetish-wear with lots of accessories like black boots and collars. They get piercings and adorn themselves with fangs. They're celebrating humanity through the blood coursing through their veins."

When the *New York Times* reporters questioned a fang-wearing man in a black trench coat who identified himself as Davyd Ventru about drinking blood, Ventru responded, "Blood is icky. There are a few who indulge in blood-drinking, usually among a small circle of donors that are carefully chosen. But the vast majority of us aren't into that."

On May 8, 2014, Stephen Colbert, on his Comedy Central cable program *The Colbert Report*, interviewed Jake Rush, a thirty-five-year-old attorney and former Alachua County sheriff's deputy making a bid to replace Republican incumbent Ted Yoho as the party's congressional representative from Florida's third district in north central Florida. Rush had gone by the names Chazz Darling and Staas van der Winst when he was a member of the Mind's Eye Society, or "Camarilla," a nationwide community of goth-punk role players, in which Rush took on the role of a vampire. Colbert asked, "What's your core message as a small government conservative who also pretends to be a vampire?" Rush responded, "Privacy rights, personal freedom." Rush clearly wanted the personal freedom to pursue his vampire role-playing, though once he began his congressional bid, he also exercised his privacy rights by deleting lots of photos of himself in vampire garb from Internet sites. In the primary election, incumbent Yoho received 79.4 percent of the vote to Rush's 20.6 percent. It was bad news for Rush, but good news for the residents of Alachua County—they now knew what percentage of their population were probably vampires.

28

What Music They Make

Songs About Dracula and Other Vampires

Monster Mash

Dracula began appearing on records as early as 1958, when TV horror host John Zacherle recorded the novelty single "Dinner with Drac," which rose to number six on the U.S. singles chart. In his persona as horror host Zacherle, he delivered a recitation about having dinner with Dracula, and finding out that *he* was on the menu. The single was recorded by the Philadelphia label Cameo with their house band, Dave Appell and the Applejacks. Dick Clark played it on his *American Bandstand* TV show, but requested that Zacherle record a less-violent version. Zacherle complied, and when audiences demanded the *American Bandstand* version, it was released as a single with the original as "Dinner With Drac, Part 1" on one side, and the *Bandstand* version as "Part 2" on the B-side.

In April of 1959, Victor released an album called *Monster Rally*, which featured Frank N. Stein conducting such tunes as "What Do You Hear from the Red Planet Mars?" "The Dracula Trot," and "Mostly Ghostly." Hans Conreid and Alice Pearce provided voices for the album.

Sheldon Allman, a songwriter and actor who was the singing voice of *Mr. Ed* (writing songs like "The Pretty Little Filly with the Pony Tail" and "The Empty Feed Bag Blues") also composed the theme songs to *George of the Jungle, Super Chicken, Tom Slick*, and the game show *Let's Make a Deal*. In 1960, he made a comedy album, *Sing Along with Drac*, on which he sang monster-themed parodies of popular songs, including "Fangs for the Memory."

In 1962, Bobby "Boris" Pickett and the Crypt-Kickers released their smash-hit single, "Monster Mash." Pickett wrote the song as a spoof of the then-popular Mashed Potato dance craze (itself promoted by songs such as Dee Dee Sharp's "Mashed Potato Time," Nat Kendrick and the Swans' "[Do the] Mashed

Potatoes," and James Brown's "Mashed Potatoes USA"). Pickett performed the song imitating Boris Karloff's voice, with a brief cameo from Dracula, who asks in a Bela Lugosi accent, "What ever happened to my Transylvanian Twist?" Produced by Gary S. Paxton (who later wrote songs for The Gaithers gospel group), the song became a number-one hit.

In 1966, Pickett collaborated with Sheldon Allman on a musical about Frankenstein, Dracula, and the Wolf Man called *I'm Sorry, the Bridge Is Out, You'll Have to Spend the Night.* By the end of the decade, he was driving cabs and playing occasional gigs at ski lodges with his wife, singer Joan Payne. Then, in 1973, "Monster Mash" inexplicably rose from the vaults to become a hit again. This time, Pickett took his act on the road, touring the country with Bobby Pickett and the Crypt-Kickers Graveyard Revue.

Dracula's Greatest Hits, an album released by Victor in 1964, had voice characterizations by Gene Moss and a sing-along chorus by The Monsters. Among the compositions were "I Want to Bite Your Hand," "The New Frankenstein and Johnny Song," "Drac the Knife" and "Carry Me Back to Transylvania." The record included an added bonus—fifteen monster trading cards.

A few years later, Decca released *An Evening with Boris Karloff and His Friends*, including Frankenstein, the Wolf Man, Dracula, and the Mummy.

Originally released on Garpax Records in 1962, the seven-inch single "Monster Mash" charted in the U.S. on three different occasions: in 1962, 1970, and 1973. *Author's collection*

Released on both the Decca and MCA labels in 1967, *An Evening with Boris Karloff and His Friends* featured audio clips from several Universal Pictures horror films, including Bela Lugosi from 1931's *Dracula*. *Author's collection*

Vampire Rock and Roll

A fusion of monsters and rock 'n' roll occurred in Paris in the mid-'60's, when a nightclub called Dracula opened at 77 Rue Pigalle. The decor consisted of blank walls on which old horror movies were projected, while pop singers, imported from Britain, performed, sometimes in ghoulish makeup.

A more direct fusion came along with performers like Alice Cooper, who combined elements of a horror stage show with his rock concerts in the early 1970s. Cooper's decidedly macabre shows included an eleven-foot boa constrictor named Yvonne, garish makeup, colored smoke and fireworks, the chopping-to-bits of a baby doll with an axe, and climaxed with a mock hanging.

Some of his stage shows included Cooper chasing live chickens about the stage, which led to some unsavory rumors. "There were some press stories implying that we killed the chickens," Cooper told Don Heckman of the *New York Times*, "but we never did anything more than run them around the stage and give them to people afterward for pets. Later we read stories that we had cut off the chickens' heads and sucked their blood, and of course even though it wasn't true I didn't deny anything, because it was great publicity. People seem to like to hear about Alice doing things like that. Look what the same kind of publicity did for Dracula."

Other performers also plugged in to vampire imagery. "I'm a black bat, babe, I need my high octane," sings Neil Young in his song "Vampire Blues," which uses vampirism as a metaphor for the greed of the oil industry. The song appeared on his 1974 album *On the Beach.*

Fans of Blue Öyster Cult have long been aware of the rock band's affinity for vampires, with many songs that explore vampirism, such as "Tattoo Vampire," "Harvest Moon," "After Dark," and their signature hit, "Don't Fear the Reaper." Their fifth album, 1977's *Spectres,* contained—besides the hit "Godzilla"—two overt vampire songs, "I Love the Night" and the album's final song, "Nosferatu," with lyrics inspired by the 1922 horror film, such as,

> Only a woman can break his spell . . .
> Pure in heart, who will offer herself . . . to Nosferatu.

Playing up the vampire connection, the 1979 debut single of the British group Bauhaus was a song titled "Bela Lugosi's Dead." The band later performed the song at the beginning of Tony Scott's stylish vampire film, *The Hunger* (1983), and it has since been featured in the TV series *True Blood.* When Bauhaus made their U.S. debut at New York's Club 57 on February 28, 1981, Stephen Holden of the *New York Times* remarked that lead singer Peter Murphy, in his cadaverous makeup, "suggested a punk Dracula, and his fierce vocals, inflected with a Transylvanian drawl, were made all the more gimmicky by heavy echo-boosting."

Rap songs also borrowed imagery from horror films, beginning with the Sugar Hill Gang mentioning Dracula in their 1979 hit "Rapper's Delight":

> Like Dracula without his fangs,
> Like the boogie to the boogie
> without the boogie bang . . .

Released in 1981, psychedelic rock pioneer Roky Erickson's album *The Evil One*, produced by Creedence Clearwater Revival's Stu Cook over a two-year period when Erickson was struggling to cope with drugs and life outside a mental institution (he was schizophrenic), is a masterful collection of songs about zombies, demons, and vampires. "Night of the Vampire" is an earnest ode to classic Vincent Price horror movies, mixing guitar and pipe organ, with Erickson singing excitedly about Dracula.

The post-punk band The Birthday Party, considered one of the first Goth bands, unleashed their single "Release the Bats" in 1981, with a young Nick Cave singing about a young lady who is either turned on by vampires and bats, or is a vampire herself, with Cave wailing phrases like, "sex vampire, cool machine!"

The New Jersey punk band the Misfits released their debut album, *Walk Among Us*, in 1982, featuring the song "Vampira," in which frontman Glenn Danzig sings of hooking up with a vampire woman in a cemetery.

In 1982, RCA released a mini-LP, *Count Floyd*, featuring Joe Flaherty as his "Count Floyd" character from NBC's *SCTV* comedy show, which regularly featured "Count Floyd" as host of "Monster Chiller Horror Theater," a spoof of 1950s and '60s TV horror movie hosts. The mini-LP has Count Floyd singing and talking his way through four songs, including "Reggae Christmas Eve in Transylvania" and "Count Floyd is Back," in which he attempted to fill in for the Rolling Stones with disastrous results.

In their song "At Dawn They Sleep," from their 1985 album *Hell Awaits*, Slayer turned their focus away from their usual

Considered to be the first Goth rock group, Bauhaus appeared in the 1983 film *The Hunger*, singing "Bela Lugosi's Dead." The song had been their debut single in August 1979.   *Author's collection*

subjects (serial killers, Satan, and hell) to sing about vampires in a song about someone who wakes up as a bloodsucker.

That same year, Sting's *Dream of the Blue Turtles* album was released, containing a song called "Moon Over Bourbon Street," inspired by the Anne Rice novel *Interview with the Vampire*. Sting had been given the book by his former Police bandmate Andy Summers. The song hit number forty-four on the British singles chart. It would not be the last song inspired by Rice's writings.

Queensrÿche's "Walk in the Shadows," from their 1986 album *Rage for Order*, was written at a time when the band members were reading Anne Rice's *Vampire Chronicles*. In an interview with *RIP* magazine in October 1991, guitarist Chris DeGarmo said, "That was our delving into vampirism: 'By day we'll live in a dream / Walk with me, and we'll walk in the shadows.' It's talking about joining the dark side." The song was also about infatuation, but as DeGarmo observed, "Even when we write a love song, it's usually obsessive in nature."

Johnette Napolitano, frontwoman of Concrete Blonde, sang lyrics about New Orleans vampires in the 1990 song "Bloodletting (The Vampire Song)," also seemingly inspired by the writings of Anne Rice.

Bram Stoker's Dracula (1992), directed by Francis Ford Coppola, featured an end-credits song written and recorded by Scottish singer Annie Lennox. "Love Song for a Vampire" made it to number twenty-four on the *Billboard* Hot Modern Rock Tracks chart. The song, however, was not inspired by Bram Stoker, but rather a more modern vampire. "I went and read Anne Rice," Lennox said in a blog promoting a 2009 greatest hits album. "The vampire is the ultimate metaphor for compulsive addictive behavior. Vampire and victim are the ultimate co-dependents, doomed for eternity." The song hit number three on the UK charts.

The Goth/doom metal band Type O Negative recorded the song "Suspended in Dusk" for their 1993 album *Bloody Kisses*. The song concerns a man who has regrets after being turned into a vampire, realizing how much he's given up for the sake of immortality. With songs focusing on death and depression, the band earned the nickname "The Drab Four."

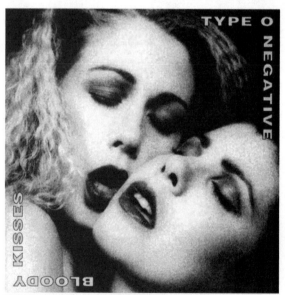

Released in August 1993, *Bloody Kisses*, the third album of Brooklyn band Type O Negative, featured the song "Black No. 1 (Little Miss Scare-All)," which parodied Goth stereotypes.   *Author's collection*

Before she sang with Wild Flag, Mary Timony was the frontwoman of Helium, an indie band from the '90s. Their first EP, 1994's *Pirate Prude,* featured multiple songs referencing vampires. One of the best was "Baby Vampire Made Me," in which Timony sings from the point-of-view of a hungry vampire out to devour and infect everyone she meets.

Also in 1994, Cher wrote the song "Lovers Forever" with Canadian songwriter Shirley Eikhard, intended to be part of the soundtrack of the film adaptation of Anne Rice's *Interview with the Vampire.* Cher told *USA Today,* "They didn't love it and there were no other vampire outlets then, so I held

Cher's 2013 album *Closer to the Truth* featured a song originally recorded for *Interview with a Vampire.*
Author's collection

it." It was eventually released on her 2013 album, *Closer to the Truth.*

In her 1995 song "Dracula Moon," Joan Osborne sings about a woman who may be dying who meets a lover and insists, "Stop feeling sorry for me."

"Do you wanna die?" became a pickup line in The Toadies 1995 alt-rock single "Possum Kingdom," sung from the point-of-view of a vampire promising eternal youth and beauty to a young girl beside a lake.

In 2002, the New Jersey rockers My Chemical Romance released their debut single, "Vampires Will Never Hurt You," which immediately established the band as one that mixed horror and sci-fi with emo melodrama. Their song "Early Sunsets Over Monroeville," from the 2002 album *I Brought You My Bullets, You Brought Me Your Love,* is about a man and woman on the run from vampires, or maybe zombies. When the woman gets bitten, the man is forced to kill her before she turns into a monster herself, even though she says she loves him very much. In 2010, their album *Danger Days: True Lives of the Fabulous Killjoys* featured the song "Vampire Money," a satire of bands that write vampire songs just so they can get spots on the soundtracks of Twilight films. My Chemical Romance had been offered lots of money to contribute a song to one of the Twilight film soundtracks, but steadfastly refused, saying they loathed that Goth had become mainstream. "We were the only kids in black wearing mascara playing heavy music in the punk clubs where we were from," said singer Gerard Way. "With things like *Twilight* the idea of anything gothic like vampires wasn't scary any more, they were sexy or contemplative. To me vampires are the new Jonas

The British band Morcheeba's song "Blood Like Lemonade," from their 2010 album of the same name, features the refrain, "He drank the blood like lemonade."
Author's collection

Brothers. So we've gone the opposite way."

The most gothic of Radiohead's songs was "We Suck Young Blood," which appeared on 2003's *Hail to the Thief*, the sixth album by the alternative rock band. In the creepy, piano-led tune, lead singer Thom Yorke portrays old, powerful people as vampires sucking the life from the young and weak, with lines like, "We want the sweet meats."

The 2003 Outkast album, *The Love Below*, featured André 3000 singing "Dracula's Wedding," with the lyrics, "My castle may be haunted, but I'm terrified of you," a song that illustrated that falling in love could be more frightening than any monsters.

"Closer," a 2008 hit by Kings of Leon, was about a lovesick two-hundred-year-old vampire who didn't feel remorse when he drained his victims dry; the listener was invited to empathize with the bloodsucker through singer Caleb Followill's soulful singing.

The song "Morning After Dark" by Timbaland, the first single from his 2009 album *Shock Value II*, was partly inspired by the Twilight franchise. Timbaland told *MTV News*, "The song, I can't describe it, it's so different. It's not different for me, but I can tell you this—it fits everything going on with the vampire theme. It fits everything with *Twilight*." The song featured vocals from French-American singer SoShy, with Nelly Furtado also singing a verse. The video also used vampire iconography, with predatory vampires walking on the sides of walls and disappearing into thin air.

"Blood Like Lemonade," from the 2010 album of the same name by British electronica/soul group Morcheeba, was about an "ex-priest vampire bounty hunter," said the group's Ross Godfrey, "who goes around seeking revenge on bad guys and bandits, whose blood he drinks like lemonade. . . . Vampires are pretty hip nowadays—all those movies where the music is really loud and the characters just whisper the screenplay."

Stevie Nicks's 2011 album *In Your Dreams* featured the song "Moonlight (A Vampire's Dream)." Nicks began writing the song in the mid-1970s, when she was involved in a relationship with Lindsey Buckingham. The song remained unfinished until 2009, when she was inspired to complete it after seeing the film *Twilight: New Moon.* She told *Spinner UK,* "The chorus—'It's strange, she runs from the ones she can't keep up with'—is all about the love affair between Bella and Edward. But 'Some call her strange lady from the mountains / Others say she's not really real,' that's written in 1976." The third verse was also written about Buckingham: "He loves her, but he loves his life alone as well." Nicks said, "This really is an ancient song that encompasses my strange and everlasting relationship with Lindsey Buckingham, and Bella and Edward, all mixed into one." A video for the song was released on October 13, 2011.

29

There Are Such Things

Real-Life Vampires

Elisabeth Bàthory

In 1983, Boston professor Raymond T. McNally, who had earlier brought to light the deeds of Vlad the Impaler, published *Dracula Was a Woman: In Search of the Blood Countess of Transylvania*, which delved into the story of Hungarian Countess Erzebet de Ecsed (Elisabeth) Bàthory. Between 1585 and 1610, in the dungeons of her remote Carpathian castle, Bàthory allegedly murdered more than six hundred girls, though it may have been as few as thirty-six. Accounts written after her death, likely exaggerated, claimed that she drained the blood of her victims and bathed in it, in the belief that this would help her maintain her youthful looks. In 1610, Bàthory and four accomplices were tried and found guilty. The accomplices were put to death, but Bàthory, because of her royal status, was spared. She was walled up in Csejte Castle, with only a hole for air and food. She died four years later.

British Bloodsuckers

One of the earliest accounts of a British vampire comes from the town of Berwick-upon-Tweed in Northumbria, where during the mid-twelfth century, writer William of Newburgh said, "A great rogue, having been buried, after his death sallied forth (by the contrivance, as it is believed, of Satan) out of his grave by night, and was borne hither and thither, pursued by a pack of dogs with loud barkings; thus striking great terror into the neighbors, and returning to his tomb before daylight." After finding the resting place of the "great rogue," the locals set his corpse alight.

In the Middle Ages, a hunchbacked vampire was said to stalk the grounds of the castle at Alnwick in Northumberland, spreading terror and disease. Growing tired of his nocturnal raids, the local peasants, it is said, descended on him with pitchforks and torches and burned him to ash.

In the years after the English Civil War, a monster with a brown shriveled face and bony hands was said to have attacked young girls in the Cumbrian village of Croglin. According to local legend, after a horrifying creature climbed through her bedroom window, a Miss Cranswell was forced to the ground and bitten on the neck. Her two brothers chased the attacker, but it was too fast for them. The attacker was dismissed as a lunatic, until it returned and attacked again. On that occasion, one of the brothers shot it in the leg as it was escaping. A group of villagers proceeded to the local graveyard, where they found a vault in which all the coffins were smashed except one. Inside that box was a shriveled, mummified corpse—with a leg damaged by a pistol ball.

Countess Elisabeth Bàthory is thought to be the most prolific female serial killer in history, though the exact number of her victims is unknown. *Wikimedia Commons*

Vampire hysteria was so rampant in England in 1824 that King George outlawed the practice of staking suicide victims through the heart and burying them at crossroads.

Residents of northeast London in the summer of 1945 were told to bolt their doors and lock their windows to protect themselves from a mysterious bedroom prowler described as a "Dracula man" whom police said might be a potential killer. Scotland Yard issued the warning after several women and young girls reported they had awoken to find a man with staring eyes and a throaty voice gripping their necks. In one instance, the slightly built intruder, wearing a heavy overcoat, was caught tying a rope around the neck of a fourteen-year-girl. When discovered, he ran off.

Sightings of a vampire with iron teeth were reported by a group of local schoolboys in Glasgow in 1954. It was said to have "strangled and devoured" two small boys, but there were no reports of missing children in the town. Hundreds of schoolchildren became amateur vampire hunters, descending on the city's graveyards and causing a nuisance for the authorities, who blamed the vampire mania on the popularity of an American comic book that contained vampire stories.

The Vampire of Hanover, Fritz Haarmann, executed by guillotine on April 15, 1925.
Wikimedia Commons

In 1969, dead animals drained of blood began showing up in the under-growth of London's Highgate Cemetery. Witnesses, some of whom claimed to have been attacked, told of a "tall dark figure" with "hypnotic red eyes." Rumor said that a king vampire had been brought over from Romania and buried in the Highgate grounds, but modern Satanists had brought the bloodsucker to life. In the resulting vampire craze, amateur vampire hunters dug up a number of graves until eventually the sightings died out.

Ghost hunter Tom Robertson had a hair-raising encounter at Lochmaben Castle near Lockerbie in 1991. After hearing the locals tell stories of animals being drained of blood, Robertson and his wife went to the castle to try and determine the cause. Leaving his wife in the car, Robertson walked into the woods around the castle. He soon encountered the bodies of small animals, and met a tall figure dressed in sacking with a hood over its head, which leapt into a tree and swung away. Fearing for his wife's safety, Robertson ran back to her. He later told Rod McPhee of London's *Daily Mirror*, "There is a creature slinking around in those woods, baying for blood."

In January 2005, in the Saltley, Small Heath, and Alum Rock areas of Birmingham, residents were attacked by a man who bit them. In one instance, neighbors came to the rescue of a potential victim, but the attacker, who was said to have unusual strength, fought them off and escaped.

The Vampires of Hanover and Düsseldorf

Between 1918 and 1924, Fritz Haarmann killed up to twenty-seven young boys in Hanover, Germany. Haarmann met his victims at the train station, offered them work or a place to stay, took them back to his flat, and killed them by biting through their windpipes, giving him the nickname "The Vampire of Hanover." Haarmann was known to deal in black market pork; after his trial, it was speculated that the meat he sold may have come from his victims. On April 15, 1925, Haarmann, having been found guilty of murdering twenty-four young men, was beheaded. His story was one of the inspirations for Fritz Lang's 1931 film, *M*.

Serial killer Peter Kürten was known as "The Vampire of Düsseldorf" after committing a series of murders and sexual assaults in the German city between February and November of 1929. In 1913, he strangled a ten-year-old girl during the course of a burglary and served eight years in prison. Released in 1921, he moved to Altenburg, and took a wife. Four years later, he returned to Düsseldorf, where he began the series of crimes. He assaulted a woman and molested and murdered an eight-year-old girl on February 8, 1929. Five days later, he murdered a middle-aged mechanic, stabbing him twenty times. Six months passed before he struck again, stabbing three people in separate attacks on August 21. Two days later, he murdered two foster sisters, aged five and fourteen. He stabbed another woman on August 24. In September, in the woods outside Düsseldorf, he raped a servant girl and beat her with a hammer, killing her. The following month, he attacked two women with a hammer. On November 7, he murdered a five-year-old girl, strangling her and stabbing her thirty-six times with scissors. Following the crime, he sent the local newspaper a map to the girl's grave.

Police believed the crimes were the work of several murderers, given the variety of victims and murder methods. From February to March 1930, Kürten engaged in a series of hammer attacks, none of which proved fatal. In May, he took a young woman to his home and assaulted her, then took her to Grafenberger Woods, where he raped her. For some reason, he chose not to kill her. She led police to Kürten's home. He managed to avoid the police, but confessed the crime to his wife, aware that they knew his identity and thinking that if his wife turned him in, she would receive a reward.

Peter Kürten, the German serial killer known as the Vampire of Düsseldorf.   *Author's collection*

He was found and arrested on May 24. Once in custody, he admitted to drinking the blood of at least one of his victims. Eventually confessing to seventy-nine offenses, he was charged with nine murders and seven attempted murders. Tried in April 1931, he was found guilty and sentenced to death. While awaiting execution, he was interviewed by Dr. Karl Berg. Kürten told Berg he received sexual pleasure from the murders; the more stab wounds, the longer it took him to achieve orgasm. He was executed by guillotine in Cologne on July 2, 1931. His head was dissected and mummified, and is now on display at the Ripley's Believe It or Not! Museum in Wisconsin Dells, Wisconsin.

American Vampires

In Exeter, Rhode Island, in 1892, Edwin Brown seemed to be wasting away, just as his sister Mercy had three months earlier, and his mother and elder sister had several years before that. When no medical remedies seemed to be working for Edwin, the other family members concluded that he was being plagued by a vampire demon, which was probably inhabiting the corpse of one of the dead women. The caskets of all three were exhumed. Two contained skeletons, but in the third they found Mercy, looking much as she had when they buried her, and with blood still in her heart. The heart was burned to ashes, and the ashes mixed into a vampire antidote, but it was all for naught; Edwin died not long afterwards, of tuberculosis.

In the spring of 1933, society folk in Chicago began receiving "poison pen" letters threatening scandal from a correspondent who signed them, "Dracula." According to the *Chicago Daily Tribune*, whenever there was an announcement in the society columns of an engagement, marriage, or trip abroad by a well-known family, it triggered a "barrage of mail demanding a job, money or castoff clothing from that family." The newspaper refereed to this phenomenon as "another Depression discomfort." The "Dracula" letters were thought to be more an inside job; the writer was said to have an intimate knowledge of society gossip and the habits of the recipients. Although receipt of the letters was reported in the press, no complaints were filed with the post office inspection service or police.

In December of 1942, twenty-two-year-old cosmetics salesman and Chicago resident Stanley Znesko, who also used the name Lee Atwood, was charged with disorderly conduct after demonstrating an unusual dating habit. Two separate women, one aged twenty-two and the other nineteen, testified that when they were sitting alone in a car with Znesko, he suddenly bit them. When they protested, he asked, "Haven't you heard of Dracula?" A municipal court psychiatrist said the case merited further investigation.

One of the strangest tales of a Dracula-type figure came out of New York in 1942, when fifty-five-year-old Jeremiah Erranght was found dead in his apartment. A mechanic for the Pennsylvania Railroad, Erranght was a familiar sight on the East Side, where he walked the streets in a long black cape and black hat, causing neighborhood children to call him "Dracula." It was said Erranght would stop in his tracks and shut his eyes when a woman approached; local storekeepers said he never spoke above a whisper.

A recluse, Erranght lived in two squalid rooms he occupied for thirty-five years on 79 Allen Street. Once a month he paid his rent to the building janitor, Frank Siebert, who lived next door. Siebert said that in the five years prior to his death, Erranght had only one visitor, an insurance adjuster. Siebert always knew when his odd neighbor had arrived home from work—he heard Erranght's heavy iron door clang shut. Erranght never allowed any repairs to his flat, which contained a couple of broken tables and chairs and was lit with candles. The windows, covered with decades of grime, were nailed shut. There were two huge black trunks in the room which contained yellowed, illegible documents, a key to a safe-deposit box, and postal certificates for $150. He prepared his meals on a small gas range, and after he died, the only food found in the rooms was oatmeal.

Erranght apparently died in his sleep. He was discovered in his bed, if one can call it that; it was, in fact, a box made of two-inch thick sheets of iron riveted together. Only four-and-a-half-feet high, four feet wide and four feet long, the box was ventilated with small holes. A door was built into one end that locked from the inside. Each night, the six-foot Erranght squeezed himself into the box, sleeping in a sitting position with his knees drawn up to his chin, wearing galoshes and ear muffs to protect himself from the cold.

When Siebert didn't hear the clanging of Erranght's door one night, he suspected that something had happened. He summoned the police, who sent members of Emergency Squad 2 to the rooms. It took them an hour with hydraulic jacks to pry off one side of the box, which police described as being like a "medieval torture chamber."

In the late summer of 1959, New York newspapers were filled with the lurid story of "Dracula," also known as "Capeman," and his accomplice, "The Umbrella Man," who attacked and killed two young boys in a playground at 45th Street near 9th Avenue, stabbing them to death. The murders happened just after midnight on August 30, 1959.

The victims were two sixteen-year-olds, Robert Young and Anthony Krzesinski. While talking with friends on a playground on Manhattan's West Side, they were attacked by a group of Puerto Rican boys. Four gang members were quickly arrested on homicide charges, but not the one who was said to be the actual killer, an eighteen-year-old who—according to the *Chicago Daily News*—called himself "Dracula" and led "the Vampire gang," which the paper said was comprised of "sexual perverts." "Dracula" was said to be fascinated by films featuring the vampire king, and it was reported that he often wore a cape. The *Los Angeles Times* elaborated on the Dracula image, stating that the young hoodlum dressed "in a dark-blue, red-lined cape, black trousers and black shoes with imitation silver buckles" and swaggered "at the head of his gang carrying a cane and wielding a knife with a long blade." As it happened, the sensational reporting by the newspapers was typical of the early reports, which got almost all the particulars wrong.

The prime suspect was arrested early on the morning of September 2, after a few days of sleeping in hallways in the Bronx. He was Salvatore Agron, a sixteen-year-old Puerto Rican youth who, when paraded before the press with seventeen-year-old Antonio Hernandez, "The Umbrella Man," said defiantly, "I don't care if I burn. My mother can watch."

Agron came to New York from Mayagüez, Puerto Rico, when he was seven, joining his mother and older sister. His mother, having divorced his father, had recently married a Pentecostal minister who treated the children harshly. Salvatore asked to return to Puerto Rico to live with his father. One day, the teenager found the body of his stepmother, who had committed suicide by hanging. He returned to New York, but was often truant from school. In 1958, he joined the Mau Maus street gang, but then left them to join the Vampires after meeting Hernandez, the gang's president. On the night of the murders, the two young men and their cohorts were heading for a rumble with a rival group, an Irish gang called the Norsemen. When they came upon the teenagers in the schoolyard, they mistook them for the Norsemen. Agron, using a knife, and Hernandez, wielding an umbrella with a sharpened tip, stabbed three young men. Two of them died.

Despite the newspaper headlines, Agron wasn't accustomed to wearing the cape; he had borrowed it from another gang member on the way to the rumble. It was a blue nurse's cape with a red lining. Agron became the youngest person ever to be sentenced to death row, but after Eleanor Roosevelt, the father of one of his victims, and the mayor of San Juan campaigned for leniency, his sentence was commuted to life in prison by Governor Rockefeller in 1962. Agron was released from prison in 1979, having earned a BA degree in sociology and philosophy while in prison. A TV movie about his life was proposed; Agron took the money he was paid for it and set up a fund for the families of his victims. He became a youth counselor, speaking out against youth violence, until his death in 1986, at age forty-two.

In 1998, a Broadway musical about Agron, *The Capeman*, with songs by Paul Simon, opened at the Marquis Theater. Marc Anthony played Agron as a young man, and Ruben Blades played the older Agron. Many New Yorkers were angry about a play they saw as glorifying a killer; it closed after sixty-eight performances.

James P. "Jimmy" Riva was a troubled youngster; he killed and drank the blood of animals. From 1975 to 1978, he spent time in a mental institution. Finally, in April of 1980, Riva loaded a gun with bullets painted gold and shot his seventy-four-year-old handicapped grandmother twice in the chest as she sat in her wheelchair. He then stabbed her repeatedly and drank the warm blood gushing from her wounds because, he said, a vampire told him that was what he should do. He then burned down the house.

Confronted with his crime, he gave several explanations. He told his mother that he was a vampire who would gain strength from drinking his grandmother's blood. He also told psychiatrists that his grandmother was a vampire who came to feed on him as he slept. He believed he was satisfying his masters (or superiors) in the netherworld of vampires by making a human kill. He thought if he killed everybody who treated him badly, he would come back as a handsome man and have a car and girls and a fine life.

At the conclusion of his lengthy trial, the jury deliberated for three hours and found him guilty of second-degree murder and arson, and assault and battery on one of the arresting officers. He was sentenced to life imprisonment in Walpole State Prison on the murder charge, and, concurrently, to ten to twenty years on the arson charge. While in prison, he received several college diplomas and, in 1990, became a devout Muslim, following a doctrine of nonviolence. On August 4, 2009, Riva told the state's Parole Board that therapy and medication had enabled him to curb the mental illness that led him to believe he was a vampire and directed him to brutally kill his elderly grandmother. The six-member board was unconvinced that he was ready for release from prison. His parole was denied.

In the 1980s, serial killer Ted Bundy reportedly bit his victims and said he felt like a vampire. Richard Trenton Chase, dubbed the "Vampire Killer" in the late 1970s, reportedly drank the blood of at least one of his six victims in the belief that it would cleanse him of his sins. In 1988, three boys in Minnesota killed a vagrant, licking the blood off their hands as they beat him. One of the young murderers claimed the trio was inspired by the vampire film *The Lost Boys*.

On Thanksgiving of 1985, in Brevard County, Florida, a nude teen woman was seen crawling along the side of the road, with feet and ankles handcuffed. Several vehicles passed her by, but one stopped. She begged the driver not to take her back to "that house." When he asked where, she asked him to remember a particular house. He took note of the location, and then took her to his home, immediately calling an ambulance.

Once in the hospital, the young woman was found to be missing between 40 and 45 percent of her blood. She had ligature marks on her neck. She said she'd been hitchhiking the day before when a man picked her up and offered to take her to her destination, but said he needed to stop at home first. Upon arriving at his house, the man invited her inside. When she refused, he choked her into unconsciousness.

When she awoke, she was tied to a kitchen countertop, unable to move. A video camera was set up, with lights. With the camera rolling, the man raped her, and then inserted needles into her arm and wrist to siphon out her blood, which he drank. He said he was a vampire. Handcuffing her, he then put her in a bathtub. Sometime later, he came back, assaulted her again, and withdrew more blood. He came back again in the morning. Leaving her bound in the bathroom, he said he would be back later to rape her once more, and if she tried to leave, his brother would come and kill her. When her captor left, the victim, although weakened from blood loss, pushed out the bathroom window, jumped out, and crawled to the road.

Police issued a warrant for John Brennan Crutchley. They arrived at his house at 2:30 a.m. to find that his wife and child were away for the Thanksgiving holiday. They located the video camera, but the tape inside was partially erased. Crutchley, dubbed the "vampire rapist," was arrested.

It was noted that in the 1970s, when Crutchley lived in the area of Fairfax County, Virginia, several women, mostly teenagers, had gone missing, including, in 1977, a twenty-five-year-old woman who had been Crutchley's girlfriend. He was placed under scrutiny and questioned several times about her disappearance, but lack of evidence prevented him being charged with any crime. The woman's skeletal remains were found by a hunter the following year. There were also disappearances of young women in Pennsylvania when Crutchley lived there, with bodies turning up in remote areas of the state.

After the teen hitchhiker escaped, a police search of Crutchley's home found seventy-two three-by-five index cards on which Crutchley had written women's names and made notes of their sexual performance. Though never charged with murder, he was suspected of murdering more than thirty women.

On August 8, 1996, Crutchley was released from state prison after serving ten years of his twenty-five-year sentence. The next day, he violated the terms of his fifty-year probation by smoking marijuana at a farewell party thrown by other prison inmates. Under the three strikes law, he was sentenced to life in prison. On March 30, 2002, he was found dead with a plastic bag over his head in his cell at Hardee Correctional Institute, reportedly from autoerotic asphyxiation.

Sadly, there are numerous accounts of serial killers and other murderers who, in the course of their heinous crimes, drank their victims' blood. These individuals, clearly emotionally and mentally disturbed, present the vilest, darkest side of the vampire fantasy, a far cry from the sublimated sexuality and repressed Victorian romanticism of Bram Stoker.

30

For Your Mother's Sake

Protection from Vampires

The Basics

Know your enemy.

If your enemy is a vampire, you have to know a lot, although the vampire mythology is so rampant in our culture that most six-year-olds know the basics. The traditional vampire of the movies and TV avoids sunlight, never eats, only drinks blood, has fangs (presumably hollow, to act like straws), has pale skin, usually dark hair, and tends to dress all in black. They can exert hypnotic control, and may be telepathically linked to their victims. Vampires can dissolve into fog, or smoke, or mist, or change into a bat, or a wolf.

Most vampires appear to be anti-Christian, and are thus repelled by Christian symbols, like the cross, holy water, or Communion wafers. Even a makeshift cross, like, say, holding two brass candlesticks together, will sometimes do the trick. In *Brides of Dracula*, the vampire is killed by merely a shadow in the shape of a cross (from the vanes of a burning windmill). Holy water is like corrosive acid if splashed on the skin of a vampire. They may also be repelled by garlic.

In movies, since vampires have no soul, they cast no reflection in a mirror (though Bela Lugosi's Dracula can be plainly seen in a mirror in *Bud Abbott and Lou Costello Meet Frankenstein*), yet they might cast a reflection in a puddle of water (as in the 1979 *Dracula*). The young vampires of *Vampire Diaries* do cast reflections in mirrors, allowing them to keep their hair perfectly coiffed.

You would think that a creature that cast no reflection might also have no shadow, yet in the 1922 *Nosferatu*, when the vampire goes up to drink the blood of Ellen Hutter, we see only his shadow ascending the stairs.

Vampires cannot enter a home unless formally invited; otherwise, they are unable to cross the threshold. In the world of *True Blood*, they can be disinvited and become once again unable to enter a residence.

Vampires are supposed to sleep in their native soil, which they usually carry within a coffin or box. A vampire in his coffin will appear to be resting or

Nosferatu (1922). Count Orlock (Max Schreck) ascends the stairs to Ellen's room, but we see only his shadow.   *Author's collection*

sleeping, but they are still capable of exerting hypnotic control, which can prevent you from destroying them.

Although they are technically dead, reanimated corpses, vampires arouse erotic feelings in their victims, and apparently enjoy sex. Though in pre-1970s movies, they only use their teeth for penetration, exploitation films in the '70s and recent TV shows like *True Blood* have shown that they are capable of phallic penetration, and, in fact, have voracious sexual appetites. But can a male vampire make a human woman pregnant? After all, how can a dead body produce fresh sperm? However their plumbing works, Edward Cullen impregnated Bella Swan in *The Twilight Saga: Breaking Dawn, Part 1.*

Becoming a Bloodsucker

The mechanics of becoming a vampire differ from film to film. In most films, the victim must be bitten three times over three consecutive nights. On the final night, the victim's blood is drained; after the victim dies, they will then resurrect as a full-fledged vampire. In the 1931 *Dracula*, the vampire king says this will only happen if the victim dies not by day, but by night. They generally bite their victims on the neck, although lesbian vampires (as in *The Vampire Lovers*) may bite their victims' breasts.

Someone who has been newly bitten by a vampire can be identified by their general lethargy, paleness (from loss of blood), and two little marks (holes) on the jugular vein of their neck. If your loved one has been bitten and turned, what do you do?

Vampire Disposal

To kill a vampire, there are several methods:

Forget guns. They cannot be harmed by bullets; in *Son of Dracula*, when the hero shoots at the vampire, the bullets pass through him and kill the woman behind him. Modern films, however, as in *Blade* or *Only Lovers Left Alive*, have introduced the innovation of wooden bullets that seem to do the trick. But the old ways are best: the foolproof way to kill a vampire is a stake through the heart. But one couldn't use just any old stake. In Russia and the Baltic states, ash was believed to be the most potent wood, except in Serbia, where they preferred hawthorn, and Silesia, where they used oak. There were also variant beliefs about *where* to stake the vampire. Though most cultures drove the stake through the revenant's heart, in Russia and northern Germany vampires were staked through their mouths. Some Serbs thought the stomach best. Whatever the location, most traditions held that the stake had to completely penetrate the vampire's body and the bottom of his or her coffin (if one was used) and go into the ground, in effect nailing the vampire to the earth to prevent it from rising again. Consequently, the stakes used were quite long; in Stoker's *Dracula*, Lucy is impaled with a round stake three feet long and three inches thick, considerably larger than the wooden spikes used in most horror films. In the prologue of *Dracula A.D. 1972*, Dracula is killed after the spoke of a broken wagon wheel enters his heart, and in modern horror films, arrows through the heart are also effective, so today's vampire hunters often carry crossbows.

In Stoker's *Dracula*, vampire hunter Van Helsing recommends not only staking the vampire but cutting off its head. In films, this happened to Carmilla Karnstein in *The Vampire Lovers*. Supposedly, this makes it easier for the

Dracula (Christopher Lee) cowers from the cross in *Taste the Blood of Dracula* (1970).
© *1970 Hammer Film Productions/Warner Bros. Author's collection.*

Le Vampire, lithographie de R. de Moraine, tirée
des *Tribunaux secrets.*

"The Vampire," a drawing by R. de Moraine, from *Secret Tribunals* (1864).   *Author's collection*

reanimated corpse's soul to leave its body and go on to its afterlife. In German and Slavic states, after decapitation, the head was placed behind the buttocks, between the feet or otherwise away from the body and the corpse reinterred. The Romani (gypsies) drove steel or iron needles into a dead person's heart and placed bits of steel about their head and between their fingers when the corpse was buried, in addition to placing hawthorn in the sock of the deceased or driving a hawthorn stake through their legs. Cremation was another way of disposing of a vampire, with one variation being to pour boiling water over the grave to incinerate the corpse, or at least parboil it. In the Balkans, vampires could be killed by being shot or drowned or by having holy water sprinkled on the body, while in Romania, just to be sure a corpse would not rise back up and terrorize the village, it might be buried with garlic in its mouth (a lemon was used in Germany), or better yet, have a bullet fired through the lid of its closed coffin before burial—the eternal kill shot.

A vampire who has been staked will crumble to dust, or turn into a skeleton. In films made prior to the 1960s, removing a stake from a skeleton, or pouring blood on the dusty remains of a vampire, will not only revive them, but also often makes their clothes magically reappear, presumably saving them from undue embarrassment in their first moments of revivification.

In most films, vampires can be destroyed by direct exposure to sunlight, an innovation introduced by the 1922 film *Nosferatu*; in Stoker's 1897 novel, Dracula is seen in daylight in London. In some later films and TV programs such as *Vampire Diaries* and *True Blood*, exposure to sunlight first causes blistering of the vampire's skin, then the body begins to smoke, and then it bursts into flames.

Cremation seems to work on some vampires; Dracula's staked body is burned in *Dracula's Daughter*, and the title vampire perishes in flames at the conclusion of *Son of Dracula*. Other films, like *Twins of Evil*, suggest that if a vampire is burned, its spirit will simply leave the body and seek a fresh human host. Electrocution, in extreme cases, will work, as in *Scars of Dracula*, wherein Dracula is impaled with an iron rod that is then struck by lightning, and falls off his castle in flames.

Some vampires are vulnerable to silver. A silver dagger through the heart may be as effective as a wooden cross; in *Billy the Kid Versus Dracula*, the vampire is done in by a surgeon's knife.

Film vampires are often susceptible to running water, as in a lake or a stream. In *Dracula, Prince of Darkness*, Dracula ends up in the running water beneath the ice of a frozen stream. In *Dracula A.D. 1972*, Van Helsing does away with one of Dracula's acolytes in a bathtub shower. A fire sprinkler system kills several disciples in *The Satanic Rites of Dracula*. This would seem to suggest that vampires should avoid rainstorms, which raises the question—why are the Cullens of *Twilight* living in the perpetually raining Pacific Northwest?

In films, if a vampire regent (head vampire) is destroyed, all his victims revert back to normal human status, or—if they've been vampires for a very long time—instantly crumble to dust.

31

Enter Freely and of Your Own Will

Vampire Societies

One of the earliest Dracula groups was founded by twenty-seven-year-old Donald A. Reed in Los Angeles in 1962. The Count Dracula Society celebrated classic horror films and often held meetings with horror and sci-fi actors, filmmakers, and authors who were in attendance. Each year they presented the Ann Radcliffe Award (named after the nineteenth-century author of gothic horror novels) to notables in the field, such as Boris Karloff. Ten years later, Reed, who by then had received his doctorate, began the Academy of Science Fiction, Fantasy and Horror Films, which eventually supplanted the Count Dracula Society. Dr. Reed died in Los Angeles on March 18, 2001, from complications from anemia, a condition in which the blood doesn't have enough healthy red blood cells. How appropriate that the founder of the Count Dracula Society should die of a blood ailment! His legacy, the Academy of Science Fiction, Fantasy and Horror Films, is still in existence, giving out yearly Saturn Awards to outstanding genre films.

The Academy of Science Fiction, Fantasy and Horror Films
334 West 54th Street
Los Angeles, CA 90037
Email: Saturn.awards@ca.rr.com
Website: www.saturnawards.org

The Bram Stoker Memorial Association was founded by Dr. Jeanne Youngson in 1985. The organization publishes a quarterly newsletter, and Dr. Youngson has led members on Stoker walks in Dublin, Ireland, touring sites relevant to the author's life.

The Bram Stoker Memorial Association
Penthouse North, Suite 145
29 Washington Square West
New York, N.Y. 10011-9180
Email: bramstoker145@yahoo.com or countdracula145@hotmail.com
Website: http://wiki2.benecke.com/index.php?title=Bram_Stoker
_Memorial_Assn

The Dracula Society was founded in October 1973 by two London-based actors, Bernard Davies and Bruce Wightman. Originally founded to enable its members to travel to remote regions in Transylvania, its emphasis now is on London-based meetings of like-minded vampire enthusiasts.

The Dracula Society
213 Wulfstan Street
East Acton
London W12 0AB
United Kingdom
Email: info@thedraculasociety.org.uk
Website: http://www.thedraculasociety.org.uk/

The Highgate Vampire Society is a London-based organization, founded by occult researcher David Farrant, who is president of the British Psychic and Occult Society. Members receive the society's newsletter, *Suspended in Dusk*.

The Highgate Vampire Society
P.O.Box 1112
London N10 3XE
England

The Transylvanian Society of Dracula, founded in Romania in 1991, is dedicated to the study of both Bram Stoker's fictional Dracula and the historical Vlad III. There are chapters of the society throughout Romania and Europe, but no active chapter in the United States; Americans are encouraged to join the Canadian chapter, formed in 1995 by Dr. Elizabeth Miller. The society hosts an annual Symposium and World Dracula Conference in Romania.

The Transylvanian Society of Dracula
(North American Chapter)
Elizabeth Miller, TSD
249 Beatrice St.
Toronto, ON
Canada M6G 3E9
Website: http://www.ucs.mun.ca/~emiller/

The Vampire Research Society formed as a part of the British Occult Society in 1967. In 1970 it gained autonomy and is now Britain's longest-established organization for vampire research. It publishes books and reports under its own imprint, Gothic Press.

Vampire Research Society
P.O. Box 542
Highgate, London N6 5FZ
Contact: International Secretary, Dennis Crawford
Email: vampireresearchsociety@gothicpress.freeserve.co.uk
Website: www.gothicpress.freeserve.co.uk

The Vampyre Connexion, formed in 1998, brings together those interested in the vampire genre for fun, fantasy, and friendship. Members are encouraged to contribute to the group's journal, *Dark Nights.*

The Vampyre Connexion
The Membership Secretary
10 Ravensbourne Mansions
40 Berthon Street
Greenwich SE8 3EB
United Kingdom
Email: Info@AlexMasi.co.uk
Website: http://www.vampyreconnexion.co.uk/

The Whitby Dracula Society was formed in 1994 in response to requests for a society based around Whitby's Dracula Experience attraction. It is now the largest society for vampirophiles in the United Kingdom, producing a quarterly newsletter and hosting the annual Vamps and Tramps ball.

Angela Woodcock
The Whitby Dracula Society
16 Grove Street
Whitby
England, YO21 1PP
Email: WhitbyDraculaSociety1897@yahoo.com
Website: http://www.whitbydraculasociety.org

Selected Bibliography

One of the joys of writing this book was that it gave me an excuse to delve back into books about Dracula, Bram Stoker, Vlad Tepeş, horror movies, and gothic literature. It is a fertile field, with hundreds of fine books from which to choose. Add to that newspaper and magazine research, and it is easy to see how, for months on end, all I did was consume Dracula and vampire information. I would like to list every source I consulted, but that would be a book in itself. Below are the most notable and useful references which, while extensive, represents just the tip of the fang.

Books

Belford, Barbara. *Bram Stoker and the Man Who Was Dracula*. Cambridge, MA: Da Capo Press, 1996.

Dawidziak, Mark. *The Bedside, Bathtub & Armchair Companion to Dracula*. New York: The Continuum International Publishing Group, Inc., 2008.

Eyles, Allen, Robert Adkinson, and Nicholas Fry. *The House of Horror*. London: Lorrimer Publishing, 1973.

Florescu, Radu, and Raymond T. McNally. *Dracula, Prince of Many Faces*. Boston: Little, Brown, 1989.

Frayling, Christopher. *Nightmare: The Birth of Horror*. London: BBC Books, 1996.

Glut, Donald. *The Dracula Book*. Metuchen, NJ: Scarecrow Press,1975.

———. *The Frankenstein Archive: Essays on the Monster, the Myth, the Movies, and More*. Jefferson, NC: McFarland, 2002.

Karg, Barb, Arjean Spaite, and Rick Sutherland. *The Everything Vampire Book*. Avon, MA: Adams Media, 2009.

Langella, Frank. *Dropped Names: Famous Men and Women As I Knew Them*. New York: HarperCollins Publishers, 2012, 2013.

Lee, Christopher. *Tall, Dark and Gruesome: An Autobiography*. London: Victor Gollancz, 1997.

Lennig, Arthur. *The Immortal Count: The Life and Films of Bela Lugosi*. Lexington: The University Press of Kentucky, 2013.

Mank, Gregory William. *It's Alive! The Classic Cinema Saga of Frankenstein*. San Diego, CA: A. S. Barnes & Co., 1981.

Maxford, Howard. *Hammer House of Horror: Behind the Screams*. New York: The Overlook Press, 1996.

Meikle, Denis. *A History of Horrors: The Rise and Fall of the House of Hammer*. Lanham, MD: Scarecrow Press, 1996.

Miller, Elizabeth, ed. *Bram Stoker's* Dracula: *A Documentary Journey Into Vampire Country and the Dracula Phenomenon.* New York: Pegasus Books, 2009.

Rigby, Jonathan. *Christopher Lee: The Authorised Screen History.* London: Reynolds & Hearn, 2001.

Skal, David J. *Hollywood Gothic: The Tangled Web of Dracula from Novel to Stage to Screen.* New York: W. W. Norton & Co., 1990.

Wolf, Leonard, ed. *The Essential Dracula: The Definitive Edition of Bram Stoker's Classic Novel.* New York: Plume Books, 1993.

Newspapers and Magazines

"Ad for 'Bud Abbott and Lou Costello Meet Frankenstein.'" *New York Times,* July 27, 1948, p. 17.

"Ad for 'Bud Abbott and Lou Costello Meet Frankenstein.'" *Los Angeles Times,* August 2, 1948. p. A7.

"Ad for 'Dracula's Daughter.'" *Los Angeles Times,* June 2, 1936, p. 13.

Ames, Walter. "Bing to Sub for Injured Son; Richfield Takes Bow for New Refinery." *Los Angeles Times,* May 28, 1954, p. 30.

———. "Pinky's Daughter in TV Debut; Gleason Set for Live Shows." *Los Angeles Times,* May 11, 1956, p. B-10.

"At the Box-Office: Top-Grossing Films." *New York Times,* December 15, 1992, p. C-18.

Banks-Smith, Nancy. "Television: Dracula." *Guardian* (London, UK), December 23, 1977, n.p.

Bannon, Aoife. "Vampire Role Was the Pitts." *Sun* (London, UK), September 19, 2011, p. 18.

Barricklow, Denise. "A Love Story You Can Sink Your Teeth Into." *St. Petersburg* (FL) *Times,* November 13, 1992, p. 18.

Bernheimer, Martin. "California Ballet Offers 'Dracula' in San Diego." *Los Angeles Times,* November 2, 1987, p. G-7.

Bianco, Robert. "This 'Dracula' Sucks Out the Fun and Fear." *USA Today,* October 25, 2013, p. D-6.

Bierly, Mandy. "'Sons of Anarchy' Star Charlie Hunnam Talks About His Screenplay for 'Vlad' (Sorry, No Vampires)." *Entertainment Weekly,* December 9, 2009. http://insidemovies.ew.com/2009/12/09/charlie-hunnam-vlad-dracula-movie/ (Accessed September 20, 2014).

Bledsoe, Wayne. "The Evolution of Elvira: Cassandra Peterson Is Not So Dark." *McClatchy-Tribune Business News* (Washington, D.C.), May 31, 2013.

Boylan, Jane. "So Now There's a New Sexy Rexy." *New York Times,* November 23, 1969, p. D-15.

Bradshaw, Peter. "Within the Pale: Tim Burton Plays the Jokey 'Darkness' of His Style to Totally Predictable Effect in His Latest Oddity-Comedy." *Guardian* (London, UK), May 11, 2012, p. 18.

Brady, Thomas F. "Abbott, Costello Signed for Satire." *New York Times*, July 29, 1947, p. 18.

Brantley, Ben. "It Ain't Over Till the Goth Vampire Sings." *New York Times*, December 10, 2002, p. E-1.

Breslauer, Jan. "Theater: Old Tale, New Blood: An Experienced Team of Creators Has Gone Back to Bram Stoker's Novel for a Musical Look at the Infamous Count." *Los Angeles Times*, October 21, 2001, p. F-3.

Broeske, Pat H. "Face-off." *Los Angeles Times*, October 2, 1988, p. K-25.

———. "Hollywood Goes Batty for Vampires." *New York Times*, April 26, 1992, p. H-23.

Bruni, Frank. "Modern Bite of the Occult." *New York Times*, August 10, 1996, p. B-9.

Burr, Ty. "In third Installment, 'Blade' Lacks Fresh Blood." *Boston Globe*, December 8, 2004, E-1.

Byrnes, Robert B. "'The Game' Chief Attraction." *Los Angeles Times*, October 9, 1965, p. A-10.

Canby, Vincent. "Screen: 'Nosferatu,' Herzog's Dracula." *New York Times*, October 1, 1979, p. C-15.

Carr, Jay. "Coppola Puts the Bite Back in 'Dracula.'" *Boston Globe*, November 8, 1992, p. A-1.

———. "Murphy Makes a Bloodless 'Vampire.'" *Boston Globe*, October 27, 1995, p. 57.

Cheney, Alexandra. "Media—On the Horizon: Dracula Is Revived, with Shades of Elon Musk and Vlad the Impaler." *Wall Street Journal*, September 16, 2013, p. B-6.

Church, Michael. "Count Dracula." *Times of London*, December 23, 1977, p. 7.

Coates, Paul. "Vampira and Voluptua, the Chill and Charm Girls, Try a New Life." *Los Angeles Times*, April 17, 1962, p. A-6.

Counts, Kyle. "'Elvira, Mistress of the Dark': TV Horror Hostess Cassandra Peterson Makes Her Character the Stuff of Legend—and Feature Films." *Cinefantastique*, January 1989, p. 105.

Craig, Amanda. "New-Age Vampires Stake Their Claim." *Times of London*, January 14, 2006, p. 17.

Crowther, Bosley. "Old Black Magic." *New York Times*, June 13, 1943, p. X-3.

"Dance of the Vampires." *London Daily Mail*, December 10, 2002, p. 35.

Daniels, Mary. "Celebrity Profile: Vampire Sheds Light on 'Shadows.'" *Chicago Tribune*, October 2, 1970, p. B-15.

Dawson, Greg. "'Dark Shadows' Has Vampire But No Bite." *Orlando Sentinel*, January 13, 1991, p. F-1.

Dedert, Arne. "Elton's Vampire Musical 'Sucks.'" *London Sunday Times*, January 22, 2006, p. 23.

Del Olmo, Frank. "Bela Lugosi Just 'Dad'—Afraid of Dracula? His Son Never Was." *Los Angeles Times*, July 19, 1971, p. A-1.

Dello Stritto, Frank J. "'Lugosi'—A Play for the Stage by Michael Theodorou." *Vampire Over London: The Bela Lugosi Blog.*

Dowd, Maureen. "The Chelsea Hotel, 'Kooky but Nice,' Turns 100." *New York Times*, November 21, 1983, p. B-1.

"'Dracula' Breaks Box-Office Records." *Los Angeles Times*, March 24, 1931, p. A-11.

"'Dracula' in Spanish Opens at California." *Los Angeles Times*, May 11, 1931, p. A7.

"Dracula Without His Cape." *New York Times*, July 7, 1935, p. X-2.

Driscoll, Kathi Scrizzi. "Should Gothic TV Soap 'Dark Shadows' Be a Comedy Film?" *McClatchy-Tribune Business News*, May 12, 2012, n.p.

Dunning, Jennifer. "'Dracula,' Beyond Bram Stoker's Darkest Dreams." *New York Times*, March 17, 1997, p. C-14.

Durrant, Nancy. "Get Your Teeth into a Dracula Spectacular." *Times of London*, December 23, 2006, p. 52.

Ebert, Roger. "'Blade' Would Be a Great Comic Book." *Denver Post*, August 20, 1998, p. E-05.

Edwards, David. "Day of the Undead: DVDs." *Daily Mirror* (London, U.K.UK), March 9, 2012, p. 6.

"English Audience Is Horrified by Drama." *Weekly Variety*, June 18, 1924, p. 2.

"Erstwhile Dracula at First National." *Los Angeles Times*, February 13, 1929, p. 11.

Faris, Gerald. "Pierce Professor Sinks Teeth Into Vampire Legends." *Los Angeles Times*, November 15, 1981, p. V-1.

Farley, Ellen. "Langella's Dracula, with Just a Nip of Sensuality." *Los Angeles Times*, July 15, 1979, p. O-45.

Feldberg, Robert. "Back in Old Transylvania, They'll Be Rockin' the Night Away." *Record* (Bergen County, NJ), September 8, 2002, p. 3.

———. "Blood Flows Like Treacle in the New 'Dracula': Terrifying Burst of Song from Vampire and Friends." *Record* (Bergen County, NJ), August 20, 2004, p. G-15.

"From Two Wide-Apart Rialtos." *New York Times*, January 25, 1931, p. X-1.

Gelder, Lawrence Van. "Theater Review: Frankenstein Relinquishes His Creature Comforts." *New York Times*, January 14, 2000, p. E-5.

George, Manfred. "Undiluted Poison." *New York Times*, June 8, 1958, p. X-5.

Gilford, Barbara. "'Dracula' in Turns and Leaps." *New York Times*, October 20, 1991, p. NJ-13.

Greenspun, Roger. "Alan Gibson Horror Films Congeal into Double Bill." *New York Times*, November 30, 1972, p. 55.

———. "Screen: A Vampire's Lot." *New York Times*, July 19, 1973, p. 31.

———. "Vampires of 'Jonathan' Strike a Metaphoric Blow Against Fascism." *New York Times*, June 16, 1972, p. 13.

Gussow, Mel. "Nosferatu." *New York Times*, February 15, 1985, p. C-21.

Haber, Joyce. "Doris Day Denies Rumored Fling." *Los Angeles Times*, May 3, 1973, p. G-14.

———. "Odd Inventory of Uneven Year." *Los Angeles Times*, January 26, 1975, p. R-25.

Hall, Mordaunt. "The Screen." *New York Times*, February 13, 1931, p. 21.

———. "The Screen." *New York Times*, June 4, 1929, p. 40.

Hamilton, George. "Operetta Renaissance Goes On." *Financial Times*, November 16, 1999, p. 6.

Hamrick, Craig. "Lara Parker." *Dark Shadows Online*. http://www.darkshadowsonline.com/where-parker.html (Accessed October 26, 2014).

Harcourt, Stewart. "Bringing Dracula Back to Life." *London Sunday Telegraph*, December 24, 2006, p. 48.

"Harlequin, a Dinner Playhouse." *Los Angeles Times*, September 20, 1985, p. OC–E20.

Heckman, Don. "Alice Cooper Plays Rock to Sink Your Fangs Into." *New York Times*, August 12, 1972, p. 17.

Herold, Charles. "Game Theory: A Design for a Little Fun: Easy to Play and to Forget." *New York Times*, August 31, 2000, p. G-10.

Hiatt, Brian. "Eddie Murphy Speaks: The Rolling Stone Interview." Brian Hiatt. *Rolling Stone*, Issue 1143, November 10, 2011. http://www.rollingstone.com/movies/news/eddie-murphy-the-rolling-stone-interview-20111109?page=4 (Accessed September 29, 2014).

Holden, Stephen. "Bauhaus, English Rock." *New York Times*, March 4, 1981, p. C-19.

———. "Eerie, Flickering Images of a Vulnerable Dracula." *New York Times*, May 14, 2003, p. E-3.

Holland, Bernard. "Concert: 'En Famille.'" *New York Times*, February 27, 1983, p. 48.

"Hollywood Gothique: News & Notes," *Hollywood Gothique*. December 10, 2004. http://hollywoodgothique.bravejournal.com/entry/8006 (Accessed November. 12, 2014).

Horovitz, Bruce. "'Elvira, Mistress of the Dark'—Green, That Is." *USA Today*, October 25, 2012, p. A-.2.

Howell, Peter. "Supernatural Soap." *Toronto* (Ontario) *Star*, November 18, 2011, p. E-1.

http://beladraculalugosi.wordpress.com/2011/06/12/lugosi-a-play-for-the-stage-by-michael-theodorou/ (Accessed October 24, 2014).

Hughes, Sarah. "Interview with the Vampire." *Independent* (London, UK), October 19, 2013, p. 9.

Hunt, Dennis. "VideoLog: Releases of Major Oscar Nominees Delayed; CBS, Warner Out With 'Nerds II,' 'Lost Boys.'" *Los Angeles Times*, February 26, 1988, p. G-25.

"Hunt Poison Pen Writer Preying on Society Folk." *Chicago Daily Tribune*, May 23, 1933, p. 12.

Jackson, Carlton Jr. "'Blade' a Good Vampire Flick." *New York Amsterdam News*, August 20, 1998, p. 26.

James, Caryn. "Film: 'The Lost Boys.'" *New York Times*, July 31, 1987, p. C-21.

Jeffries, Mark. "Jonathan Rhys Meyers on Dracula and Kicking Booze." *Daily Mirror* (London, UK), November 1, 2013, p. 20.

Johnson, Malcolm. "'Dracula' Musical Drained of Life." *Hartford* (CT) *Courant*, August 20, 2004, p. D-1.

"Jonathan Frid: Actor Who Burst From the Crypt into the Spotlight as a Lovelorn Vampire in the TV Soap 'Dark Shadows' and Enjoyed a Devoted Following." *Times of London*, May 18, 2012, p. 49.

———. "'Vampires' a Phantom of Its Former Self; Musical Based on Polanski Film Suffers from Genre Confusion, Light Profusion." *Hartford* (CT) *Courant*, December 10, 2002, p. D-6.

———. "A Ludicrous, Lifeless 'Lestat.'" *Hartford* (CT) *Courant*, April 26, 2006, p. D-5.

Jones, Chris. "Lack of Clear Purpose Helps Make 'Lestat' a Costly Mess." *Chicago Tribune*, April 26, 2006, p. 5.1.

Jones, Jack. "Only in L.A./People and Events." *Los Angeles Times*, September 13, 1988, p. 2.

Kellerman, Stewart. "Other Incarnations of the Vampire Author." *New York Times*, November 7, 1988, p. C-15.

Kelley, Bill. "Christopher Lee: King of the Counts." *Dracula: The Complete Vampire*. *Starlog Movie Magazine* #6, 1992, p. 46.

Kellogg, Carolyn. "Anne Rice Talks About Reviving Vampire Creations in 'Prince Lestat.'" *Los Angeles Times*, October 23, 2014, http://www.latimes.com/books/jacketcopy/la-ca-jc-anne-rice-20141026-story.html. (Accessed October 24, 2014.)

Kendrick, Walter. "Better Undead Than Unread: Have Vampires Lost Their Bite?" *New York Times*, October 18, 1992, p. BR-55.

Kermode, Mark. "Observer Review: Critics: Film: DVDs: Scary Movies? You Should See the Fans." *Observer* (London, UK), March 21, 2010, p. 30.

Kilday, Gregg. "Cheech & Chong Picture Show." *Los Angeles Times*, April 23, 1977, p. B-6.

King, Susan. "Heydays in Hollywood: Eva Marie Saint and Jean Simmons Recall the Past, Revel in the Present." *Los Angeles Times*, May 13, 1990, p. 80.

Kissel, Howard. "Elton's 'Lestat' on B'Way: Fangs But No Fangs." *New York Daily News*, April 26, 2006, p. 38.

———. "Vampire Show Down for Count." *New York Daily News*, December 10, 2002, p. 50.

Klein, Alvin. "Musical 'Dracula' on Teaneck Stage." *New York Times*, December 20, 1987, p. NJ-19.

Klemesrud, Judy. "Frank Langella Gets His Teeth into a Winning Role." *New York Times*, November 27, 1977, p. 4.

Koch, Jim. "Transforming a Ghoul into a Leading Man." *New York Times*, November 6, 1994, p. "'Lovers Forever' by Cher." Songfacts. http://www.songfacts.com/detail.php?id=2013 (Accessed November. 19, 2014).

Lawson, Terry. "'Blade: Trinity' Director Makes Comics Come Alive." *Knight Ridder Tribune News Service*, December 6, 2004, p. 1.

————. "Wesley Snipes Parties Across the Country to Hype 'Blade II.'" *Knight Ridder Tribune News Service*, March 18, 2002, p. 1.

Lewis, Fiona. "I Was Famous for 15 Minutes. Then I Put My Clothes On: Confessions of a B-Movie Actress." *Observer* (London, UK), May 3, 1998, p. 2.

Lyon, Jeff. "Without His Fangs, Dracula's a Nice Guy." *Chicago Tribune*, February 16, 1979, p. 1.

Lythgoe, Dennis. "Vampire Book Series Started with Vivid Dream." *Deseret News* (Salt Lake City, UT), September 10, 2006, p. E-9.

"Lugosi Complains of Shortness of Life." *Los Angeles Times*, June 28, 1928, p. A-9.

Maher, Kevin. "How Tim Burton Resurrected the Vampire Movie." *Times of London*, April 7, 2012, p. 40.

Manchester, William. "How the Movies Chased the Blues Away in the Last Depression." *New York Times*, March 16, 1975, p. X-17.

Mann, Roderick. "A Mercedes in Cybill's Future?" *Los Angeles Times*, October 6, 1978, p. F-36.

————. "George Hamilton Gives Up Leisure for 'Dynasty.'" *Los Angeles Times*, August 4, 1985, p. W-20.

————. "Hamilton Sinks Teeth Into Film." *Los Angeles Times*, July 6, 1978, p. I-13.

————. "Less Moore is More Moore." *Los Angeles Times*, November 2, 1978, p. H-16.

————. "Movies: Langella Sheds Cloak for 'Sphinx.'" *Los Angeles Times*, March 9, 1980, p. L-29.

Markoutsas, Elaine. "'Bite' the Juicy Comic Role Hamilton Was Waiting For." *Chicago Tribune*, April 6, 1979, p. B6.

Marks, Peter. "'Dracula' Has Little Bite." *Washington Post*, August 20, 2004, p. C-01.

Martin, John. "Dance: Review—Events of Past Season Not To Be Ignored." *New York Times*, June 21, 1959, p. X-12.

Maslin, Janet. "Giving New Fangs to an Old Vampire." *New York Times*, December 22, 1995, p. C-35.

————. "Neither Dracula Nor Rumor Frightens Coppola." *New York Times*, November 15, 1992, p. H-24.

————. "Screen: 'Love at First Bite,' Dracula's 'Plaza Suite.'" *New York Times*, April 13, 1979, p. C-10.

McArdle, Helen. "The Highland Heritage of Depp's Debonair Vampire." *Sunday Herald* (Glasgow, Scotland), May 6, 2012, p. 3.

McDowell, Edwin. "Remarque's Diaries Given to N.Y.U." *New York Times*, February 17, 1984, p. C-30.

McPhee, Rod. "Vampire Britain: UK Could Be Home to More Blood-Sucking Nightfeeders Than Dracula's Homeland." *Daily Mirror*, September 16, 2014. http://www.mirror.co.uk/news/uk-news/vampire-britain-uk-could-home-4272342. (Accessed October 9, 2014).

Mitchell, Steve. "Badham Directing a Bat Out of Hell." *Fantastic Films* (Vol. 2, No. 7), January 1980, p. 30.

Mittelbach, Margaret, and Michael Crewdson. "To Die For: Painting the Town Red, and the Capes and Nails Black." *New York Times*, November 24, 2000, p. E-13.

"Moonlight (A Vampire's Dream)" by Stevie Nicks. *Songfacts.* http://www.songfacts.com/detail.php?id=20018 (Accessed November. 19, 2014).

"Movie Briefs." *Chicago Defender*, March 6, 1973, p. 10.

Morris, Deborah. "Sci-Fi & Fantasy Briefly." *Dominion Post* (Wellington, New Zealand), July 14, 2007, p. ID-21.

Munoz, Lorenza. "A Star Cools Down: Action. Drama. Comedy. Wesley Snipes Sizzled. And Then . . . He Didn't." *Los Angeles Times*, August 1, 2004, p. E-1.

Murphy, Ryan. "How a Scribe and a Damsel Saved 'Dracula' from Cable." *Los Angeles Times*, November 8, 1992, p. 19.

———. "More Murphy: Something to Sink His Teeth Into." *Los Angeles Times*, October 18, 1992, p. 28.

Naval-Shetye, Aakanksha. "'I Do Not Know What Is Sexy About Me!' . . . Says Hollywood Hottie Johnny Depp." *DNA: Daily News & Analysis* (Mumbai), May 21, 2012.

Nestruck, J. Kelly. "A Theatrical Curse Fit for the Undead." *National Post* (Don Mills, Ontario), May 25, 2006, p. AL-2.

"News and Comment of Stage and Screen." *Fitchburg* (MA) *Sentinel*, May 9, 1936, p. 5.

Nichols, Peter M. "Home Video: A Light Year for Laser Disks, But Things May Pick Up with Smaller Ones." *New York Times*, June 3, 1993, p. C-18.

Nugent, Frank S. "The Screen." *New York Times*, May 18, 1936, p. 14.

"Obituary: Maila Nurmi." *Times of London*, January 24, 2008, p. 67.

O'Connor, John J. "The Enduring Fascination of 'Dracula.'" *New York Times*, March 5, 1978, p. D-27.

Olsen, E. "The Voice of the Fan." *Chicago Daily Tribune*, June 28, 1931, p. C-10.

"Paperback Best Sellers." *New York Times*, December 13, 1992, p. BR32.

"Paperback Best Sellers." *New York Times*, December 6, 1992, p. BR86.

"People." *Chicago Tribune*, July 11, 1979, p. 20.

"Revival of the Undead." *New York Times*, October 16, 1938, p. 160.

"Rockefeller Calls FBI in Teen-Age Crisis." *Los Angeles Times*, September 2, 1959, p. 10.

"Romanian Film to Whitewash Prince Vlad, Model for 'Dracula.'" *Los Angeles Times*, September 9, 1977, p. G-20.

"Screen News." *New York Times*, March 14, 1945, p. 22.

"Screen News Here and in Hollywood." *New York Times*, April 29, 1944, p. 12.

"Screen News Here and in Hollywood." *New York Times*, June 9, 1942, p. 27.

"Summary of Current Legit Shows in London's West End." *Weekly Variety*, April 27, 1927, p. 3.

"Today's Best Bets." *Los Angeles Times*, February 8, 1974, p. E-25.

"Two Plays in London Make Many Faint." *New York Times*, March 11, 1927, p. 24.

"Universal to Make 55 Feature Films." *New York Times*, June 12, 1944, p. 16.

Pacheco, Patrick. "Play by Play: Vampires Are In, Salami to Go on Broadway." *Newsday*, May 24, 2001, p. B-09.

Pall, Ellen. "Nicolas Cage, the Sunshine Man." *New York Times*, July 24, 1994, p. H-1.

Panec, Richard. "Tribune Books: Rice's Vampires Again Take Flight." *Chicago Tribune*, October. 27, 1988, p. C-3.

Parisi, Albert J. "An Influential Writer Returns to Fantasy." *New York Times*, April 10, 1994, p. N–J3.

Patterson, Alex. "Much at Stake for Coppola's Dracula Film." *Globe and Mail* (Toronto, Ontario), November 6, 1992, p. D-1.

Patterson, Alex. "Video Puts Vampy Elvira Back Where She Started." *Toronto* (Ontario) *Star*, February 12, 1989, p. C-6.

Penn, Jean Cox, and Jill Barber. "The New Draculas Become the Kinkiest Sex Symbols Ever." *US Magazine*, July 24, 1979. http://franklangella.net/files/interviews/US_Mag.txt. (Accessed October 5, 2014).

Persall, Steve. "So Little Time, So Many Bad Movies." *St. Petersburg Times*, December 29, 1995, p. 8.

Prelutsky, Burt. "Dream to Build a Series On." *Los Angeles Times*, September. 22, 1974, p. N-18.

Pryor, Thomas M. "U-I Plots Movie About a Vampire." *New York Times*, February 23, 1953, p. 21.

Quill, Greg. "Dark Shadows Returns and Network Is Betting Viewers Will Be Charmed Enough to Keep It Around for a While." *Toronto Star*, January 13, 1991, p. C-1.

Rea, Steven. "Francis Ford Coppola Behind the Camera for 'Dracula.'" *Las Vegas Review-Journal*, October 28, 1991, p. D-4.

Reed, Rex. "Rex Red Reports: Ringo the Pop Pariah . . . From Limbo to Film Mogul." *Chicago Tribune*, December 24, 1972, p. J-7.

Rees, Jasper. "Bram Stoker Would Plunge a Stake Through This Show." *Daily Telegraph* (London, UK), November 1, 2013, p. 40.

Rich, Frank. "The New Blood Culture: Fantasizing of Sex and Death, America Sees Its Enemy: AIDS. Enter Dracula." *New York Times*, December 6, 1991, p. V-1.

Riedel, Michael. "'Dracula' Back from the Dead." *New York Post*, March 10, 2004, p. 73.

———. "Bloodied, Not Bowed; Vampire Tale Nailed But Vows to Live On." *New York Post*, January 11, 2006, p. 61.

Robey, Tim. "I've Been Through Hell. But There's a Brighter Day." *Sunday Telegraph* (London, UK), August 10, 2014, p. 10.

Rockwell, John. "Few Mourn as BBC Soap Is Put Out of Its Misery." *New York Times*, August 9, 1993, p. C-12.

Romney, Jonathan. "The Monster Man: Does the Mexican Director Guillermo del Toro Make Fantasy, Action or Art-House Cinema? The Answer Is All Three—And Often in the Same Breathtaking Film." *Independent on Sunday* (London, UK). November 19, 2006, p. 6.

Rose, Chris. "Bloody Good Show Another 'Dracula' Movie, Another Day in the Quarter." *New Orleans Times-Picayune*, August 26, 2000, p. E-1.

Rosenberg, Howard. "'Dark Shadows' Takes a Bite Out of Prime Time." *Los Angeles Times*, January 12, 1991, p. 12.

Rossman, Martin. "Hollywood Hype in Full Cry: Dracula Drops In—with Hokum." *Los Angeles Times*, May 1, 1979, p. E-5.

Roush, Matt. "'Shadows': Ghoulish Shades of Camp." *USA Today*, January 11, 1991, p. D-3.

Rowat, Alison. "Interview with the Vampires." *Herald* (Glasgow, UK), November 8, 2012, p. 20.

Rubin, Mike. "'Dracula' Takes Dancing Lessons." *New York Times*, May 18, 2003, p. AR-23.

Rush. "New Acts of the Week." *Variety*, March 2, 1907, p. 10.

Salem, Rob. "Mel Brooks Ready to Retake Farce Throne, Dracula Flick Takes a More Subdued Run at Director's Usual Anarchical Schtick." *Toronto Star*, December 22, 1995, p. D-3.

Schallert, Edwin. "Abbott, Costello Plan Novel Stage Enterprise." *Los Angeles Times*, December 3, 1942, p. A-11.

———. "Drama and Film: 'Bride of Vampire' Chiller Sequel." *Los Angeles Times*, December 9, 1943, p. 12.

———. "Three Horror Experts Placed in Same Movie." *Los Angeles Times*, October 25, 1938, p. 10.

———. "Vampire Story to Be Filmed at R.K.O." *Los Angeles Times*, October 9, 1943, p. 9.

Scheuer, Philip K. "Adventures of 'Dracula' Now in Film Form." *Los Angeles Times*, March 30, 1931, p. A-7.

———. "Gay Pirates Dance in New Radiant Film." *Los Angeles Times*, June 4, 1936, p. 13.

Schiro, Anne-Marie. "Patterns." *New York Times*, November 10, 1992, p. B-9.

Schwardz, K. Robert. "Moran: 'The Dracula Diary.'" *New York Times*, December 18, 1994, p. H-44.

Scott, A. O. "New Videos Resonate Darkly." *New York Times*, July 19, 2002, p. E-1.

Scott, John L. "Thriller Bill Now on View." *Los Angeles Times*, February 7, 1946, p. 9.

———. "Thriller Stars Convene." *Los Angeles Times*, December 23, 1944, p. 5.

Shabecoff, Philip. "Advertising: Monster Market Creeping Up." *New York Times*, August 30, 1964, p. F-12.

Shaffer, Rosalind. "Foreign Actor Hurdles Talkie Language Bar." *Chicago Daily Tribune*, July 28, 1929, p. F-9.

Shanklin, Ricky L. "Fangs for the Funny Books: Or, Dracula in the Comics." *Dracula, the First Hundred Years*. Baltimore: Midnight Marquee Press, 1997.

Siegert, Alice. "Dracula Is Alive and Well in Munich." *Chicago Tribune*, September 2, 1979, p. 3.

Siskel, Gene. "'Gold' Mines the Adventure Lode." *Chicago Tribune*, November 26, 1974, p. B-4.

———. "'Nosferatu' Puts Dracula in New Light." *Chicago Tribune*, October 25, 1979, p. A-6.

———. "In Langella's Hands, Dracula Is Not a Bit Part." *Chicago Tribune*, July 13, 1979, p. C-3.

———. "Movie Review: 'Vampire in Brooklyn.'" *Chicago Tribune*, October 27, 1995, n.p.

———. "Tempo Entertainment: 'Bell Jar' is a Movie Many Will See Through." *Chicago Tribune*, April 10, 1979, p. A-6.

Smith, Cecil. "'Dracula' to Rise Again on Friday." *Los Angeles Times*, February 4, 1974, p. C-13.

———. "'Sweet Charlie,' Where Are You?" *Los Angeles Times*, October 23, 1973, p. C-15.

———. "Dan Curtis Becomes New Pied Piper of Monster Tales." *Los Angeles Times*, January 14, 1973, p. N-2.

———. "Jourdan Plays Count Dracula." *Los Angeles Times*, March 1, 1978, p. F-13.

Smith, Mark. "Stage Review: 'Dracula': A Musical Comedy of Terrors." *Los Angeles Times*, June 2, 1988, p. AG-10.

Smith, Sid. "Variety: Ping Chong's Work Defy Categories, but Whatever They Are, They're Wild." *Chicago Tribune*, April 7, 1985, p. K-15.

Sondak, Eileen. "Count Dracula Will Dance His Way Through Transylvania." *Los Angeles Times*, October 30, 1987, p. S-D; E-25A.

Spelling, Ian. "Night Hunter: As Blade: Wesley Snipes Stays Sharp as Ever While Slaying Vampires." *Starlog*, October 1998, pp. 49, 50.

———. "Playing Dracula for Laughs." *Denver Post*, December 19, 1995, p. E-8.

Stewart, Jocelyn. "Created Glamour Ghoul: Vampira. Won Actress a Cult Following." *Montreal Gazette*, January 17, 2008, p. B-7.

Stuever, Hank. "'Dracula' on NBC Review." *Washington Post*, September 14, 2013, n.p.

Sullivan, Dan. "Stage Review: 'Dracula' at the Bat at Royce Hall." *Los Angeles Times*, January 10, 1985, p. K-4.

Sullivan, Ed. "Looking at Hollywood." *Chicago Daily Tribune*, January. 10, 1939, p. 11.

Taylor, Frank. "Easter Week at the Movies." *Los Angeles Times*, April 11, 1979, p. OC–D2.

Thomas, Kevin. "'Blacula' Has Effect on Marshall." *Los Angeles Times*, September 9, 1972, p. A7.

———. "'Dracula' a Bloody Good Film." *Los Angeles Times*, April 15, 1966, p. C-15.

———. "'Dracula's Castle' and 'Nightmare in Wax' Open." *Los Angeles Times*, December 12, 1969, p. I-23.

Thompson, Howard. "Dracula Returns." *New York Times*, March 27, 1969, p. 54.

———. "Screen: Czech 'Valerie.'" *New York Times*, March 11, 1974, p. 34.

———. "TV: C.B.S. 'Dracula' Film Loses Bite." *New York Times*, October 12, 1973, p. 86.

Tinee, Mae. "Awed Stillness Greets Movie, About 'Dracula.'" Chicago Daily Tribune, March 21, 1931, p. 21.

———. "Film 'Dracula's Daughter' Has Horror Aplenty." *Chicago Daily Tribune*, July 4, 1936, p. 7.

———. "Usual Horrors Abound in 2 Horror Films." *Chicago Daily Tribune*, January 1, 1946, p. 29.

Tolin, Lisa. "Tom Hewitt Profile." *Deseret News* (Salt Lake City, UT), August 15, 2004, E-12.

Trachtenberg, Jeffrey A. "Booksellers Find Life After Harry in a Vampire Novel." *Wall Street Journal*, August 10, 2007, p. B-1.

Trachtenberg, Nancy. "For a Delightfully Horrifying Halloween." *New York Times*, October 24, 1979, p. C-12.

Travers, Peter. "Can Frank Langella Re-Vamp 'Dracula?'" *New York Times*, July 8, 1979, p. D-1.

Turan, Kenneth. "A 'Dark' Lesson in Tim Burton; Best and Worst of the Director Are on Display in the Fitfully Fun But Flawed 'Shadows.'" *Los Angeles Times*, May 11, 2012, p. D-1.

Turan, Kenneth. "Movie Review: 'Dracula': Letting the Blood Flow." *Los Angeles Times*, November 13, 1992, p. 1.

Turchiano, Danielle. "'On Writing' with 'Dracula's' Cole Haddon." *Examiner. com.* October 23, 2013. http://www.examiner.com/article/on-writing-with-dracula-s-cole-haddon (Accessed November 11, 2014).

Verhoek, Sam Howe. "Houston Ballet Knows How to Use a Dracula." *New York Times*, March 13, 1997, p. C-13.

Weiler, A. H. "At the Rialto." *New York Times*, December 16, 1944, p. 19.

Whitaker, Alma. "Lugosi, Creator of Dracula Role, Is Courtly Hungarian." *Los Angeles Times*, June 17, 1928, p. C-11.

Wilmington, Michael. "'Vampire' One Eddie Murphy Movie Viewers Can Sink Their Teeth Into." *Chicago Tribune*, October 27, 1995, p. C.

Wooley, John. "Comic Screams." *Dracula: The Complete Vampire. Starlog Movie Magazine*, #6, 1992, p. 56.

Zeidner, Lisa. "When a Kiss Isn't Just a Kiss: A Lip-Smacking Top 10." *New York Times*, April 30, 2000, p. MT-19.

Ziaya, Christine. "Elvira vs. Vampira: Tale from the Crypt." *Los Angeles Times*, October 25, 1987, p. K-19.

Zurawik, David. "'Dark Shadows': Neck-Deep in Romantic Ambience." *Baltimore Sun*, January 11, 1991, p. E-1.

Index

THE FAQ SERIES

Morrissey FAQ
by D. McKinney
Backbeat Books
978-1-4803-9448-3........... $24.99

Nirvana FAQ
by John D. Luerssen
Backbeat Books
978-1-61713-450-0 .... $24.99

Pink Floyd FAQ
by Stuart Shea
Backbeat Books
978-0-87930-950-3 .... $19.99

Elvis Films FAQ
by Paul Simpson
Applause Books
978-1-55783-858-2 .... $24.99

Elvis Music FAQ
by Mike Eder
Backbeat Books
978-1-61713-049-6 .... $24.99

Prog Rock FAQ
by Will Romano
Backbeat Books
978-1-61713-587-3 .... $24.99

Pro Wrestling FAQ
by Brian Solomon
Backbeat Books
978-1-61713-599-6 .... $29.99

Rush FAQ
by Max Mobley
Backbeat Books
978-1-61713-451-7 .... $24.99

Saturday Night Live FAQ
by Stephen Tropiano
Applause Books
978-1-55783-951-0 .... $24.99

Prices, contents, and availability
subject to change without notice.

Seinfeld FAQ
by Nicholas Nigro
Applause Books
978-1-55783-857-5 .... $24.99

Sherlock Holmes FAQ
by Dave Thompson
Applause Books
978-1-4803-3149-5 .... $24.99

The Smiths FAQ
by John D. Luerssen
Backbeat Books
978-1-4803-9449-0 .... $24.99

Soccer FAQ
by Dave Thompson
Backbeat Books
978-1-61713-598-9 .... $24.99

The Sound of Music FAQ
by Barry Monush
Applause Books
978-1-4803-6043-3 .... $27.99

South Park FAQ
by Dave Thompson
Applause Books
978-1-4803-5064-9 .... $24.99

Bruce Springsteen FAQ
by John D. Luerssen
Backbeat Books
978-1-61713-093-9 .... $22.99

Star Trek FAQ
(Unofficial and Unauthorized)
by Mark Clark
Applause Books
978-1-55783-792-9 .... $19.99

Star Trek FAQ 2.0
(Unofficial and Unauthorized)
by Mark Clark
Applause Books
978-1-55783-793-6 .... $22.99

Star Wars FAQ
by Mark Clark
Applause Books
978-1-4803-6018-1 .... $24.99

Quentin Tarantino FAQ
by Dale Sherman
Applause Books
978-1-4803-5588-0 .... $24.99

Three Stooges FAQ
by David J. Hogan
Applause Books
978-1-55783-788-2 .... $22.99

The Who FAQ
by Mike Segretto
Backbeat Books
978-1-4803-6103-4 .... $24.99

The Wizard of Oz FAQ
by David J. Hogan
Applause Books
978-1-4803-5062-5 .... $24.99

The X-Files FAQ
by John Kenneth Muir
Applause Books
978-1-4803-6974-0 .... $24.99

Neil Young FAQ
by Glen Boyd
Backbeat Books
978-1-61713-037-3 .... $19.99

HAL•LEONARD®
PERFORMING ARTS
PUBLISHING GROUP

FAQ.halleonardbooks.com

0815